FOREIGN INTERVENTION IN THE
RIO DE LA PLATA

FOREIGN INTERVENTION
IN THE
RIO DE LA PLATA
1838-50

*A Study of French, British, and American Policy in
Relation to the Dictator Juan Manuel Rosas*

BY

JOHN F. CADY

AMS PRESS
NEW YORK

Dedicated
to
MY MOTHER

PREFACE

This study of European-South American relations began as an examination of a phase of the diplomatic history of the United States. The inadequacy of the original point of view was quickly revealed, and continued research carried the story into ever-widening ramifications which seemed to baffle every attempt to set a boundary to them. Exhaustive research, the writer has learned, has little or no meaning in any absolute sense of that term; even within the more or less arbitrary limits which one is forced to adopt, it seems to apply more accurately to the student himself than to the topic which he explores. But the result as here given should at least demonstrate how unsatisfactory is much that has been written in a superficial way concerning Latin-American history. It will also show the way into a great mass of archival material on the subject, which gives promise of rich returns for future effort.

Obligations are incurred in the course of such an undertaking which are too numerous to catalogue. Only the most important ones can be recognized. Very special acknowledgment must be made for the assistance which the writer has enjoyed from the Albert J. Beveridge Foundation of DePauw University, assistance which has granted him a full year's time, unencumbered by other responsibilities, for the arduous task of preparing the manuscript. The author would express his appreciation for the many privileges and courtesies which have been extended to him by the Bibliothèque Nationale and the Foreign Office on the Quai d'Orsay in Paris, by the Public Record Office and the British Museum in London, by the State and Navy Departments and the Library of Congress in Washington. He is under obligation for help afforded by the Pan American Union, for access to rare material in the New York Public Library and in the Church Collection of the John

Hay Library of Brown University. A word of thanks is due to M. Abel Doysié, Mr. Oren J. Hale, and Mr. Charles L. Chandler for valued assistance. Finally, the writer is inestimably indebted to his friends and teachers, Professor St. George L. Sioussat and Professor W. E. Lingelbach of the University of Pennsylvania for their untiring counsel and encouragement.

JOHN F. CADY

Philadelphia,
June, 1929

CONTENTS

MAPS

FOREWORD

In any treatment of international relations which involves live questions of policy, protestations on the part of a writer that he has maintained an objective point of view are always unconvincing. They usually convict him immediately of that most subtle of all errors, self-deception. Indeed, perhaps one of the most serious obstacles in the road to international understanding is this very failure to recognize and admit the premises and assumptions which enter into any discussion of such questions. The point of view always colors the interpretation, and operates as well to limit both one's perception of fact and the scope of his inquiry. Until we willingly attempt to define and criticize these underlying assumptions and seek to understand an opposing point of view, discussion is obviously futile. Neither statesmen nor historians can do their thinking in a neutral vacuum.

Concerning perhaps no other phase of international relations has more ink and paper been vicariously wasted than in the endeavor of the United States to prove to our Latin-American neighbors that the successive Governments at Washington have pursued a consistent, definable, and for the most part benevolent policy toward them. The Monroe Doctrine has come to be such a fundamental part of our mental machinery that South American diplomacy has largely been relegated to the menial task of providing illustrative material for it. That which did not illustrate was ignored. Thus it happens that one of the most significant periods in the international relations of Argentina is almost entirely unknown in North America. What little aid and comfort the Monroe Doctrine enthusiasts have gleaned from the era of Rosas has been misappropriated. Until we doff our colored spectacles, therefore, and come to regard Latin-American diplomacy in a truer light, there is little hope that we shall understand the attitude of our neighbors in this hemisphere.

The story of the initiation and the defeat of two determined efforts on the part of European powers to interfere in the political affairs of the countries of the Rio de la Plata is far from a simple one. In the aggressive rivalry of the British and French Governments in this quarter, commercial and financial interests are factors constantly to be taken into account. The policy which either pursued in the Plata at any particular time was nearly always influenced by important political considerations of an international character which had precious little to do with South American affairs themselves. The very complexity of these many cross-currents contributes a large measure of the significance which attaches to the narrative. That the Argentine policy of Paris or London was often a pawn in the chess game of international affairs does not, therefore, rob it of a more general importance; the move of the pawn may often reveal the hidden purposes of the queen.

It is hardly necessary to say that the narrative cannot pretend to make more than an incidental contribution to the story of the travail suffered by the Plata countries in the birth of their national and political unity. That subject merits a thorough investigation, but the present study must confine itself to a more limited task.

CHAPTER I

THREE DECADES OF ARGENTINE INDEPENDENCE

The power of Spain in America began to decline long before the fateful invasion of the Iberian peninsula by Napoleon. With the passing of her naval power, the old monopolistic system was doomed. Other nations forced their way into a share of the trade of the Spanish colonies. The prosperous Creole mercantile communities in America became progressively more restive under the galling commercial regulations and the domination of the Spanish bureaucracy. It was only a question of time till the dissatisfaction should get beyond control. The decay of the political authority of the mother country was evidenced by the decentralization of the colonial administration and by the relaxation of the mercantile policy during the last years of Spanish sovereignty.[1]

Alongside of this fact of the steady decline of the Imperial authority stands the even more significant one that the separation of the Colonies came before it was due. No indigenous political institutions had developed to take the place of the Spanish system.[2] Had the promoters of independence been obliged to wrest their commercial and political rights from a vigorous power in Europe, the development of a considerable capacity for organization and co-operation would have been a prerequisite for their success. Even if the crumbling empire had been allowed by Napoleon to die a natural death, the conservative Creole elements would have seen to it that the separation movement was postponed until some adjustment had been made which would not have left their interests at the

---

[1] Bernard Moses, *Spain's Declining Power in South America, 1730-1806.* (Berkeley 1919), pp. 153-155.
[2] *Ibid.,* p. xix.

mercy of a people who were clearly incapable of orderly self-government. When both loyalist and patriot, conservative and radical were enlisted almost indiscriminately in the independence movement as a result of the French occupation of Spain, no stabilizing element remained. The new independent communities were, without exception, caught in the current of the same disruptive forces with which the Imperial agents had been struggling, and were quickly carried beyond their depth. The population lacked unity in blood, language, and culture. The conception of political activity among most of the people did not go beyond their loyalty to the nearest *caudillo*, or local chieftain. The first leaders who attempted to form governments found neither national consciousness, representative institutions, nor any recognized authority which could provide them with a foundation.

Associated with the universal problem of creating a government from meager resources was another of equal difficulty, namely, that of apportioning between the new states a continent and a half of territory. Not a single boundary line was established beyond dispute. Faced with such difficulties, it is small wonder that the heroes of the independence movement and their immediate successors only partially succeeded. One after another, they broke down under the crushing burdens imposed upon them. The political history of most of the states for more than a generation took the form of successive dictatorships, punctuated by revolutionary explosions and international strife.[3]

In no quarter of South America did the making of a nation present problems more baffling than in the territory which had comprised the Viceroyalty of the Rio de la Plata. With the exception of the populous mission province of Paraguay, the lower reaches of the great valley constituted a comparatively new country.[4] There was little that the Spanish had

[3] W. R. Shepherd, *The Hispanic American Nations of the New World.* (New Haven 1920). L. S. Rowe, *The Federal System of the Argentine Republic.* (Washington 1921), p. 3-4.
[4] Moses, *op. cit.,* pp. xvi-xvii. Rowe, *op. cit.,* pp. 15-21.

been able to exploit with profit in the Pampas. For two centuries, the European influence had been confined to the scattering settlements of the interior—outposts of Peru and Chile—and the backward frontier river ports of Santa Fé and Buenos Ayres. These were distinctly outside the main current of affairs, being, as one writer has said, scarcely more than "oases of Spanish population in a savage country."[5] The intervening plains had been covered in the course of time with immense herds of cattle and horses. They were overrun by untamed wandering Indian tribes and by the scarcely less uncivilized half-breed *gaucho* horsemen, who manned the frontier ranches near the settlements.[6] The civilizing agencies of the religious orders, so effective elsewhere in Spanish America, had made little progress among the warlike nomads of the Pampas. Their influence was entirely removed when the Jesuit orders were expelled in 1767.[7] The towns were isolated frontier communities, with a minimum of political organization. They managed local concerns through an appointive *cabildo*, or council, and suffered comparatively little interference from the central authorities.[8]

The real development of the river may be said to date from the establishment, in 1776, of the Viceroyalty of the Rio de la Plata. The new center of authority at Buenos Ayres was intended to serve as a bulwark against the encroachments of the Portuguese on the *Banda Oriental*, or eastern bank of the Plata and Uruguay rivers.[9] The reduction of the Portuguese stronghold of Colonia in the following year, a port which

[5] Ernesto Quesada, "Social Evolution of the Argentine Republic." *Annals of the American Academy*, 30, pp. 707-721.

[6] See Oscar Schmeider, "Alterations of the Argentine Pampa in the Colonial Period." Vol. 2, No. 10 of the *University of California Publications in Geography*. (Berkeley 1927), pp. 303-308.

[7] *Ibid.*, pp. 308-318; Moses, *op. cit.*, pp. 106, 152.

[8] Quesada, *op. cit.*, pp. 707-715. Rowe, *op. cit.*, pp. 23-31.

[9] For the earlier contact between Spanish and Portuguese, see Schmeider, *op. cit.*, p. 319, and E. G. Bourne, "The History and Determination of the Line of Demarcation established by Pope Alexander VI between the Spanish and Portuguese Fields of Discovery and Colonization." *Annual Report of the American Historical Association for 1891.* (Washington 1892), pp. 119-122.

had been for many decades the center of a thriving contraband trade, was followed by the promulgation of a liberalized commercial code. A powerful impetus was thus given to the development of Buenos Ayres.[10] By 1810, it had become the foremost city of Spanish America, with a population, predominantly white, almost double its former size and rapidly increasing.[11] It possessed a wealthy and cultured Creole community which would have been an ornament to the society of any state. Its prosperity was the envy of Montevideo and Santa Fé, and the cause of hatred on the part of the now decadent though far more populous inland city of Asunción.[12] The Viceroyalty was far from being unified in spirit.

The increased vitality which the new commercial code had brought to Buenos Ayres manifested itself in the rapid expansion of the cattle industry across the Pampas. During the two decades following 1790, the Creole *estancias*, or ranches, manned by the half-savage *gauchos*, swept beyond the old lines of the Indian frontier, crowding the natives into the less desirable mountain regions and the barren areas of the south.[13] Although this rural population contained much of the blood of the European [14] and provided the staple export commodity of hides for the commerce of Buenos Ayres, there was little else that it had in common with the civilized metropolis. The *gaucho* was the product of an idle, disorderly, pastoral society. He had been for many generations a foreigner to the political, educational, and religious institutions of his white forebears. His law was personal vengeance; fighting and gambling were his amusements; his political allegiance was the primitive loyalty to a popular chieftain; his *mores* were the product of the

[10] Moses, *op. cit.*, pp. 26-34; 95-106; 159-168. This contraband trade through Colonia was greatly to the profit of the British and Dutch, and Spain was repeatedly obliged to restore the place to Portugal during the eighteenth century because of pressure exerted in Europe.

[11] Schmeider, *op. cit.*, p. 319; Moses, *op. cit.*, pp. 153-155. The population was approximately 25,000 in 1778, 46,000 in 1810, and 70,000 in 1832. See S. D. Arg. Rep., Desp., 4, Baylies to Livingston, July 24, 1832.

[12] Moses, *op. cit.*, p. xvii.

[13] Schmeider, *op. cit.*, pp. 317-318. The southern Indian frontier of Buenos Ayres did not pass beyond the Salado river until the 19th century.

[14] W. R. Shepherd, *Latin America*. (New York and London 1924), p. 32.

ranch and the slaughter-pen. He dealt as harshly with the robber as he was tolerant of the murderer.[15]

There was little love lost between these two divergent social groups who were suddenly called upon to team together in the formation of the Argentine state. The Creoles of the city entertained no illusions concerning the savage character of the untutored and bloodthirsty plainsmen. The contempt of Buenos Ayres was heartily reciprocated on the part of the *gaucho*, who exhibited to a marked degree that antipathy toward the trade and civilization of urban life so characteristic of the child of the soil. There was nothing in the independence movement (almost entirely urban in character) which served to bridge the dangerous gap between these two elements of the Argentine population.[16] Neither of them would voluntarily submit to the control of the other, and it is, therefore, difficult to imagine how a conflict for the mastery could have been avoided.

The immediate effect of the collapse of the authority of Spain at Buenos Ayres was an alarming movement toward the disintegration of the territory of the old Viceroyalty. High Peru became Bolivia. The Portuguese authority was extended over large areas of São Paulo, Santa Catharina, and Rio Grande do Sul, the possession of which had long been disputed with Spain.[17] So jealous was Paraguay of the leadership assumed by Buenos Ayres, that the up-river province repelled an expedition directed against it in 1810-1811 for the purpose of forcing Asunción to throw out the Spanish official. Yet the victors immediately conceded the point at issue when an armistice was arranged. By a treaty which was concluded in October, 1811, Paraguay became nominally a part of the United

[15] S. D. Arg. Rep., Desp., 4, Baylies to Livingston, July 24, 1832. Sarmiento, *Life in the Argentine Republic in the Days of the Tyrants.* (New York 1868), pp. 48-51.

[16] Rowe, *op. cit.,* pp. 15-21. The often repeated statement that the successful resistance of Buenos Ayres to the British expeditions of 1806 and 1807 (see Moses, *op. cit.,* pp. 356-371) created the Argentine nation must be considerably qualified. It contributed much more to the independence movement than it did to national consciousness within the Viceroyalty.

[17] Quesada, *op. cit.,* p. 716.

Provinces of the Rio de la Plata.[18]   But Dr. Francia, the Dictator at Asunción, soon isolated it; the state was kept almost hermetically sealed from outside contacts until the death of Francia in 1840.[19]

The Spanish were not driven from the Oriental Province of Uruguay until 1814.[20]   Difficulties immediately arose with Buenos Ayres over the representation of the new territory in the Argentine Assembly, with the result that the jealous Montevideo severed its connection with the United Provinces in 1815.[21]   This demonstration of hostility between the two banks of the Rio de la Plata was an invitation to the authorities at Rio de Janeiro to continue their expansionist program by the absorption of the *Banda Oriental.*   Uruguay was accordingly invaded in 1817, and four years later duly incorporated into the Portuguese dominions as the Cisplatine Province.   It passed into the hands of independent Brazil in 1822.[22]

The rapid splitting-up of the old Viceroyalty threatened to extend itself even to the provinces of the Pampas.   For more than a decade, the outlying settlements were practically independent communities, each dominated by a local chieftain who was extremely jealous of his power.   The strife was interminable.   If trade was to be carried on and property protected, some more effective central government had to be devised.

In regard to this problem of a government for Argentina, there were two more or less distinct parties.   The Federal ideal of local autonomy was regnant generally outside of Buenos Ayres.   But the more capable political leaders of the metropolis were convinced that the only safe policy was to entrust authority to the civilized elements of the population.

[18] W. H. Koebel, *Paraguay.* (London 1917), pp. 166-178. *Archivo Diplomático y Consular de Paraguay.* Published by the Ministerio de Relaciones Exteriores. (Asunción 1909), pp. 5-8. Article 5 of the treaty.
[19] C. A. Washburn, *The History of Paraguay.* 2 vols. (Boston 1871), v. 1, pp. 267-333.
[20] Augustín de Vedia, *Martín García y la Jurisdicción del Plata.* (Buenos Ayres 1908), p. 27.
[21] L. S. Rowe, "The Centenary of the Republic of Uruguay." *Bulletin of the Pan American Union* 59: 865-879.
[22] W. R. Manning, "An early diplomatic controversy between the United States and Brazil." *Hispanic American Historical Review,* I, pp. 126-127. Vedia, *op. cit.,* pp. 27-33.

THE LOWER VALLEY
OF THE
RIO DE LA PLATA
AND ITS TRIBUTARIES

They would make the capital the seat of a unitary administrative system like that of France. This *Unitarian* party was able to secure control of the revamped Argentine Confederation in 1826. Under the leadership of President Rivadavia, they promulgated a Constitution which would have made the various Provincial Governors virtually the Intendants of the President.[23]   But the system could not be put into operation. Rivadavia encountered so much opposition that he was obliged to retire in 1827 in favor of a Federalist leader named Dorrego. The change was partly due to circumstances connected with a war which had broken out with Brazil meanwhile over the possession of Uruguay.[24]

The control of the Province of Uruguay was a question of transcendent importance to the two rival states, Argentina and Brazil. The great valley of the Plata which found its only practicable commercial outlet down the rivers included some of the most valuable portions of the Brazilian Empire. For Rio de Janeiro to surrender control of both banks of the Plata into unfriendly hands, without securing for herself free use of the rivers, would prejudice for all time the economic development of this region.[25]   On the other hand, the domination of the Oriental Province by Brazil was intolerable from the Argentine point of view, because of historical and racial considerations, as well as commercial. The matter was of even greater importance because of the fact that the province then included the Isle of Martín García, which commanded the only navigable passage of the river at that point.[26]

When the Orientals themselves, under the leadership of Lavalleja, revolted against the Portuguese authority in April, 1825, they found ready sympathy from their Spanish brethren

[23] S. D. Arg. Republic, Desp. 4, Baylies to Livingston, July 24, 1832. W. S. Robertson, "South America and the Monroe Doctrine, 1824-1828." *Political Science Quarterly*, 20:82 ff. Juan P. Ramos, *El poder ejecutivo en los estatuos, reglamentos, y constitucionales de la nación y las provincias.* (Buenos Aires 1912), p. 146 ff.

[24] Antonio D. Pascual, *Apuntes para la historia de la República Oriental de Uruguay.* 2 vols. (Paris 1864), v. 1, pp. 321-335. See also W. A. Hirst, *Argentina.* (New York 1910), p. 88.

[25] Carlos Oneta y Viana, *La Diplomacia del Brasil en el Río de la Plata.* (Montevideo and Buenos Aires 1903), pp. 5-12.

[26] Manning, *op. cit.,* pp. 127-129.

across the river. War broke out between the two larger states in 1826. After two years of active fighting, in which the Argentine forces had somewhat the best of it, a "preliminary Convention of peace" was arranged under British mediation in August, 1828.[27] They agreed to compromise the question by creating a new state out of the territory in dispute. Both parties pledged themselves to intervene disinterestedly on behalf of the legal Government of Montevideo in case of civil war, until five years subsequent to the adoption of a Constitution. The contracting parties further agreed to appoint other plenipotentiaries for the purpose of concluding a *definitive* treaty of peace, which would specify the occasion and the manner in which each would be bound to defend the independence of the new state. The two governments also promised to employ every effort to preserve the free navigation of the Plata river system for a period of fifteen years, "in the form which will be arranged in the definitive treaty of peace." [28]

This settlement of 1828 by no means solved the problem. The principal defects arose from the fact that the intended definitive treaty, which was to have regulated the purposes set forth, was never concluded. The free navigation of the rivers was not recognized, and the occupation of Martín García by Buenos Ayres gave to that government the power to interdict up-river traffic at will. No plan was devised whereby their mutual guarantee of the independence of Uruguay could be enforced, and the limits of the new state were left undetermined.[29]

The Republic of Uruguay embarked upon its national career in a rather auspicious manner. The first President, Fructuoso Rivera, was popular with the masses of the people, and managed to maintain his authority throughout his five-year term. He secured the choice of his lieutenant, Manuel Oribe, as his

[27] Adolfo Saldías, *Historia de la Confederación Argentina; Rosas y su época.* 5 vols. (Buenos Aires 1892), v. 2, pp. 281-297. H. W. V. Temperley, "The Latin American Policy of George Canning," *American Historical Review,* 11, pp. 783-785.
[28] Pascual, *op. cit.,* 1, pp. 347-353.
[29] Vedia, *op. cit.,* pp. 54-58; 78-87.

successor in 1835.[30]   But evil days were in store.   Uruguay soon found herself swept into the orbit of the political upheavals of Argentina, from which she emerged fifteen years later in a state of complete desolation and ruin.

Scarcely had the military operations against Brazil ended in 1828, when political affairs in Argentina were again thrown into confusion by the collapse of the Dorrego Government. This leader had been able neither to gain the respect of his Federalist associates, nor to reconcile himself with Generals Lavalle and Paz, two capable Unitarian leaders who were heroes of the late war.[31]   The power of Dorrego quickly evaporated in 1829, when Lavalle engineered an insurrection.   But Lavalle sacrified the opportunity which was his.   Coming in as a popular hero at a time when the Federalist party was divided and the country as a whole desirous of peace, it is possible that he might, by a conciliatory policy, have gained acceptance by both parties.   Instead, he immediately proceeded to the extreme of executing his predecessor, an act which again released all the forces of civil war.

In the struggle that ensued, the more numerous rural party was almost bound to win.   Although General Paz was able to hold in check the Federalist forces of the interior, the new President proved to be no match for General Juan Manuel Rosas, an influential cattle owner, formerly Commander-in-chief of the Provincial militia under Dorrego, who advanced upon Buenos Ayres at the head of a multitude of worshipping *gaucho* followers.[32]   Lavalle came to a tentative personal agreement with Rosas in June, 1829.   The former remained as the

[30] Alfred de Brossard, *Considérations historiques et politiques sur les républiques de La Plata dans leur rapports avec la France et l'Angleterre.* (Paris 1850), pp. 171-175.   For the 1829 Constitution of Uruguay, see José Ignacio Rodríguez, *American Constitutions.* 2 vols.   (Washington 1907), v. 2, pp. 158-202.

[31] Sarmiento, *op. cit.,* pp. 154-161.   Pascual, *op. cit.,* p. 335.   For a more appreciative account of the work of Dorrego see M. A. Pelliza, *Dorrego en la historia de las partidos Unitario y Federal.* (Buenos Ayres 1878.)

[32] Sarmiento, *op. cit.,* pp. 178-186.   Rosas was a wealthy rancher of pure Spanish descent who had spent almost his entire life among the rural inhabitants.

nominal head of the Government for the following six months, but his tenure was manifestly dependent upon the will of Rosas. The American *Chargé d'affaires* saw only hopeless anarchy ahead. He wrote in July, 1829, as follows:

> "The whole of these once flourishing Provinces are now on the verge of falling into the unqualified possession of countless hordes of savages, associated with a race of men . . . at the head of which may be found an indiscriminating thirst [*sic*] of blood and rapine." [33]

The leader whom this new convulsion had brought to the surface proved, however, to be not merely the idol of the *gauchos* but their master as well. Contemporary witnesses agree that it was Rosas alone who saved the Province of Buenos Ayres from falling into a state of utter chaos. The American agent, writing some four months after his earlier pessimistic account, was most extravagant in his praise of the moderation and magnanimity displayed by the new leader in his hour of triumph.[34] Rosas intervened personally in December, 1829, to reconvene the old *Junta* of Dorrego, by which body he was immediately elected as Captain-General of the Province of Buenos Ayres with extraordinary powers, for a term of three years. The resistance of General Paz did not long survive the attacks of his Federalist opponents. Rosas became, as leader of the Federalist party and Dictator of Buenos Ayres, the most powerful individual in the Confederation.[35]

The reasons for the remarkable influence which Rosas exercised among the rural population are set forth in part in the following rather flattering statement of the United States Chargé, made at the time of the Dictator's election:

> "He is . . . a man of moderate education, but like many of those strong minded farmers which abound in our own Country, and are justly considered to be the best guarantees of our national liberty. Rosas however, differs from anything we have in our Country inasmuch as he owes his great popularity among the *gauchos,* or common peasantry, to his having assimilated himself

[33] S. D. Arg. Rep., Desp., 3, Forbes to Van Buren, May 25, July 1, 26, 1829.
[34] *Ibid.,* Nov. 12, 1829.
[35] Brossard, *op. cit.,* pp. 177-183.

to the greatest extremity to their most singular mode of life, their dress, their labors, and even their sports; and it is said that he excells in every gymnastic exercise, even the most active and adroit, of that half-savage race of men. . . . He affects no display of learning, but shows in all his conversation a full share of excellent judgment and knowledge of the affair of his Country, and a most cordial and sincere patriotism." [36]

The task of devising some scheme of central government now devolved upon the Federalist leaders. The first step was taken in 1830 when a preliminary convention was agreed to by the representatives of the four principal Provinces of Buenos Ayres, Entre Rios, Corrientes, and Santa Fé. The arrangement provided for a subsequent meeting in Santa Fé of an Assembly of Provincial delegates chosen for the purpose of drawing up a plan for a central government of the Confederation. The conduct of foreign affairs was temporarily assigned to the Governor of Buenos Ayres until further provision should be made.

The work of this Constitutional Assembly, which concluded its sessions on January 4, 1831, left much to be desired. The net result was a treaty between the four Provinces, which provided for little more than a commercial agreement and an offensive and defensive alliance. The other Provinces were invited to adhere to the same treaty. The control of the foreign relations of the Confederation was to be confided to a representative Commission with its seat at Santa Fé, all treaties with foreign powers being subject to the ratification of the several governments of the allied provinces. In 1832, several prominent leaders outside of Buenos Ayres succeeded in convening this Foreign Affairs Commission; but friction and jealousy immediately arose and the body dissolved after Rosas withdrew his representative. The convoking of the representative Federal Assembly, which had also been agreed upon, was repeatedly postponed because of political unrest, and the body never came together.[37]

[36] S. D. Arg. Rep., Desp., 3, Forbes to Van Buren, Dec. 9, 1829.
[37] Brossard, *op. cit.*, pp. 177-190; 244-245.

An important result of this failure to establish a real Federal Government was that the incumbent in the office of Governor of the Province of Buenos Ayres continued to consider himself as charged with the conduct of the foreign relations of the Confederation.   Along with the traditional primacy of his province, this power constituted practically his only claim to legal superiority over his fellow governors.   It came to be, in the hands of General Rosas, one of the principal means by which he maintained his personal ascendency throughout the Confederation and his unchallenged leadership in the Province of Buenos Ayres.

At the end of his first three years of dictatorship, Rosas was invited to continue as Governor of the Province, but without his former exercise of extraordinary powers.   He refused to accept the responsibilities of the office under these terms, however, and soon departed with an army of his followers to the south for the purpose of subduing some troublesome Indians.   A more liberal faction came into control.   They repealed many of the harsh measures of Rosas, and promulgated a Constitution in July, 1833, which declared the Province of Buenos Ayres free from all Confederation government and explicitly forbade the repetition of the granting of unlimited authority to the governor.[38]

The new Government quickly found itself engulfed in popular disorders which it was powerless to curb.   The allegation may be true that these troubles were deliberately fomented by the agents of Rosas, but, aside from this question, it soon became evident that no government could maintain itself without his powerful support.   When Rosas returned to the city at the head of his victorious army after an absence of two years, he persisted in his refusal to take control of affairs unless he was granted his former undefined powers.   This the Assembly was loath to do.   The expedient was tried of electing Rosas' most intimate associates to governmental positions, but the disorderly rural population which had invaded the city knew but one master.   Complete anarchy again threatened the

[38] Brossard, *op. cit.*, p. 184 ff.

place. It was with the approval of some of the most intelligent conservative citizens of Buenos Ayres that Rosas was finally invited on March 7, 1835, to assume for five years the duties of Governor, with authority that comprehended the sum total of the public power.[39]

Still the *gaucho* leader was not satisfied. He demanded of the *Sala*, or Chamber, that his election under these wide powers should be approved by a plebiscite. This was accordingly done, with the result that the proposition was accepted by a vote of 9320 to 4.[40] The *Sala* then reaffirmed its previous action, and on April 1, 1835, General Rosas, the "Illustrious Restorer of the Laws," assumed his post with the official title of "Governor and Captain-General of Buenos Ayres, charged with the Foreign Relations, and General-in-chief of the Armies of the Argentine Confederation." [41]

The power of the Dictator soon made itself felt throughout the Confederation. He proceeded to stamp out disorder and to crush all opposition with a heavy hand. His Federalist rivals disappeared one by one, usually under suspicious circumstances. Most of the Provincial Governors became his creatures. Prominent leaders and wealthy men of Unitarian convictions sooner or later experienced the iron hand of his despotism and either followed Lavalle into exile across the Plata, joined General Paz on the northern frontier, or accompanied Sarmiento and Alberdi to other parts of South America. From their various places of refuge, these emigrés began eventually to attack the Dictator by every means at their disposal. The press of Buenos Ayres was, of course, subjected to the direct control of Rosas, and the Assembly became entirely subservient.[42]

There was little place for the niceties of civilization in the *gaucho* state. Not only did educational and religious institu-

[39] Brossard, *op. cit.*, pp. 184-192. Saldías, *op. cit.*, 2, pp. 256-257.

[40] S. D. Buenos Ayres, Consular Letters, 4, Dorr to Forsyth, April 5, 1835. The plebiscite was, of course, the merest farce. All kinds of irregular tactics were used, and the vast majority of the people were too much cowed to express their views.

[41] Brossard, *op. cit.*, p. 408.

[42] *Ibid.*, pp. 194-203.

tions, hospitals, and public works generally languish under the new régime; Rosas was also contemptuous of the value of trade, and repeatedly demonstrated his willingness to sacrifice the commercial and financial interests of his province for the sake of personal and party ends.[43]

It is more important that the dictatorship of Rosas be understood than that judgment be passed upon it. His faults and his virtues were those of the people from whom he sprang, and his policies were elicited by the problems which he was obliged to confront. If his Government was blighting to prosperity and based on terrorism, it was at least effective, and no one could have envied him his task. It undoubtedly cost him prodigious physical toil, and it has never been charged that he was other than scrupulously honest and sincerely patriotic in the discharge of his duties.[44] He certainly bridged a dangerous social gap between the two elements of the population and arrested the disintegration of the Argentine state.[45] Who will condemn him because he enjoyed the exercise of authority, or because he turned, with unusual cleverness, the machinations of his arrogant and intriguing enemies to his own advantage? [46]

[43] Sarmiento, *op. cit.*, pp. 271-272. See also an article in *Fraser's Magazine*, 42, p. 598 ff. "Rosas, the Dictator of Buenos Ayres." (May, 1852.) It is difficult to reconcile the fact of Rosas' contempt for trade with the contention which some have advanced that the Dictator set out deliberately to ruin Montevideo as the commercial rival of Buenos Ayres.

[44] José Manuel Éstrada, *La Política Liberal bajo la Tiranía de Rosas.* (Buenos Aires 1897, 1927), p. 37.

[45] Bartolemé Mitre, *Historia del Belgrano y la independencia de Argentina.* 3 vols. (Buenos Aires 1887), v. 3, p. 438.

[46] Quesada, *op. cit.*, pp. 716-721. The following statement of a Commodore of the United States navy who had intimate dealings with Rosas in 1838 may be à propos:

"He [Rosas] is a man who has much cunning as well as determination, and I believe would not hesitate to commit any act to carry into effect his views. . . . To do the Governor justice, he has a police which he makes respected, not only in Buenos Ayres, but in every part of his Dominions, and among his before wild and lawless people. The Assassin and Robber find in him a severe Judge, and you may traverse the streets of the Cities as well as the solitudes of the Pampas in perfect safety from his former ruthless subjects; they are tamed; for this he deserves the blessings and thanks of all good men. I must and do acknowledge him to be a man well calculated for his country as it is.—He has Talents, Honesty, and firmness, and if he would enlighten his Countrymen

With the domestic policy of the Dictator, we shall have little to do, for our narrative concerns especially his direction of the foreign policy of the Confederation.

The fact that Uruguay was the natural asylum for refugees from Buenos Ayres inevitably brought that state within the scope of the policy of Rosas. Much of the trouble which Rivera had encountered as President, from 1830 to 1835, had been instigated from Buenos Ayres because of the fact that he had refused to curb the activities of the Unitarian emigrés.[47] Rather than run the risk of similar opposition, President Oribe preferred to come to terms with the powerful Dictator. It was agreed between them that each government should oppose within its own borders all activities directed against the legal authority of the other. As a result of this arrangement, the Argentine refugees at Montevideo soon found themselves frustrated in their political activities. They were placed under such strict surveillance that they came to regard Oribe also as their enemy.[48] When a quarrel developed between Oribe and Rivera and the latter raised the banner of revolt in July, 1836,[49] the small group of persecuted Unitarians, led by Lavalle, had little choice but to cast their lot with the insurgents. This action was taken in spite of the fact that they had but little respect for the mendacious and untrustworthy ex-President.[50] Both rebel leaders were immediately declared outlaws, and were obliged to flee across the Brazilian border.

by introducing Knowledge, Science, Agriculture, and Commerce— He would as he calls himself) be another Cincinnatus." [sic] See N. D. Captain's Letters, April, 1839. From Com. Nicolson, April 22, p. 65.

[47] Pascual, op. cit., 2, pp. 51-55. Vicente Lopez, Manual de la historia argentina. (Buenos Aires 1920), pp. 475-480.

[48] M. A. Pelliza, Historia Argentina. 2 vols. (Buenos Aires 1910), v. 2, pp. 176-179. Pelliza, La Dictatura de Rosas. (Buenos Aires 1917), pp. 94-99.

[49] Julian D. Miranda, Compendio de historia nacional, 1830-1894. (Montevideo 1905), pp. 27-36.

[50] Lopez, op. cit., pp. 475-480.

Rosas stood ready to give the legal President material assistance if it should be necessary.[51]

This more or less accidental collusion between Rivera and Lavalle was admirably designed to serve the purposes of Rosas. In the first place, it enabled him to identify the cause of Rivera with that of his Unitarian enemies, thus providing him with a ready excuse for his interminable interference in the internal affairs of Uruguay. The real seat of the Federalist-Unitarian controversy could be shifted to the conveniently distant territory of Uruguay. Again, by a clever use of the press, Rosas could picture the chronic unrest in the Oriental Republic with its occasional repercussions in Argentina, as an insidious attack directed at the heart of the Federal cause. By this means he was able to maintain the spirit of factional bitterness among his own followers at a very high pitch and to divert attention from his own arbitrary actions. Whether as accomplice or simply as tool, Oribe co-operated from this time forward, hand in glove, with the policy of Rosas.[52]

The government at Rio de Janeiro was in no position to take measures to counteract the predominance which Rosas was acquiring in the Oriental state. The preoccupation of Dom Pedro I with the interests of his daughter in Portugal had allowed the numerous insurrectionary movements throughout his vast Empire to get beyond control. His abdication in 1831 had left a six-year-old boy as head of the government. The successive regencies under the new régime made little progress in restoring the Imperial authority. The situation in the southern Province of Rio Grande do Sul was particularly complicated because of the fact that the Riverista group in Uruguay was fraternizing with the Brazilian rebels across the frontier. If either party was hard pressed, it could easily find refuge within the boundaries of the neighboring country. As long as such a relationship obtained, the Imperial Govern-

[51] Miranda, *op. cit.*, pp. 27-36. S. D. Consular Letters, Buenos Ayres, 5, Dorr to Forsyth, Aug. 14, 21, 1836. Some assistance was actually furnished Oribe by Rosas.

[52] S. D. *ibid.*, Sept. 14, Oct. 11, 1836. Pelliza, *Historia Argentina*, 2, pp. 176-179. Oribe made the arrest of 18 peaceful Argentine residents at Montevideo at the instance of Rosas.

ment could not afford to alienate President Oribe at Montevideo, no matter how much that leader might be dominated by
the Buenos Ayres Dictator.[53]
It is not surprising, under these circumstances, to learn that
Brazil turned her attention to Paraguay. This populous inland state would be the logical ally of the Imperial Government in the cause of free navigation of the rivers, when the
isolation policy imposed upon it by the aged Dr. Francia should
be cast aside. The Brazilian Government set about deliberately, therefore, to foment hostility between Asunción and
Buenos Ayres. Even before the death of the Paraguayan Dictator in 1840, a Brazilian consul had gained access to Asunción, and had made a beginning of such a policy.[54]

In the Rio de la Plata, as elsewhere in Spanish America, the
foreign policy of Mr. Canning had given to Great Britain an
unquestioned leadership as far as the influence of the North
Atlantic states was concerned. England had not only protected the new republics by her fleet, but had also provided
Buenos Ayres in particular with a large loan from Baring
Brothers of London in 1824. Her merchants had been willing to furnish the munitions and supplies so badly needed on
easy initial payments and long term credit. England alone
of the nations of Europe was trusted in Spanish America, and
she had a commercial stake in the Plata in 1830 which dwarfed
that of her nearest rival.[55] Her trading position was guar-

[53] E. Lavisse et A. Rambaud, *Histoire Générale*. 12 vols. (Paris 1893-
1901), v. 10, pp. 863-864. The constant ferment on the Oriental-Brazilian
frontier and the activities of the Rio Grande privateers, who were commanded by Guiseppe Garibaldi, were a nuisance to neutrals as well as to
the parties primarily concerned. See F. O. 6, Argentina, 56, from the
British consul at Montevideo, Nov. 8, 1837.
[54] Oneta y Viana, *op. cit.*, pp. 16-18.
[55] H. W. V. Temperley, *The Foreign Policy of Canning, 1822-1827*.
(London 1925), pp. 133-144. L. A. Lawson, *Relation of British Policy to
the Declaration of the Monroe Doctrine*. (New York 1922), pp. 84-86.
British commerce to the Rio de la Plata jumped from 660,000 pounds in
1823 to more than 1,140,000 in 1824, at the time of the Baring loan.
The total trade of Britain with South America in 1825 was over 8½ million pounds. See vol. 3, p. 555 of *Hunt's Merchant's Magazine and Commercial Review*.

anteed by the commercial treaty which she had secured from
Argentina as the price of her recognition in 1825. By its
terms British merchants were placed on a status of absolute
equality with Argentine citizens in the matter of trading privileges, port and tonnage dues, etc.   Furthermore, resident
British nationals were expressly exempt from all forced loans,
military requisitions, and from compulsory military service.[56]
This latter exemption was particularly important because it
repealed, as far as British subjects were concerned, a Buenos
Ayres law of April 10, 1821, making all foreigners liable for
service in the Provincial militia.[57]

The United States really made no effort to keep pace with
Great Britain in the race for the leading position in South
America. After the Panama Congress fiasco, even Adams and
Clay lost much of their earlier enthusiasm for the new republics.[58] The principal concern of the Washington Government
was to avoid at all costs becoming entangled in the turbulence
of South American affairs. During the Argentine-Brazilian
war, which was brought to a close by the friendly interposition
of Great Britain, the State Department found itself engaged in
an acrimonious quarrel with Brazil over neutral rights during
blockade.[59] At the same time, Secretary Clay emphatically
rebuffed an Argentine attempt to invoke the Monroe Doctrine
against monarchist Brazil, by explaining that an executive
declaration such as that of 1823 did not constitute a pledge
to Latin America which the United States Government could
be called upon to fulfill. He even went further to volunteer the
affirmation that there was no longer any danger of the development of the contingencies contemplated by the message of

[56] Florencio Varela, *Tratados de los estados del Río de la Plata.* (Montevideo 1847-1848), pp. 847-848.

[57] A copy of this military service law can be found in N. D. Captain's
Letters, April 1839. Nicolson to Paulding, April 22.

[58] S. F. Bemis, *The American Secretaries of State and their Diplomacy.*
10 vols. (New York 1928-9), v. 4, pp. 142-146; 154.

[59] Temperley, *op. cit.,* pp. 163-167, 181-184, 211-222. London feared very
much that the Republicanism of Bolívar would be enlisted in support of
Argentina, and that the Brazilian Monarchy might be overthrown. For
the United States quarrel see *British Foreign and State Papers,* 16, pp.
1099-1160, and Manning, *op. cit.,* pp. 129-144.

Monroe.[60] In decided contrast to the British agent, the United
States Chargé at Buenos Ayres kept himself strictly aloof
from local political controversies. President Jackson later refused to take advantage of an opportunity to establish by
treaty the tacit understanding whereby United States citizens enjoyed personal and trading privileges equal to those of
the British, so little interest did he take in Argentine affairs.[61]

But this lack of interest on the part of the United States
President cannot under any consideration justify the disaster
which befell North American prestige in Argentina in 1831
and 1832. The occasion of the debacle was a quarrel over the
exercise of alleged fishing rights of a prescriptive nature by
non-Argentine vessels near the Falkland Islands. When several American ships off the Islands ignored the summons of
the commissioned Argentine authorities to cease their operations, the vessels were taken into custody. The tactless United
States consul at Buenos Ayres, who was in charge of the legation at the time, was highly incensed upon learning of the
incident. His peremptory demand that the acts of the Island
"pirates" be disavowed and that fitting restitution be made soon
took the form of an ultimatum. When a satisfactory reply
was not promptly forthcoming, an American war vessel proceeded to make reprisals by destroying considerable property
on the Islands and bringing the offending Argentine representatives back to the Plata in irons. The affair immediately
assumed a very serious aspect.[62] This hasty action was entirely unauthorized and could easily have been disavowed if
the Washington Government had desired to avoid offense. But
nothing of the sort was done. The new Chargé sent to Buenos

[60] W. S. Robertson, op. cit., Political Science Quarterly 30, p. 82 ff. J. B.
Moore, Digest of International Law. 8 vols. (Washington 1906), v. 6,
p. 434.
[61] S. D. Brazil, Desp., 11, Hunter to Forsyth, Apr. 16, 1838. S. D. Arg.
Rep., Desp., 3, Forbes to Van Buren, Nov. 12, 1829. Mr. Forbes thought
that the advantages of a treaty would be all on the side of Argentina since
the United States could not expect Buenos Ayres to fulfill its engagements.
[62] Julius Goebel, The Struggle for the Falkland Islands. (New Haven
1927), pp. 437-442. British Foreign and State Papers, 20, pp. 316-317.
Goebel maintains that the designation of the Island authorities as pirates
was utterly unwarranted. He also says that the United States consul was
probably encouraged in his defiant attitude by the British Minister at
Buenos Ayres.

Ayres was directed to support the previous demands of the consul. Rosas refused to treat concerning the original question until atonement had been made for the subsequent attack on the Islands. After several weeks of fruitless negotiation, the Chargé left Buenos Ayres in a huff, recommending that the United States chastise the insolent Government.[63]

The resentment which Argentina entertained toward the North American republic for attacking the Falkland Islands was made much more intense by the fact that the British moved in and took possession of them in January, 1833, before Buenos Ayres had had opportunity to re-establish control. Diplomatic relations were not restored between the two American nations until 1844.[64]

The elimination of the United States from the affairs of the Plata left the British more dominant than ever, notwithstanding London's refusal to see the Argentine point of view in regard to the ownership of the Falkland Islands. Britain's trade with Buenos Ayres, which far surpassed that of her nearest rival,[65] was protected by the treaty of 1825, and the London Government was not backward in insisting that the claims and personal rights of her citizens be duly honored.[66] British agents continued to take an active interest in local politics.[67] So high was England in the esteem of some parties in Uruguay that the British consul was approached unofficially in 1838 with the proposition that his Government should cut the Gordian knot of their interminable civil strife by taking

[63] S. D. Arg. Rep., Desp., 4, Baylies to Livingston, Sept. 26, 1832.

[64] Goebel, *op. cit.,* pp. 454-459. In reply to the Argentine charge that the United States here connived at England's spoliation of Argentina in violation of the Monroe Doctrine, the State Department has since declared that the Doctrine was not affected because the British claims to the Islands antedated 1823. For further discussion of the question, see C. E. Martin, *The Policy of the United States as Regards Intervention. Columbia University Studies,* 93, No. 2, pp. 125-126, and Daniel Antokoletz, *La Doctrine de Monroe et l'Amérique latine.* (Paris 1905), pp. 25-26.

[65] *Hunt's Merchant's Magazine* 8, pp. 132-133; 1, pp. 184-185.

[66] *British Foreign and State Papers* 28, pp. 1012-1015; F. O. 6, 56, Instructions to Mandeville, Aug. 2, Nov. 8, 1837; vol. 62, to same, June 6, 1838. The British Minister was also pressing vigorously to secure a slave-trade treaty.—F. O. 6, 56, to same, July 18, 1837.

[67] *Ibid.,* to Mandeville, July 5, 1837, Sept. 4 and 6, 1838.

the Oriental state under its protection.[68] Lord Palmerston refused to discuss the question until the offer came from an authoritative source.[69] At the same time, however, the British Government was taking precautions against all eventualities, particularly in view of the stream of French Basque immigration which had begun to flow to Montevideo. An English naval officer had secretly gathered detailed information concerning the strategic aspects of all the important ports of the Oriental Republic.[70] Britain had come to see in France a new rival in Argentine affairs who was ready to go to extreme lengths to attain a position of equality with her.[71]

[68] F. O. 6, 63, Mandeville to Strangeways, Feb. 14, 1838. The matter was suggested to consul Hood by one Señor Muños, an ex-Minister of Finance under Oribe.

[69] F. O. 6, 62, Palmerston to Mandeville, June 4, 1838.

[70] F. O. 6, 63, Mandeville to Palmerston Jan. 12, 1838. The extended report here submitted covered such questions as anchorage facilities, strategical importance, means of defense, water, food, pasturage, etc.

[71] The French secured a treaty with Montevideo in 1836, but it was not ratified until Oribe had been thrown out of control, in 1839. See *Colección de tratados . . . de . . . Uruguay.* 3 vols. (Montevideo 1923), v. 1, pp. 19-23. Brossard, *op. cit.,* pp. 381, 147-156. French trade to the Plata from 1831 to 1841 increased 67%, but was still smaller than that of the United States. *Hunt's Merchant's Magazine* 8, pp. 445-447.

CHAPTER II

THE FRENCH COME TO BLOWS WITH ROSAS, 1838-1839

The July Monarchy embarked upon its diplomatic relations with Argentina in 1830 under very unfavorable auspices. Not only did France suffer in standing from the general suspicion occasioned by the fact that she had sided with reactionary Europe in the hour of American need, but she was also engaged, even then, in a special quarrel with Buenos Ayres. During the short struggle between Lavalle and Rosas in May of 1829, a French Admiral stationed off the city had taken advantage of Lavalle's embarrassment to exact, by a demonstration of force, the promise that resident French nationals would not be impressed into Argentine military service.[1] This act of violence had excited universal popular indignation at the time,[2] and the promise made by Lavalle was promptly repudiated when Rosas took control. The strenuous protest of the French consul against this action only aroused further the ire of the stubborn Dictator. The question was finally allowed to drop unsettled in November 1830.[3] The incident augured nothing of good for the future of Franco-Argentine relations.

One of the first diplomatic actions of the Government of Louis Philippe was to break with the policy of the previous Legitimist régime by gratuitously according French recognition to the

---

[1] *British Foreign and State Papers,* 16, pp. 917-937. Orators in the French Chambers later held up this incident as an example of the way France should act. See *Le Moniteur Universel,* Feb. 9, 1841.

[2] S. D. Arg. Rep. Desp., 3, Forbes to Van Buren, May 25, June 4, 1829. The French Admiral captured the entire Argentine fleet and liberated several hundred political prisoners.

[3] Saldías, *op. cit.,* 3, pp. 8-9; C. Pereyra, *Rosas y Thiers.* (Madrid 1919), pp. 24-25.

"illegitimate" republics of the new world.[4] Paris was doomed to discover, however, that a common illegitimacy was not much of a family tie. Instead of winning the good will of the American states by this magnanimous gesture, as the Government had expected to do, France simply weakened her own bargaining position in the establishment of advantageous treaty relations with the various states. In the face of their previous estrangement from Rosas, the French now found themselves under the humiliating necessity of begging for commercial concessions with nothing to give in return.[5]

The diplomatic agents which the Paris Government sent to Buenos Ayres encountered the most exasperating difficulties. The first, M. de la Forêt, was rejected unconditionally on personal grounds. The second appointee, M. Vins de Paysac, was obliged to resign himself to a year of the most humiliating delay. He was finally received only when pressure was brought to bear upon Rosas by the British Minister, and then on the condition that the action should not serve as a precedent for the future.[6] It was with great difficulty that Paysac maintained himself in friendly relations with Rosas; in executing his instructions to secure for French nationals a treaty position on a par with that enjoyed by the British he was able to make no progress at all. After the death of Paysac in May, 1836, relations were again suspended. Rosas refused to converse on diplomatic questions with the vice-consul, M. Aimé Roger, who was left in charge of the French legation.[7] The quick-tempered young Frenchman interpreted his treatment as both a personal and a national insult. When a change of attitude on the part of the authorities at Paris gave him the opportunity

---

[4] Brossard, op. cit., pp. 144-146. F. A. M. Mignet, "Des Rapports de la France et de l'Europe avec l'Amérique du Sud." Revue des Deux Mondes, 1838, v. 3, pp. 48-50. Brazil had already been recognized by France in 1826 and Mexico had in 1827.

[5] Aff. Etr., Bolivie, 1, pp. 112-114. Instructions dated October 18, 1830. Brossard, op. cit., pp. 143-146. Mignet, op. cit., pp. 48-50. The first South American treaties were secured with Uruguay in 1836, Bolivia in 1837, Chile in 1838, and Argentina in 1840.

[6] Aff. Etr., Buenos Ayres, 24, pp. 18-22, a memorandum signed by Molé. Thomas Page, "Affaires de Buenos Ayres," Revue des Deux Mondes 25, (1841, v. 1), pp. 301-303.

[7] Brossard, op. cit., pp. 217-220.

in 1838, Roger needed no encouragement to engineer a break with the insolent Dictator.[8]

The situation which had thus arisen in Argentina in 1837, so prejudicial to the prestige of the French Government, was not an isolated instance. France was encountering similar difficulties elsewhere in Spanish America,[9] and she was still smarting from the indignity of President Jackson's treatment in regard to the indemnity.[10] The position which she occupied in Europe was hardly more satisfactory. Louis Philippe had grown frightened at his own boldness in following the lead of England, especially in Spain, and with the Molé Government in power in 1836-1837 had definitely broken with the policy of his former ally.[11] But the Molé Government had not gone far on the alternative road of making its peace with conservative Europe, which seemed so necessary if the matrimonial blockade of the House of Orleans was to be broken,[12] before it was challenged by the damning charge that it was betraying the principles of the July Revolution and sacrificing national interests in deference to the personal wishes of the King.[13] The opposition in the Chambers which had previously been centered in the nationalistic Third Party, quickly spread to other quarters. Thiers and Guizot began to attack from the Center and even the Legitimist Right took up the cry against the Orleans dynasty.[14] These conservative elements were backed by powerful commercial interests who thought they perceived that their trade was suffering from the neglect of the Government.[15] The charge that Molé was pursuing a spine-

[8] *Aff. Etr.*, Bolivie, 2, pp. 157-160, Instructions, Nov. 17, 1837; *ibid.*, Buenos Ayres, 23, pp. 82-85. From Aimé Roger, April 24, 1837.

[9] Antonio de la Peña y Reyes, *La Primera Guerra entre México y Francia. Archivo Histórico Diplomático Mexicano*, No. 23. (Mexico 1927.)

[10] *Archives Parlementaires*, Deuxième Série, 99, p. 425. Jan. 6, 1838.

[11] Major John Hall, *England and the Orleans Monarchy*. (New York 1912), pp. 103-144.

[12] Beckles Willson, *The Paris Embassy, a narrative of Franco-British Relations, 1814-1920*. (London 1927), pp. 146-147.

[13] *Archives Parlementaires*, Deuxième Série, 106, pp. 377-507. This debate of January, 1837, especially concerned Switzerland and Spain. Charles de Mazade, *Monsieur Thiers, cinquante années d'histoire contemporaine*. (Paris 1884), pp. 123-133.

[14] John M. Allison, *Thiers and the French Monarchy*. (Boston 1926), pp. 185-193, 208, 238-239, 254-261. Hall, *op. cit.*, pp. 202-212.

[15] *Archives Parlementaires*, Deuxième Série, 114, pp. 723-724.

less and impotent foreign policy had to be refuted by tangible evidence if the Government was to survive these recurring attacks.

The search for some new enterprise which would provide the Ministry with its needed means of defense led the Government far afield. It was necessary that the effort be directed toward ends which were both intelligible and easily attainable; it must be assertive enough to gratify the national pride, without at the same time endangering the precarious position which France occupied in Europe.[16] It was under these circumstances that the irritating, though minor, grievances which France was suffering in Spanish America became matters of primary diplomatic concern demanding immediate correction. The resulting action in America marked the inauguration of a restless, incoherent foreign policy. The July Monarchy found itself engaged, throughout the remainder of its tenure, in a series of similar enterprises in every quarter of the world.[17]

An appeal of a spokesman of the Government for increased naval strength during the debate on the address to the King in January, 1838, may be taken as a sort of preface for the new program. He said, in part:

"It is from the support of a powerful marine that some new markets will be opened to French products. . . . With the naval forces which are now being made ready, the Government has the means of guaranteeing the property of our fellow citizens against the hostile designs of certain Governments. To contribute to our

[16] An eminent French historian, writing in the semi-official *Revue des Deux Mondes* in July, 1838, was frankly in favor of an active but safe foreign policy designed for purposes of national expression and entertainment. One paragraph ran as follows:
"According as the chances of war are distant, it becomes more indispensable to prepare some food for the national character. One cannot pretend to concentrate all activity within the country, not that it ought not to find useful employment, but more because the results are not of a nature to arouse the imagination sufficiently. . . . It is necessary to consider how to satisfy that imagination, which has made France do such great things in the world. Order and economy in State finances, honest and wise laws, these are doubtless good and necessary. But with such one does not impassion the people, one does not strike the heart of the great masses of men, one does not excite their imaginations."
See Mignet, *op. cit.,* pp. 60-61.
[17] Hall, *op. cit.,* pp. 103-144. In regard to the French policy in Algeria, see Camille F. M. Rousset, *Les Commencements d'une conquête. L'Algérie de 1830 à 1840.* 2 vols. (Paris 1887), v. 2, p. 490.

commercial relations it is necessary to maintain perfect security for distant expeditions. Now, in some states of South America, the rights of French citizens have been ignored, their property has been seized by measures similar to those which, under the name of insults, one endured in former times in the East." [18]

The Republic of Mexico, which had recently refused to honor some French claims relative to losses sustained during a civil war,[19] was chosen as the principal victim of the new policy. The action of the considerable naval force which was sent to Vera Cruz was to be accompanied by a more vigorous assertion of French rights elsewhere in Spanish America, it being hoped that the example which was to be made of Mexico would make it unnecessary to go to similar extremes in other quarters.[20]

The quarrel between Consul Roger and Governor Rosas had become increasingly bitter during 1837. Instead of applying to Paris for the diplomatic credentials which the punctilio of Rosas demanded, Roger seized upon every new grievance to become more defiant in his attitude. The specific claims which he urged were neither numerous, important, nor particularly well founded. Two of them concerned instances of enforced service in the Argentine army. Another was the case of a French sutler in Rosas' army, Lavie by name, who had been summarily imprisoned for six months for possession of property belonging to the Government. The most serious claim was that of the widow of a Swiss printer named Bacle, claiming French protection, who died at his home in January, 1838, from illness contracted while serving a prison term for revolutionary intrigue. A fifth concerned an acknowledged claim of a French citizen named Despouy, who had sustained, in the

---

[18] *Archives Parlementaires, op. cit.,* 114, pp. 723-724. The speaker was referring to happenings in Chile on this occasion.

[19] Peña y Reyes, *op. cit.,* pp. xxvii-xxx. The quarrel concerned the famous question in International Law of whether a state was responsible for damage suffered by alien property during civil war.

[20] Saldías, *op. cit.,* 3, pp. 20-21. As late as March 31, 1838, the Paris Government was only acknowledging the possibility that armed intervention in the Plata might be necessary. See *Aff. Etr.,* Argentine, 23. Demonstrations were also staged in Chile and Ecuador. In Rio de Janeiro the new spirit of the French Government was markedly reflected in a more pretentious legation and an increased naval force. S. D. Brazil, Desp., 11, Hunter to Forsyth, Jan. 16, 1838.

disorder of 1821, considerable damage to his business.[21] The
particular merits of the claims were never, however, the primary
subject of the dispute, because of the fact that Rosas refused
to discuss them except with a regularly accredited diplomatic
agent. With a will for peace on either side, a settlement might
easily have been arranged; in reality, it became a point of
honor with each party not to surrender to the formal demands
of the other.

The outbreak of a war between Argentina and Bolivia in
1837 and a general revival of the local opposition to Rosas
led the French consul to commit himself to a position from
which he could hardly withdraw.[22] On November 30, 1837,
Roger presented a formal demand to the Buenos Ayres Government. He set forth at some length the various claims of
French nationals enumerated above against the Argentine authorities. He declared, furthermore, that the French Government felt itself entitled to require for its subjects the same
privileges enjoyed by British residents under the treaty of
1825.[23]

The dilatory reply of Foreign Minister Arana, dated Dec.
12, served only to increase the irritation of the consul. Arana
promised only that the Government would examine into the
precedents of the several claims presented. Roger replied on
the following day that he would not permit the discussion to
be postponed unless the discriminatory liabilities to which
French nationals were subjected were declared suspended during the interim.[24] The question of equal status with the British
became, therefore, the real subject of the dispute, and the old

[21] Aff. Etr. Argentine Republic, 23, pp. 80, 333-335. F. O. 6, Buenos
Ayres, Mandeville to Strangeways, Sept. 29, 1838. T. Page. op. cit., Revue
des Deux Mondes, 1841, 1, p. 311. Pereyra, op. cit., pp. 27-31. The last
reference presents a rabidly pro-Rosas point of view. Bacle had been
sentenced to death in April, 1837, for treason, at which time the intervention of the British Minister had saved him.
[22] S. D. Buenos Ayres, Consular Letters, Dorr to Forsyth, May 22,
June 8, 1838. Aff. Etr. Argentine, 23, pp. 108-111. Niles Register 53, pp.
37-38. The Bolivian war was partly to prevent the union of that country
with Peru under the dictator, Santa Cruz. Chile also attacked Santa Cruz.
[23] Saldías, op. cit., 3, pp. 9-12.
[24] Ibid. Also in the Correspondence Officielle; Ultimatum of M. Aimé
Roger . . . to the Government of Buenos Ayres; its answer and relative
documents. (Buenos Ayres 1838), pp. 5-9.

quarrel of 1829-1830 was brought out into the open again. During the four weeks of delay before Arana's second reply was received, the despatches which Roger sent to Paris breathed fire. He denounced the Dictator to Molé as a cruel and inhuman tyrant and begged for instructions adequate to bring to an end the exasperating treatment which he was encountering. The consul tactfully suggested that force was probably the only reasonable method of treating with Rosas.[25]

The second letter which Roger received from Arana, on January 8, was even more unsatisfactory than the previous one had been. The Argentine Minister contended that the existing military service law of 1821 had been acquiesced in by France ever since the recognition of the independence of the Confederation in 1831, and he affirmed that, under the circumstances, the Buenos Ayres Government would not even discuss the alteration of the law except with a regularly authorized diplomatic agent.[26] The issue was clearly drawn, with no grounds on which negotiations could be continued unless Roger withdrew from the picture.

The deadlocked affair took a definite turn in late January, when the consul received permission from Paris to ask for the assistance of two war vessels from the fleet of Admiral Leblanc at Rio de Janeiro in recovering the claims with which he was charged. The appeal to the Admiral was immediately made. At the same time, Roger replied to the Paris despatch, assuring Molé that the measures authorized were entirely insufficient to meet the situation. He complained, particularly, of the fact that his principal demand, in regard to most-favored-nation treatment for French nationals, had not been comprehended in his instructions.[27]

The attitude of the two French agents is clearly revealed in the account of the conference which they held at Montevideo soon after the arrival of Admiral Leblanc on February 21. Since the Admiral himself had already been ordered to support

[25] *Aff. Etr.*, Argentine, 23, pp. 190-193; 241-242. From Roger, Dec. 2 and 31, 1837.
[26] Saldías, *op. cit.*, 3, pp. 9-12. *Ultimatum of M. Roger, op. cit.*, pp. 5-9.
[27] *Aff. Etr.*, Argentine, 23, pp. 247-259. From Roger, Jan. 26, 1838.

the claims of the consul, he made no effort to go behind Roger's rather distorted version of the quarrel.[28] It was therefore agreed between them that the refusal of the Buenos Ayres authorities to atone for the outrages already inflicted upon French nationals would justify an immediate break with the Dictator. Roger also triumphed in his contention that the political situation prevailing among the Plata countries at that particular time made a forcible demonstration especially apropos. Rosas was at war with Bolivia,[29] and it was known that he was embarrassed by serious financial difficulties and by discontent within his own army. Evidence had recently come to light that the interior Argentine Provinces were much displeased over the appropriation of receipts of the custom's house at Buenos Ayres by that Government alone. An additional consideration appeared in the fact that President Oribe in Uruguay had been suffering serious reverses at the hands of the insurrectionary Riverista party.[30] The time seemed ripe for French action.

Difference of opinion arose between the consul and the Admiral, however, when it came to determining the nature of the measures to be undertaken. Roger insisted that continued patience was worse than useless, and that they should immediately declare a blockade of the port of Buenos Ayres. Such a move, he argued, would provide the enemies of the Dictator with the very encouragement which they now needed to free themselves from his tyranny. The Admiral was not as rash as his young associate. Admitting the propriety of the blockade, Leblanc was in doubt as to his own authority to adopt such an extreme measure.[31] A compromise was finally agreed upon

[28] T. Page, op. cit., p. 311. Aff. Etr., Argentine, 23, p. 328.

[29] The Chilean forces had recently withdrawn from the Bolivian war because of an epidemic of small-pox among them. Their attack was later renewed. See Aff. Etr., Argentine, 23, pp. 244-245. From Roger, Jan. 2 and 3, 1838. S. D. Buenos Ayres, Consular Letters, 5, Dorr to Forsyth, Jan. 2, 1838.

[30] Aff. Etr., Argentine, 23, pp. 328-332. From Roger, Feb. 24, 1838. Rivera in Uruguay had reviewed his troops under the very walls of Montevideo in January, as a demonstration of the impotence of Oribe. See F. O. 6, Buenos Ayres, 63, Mandeville to Palmerston, Jan. 31.

[31] Aff. Etr., ibid.

whereby Roger should return to Buenos Ayres for another attempt to negotiate with the Governor.

The consul returned to the Argentine capital more haughty than ever.[32] He arranged for an audience with Rosas on March 7. The two hour conference between the two men accomplished nothing, for the Governor would not budge in his demand for the missing diplomatic credentials. He also pretended that the repeal of the 1821 military law was beyond his power as executive head of the Buenos Ayres Government. The conversation developed into an open quarrel, culminating in a threat by the consul that France would ally herself with the enemies of the Dictator. Rosas replied that in such a case the country would unitedly support him and there would be no Unitarians. The French might take the city, but it would be a heap of worthless ruins when they entered it. Roger closed the matter by reasserting his former demands in the form of an ultimatum. The consul received his passports on March 13. He was assured, at the time, that the Argentine Government would regret any break in the harmonious relations with France and would be glad to treat on the questions at issue when he could show the proper credentials. Roger again departed from the city on the 16th.[33]

Both parties were considerably to blame in this petty quarrel. The exasperating insistence on formality, so characteristic of Rosas, was but his natural reaction to the arrogant and tactless attitude of the consul. The threat of coercive measures merely increased the determination of the Dictator not to surrender to an insignificant consul. Rosas would have nothing to do with the suggestion made to him by the British agent, Mr. Mandeville, that some accommodation should be offered for the most valid of the French demands.[34]

The affair moved rapidly to an open rupture. On March 24, Admiral Leblanc appeared before the city and presented three

[32] *Aff. Etr.,* pp. 333-335. From Roger, Feb. 28. Immediately upon his return to the city, Roger found other matters of which to complain.

[33] F. O. 6, 63, Mandeville to Palmerston, March 14, 1838.

[34] F. O. 6, Buenos Ayres, 63, Mandeville to Palmerston, March 17, reporting a confidential conversation with Arana in which it was learned that Roger had disclosed to his friends every detail of the negotiation.

demands to which he gave the Government two days to reply:
(1) The military service law must be suspended in its application to French nationals, they being guaranteed most-favored-
nation treatment until the conclusion of a treaty.   (2) The
right of French citizens to seek indemnity for injuries suffered at the hands of the Argentine Government should be
acknowledged.   (3) Pierre Lavie, the alleged sutler-thief, must
be accorded an immediate trial.[35]   Mr. Mandeville urged Rosas
to make a statement in reply to the effect that there was no
Frenchman serving in the army against his will, and containing
appropriate explanations concerning the other two demands.
But it was all to no avail.   The Governor replied defiantly that
the questions at issue would remain undiscussed as long as he
was thus summoned:

"in a military way to consent to Demands, which, if brought forward by a person authorized to treat upon them, would encounter
little difficulty in being agreed to. . . . At the Cannon's mouth to
ask for Privileges which can only be granted by a Convention is
what this Government—insignificant as it may be considered—
will never yield to." [36]

The port of Buenos Ayres was accordingly declared to be in a
state of blockade on March 28.   Vessels then in the port were
granted until June 15 to depart.[37]

There is conclusive proof to show that the French leaders
did not anticipate great difficulty in securing an acquiescence
to their demands, which seemed indeed a small price for Rosas
to pay to be rid of the considerable inconvenience of the
blockade.   Roger was confident, upon his departure from
Buenos Ayres, that he would be back at his post within a fort-

[35] F. O. 6, Buenos Ayres, 63, Mandeville to Palmerston, March 28;
Pereyra, *op. cit.*, pp. 44-45.
[36] F. O., *ibid.* Rosas published this dramatic utterance in *La Gaceta
Mercantil* of March 31, 1838. For a discussion of this effective propaganda
agency, see Antonio Zinny, *La Gaceta Mercantil de Buenos Aires, 1823-
1852.* 3 vols. (Buenos Aires 1912), vol. 2, p. 335 ff. Carlos Calvo, *Le
Droit International.* 2 vols. (Paris 1870), vol. 1, pp. 226-227. *Aff. Etr.,*
Argentine, 25, p. 401,—a memorandum of the French Government at the
end of 1838.
[37] *Aff. Etr.,* Argentine, 25, p. 401.

night,[38] and he informed the authorities at Paris that he believed that no great effort would be required. The consul nevertheless insisted emphatically that the time had come when Americans should be made to understand that equity and international rights must be respected. The dignity of France, he wrote, could no longer permit the continuance of the preferential treatment enjoyed by the British in commercial and financial matters. The punishment of Buenos Ayres would be a salutary lesson to the other American states.[39]

The acute distress at Buenos Ayres occasioned by the blockade gave promise for a time that the expectations of the French would be realized. The lack of firewood alone was a serious inconvenience. Widespread unemployment followed the suspension of commerce. The finances of the state collapsed; all Government departments were thrown badly in arrears,[40] and all schools, hospitals, and other public institutions which had managed to survive the previous era were closed. A man less feared than was Rosas would have been in danger from a popular uprising.[41] The Governor was obviously worried. Through his press he broadcast his contention that the action of the French was both unauthorized and illegal,—unauthorized because no government would order the adoption of a warlike program before the differences had been discussed, and illegal because the blockade had not been accompanied by the required declaration of war.[42] In order to create a still better basis on which he could defend his policy, Rosas informed the French Admiral on April 26 that he had released Lavie from prison and had discharged all French subjects from the militia. The Governor accompanied this information with personal assurances as to the proper treatment of French nationals in

[38] F. O. 6, 63, Mandeville to Palmerston, March 14, 1838. See also F. Durand, *Précis de l'histoire politique et militaire des États de la République de la Plata.* (Paris 1853), pp. 64-69.
[39] *Aff. Etr.,* Argentine, 24, pp. 4-8.
[40] F. O. 6, 63, Mandeville to Strangeways, April 4, 1838; *ibid.,* 64, same to Palmerston, May 2. The British Minister thought that the city would not submit to the inconveniences of the blockade.
[41] S. D. Buenos Ayres, Consular Letters, 5, Dorr to Forsyth, May 3, 1838.
[42] F. O. 6, 63, to Palmerston, April 15. See also Saldías, *op. cit.,* 3, p. 17.

the future.   The hope that Leblanc might seize this opportunity to reopen negotiations was disappointed.   The Admiral
declared that official guarantees, not mere personal assurances,
would be required, along with an explicit renunciation by Rosas
of the power to act similarly in the future.[43]   An excellent
chance to reach an accommodation was passed up in this
manner.

The most serious opposition to the policy of Rosas came
from the up-river provinces, whose interests were being unnecessarily injured by a quarrel in which they themselves had
no part.   Santa Fé and Corrientes were the leaders in the protest, and they found support in Mendoza, Cordova, Santiago
del Estero, and in other interior provinces.[44]   The principal
promoter of this dissatisfaction movement was a man named
Domingo Cullen, the deputy Governor of Santa Fé, who made
no secret of his partisanship for the French.   He had prevailed
upon the Governor of Santa Fé, Estanislao Lopez, to commission him to remonstrate with Rosas at Buenos Ayres for engaging the Argentine Confederation in hostilities with France
over grievances and regulations which were peculiar to the
Province of Buenos Ayres.[45]   Cullen even threatened, so it
was reported, that the river provinces would withdraw from
the Dictator his authority to manage foreign affairs if a
prompt adjustment with France were not made.   Through the
mediation of a North American naval officer, the promoter of
the opposition secured a statement from the French Admiral
agreeing to suspend the blockade provisionally if assurance
could be had of official sanction to the recent promises of
Rosas.[46]

But this second promising development quickly ran aground.
When Cullen communicated his proposition to Rosas on May

[43] F. O. 6, 63, M. to P., May 18; S. D. *op. cit.,* Dorr to Forsyth, May 3,
1838.

[44] *Aff. Etr.,* Buenos Ayres, 24, p. 25.   From Roger, April 23, 1838.   The
French agent was confident at this time that Rosas was doomed to succumb
to the opposition which was gathering around him.

[45] F. O. 6, 64, Mandeville to Palmerston, June 18; Saldías, *op. cit.,* 3, pp.
38-40.

[46] S. D., Buenos Ayres, Cons. Letters 5, Dorr to Forsyth, June 1, 1838.
F. O. 6, 63, M. to P., June 19.

18, the Governor flew into a rage. Rosas was exasperated that anyone should dare to interfere with his exclusive prerogatives as director of foreign affairs, and berated Cullen vigorously for his recent activities.[47] On the following day, May 19, news reached the capital concerning the rather mysterious death of Governor Lopez at Santa Fé, who happened to have been under the care of the personal physician of Rosas at the time. Cullen was obliged to depart immediately for his Province in order to keep control of the situation,[48] and Rosas was relieved for the time being from all danger of up-river interference.[49]

The Dictator moved quickly to consolidate his power at home. He made the issue that of the defense of the honor and independence of the country, and laid the matter before the Buenos Ayres Assembly on May 25. The correspondence with the French agents was published practically in its entirety. Some little opposition within the Assembly made itself heard during two days of discussion, but the Committee to whom the question was referred brought back a resolution approving the policy of Rosas and recommending that reparations be claimed for all injuries received from the French blockade. When four brave assemblymen brought forward a counter resolution to the effect that all resident foreigners should be granted equal treatment with that enjoyed by British subjects, they were threatened with physical violence within the *Sala* itself. On the following day placards were distributed over the city suggesting that the throats of such traitors should be cut. The policy of Rosas was solemnly approved on June 8, and with the possible exception of the four foolhardy deputies, who persisted in voting against the resolution, the suffering urban population was effectively cowed.[50]

[47] F. O. 6, 64, M. to P., June 19, 1838.
[48] *Ibid.*, Aug. 25.
[49] S. D. Buenos Ayres, Cons. Letters 5, Dorr to Forsyth, June 1. The common charge of the enemies of Rosas has been that Governor Lopez was poisoned by the physician of the Dictator. N. D. Captain's Letters, August, 1838, Commodore Nicolson wrote on Aug. 3, from Montevideo: "The unfortunate death of Governor Lopez of Santa Fé destroyed all the hope which was at one time entertained of an amicable arrangement."
[50] F. O. 6, 63, M. to P., May 18 and June 15, 1838. The placards branded the four men as "assassins of American liberties."

Simultaneously with this action within the capital, Rosas appealed to his fellow governors in the Confederation, asking for their support in the defense of the country. The several governors quickly fell in line. Five of them had replied by June 3; two more approved in July, and three in August, together with the General then conducting the operations against Bolivia. It was with obvious misgivings that the Governor of Corrientes gave his consent on September 1; the last to agree were Santa Fé and Catamarca, on November 16 and 26 respectively. Cullen, by this time, had been displaced by a brother of the Lopez who had died.[51]

Instead of encouraging the opposition to Rosas, the attacks of the French had produced, for the most part, exactly the opposite effect. Rosas had made himself the champion of American liberty against the distrusted Europeans, and, in the heat of patriotic fervor, the discontent with his régime had largely evaporated.[52] The Governor also made a clever bid for British sympathy by acceding to the request of Mandeville to admit all overseas merchandise arriving at Buenos Ayres in spite of the French at a duty one-third less than it had been before the blockade.[53]

The aggressive policy which Roger and Leblanc had adopted was in perfect harmony with the temper of the Molé Government.[54] On the basis of the news from Roger up to the end of January, the Foreign Minister prepared a comprehensive memorandum on the question. The document reviewed the humiliating treatment which the French agents had endured at Buenos Ayres since 1832, and catalogued all of the discriminatory indignities which had been inflicted upon French residents. In anticipation of the adoption of the coercive measures which had already been authorized in support of the Bacle claim, Molé recorded that several additional ships had

---

[51] *Contestaciones de los Exmos. Gobiernos de las Provincias de la Confederación Argentina,* etc. pp. 12-45. (Buenos Ayres 1838.)

[52] Brossard, *op. cit.,* pp. 219-222. The French residents in Buenos Ayres had protested to Roger before the break that such would probably be the result of coercive measures. See Pereyra, *op. cit.,* pp. 96-97.

[53] F. O. 6, 64, M. to P., June 14, 1838.

[54] Brossard, *op. cit.,* pp. 217-220.

already been ordered to the Plata. Their instructions, he continued, were to support the demands which Roger had previously made, including the treatment of their nationals equal to that enjoyed by the British under the 1825 treaty. This report bears the mark of the approval of the King.[55]

Nine additional French vessels and 1400 men were ordered to the Plata in May, and Leblanc was directed to place Buenos Ayres and the Argentine bank of the Plata under strict blockade.[56] Additional instructions were sent on June 15, after news had arrived of the actual declaration of the blockade. Roger was praised for his firmness and moderation, and told that the King "understood that the dignity and the interests of France must be preserved in such a situation." [57] The Foreign Minister repeatedly expressed the hope that the vigorous measures taken by the Admiral had already terminated their difficulties with Rosas. A prolonged resistance was not to be expected.[58]

The simultaneous action of the French fleets in Mexican and Argentine waters was applauded with great enthusiasm by the French press. An article in the reputable *Revue des Deux Mondes* of July, 1838, reminded its readers of the high duty incumbent upon France to exercise her disciplinary and civilizing influence upon the "degenerate children of the Spanish heroes of the conquest." To refuse giving expression to French character in thus contributing to the material and moral wellbeing of these people would be "on the part of France, a crime both to herself and to America." France must especially guard against the domination of all America by the United States, for if the aggressive and independent spirit of the North American republic should ever spread to all these states, Europe would certainly come to rue the day.[59] The French Govern-

[55] *Aff. Etr.*, Buenos Ayres, 24, pp. 18-22. Memorandum, dated April 23, 1838.

[56] *Ibid.*, p. 401. A later memorandum of Molé near the close of 1838.

[57] *Ibid.*, p. 153. It must be constantly borne in mind that the instructions which arrived at Buenos Ayres were always based upon information which had been reported to Paris at least five months previously. To approve the program of the agents unreservedly was therefore practically to commit the whole affair into their hands.

[58] *Aff. Etr.*, Brésil, 18, p. 37; Buenos Ayres, 24, p. 153.

[59] Mignet, *op. cit.*, pp. 53-61. See also note 16 above.

ment could no longer be pilloried for a weak and faltering foreign policy in America.

The departure of the new French diplomatic agent, who had been appointed to succeed the deceased Vins de Paysac at Buenos Ayres, one Buchet de Martigny, was held up during the early months of 1838 pending the outcome of the demands of consul Roger.[60] Martigny was not actually sent until late August, when it was learned that the expected early settlement had not occurred, and when letters from Leblanc began to indicate that Roger's status as consul and the *amour-propre* of both him and Rosas were important obstacles to the agreement.[61] The demands which Martigny's instructions directed him to support were the same as those made by Roger. If the original ultimatum had already been met, the new Chargé should, upon his arrival, hasten to terminate the blockade. The measure was, at best, prejudicial to the interests of all parties, and might easily become the source of unhappy foreign complications. Whatever the situation might be, he should immediately advance in his diplomatic capacity to hasten any prospective settlement; the speedy determination of the difficulty should be the primary consideration of his mission.[62] Additional vessels were being sent so that even more vigorous measures could be undertaken, if necessary.[63]

The success which the Mexican expedition achieved was most gratifying to the July Monarchy.[64] The brilliant feat of

[60] *Aff. Etr.*, Buenos Ayres, 24, pp. 14-17. Molé to the King, April 6, 1838. Martigny had negotiated the French treaty with Bolivia in 1837.

[61] *Ibid.*, p. 401. Martigny left on August 27.

[62] *Ibid.*, pp. 177-178. To Martigny, July 24, 1838.

[63] *Ibid.*, p. 203. Molé appeared much concerned that British and United States commerce should not be unnecessarily injured.

[64] S. D. Brazil, Desp., 11, Hunter to Forsyth, Feb. 2, 1839. Mr. Hunter gave the following interesting interpretation of the purpose of France:

"France meant to conduct herself haughtily and severely both to Buenos Ayres and to Mexico. . . . England does not like this, but as France, reverting to former scenes is but her copyist, she has said less than she perhaps penitentially feels. . . .

"France means to be successful, she means in America to avenge her great American wrong, as in her pride she conceives it. . . . The bombardment and conquest of American Buenos Ayres and the American castle of St. Ulloa, will be, as it were, the conquest of New York and Charleston, and the Jackson indemnity will be repaid. Do not impute this thought so much to me as to every other neutral diplomat here."

Admiral Baudin in November, 1838, when he captured the castle of San Juan d'Ulloa in the harbor of Vera Cruz, was followed by a land attack that was almost equally decisive. The glory of San Juan d'Ulloa was made the most of both in the French Chambers and in the press.[65] The visitor to Versailles today may see it immortalized in a painting on a wall of the palace. The companion enterprise in the Plata was to have a less happy outcome.

The threats made by the French agents that they would unite with the enemies of Rosas resulted only in strengthening the hands of the Dictator among his own people.[66] The Bolivian war proved to be no serious embarrassment to Argentina,[67] and the crushing of a subversive plot in the capital in August [68] caused almost all evidence of unrest to disappear. It became perfectly evident, under these circumstances, that Rosas would not surrender to the Europeans until obliged to do so by force.[69] The policy of bluff was therefore abandoned in early August. Leblanc returned from Rio de Janeiro in disgust and immediately undertook to suppress the activity of small boats in the illicit trade with Buenos Ayres across the shallow water in front of the city.[70]

This more vigorous policy brought with it additional difficulties. A suitable base of operations had to be found, and some means provided for disposing of the prizes taken by the blockade. Finally, some allies must be secured who could provide a land force to assist the fleet. In order to satisfy these pressing needs, the French agents naturally turned their atten-

---

[65] For an account by an eye-witness of this attack on San Juan d'Ulloa, see the *National Intelligencer*, Dec. 15, 1838.

[66] F. O. 6, 64, M. to P., Aug. 23, 1838; F. O. 51, 14, Hood to P., Sept. 30.

[67] *Aff. Etr.*, Bolivie, 2, pp. 213-214; F. O. 6, 64, M. to P., July 9, 1838. P. to M., June 30. There was never any serious fighting on the Bolivian frontier, and Santa Cruz was soon overwhelmed by a domestic revolution.

[68] F. O. 6, 64, Aug. 21 and Sept. 25. The uprising involved several army officers, and one of the claimants supported by Roger, M. Despouy, had furnished funds for it.

[69] N. D. Captain's Letters, August, 1838. From Com. Nicolson, Aug. 3.

[70] Page, *op. cit., Revue des Deux Mondes*, 1841, 1, pp. 309-318. F. O. 51, 14, Hood to P., Sept. 30, 1838.

tion to the state of Uruguay, where the enemies of Rosas had recently obtained complete control of the country outside Montevideo.

The triumph of Rivera and Lavalle had been irresistible during 1838. The power of the rebels had been almost unchallenged in the interior from as early as February. On June 15, a decisive battle had taken place, in which the forces of Ignacio Oribe, the brother of the President, had been disastrously defeated. As a result, the military resistance of the authorities at Montevideo entirely collapsed. The British consul at Montevideo, Mr. T. S. Hood, who was an intimate friend of President Oribe, wrote as follows immediately after the battle:

"All chance of putting down General Rivera seems hopeless, and it is evident that any Force that may be possible to collect [sic] can only be looked upon as a defense measure which may protract the war to the end of the present Presidency, which will expire on the first of March next. [1839]" [71]

So desperate was the position of Oribe that he was obliged, on July 7, to convene the Legislative Assembly at Montevideo and ask its advice. A Commission of Inquiry reported unanimously that negotiations for peace should be entered into. Three influential citizens were accordingly chosen on July 11 to visit the camp of Rivera, who was then at some distance from the city. They were directed to propose an armistice with freedom of transit and the release of all prisoners, while the two forces remained *in statu quo* until the expiration of Oribe's term of office. An arrangement guaranteeing to the insurgents a fair portion of the revenue was to be administered by the French and British consuls.[72]

The reply which Rivera gave to this offer on August 9 left no hope for the city. He demanded that Oribe should immediately retire, and that the "Executive power should declare to the Chambers its inability to resist any longer the power and Influence [sic] of General Rivera." When the Commission returned to the capital on August 29, Rivera's cavalry had

[71] F. O. 51, 14, Hood to P., June 25, 1838. *Gaceta Mercantil* for June 25.
[72] *Ibid.*, Hood to P., July 13 and enclosures. The fact that the French consul was called upon to act as guarantor indicates that he was trusted by the Assembly at Montevideo.

already shut off the land communications.[73] There is not the slightest evidence, up to this point, that the struggle in Uruguay had been directly affected by the quarrel between the French and Rosas.[74] So little support did Oribe enjoy even within Montevideo, that he was obliged to overawe the Assembly with his armed partisans in order to prevent an uprising.[75] It is significant, moreover, that the principal charge raised against Oribe within Montevideo at this time concerned his employment of Argentine auxiliaries.[76]

It is perfectly clear, therefore, that the French agents were not responsible for the predicament in which the legal President at Montevideo found himself, when they embarked on their active measures in August. As long as they had expected Rosas to surrender to their threats or to yield after the first few weeks of the blockade, they took little interest in Uruguay. The fact that the French had entertained General Lavalle soon after he occupied Colonia in late July, toasting him as the man who would shortly be guiding the affairs of Argentina, did not mean that they were rendering positive aid to Rivera. This well-advertised demonstration with Lavalle seems to have been a part of their bluff.[77] A very different attitude had been assumed toward the situation two months later.[78]

By the first of September, Leblanc had collected a small prize fleet of coasting vessels, mostly Montevidean, of which he de-

---

[73] F. O., 51, 14, Hood to P., Aug. 30, 1838.

[74] The view supported by the despatches of Mr. Hood, namely, that the fall of Oribe was inevitable after the battle of Palmar in June, is ably presented by M. A. Pelliza, *Historia Argentina.* (Buenos Aires 1888, 1910), vol. 2, p. 180 ff.

[75] S. D. Brazil, Desp. 11. Hunter to Forsyth, Sept. 12.

[76] *Ibid.* Pelliza, *op. cit.,* 2, p. 180. Orestes Oranjo, *Gobernantes del Uruguay,* 2 vols., (Montevideo 1903), v. 2, pp. 94-101. N. D. Captain's Letters, Aug., 1838; from Nicolson, Aug. 3. Rivera was enjoying, in early August, active support from Brazil, because of his promise to aid the Imperial Government in Rio Grande. The charge that the French fomented Rivera's revolution (see Pereyra, *op. cit.,* p. 30 ff.) is without foundation.

[77] F. O. 6, 64, M. to P., Aug. 23, 1838. Mandeville comments: "When Genl. Rivera gets possession of Montevideo, which, if he does not soon it will be very extraordinary, the Unitarians under General Lavalle, with Rivera's support will run Rosas very hard."

[78] Durand, *op. cit.,* pp. 70-71. Antonio Díaz, *Historia política y militar de las Repúblicas del Plata. . . .* 10 vols. (Montevideo 1877-78), v. 4, pp. 43-51.

sired to dispose. To escort them to Europe for regular adjudication in the French admiralty courts was out of the question, as was the transshipment of their cargoes to France. The Admiral decided that he would attempt to sell them at Montevideo, and the sale was advertised in the papers of that city on September 7. Difficulties immediately arose in regard to the validity of the purchase of uncondemned prizes. On this point, the British consul sided with the local authorities in denying the legality of the procedure. The sale was postponed for a few days and then finally abandoned, when Oribe took the position that it would be a violation of his neutrality in the quarrel between France and Buenos Ayres for him to permit the sale.[79] A futile effort was made by Leblanc to get the original owners to deposit in the French consulate amounts equal to the value of the vessels, pending the action of the admiralty courts. The ships were eventually disposed of at Colonia, which was under Rivera's control.[80]

This altercation over the sale of prizes apparently marks the beginning of the friction between the French and Oribe. It was quickly followed by an action of a more serious character. The fleet of Montevideo, consisting of three schooners under the command of Admiral Brown of Argentina, was forcibly detained by the French when it essayed to leave the harbor of Montevideo.[81] Oribe was also isolated from any support which Rosas might have been able to send him.[82] But before the French went so far as to render positive assistance to Rivera's besieging army,[83] another effort was made to negotiate with Rosas.

On September 20, or thereabouts, a French proposal was secretly transmitted to the Government of Buenos Ayres through the medium of Oribe himself.[84] Rosas was asked to

[79] F. O. 51, 14, Hood to P., Sept. 15, 1838.
[80] F. O. 6, 64, M. to P., Sept. 26; F. O. 51, 14, Hood to P., Sept. 30. Montevideo was informed on Sept. 14 by the French that it must accept the consequences of its refusal to allow the sale of the prizes.
[81] F. O. 51, 14, H. to P., Oct. 30, 1838.
[82] F. O. 6, 64, M. to P., Sept. 30. The French were closely blockading the Island of Martín García.
[83] F. O. 51, 14, H. to P., Oct. 3, Díaz, op. cit., 3, pp. 24-26.
[84] F. O. 6, 65, M. to P., Oct. 12 and 14. This proposal was carried by one Garcia de Tuniga. Roger considered the terms very liberal.

give his immediate ratification to a Convention granting most-favored-nation treatment to French residents on the basis of reciprocity and containing a promise for the adjudication of claims and the payment of indemnity for injuries inflicted by the Government. Secret articles should specify the payment of $20,000 to the widow of Bacle and $10,000 to Lavie for the confiscation of his goods, and should admit the arbitration of the Despouy claim by a mixed Commission. The non-secret provisions were to be published without comment, and appropriate salutes were to be returned. Roger allowed the agents of Oribe three days to secure the consent of the Dictator to these terms. If the terms were accepted, the consul would proceed immediately to Buenos Ayres and the blockading fleet would retire out of sight. If the proposal should be refused, a more exacting ultimatum would be presented and made public.[85]

The Government of Rosas would have nothing to do with the proposal, notwithstanding the vigorous pressure of the British Minister upon it. Secretary Arana replied to Mandeville's representations that he hoped that his right arm would wither if he ever signed such an ignominious agreement. It would be equivalent, he said, to paying a fine for punishing those who had violated the law.[86] The French had no choice but to proceed to more extreme measures.

Roger's formal ultimatum of September 23 was an extended manifesto designed to set forth the French version of the quarrel. The consul undertook first to establish his own competency to conduct the negotiations. He then denied in a spirited manner the allegation that France had acquiesced in the military service law of 1821. He defended at great length each of the claims which he had previously presented, and added two additional demands. The entire Despouy claim, with interest calculated from 1828, must be paid within a year, and an officer in the Argentine army who had been particularly hostile to the French must be dismissed from the service. If a favorable reply was not forthcoming within forty-eight hours, France

[85] F. O. 6, 64, M. to P., Sept. 28.
[86] Ibid., Sept. 28, Oct. 12 and 14.

would not hesitate, he declared, "to employ all the means in its power promptly to put an end to a contest injurious to its own interests." [87]

The Argentine reply was more prompt than usual, and touched briefly, for the first time, on the merits of the various demands. Arana declared that both Bacle and Lavie were admittedly guilty as charged, and that the former had definitely forfeited his claim to French protection by accepting employment under a foreign government.[88] The Despouy claim, which totalled some $40,000, was declared both exorbitant and inadmissible, since that very man had recently been implicated in the abortive plot to overthrow Rosas. The other demands could be taken up through regular diplomatic channels, but would under no consideration, he added, be conceded under the menace of coercion. The reply concluded by suggesting the mediation of Great Britain [89] in the question.

Mr. Mandeville was more than ready to volunteer his good offices, for British trade was suffering greatly and the prospect of the triumph of the pro-French party on both sides of the river was enough to occasion serious alarm.[90] With the consent of Arana, he therefore invited Roger to come to Buenos Ayres for a conference on October 8. The consul at first indicated his acceptance of the invitation, and a special British vessel was held in readiness for him at Montevideo. But his plans were abruptly changed after a visit to the camp of Rivera outside the city. To the dismay of the would-be mediators, he announced at the last moment that the receipt of new instructions had influenced him to abandon all intention of visiting Buenos Ayres. But it was well known that no mail vessel had arrived in the meantime.[91] Roger's action at this

[87] *Ultimatum addressed by Mr. Aimé Roger, consul of France, to the Government of Buenos Ayres.* (Buenos Ayres 1838), pp. 11-37.
[88] Bacle had accepted employment under the Governments of both Buenos Ayres and Chile.
[89] F. O. 6, 65, M. to P., Nov. 15, 1838, and enclosures. Pereyra, *op. cit.,* pp. 62-64.
[90] F. O. 6, 64, M. to P., Sept. 28 and 30, 1838. Mandeville believed that the incident was being utilized to build up the French navy, and as a pretext for paralyzing British trade.
[91] F. O. 6, 65, M. to P., Oct. 12. An enclosure, Hood to Herbert, Oct. 9. Saldías, *op. cit.,* 3, pp. 46-47.

time makes one suspect that he wished to commit his government definitely to the task of overthrowing the Dictator, before Martigny should arrive to take over the negotiations.[92]

On October 11, a combined force of 265 French marines and about 150 Riverista soldiers stormed and captured the fortress on the Isle of Martín García. Both flags were run over the fortress, and an equal number from each force left to man the place. The French explained that Rivera's aid was purely voluntary, and had been accepted only to show that the Europeans had no intention of annexing the important position for themselves.[93] This attack cut short any further attempts at negotiation, and demonstrated openly that the French had allied themselves with Rivera.

Further resistance on the part of Oribe was out of the question after the French began their support of the besieging party. On October 24, the National Assembly of Uruguay accepted the resignation of the President. According to terms of the Constitution, the President of the Senate, one Sr. Vasquez, who had, however, only recently arrived from Brazil,[94] became the chief executive. On the 27th, the former President, his chief advisers, and some three hundred of his intimate followers were transferred to Buenos Ayres on European vessels. Rivera entered the city and assumed the title of General-in-chief of the army of Uruguay, leaving the nominal executive authority in the hands of Vasquez until the expiration of Oribe's term of office. On March 1, 1839, the victorious leader was duly elected President with no opposition.[95]

Oribe and Rosas naturally made the most of the interference of the French at Montevideo. Before he left that city, the deposed President issued a formal statement to the effect that

[92] See Saldías, *op. cit.*, 3, pp. 46-47; Pelliza, *op. cit.*, 2, p. 180. F. O. 6, 65, M. to P., Oct. 12.

[93] Vedia, *op. cit.*, pp. 102-5; 116-7. Durand, *op. cit.*, pp. 71-74; F. O. 6, 65, M. to P., Oct. 15.

[94] F. O. 51, 14, Hood to Palmerston, Sept. 26, Oct. 3 and 30, 1838.

[95] An excellent account of this episode, which insists that the resignation of Oribe was *bona fide,* may be found in Antonio Díaz, *Historia política y militár de las Repúblicas del Plata.* v. 4, pp. 28-43. Vedia, *op. cit.,* pp. 106-108; F. O. 6, 65, Mandeville to Palmerston, Nov. 15, 1838. Mandeville gives Oct. 25 as the date of the arrival of Oribe at Buenos Ayres; others say Oct. 27.

his opponents would have been "impotent" but for the support which they had received from the European forces.[96]   This contention was repeated and amplified in a public letter to Rosas on November 8, in which the entire responsibility for his overthrow was charged to Leblanc.[97]   Rosas addressed his ally, in his own public reply, as "His Excellency the President of the Oriental State of Uruguay," and expressed a deep sympathy for the exile who was the victim of their common enemies.[98] As far as Rosas was concerned, Manuel Oribe remained from this time forward indefinitely the legal President of the neighboring Republic.   With the alleged usurpers at Montevideo the Dictator was unalterably determined to have nothing to do.[99]

The situation encountered by Martigny upon his arrival at Montevideo in the middle of October corresponded so little to that contemplated by his instructions [100] that he did nothing to alter the program of intrigue which Roger had already inaugurated.   The new agent entertained no love for Rosas, as a result of previous experiences in Bolivia, and Roger's argument seemed sound that they could not now hope to negotiate with success until they had given an impressive demonstration of the power of France.

The task of organizing the enemies of Rosas was begun with considerable energy.   Their first outstanding success was the conclusion of an alliance, directed against Rosas, between Montevideo and Governor Astrada of Corrientes.[101]   In order to secure exemption for the trade of his Province, Astrada was later obliged, on March 6, to announce publicly its secession

[96] Pereyra, op. cit., p. 94.
[97] F. O. 6, 65, M. to P., Nov. 15, and enclosure, Jan. 10, 1839, and enclosure.
[98] Díaz, op. cit., 4, pp. 61-66.
[99] Ibid., 4, pp. 66-189.   The French consul at Montevideo prepared a counter statement in reply to the charges of Oribe, in which he went far to clear himself of complicity with Rivera before September.   He vigorously denied the existence of an alliance between them, and even attempted to justify their interference with Admiral Brown.   As a matter of fact, the only real alliance of the French was with, the Argentine Commission of Unitarian émigrés at Montevideo.
[100] F. O. 6, 65, M. to Strangeways, Dec. 14, 1838.
[101] Colección de tratados . . . de la República Oriental del Uruguay.   3 vols., (Montevideo 1923), v. 1, pp. 29-33.

from the Argentine Confederation and to revoke his previous approval of the policy of Rosas. But the revolt of other Provinces, which was expected to follow this announcement, failed to take place. Governor Echagüe of Entre Rios refused to follow the example of Astrada even when five French war vessels pushed up the Paraná river to protect these two Provinces from Rosas.[102] Elsewhere throughout the Confederation, French intrigue met with the same disappointing results. Argentine patriotism was not to be so easily discounted.[103]

The French received their only enthusiastic backing from the group of Unitarian exiles in Montevideo, who organized themselves into the so-called Argentine Commission. J. B. Alberdi, who was later to become President of Argentina, and Florencio Varela, a brilliant young journalist, were two of the outstanding leaders. It was not without considerable reluctance, however, that these joined hands with the foreigner; but the chance to strike at their arch-enemy at Buenos Ayres was too promising to be refused. Once their decision was made, however, they entered into the project with great enthusiasm.[104] Lavalle was persuaded to take command of their military forces.[105] The Commission was particularly influential in getting Rivera to declare war against the Dictator in late February, 1839, and they maintained a relentless press attack against their enemy.[106]

[102] Saldías, op. cit., 3, pp. 65-68. F. O. 6, 69, Rivera to Astrada Feb. 25, 1839. Page, op. cit., pp. 318-320.
[103] For evidence of this wide-spread French intrigue, see F. O. 6, 69, M. to P., April 18, May 16, 29, July 8, Sept. 21. Durand, op. cit., pp. 72-74. Cullen was captured by the Governor of Santiago del Estero in June, 1839, and executed.
[104] J. B. Alberdi, Escritos póstumos. 16 vols. (Buenos Ayres 1897-1901) v. 15, pp. 433-436; 468-470. Alberdi admitted in 1840 that their union with the French had been a mistake.
[105] Auto-biografía de D. Florencio Varela. (Montevideo 1848), pp. 7-8.
[106] Alberdi, op. cit., 15, pp. 513-517; 13, pp. 333, 341, 617, 622, 627, 590-1. Sarmiento, Política Arjentina, op. cit. Rivera's declaration of war was ratified by the Assembly after his election to the Presidency on March 1. From reports of disinterested parties present, the election was perfectly valid, only one vote being cast in the negative. To maintain that Oribe continued to be the legal President of Uruguay after his term had expired seems to be little short of ridiculous, even if the French alone had been responsible for his expulsion. For Rivera's declaration of war, see British F. and S. P. 27, pp. 1214-1217. For a report of Rivera's election, see N. D. Captain Letters, Nicolson to Paulding, Mar. 3, 1839.

The union which the French had made with Rivera, as had been confidently predicted by those who knew that leader, brought them almost nothing in return.[107]   They even had difficulty in securing definite permission from him to make use of Oriental ports for purposes of revictualing and for the disposition of prizes.[108]   Rivera proved to be a dangerous ally in connection with the campaign in Corrientes, where Lavalle and Astrada found themselves faced by a powerful Argentine army under Echagüe.   At the critical time, no assistance was forthcoming from Uruguay, and the allied forces suffered a disastrous defeat on March 31, 1839.   Governor Astrada was killed, and only a remnant of his army was able to escape to the north under the leadership of General Paz.   Lavalle and his followers returned to Colonia, feeling very bitter against Rivera.   Rosas quickly recovered control of the seceded Province of Corrientes, although much disaffection continued there.[109]

Within the city of Buenos Ayres, the followers of the Dictator were kept in a veritable frenzy of enthusiasm.   Rosas gave spectacular publicity to the activities of the blockading squadron and to Unitarian intrigue in the various provinces. Violence, extending even to murder, was not uncommonly inflicted upon those suspected of sympathy with his enemies.[110] Everywhere the slogans appeared: "Eternal hatred to the parricide Unitarians, killer of kin, sold out to the filthy French gold!" "Hatred and vengeance in the breast of every Federal against the incendiaries of Louis Philippe." Every newspaper and public document bore the heading: "Death to the Unitarian

---

[107] F. O. 6, 65, M. to Strangeways, Dec. 14, 1838. Neither did Rivera keep his promise to the Brazilian Government that he would oppose the Rio Grande rebels. Mandeville wrote: "Hood informs me that Rivera will cheat."

[108] F. O. 6, 69, M. to P., May 4, 1839. A copy of the treaty is enclosed. Brossard, op. cit., p. 270. Durand, op. cit., pp. 74-75.

[109] Page, op. cit., pp. 318-320. F. O. 6, 69, M. to P., March 21. Just what obligations were involved in the union in fact between Rivera and the French has never been determined. Legal obligations were claimed and denied at one time or another by both parties. Pereyra, op. cit., pp. 66-67. Rivera was at the time intriguing with Rosas behind the back of the French. Durand, op. cit., pp. 74-75. F. O. 6, 69, M. to P., Mar. 23. Rosas's Bolivian army aided Echagüe. National Intelligencer, July 19, 1839.

[110] Saldías, op. cit., 3, pp. 91-101. The most severe of these outbreaks were occasioned by the uncovering of plots against the Dictator.

Savages." The foreign attack was proving to be an important
asset to the political régime of Rosas.

The news which reached Paris concerning the complete failure of the earlier blockading efforts at Buenos Ayres was the
cause of considerable uneasiness. The question was made particularly embarrassing by continuing importunities from London. The Foreign Minister sent supplementary instructions on
October 12 directing Martigny to place himself immediately
in communication with the authorities at Buenos Ayres, and
to propose:

"an arrangement on such bases and in such form that it will appear
clearly to the eyes of all that, far from wishing to humiliate the
Republic and to impose on it some conditions incompatible with
its independence, we are asking only that which the laws of nations
entitle us to claim from it."

Since their demands were not capable of mediation, the good
offices of the British Government had been refused, but it was
very apparent that a long blockade would neutralize its own
advantages to France, and seriously compromise foreign trade.
Molé continued:

"I can only urge you again finally, sir, to hasten with all your
efforts the solution of our differences with Buenos Ayres. Certainly I do not wish to say that it is necessary to renounce for that
end the obtaining of the just satisfaction which the dignity of
France and the interests of her nationals demand. I know well
enough what would be the consequences of such an abandonment
for the future of our relations with South America." [111]

Later instructions sent by Molé were even more unqualified
in their demand for an immediate settlement. A separate communication informed Roger that the sending of Martigny was
a gesture of moderation which would serve to shift all responsibility for the continuation of hostilities to Rosas. Another letter, written on November 8, indicated increasing concern:

"It becomes more and more urgent to settle our difficulties with
Buenos Ayres; . . . you and Mr. Martigny ought not to neglect

[111] *Aff. Etr.,* Buenos Ayres, 24, pp. 215-220. To Martigny, Oct. 12. Molé
transmitted a copy of these instructions to the British Government.

any means which would not be incompatible with the interests of France." [112]

The serious apprehension which the Foreign Minister entertained in regard to the joint attack with Rivera's force upon Martín García was not immediately made known to the agents. That Molé regretted from the first the association of the French flag with that of Rivera is revealed in a suppressed portion of a despatch sent to Rio de Janeiro. That action, he feared, was liable to postpone the settlement by offending Rosas and wounding the *amour-propre* of the Argentine people.[113] The instructions which were sent in reply to Roger's version of the attack on the island a short time later, however, contained nothing of positive disapproval. The consul was assured that the authorities had lost none of their confidence in his zeal and excellent intentions, which had failed thus far only because of the blind obstinacy of Rosas. Molé definitely approved the rejection of British mediation, for reasons which will be apparent later. The French Minister also promised that he would follow out a suggestion made by Roger to invite the London government to exert its influence more effectively in securing the acquiescence of Rosas to their reasonable demands.[114]

In the meantime, the French Government had been brought face to face with a serious political crisis, largely because of the attacks in the Chamber on their foreign policy.[115] Even the news of the victory at Vera Cruz, which was of material assistance to Molé in the debates of January, 1839,[116] called up an embarrassing question as to why similar encouraging developments were not forthcoming in the Plata. The Foreign Minister was obliged to admit that he could give no information

[112] *Aff. Etr.*, pp. 295-296. Instructions to Roger Nov. 3 and 8, 1838.

[113] *Aff. Etr.*, Brésil, 18, p. 151 ff. Instructions, January 18, 1839.

[114] *Aff. Etr.*, Buenos Ayres, Jan. 25, Instructions to Roger, Feb. 2; *ibid.*, from Martigny at Montevideo, Feb. 11, 1839. The relations between Martigny and Mandeville were openly hostile and Molé seems here to have taken at face value the repeated allegations of the French agents that the stubbornness of Rosas was due to British encouragement, the latter not wishing France to do what they themselves had failed to accomplish in 1806 and 1807. These allegations are not supported by the British correspondence.

[115] *Archives Parlementaires*, 2nd Series, 122, pp. 711-712; v. 123, pp. 47-48.

[116] *Ibid.*, 123, pp. 48-55.

which would justify the hope which he had expressed for an
early settlement with Rosas.[117] When the debate shifted to
the subject of European affairs, the attacks of Thiers and
Guizot left the Government with almost no defense whatever.
On January 31, the King was obliged to prorogue the Chambers; they were dissolved two days later.[118] Molé struggled
on for several weeks longer, hoping against hope that a new
election might vindicate his policy. But the days of his Government were numbered.

The Argentine enterprise had by this time ceased to serve
any political purpose for France, and it bid fair to involve
her in serious embarrassments. In a letter of March 6, Molé
flatly refused the request that Martigny had made that troops
be sent him for disembarkation. The Foreign Minister explained his attitude in the following words:

"The Government of the King, without disapproving the expedition to Martín García from the moment that the occupation of that
point became a necessary complement of the blockade, has decidedly
regretted that the expedition should not have preserved a character
exclusively French. . . . It is important . . . that the purely
coercive measures do not longer retain that aggressively hostile
character, which is scarcely to be distinguished from a state of open
war. It is not less important to avoid all positive interference in
the domestic affairs of the Republics of Montevideo and of Buenos
Ayres. . . .

"I would have desired that you had found the means of avoiding completely all that could give to a simple connection in fact
between our action and that of General Rivera the character or
even the appearance of an offensive alliance. . . . I would not conceal, moreover, that I have been surprised to see you, MM. Roger,
Leblanc, and yourself, conclude from the rejection of the ultimatum,
sent back by the Government of Rosas, that the rejection had of
necessity to modify the character of our attitude toward the Argentine Republic, and make us by that fact in a state of war against
her. Nothing was less correct nor more contrary to our intentions." [119]

In still later instructions, the agents were criticized for having occupied themselves exclusively with the overthrow of Rosas
and the promotion of local alliances of questionable value. The

[117] *Archives Parlementaires, op. cit.,* 123, pp. 48 and 387.
[118] *Ibid.,* 122, pp. 773-774; 123, p. 88 ff., 104 ff., 401 ff.
[119] *Aff. Etr.,* Buenos Ayres, 25, pp. 63-70. Instructions to Martigny,
March 6.

securing of their own reparations had been almost completely
lost sight of.   However beneficial the fall of Rosas might be,
said Molé, a measure so injurious to commerce as was the
blockade should not be prolonged for the sake of that end.
Martigny should therefore neglect no opportunity to reach an
honorable settlement, and should separate himself from any
cause which did not directly contribute to the interests of
France.[120]

Before these instructions had reached their destination,
Paris was in a political turmoil.   The Government was badly
beaten in the new elections; but the victorious opposition was
finding it impossible to form a Ministry from its irreconcilable
elements.   A veritable interregnum ensued for a period of ten
weeks, during which time a group under the leadership of the
Duc de Montebello tried in vain to get control of the situation.
A general insurrection was very imminent.   It was averted only
by the sudden intervention of Marshal Soult on May 12,
1839.   The Ministry which he formed from the Left Center
was, as one writer has said, "less a solution than a combination
of circumstances, an expedient improvised before a sudden
danger." [121]   The news of these happenings in Paris naturally
went a long way toward discounting, in the minds of the agents
in the Plata, the final orders of Molé.

Martigny was, in fact, quite bewildered at the Government's
sudden change of heart,[122] and the instructions sent by later
Ministers only contributed to this confusion.   Montebello's
single letter to Martigny, dated May 3, was by no means as
emphatic as those of Molé had been in regard to the necessity
of avoiding local entanglements.   The Minister did express
some anxiety, however, that no opportunity should be allowed

[120] *Aff. Etr.*, Buenos Ayres, 25, pp. 68-70, March 8.   Roger returned to
France during the spring of 1839.   He was later transferred to the French
consulate at New Orleans at which post he was very active during the
Mexican War.   See *ibid.* Etats Unis, 102, p. 74 ff.
[121] Charles de Mazade, *Monsieur Thiers.* (Paris, 1884), pp. 138-156.   *Archives Parlementaires,* 124, p. 795.   The personnel of the Ministries is here
given.
[122] *Aff. Etr.*, Buenos Ayres, 25, Soult to Martigny, June 4, 1839.

to escape in bringing the affair to an end.[123] Marshal Soult
was not at all interested in the Argentine affair, and does not
seem to have had any very definite convictions on the subject.
The first instructions which he prepared for Martigny on
June 24 were in complete agreement with the final orders of
Molé, but for political reasons they were never sent. Instead,
the Minister announced that for the time being the King was
determined to pursue with energy and perseverance the satisfaction which French commerce and establishments in Argentina required.[124] This change of policy may have been due
to the fact that an appropriation of nearly six million francs
was pending before the Chambers to cover the cost of the
operations in America.[125]

The contradictory character of these various instructions
left the guiding of French policy in the Plata largely in the
hands of the agents on the spot. After the fiasco in Corrientes and an abortive mediation effort in April, 1839, by a
North American naval officer, which will be considered in a
later connection, Martigny and Leblanc resumed their none too
promising coercive program. It was proving impossible to
prevent the trade in small boats across the submerged delta in
front of Buenos Ayres, but even if this had not been the case,
it is improbable that trade considerations alone would ever
have affected the determination of the Dictator. A direct
attack upon the city was out of the question. It would only
injure the non-combatant inhabitants and bring certain ruin
upon the many foreign merchants resident in the city. Rosas
and his followers could easily flee to the Pampas and check-
mate them by driving all of the live stock away. It was clear
that the French could not force the Governor to treat with

---

[123] *Aff. Etr.*, Buenos Ayres, 25, to Martigny, May 3, 1839. Montebello
expressed the hope that the Corrientes-Uruguay alliance might have hastened the conclusion. He approved the encouragement given Corrientes,
as well as the dickering with the Argentine Commission for a commercial
treaty, this latter being done on the presumption that they would soon
be in control of the affairs of the Confederation.

[124] *Aff. Etr.*, Brésil, 18, p. 228. To Rouen at Rio, June 24, 1839. *Ibid.*,
Buenos Ayres, 25, to Martigny, June 24.

[125] *Archives Parl.*, 126, p. 493.

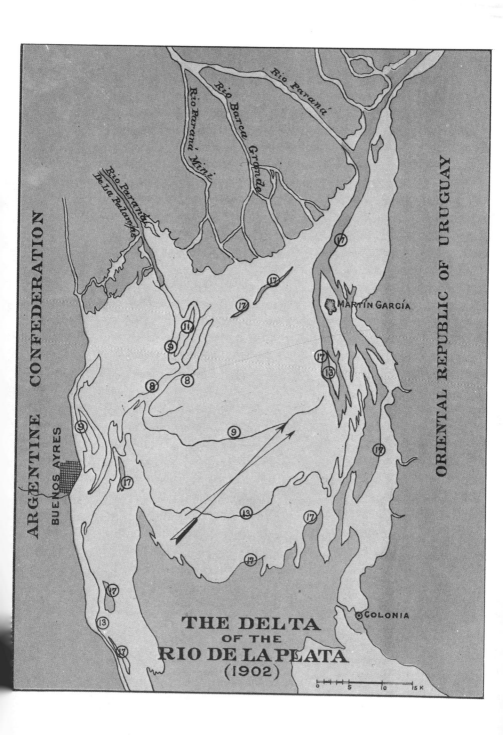

THE DELTA
OF THE
RIO DE LA PLATA
(1902)

them by the use of naval means alone. Local assistance must be secured.

Instead of making progress in their positive program, however, the interventionists found themselves actually thrown on the defensive throughout the remainder of 1839. President Rivera steadfastly refused to co-operate with them, and until September, 1839, was secretly trying to arrange a separate peace with Rosas. Lavalle and a number of his followers were obliged to depart suddenly from Montevideo in August, to avoid being seized by Rivera. The latter tried to win the favor of the Dictator by imprisoning the captain of the port, who had permitted Lavalle to escape.[126] When Rosas finally spurned these peaceful overtures and sent General Echagüe into Uruguay in September, 1839, with a powerful army, the French themselves were left the entire burden of defending the capital. Rivera's troops kept to the open country. A body of militia was hastily organized from the numerous immigrant population within the city, and 400 marines from the French squadron were sent ashore to help man the defenses. So disgusted was Leblanc with the Uruguayan Government that he secretly offered to abandon Rivera and to exempt Entre Rios from the French blockade if Echagüe would retire from Uruguay and remain neutral as between France and Rosas. This suggestion was promptly rejected.[127] It was not until December that a decisive victory for Rivera relieved the situation at Montevideo.[128]

The French leaders were meanwhile engaged upon some activities on their own account. Lavalle's small army had been transferred from Martín García up the Uruguay river, and set ashore in the Province of Entre Rios. No resistance was encountered, but efforts at recruiting failed miserably. Proceeding northward, Lavalle reached the boundary of Corrientes by early October, in which Province a recent upheaval had brought one General Ferré to the position of Governor.

[126] Saldías, *op. cit.,* 3, pp. 70-83. Lavalle even offered to serve under Rivera in April, 1839, in order to get his support.
[127] F. O. 6, 70, M. to P., Nov. 22, 1839.
[128] Durand, *op. cit.,* pp. 74-82. Page, *op. cit.,* pp. 327-335.

Ferré immediately joined hands with the Unitarian leader, and together they began to make a little progress in building up an army.[129]

The opportunities for decisive action against Echagüe's battered army were allowed to slip through the fingers of the allies. Rivera might easily have annihilated the Entre Rian force as it retired from his territory, and Lavalle himself can be charged with the same lack of initiative for failing to attack the defeated leader immediately after he returned to his own Province. The French tried desperately, in January, 1840, to persuade Rivera to transfer a portion of his army into Argentine territory. A treaty was drawn up by which the French agreed to subsidize liberally any such effort, but it came to nothing.[130] The only considerable reënforcement which Lavalle's army received came from the transfer of something under a thousand disorganized militiamen from the region south of Buenos Ayres, where a revolt, encouraged by the French, had recently failed.[131]

After two years of effort, the French had made surprisingly little progress in forcing Rosas to grant their demands.[132] Lavalle and Ferré were in control of Corrientes, with the French fleet supporting from the Paraná river;[133] but there was no

[129] Durand, op. cit., pp. 74-82. Page, op. cit., pp. 327-335.

[130] Colección de tratados . . . de Uruguay. v. 1, pp. 83-87.

[131] Ibid., M. to Strangeways, Dec. 14, 1839. A. J. Carranza, La revolución del 39 en el sur de Buenos Aires. (Buenos Aires 1880), pp. 1-21. National Intelligencer, Mar. 11, 1840. The rebellion south of Buenos Ayres fizzled out prematurely because of friction among the leaders.

[132] This action of the French fleet against Buenos Ayres, without a declaration of war on either side, has considerable significance for International Law on the question of the pacific blockade. A. H. Washburn, in the Columbia Law Review 21, pp. 227-230, has touched upon it briefly. Rosas, of course, would have been justified in issuing a declaration of war, but since his operations must have been purely of a defensive character, he preferred to allow France to force the matter. The French instructions, the ruling of their legal authorities on the prizes taken in the Plata, and many uncontradicted statements in the Chambers all admit that a state of war actually existed. The Paris Government preferred not to avow this belligerency, however, in order to avoid any embarrassment arising from the rules of war when peace should be made. During the simultaneous Mexican blockade, the American state did declare war. The British Government recognized the blockade at Buenos Ayres on the sole grounds that such action was a belligerent right. See Aff. Etr., Buenos Ayres, 26, pp. 77-83. Parliamentary Debates, 3d series, v. 53, pp. 1315-1316.

[133] Durand, op. cit., pp. 80-82; Page, op. cit., pp. 337-342.

prospect of assistance for them from any other quarter.   The Unitarian-French crusade against Rosas was opposed by Echagüe's convalescing army in Entre Rios and by the almost unanimous hostility of the people on the right bank of the Paraná and Plata rivers.

By the end of 1839, the authorities at Paris had decided definitely to extricate themselves from the interminable war with Buenos Ayres.   The glory hunt had long since lost its tang and Palmerston was making the issue a most uncomfortable one for them.   Most important of all, clouds were gathering in the Near East which had an ominous appearance, and it behooved the French Government to disentangle themselves from all embarrassing connections.   It is to this broader international aspect of the Plata affair that we must now turn our attention.

CHAPTER III

THE OUTCOME OF THE FRENCH INTERVENTION

The injury which the French blockade inflicted upon neutral commerce and the suspicious character of their intrigue with the enemies of Rosas made the intervention inevitably a matter of international interest. The important commercial and financial stake which Great Britain had in the country naturally made her the nation most concerned. The question came to be, in fact, so exclusively a Franco-British affair that a few preliminary words should be said in explanation of the surprising passivity of Brazil and the United States.

The circumstances surrounding the French intervention were such that Brazil had nothing to gain from participation in it. Rivera's victory at Montevideo gave the Rio de Janeiro authorities a much-needed respite in their quarrel with Rosas over the Oriental state.[1] But even if the domestic situation had permitted the Imperial Government to take an active part in Plata affairs, which was not the case, they had no reason to suppose that the Unitarian party, if victorious, would be more reasonable in the question of river navigation than was Rosas. The perfidious Rivera was, moreover, flagrantly violating his promises to Brazil to assist in the suppression of the Rio Grande insurrection; while at the same time, Rosas was observing a correct neutrality in that respect. The unconcealed ambition of the Uruguayan President to preside over a state extending from the Paraná river to the Atlantic suggested even more serious problems than the existing situation involved.[2] The only sensible policy for the Imperial authorities to pursue, therefore, was to let matters take their course,

[1] F. O. 6, 65, Mandeville to Palmerston, Oct. 15 and Dec. 14, 1838.
[2] F. O. 6, 68, P. to M., Dec. 21, 1839.

while they remained watchful of Rosas and prepared for eventualities after the French should withdraw.[3]

The administration at Washington paid almost no attention to the activities of France in the Plata. The diplomatic agent whom Rosas sent to the United States in 1838 to enlist the sympathy of the Government found the Falkland Island question still a barrier to official intercourse.[4] The reports which the State Department received from their consular and diplomatic agents in South America were never particularly enlightening.[5] The North American Minister at Rio de Janeiro declared from the first that the French blockade was illegal without a declaration of war. He also recognized that the overthrow of Rosas would be the principal objective of the intervention. In view of these facts, it is significant that he saw no interest of the United States in the affair not capable of being fully safeguarded by the presence of a few war vessels in the river.[6] The demonstration which Admiral Baudin staged at Vera Cruz at the same time excited much more interest in the North American republic.[7] But even in this incident, the feeling toward France was far from hostile, largely because the blockade brought much needed relief to Texas.[8]

[3] F. O. 6, 70, M. to Strangeways, Dec. 14, 1839.

[4] S. D. Arg. Rep., Notes to Legation, 6, to General Alvear, Oct. 10, 1838 and Dec. 4, 1841.

[5] The United States consul at Buenos Ayres made the ridiculous recommendation that President Van Buren should declare that, by virtue of the Constitution and the political policies of the United States, the entire estuary of the Plata was a territorial sea of Argentina. Such a declaration, he thought, would enable him to forbid the endorsement of the papers of North American vessels by the blockading squadron in the river. See S. D. Buenos Ayres, Consular Letters, 5, B. C. Foster to Van Buren, April 2, 1838.

[6] S. D. Brazil, Desp., 11, Hunter to Forsyth, May 4 and 27, 1838; Feb. 2, 1839; v. 12, same to same, Dec. 29, 1839. While Hunter saw no grounds for protest against the intervention, he did suggest that a French-Brazilian royal marriage might involve too great a degree of French domination over Brazil. Such a development, he thought, would bring into operation the uncontradicted declaration of Monroe.

[7] S. D. France, Notes to Legation, July 19, 1838, Jan. 2, 7, 9, 1839.

[8] *Niles Register,* 54, p. 355 ff., June 28 and Aug. 4, 1838. R. C. McGrane, *Correspondence of Nicolas Biddle.* (New York 1919), pp. 331-332, Clay to Biddle, Sept. 14, 1838. A. Peña y Reyes, *La Diplomacia Mexicana.* (Mexico 1923), p. 21. E. B. White, *American Opinion of France from LaFayette to Poincaré.* (New York 1927), pp. 111-112. The United States made a friendly offer of mediation in October, 1838.—See S. D. France, Instructions, 14, p. 51. To Louis Cass, Oct. 29, 1838. *National Intelligencer,* Oct. 27, 1838.

Congress and the United States press were equally apathetic in regard to the Argentine intervention. Only two references to the affair were made in Congress, both of them by Caleb Cushing. In a motion which he introduced in the House on December 31, 1838, asking for information from the President concerning the French blockade of Mexico, Cushing inserted as an afterthought a phrase which extended the inquiry to include the action in the Plata as well.[9] The other instance was in July, 1840, when he declared before the House that the so-called pacific blockade of France at Buenos Ayres was illegal, and should never have been acquiesced in by the silence of neutral powers.[10] There was no suggestion at either time that any peculiar American policy was being violated by the French program. Complaining commercial interests received scanty attention from the Government.[11] The press was content to report with evident gratification, that the French were encountering unexpected difficulties in Argentina. It was generally conceded that the only hope of a settlement lay in the acceptance of the mediatory offices of Great Britain.[12]

The naval forces of the United States which were stationed in the Plata had a most difficult time maintaining the neutrality which their instructions enjoined. The strong feeling of hostility toward the blockading force which prevailed among the under-officers and crews made the Americans extremely touchy in regard to any infringement of their shipping rights. More than once Commodore Nicolson, the commanding officer, paid tribute to the extraordinary patience and courtesy of Admiral I eblanc in meeting such instances.[13] A vessel from each squadron went so far in December, 1838, as to clear its deck for

[9] 25th Congress, 1st Session, House Journal, pp. 159, 520; 25, 3, House ex. doc. 211, v. 5, pp. 1-70. The United States was also having difficulty in collecting Mexican claims.

[10] Niles Register, 58, p. 316, July 18, 1840.

[11] National Intelligencer, July 24, 1840.

[12] Ibid., Aug. 27, 1839.

[13] N. D. Captain's Letters, December, 1838. Nicolson to Paulding, Dec. 3 and enclosures. 25, 3, H. ex. doc. 211, p. 33 ff. In connection with this incident, Nicolson made the following observation: "I admire both the gentlemanly manner of the Admiral, as well as his courtesy throughout the correspondence, and must confess, I doubt very much whether I should have had the forbearance which he has shown had circumstances placed me in his position."

action. A clergyman on the American vessel at the time declared later that he alone on board was not disappointed when the intervention of higher officers prevented the fight.[14] A more serious difficulty arose in March, 1839, between the French Admiral and Commodore Nicolson himself, concerning the legal limits of the blockade of the Argentine coast. Trouble was avoided only when Leblanc released two captured American vessels.[15]

The frequent recurrence of such disagreeable incidents influenced the United States commander to undertake a mediation between the two parties. After several preliminary conferences,[16] Nicolson announced to Rosas on April 4, that he was authorized by the French agents to propose the following terms as a basis for discussion: (1) most-favored-nation treatment for French nationals pending the conclusion of a treaty; (2) their permanent exemption from Argentine military duty; (3) the payment of the claims of injured Frenchmen; (4) reference of the indemnity question to a neutral commission and its inclusion in secret articles, in case the matter could not be arranged by direct negotiation.[17]

Rosas assumed a most unreasonable attitude in his reply. As a substitute for the Nicolson terms, he suggested the following bases: (1) French citizens should continue to enjoy, as they had up to the present time, equal treatment as regard legal protection and military service with nationals of other countries not having treaties with Argentina.[18] (2) Rosas would admit the obligation to meet the claims of injured French citizens only on condition that France should agree in turn to

[14] F. O. 6, 65, M. to P., Dec. 14, 1838 and enclosures.
[15] F. O. 6, 69, M. to P., Mar. 23, 1839 and enclosures; M. to Strangeways, April 8, 1839. *National Intelligencer,* June 10, 1839. S. D. France, Instructions, 14, p. 257. To Cass, Oct. 31, 1839. This incident was considered serious enough by the Washington authorities for the Secretary of State to ask Mr. Cass in Paris "to invite a disavowal of any intention on their part to wantonly harass our commerce."
[16] F. O. 6, 69, M. to P., April 20, 1839.
[17] N. D., Captain's Letters, April, 1839; *Correspondence sustained between the Government of Buenos Ayres and Capt. John B. Nicolson.* (Buenos Ayres 1839), pp. 5-21.
[18] Rosas had at first wanted to make an express exception of the position of the United States as well, but Mandeville dissuaded him. F. O. 6, 69, M. to P., April 20, 1839.

indemnify the Argentine Republic for all injuries sustained as
a result of the blockade and its attendant hostilities. In case
of failure to reach agreement on the amount of this indemnity,
it should be left to the determination of the British Government. (3) Martín García should be restored to the Argentine
Government as it had been when occupied.[19] In vain did
Nicolson strive, with the assistance of Mandeville, to secure
alterations which would have removed some of the most inadmissible of Rosas' demands—namely, that the French be
treated as were North Americans, and that the indemnity demand be restricted to the actual losses sustained by the citizens
of Argentina. The Dictator refused to alter his terms in the
least particular.[20]

The rejection of Nicolson's proposals seriously prejudiced
the standing of Rosas in the eyes of neutrals. Even when one
takes into consideration the fact that the mediation followed
directly upon the collapse of Astrada's insurrection in Corrientes, it cannot be denied that there was good ground on
which to denounce the unreasonable obstinacy of the Governor.
Roger left for Paris immediately to insist upon the despatch
of a military force sufficient to bring the Dictator to terms.[21]
Nicolson's own comment was as follows:

"Rear Admiral Leblanc will no doubt transmit this correspondence to his Government and urge upon them the necessity of fitting
out a Competent Force to compel these people to do them Justice.
. . . This is the only Course to be pursued, and until some such
strong measures [sic], I see no probable termination of this War
and Blockade which is so injurious to the Commerce of all Neutrals." [22]

The disinclination of the Governor to make peace with the
French was attributed to a variety of causes. Nicolson thought
that the Dictator wished to continue the prevailing unsettled

[19] *Nicolson's Correspondence, op. cit.,* p. 23. *National Intelligencer,* Aug.
6, 1839.
[20] *Ibid.,* pp. 39-53; F. O. 6, 69, M. to P., April 20; *British For. and S. P.,*
31, pp. 1089-1091; *National Intelligencer,* July 4, 1839.
[21] N. D. Captain's Letters, April, 1839. Nicolson to Paulding, April
22; an enclosure, Martigny to Nicolson, April 29. Durand, *op. cit.,* pp. 75-76.
In November of 1839, Rosas also refused to accept the mediation of Chile.
F. O. 6, 70, M. to P., Nov. 18, 1839.
[22] N. D. Captain's Letters, Nicolson to Paulding, April 22, 1839.

state of affairs until after he had been elected in 1840 to another five-year term of dictatorship. His political advantage in the situation was obvious.[23] On the other hand, Arana told Mandeville that Rosas was so utterly exasperated at the recent French intrigues that he would make no concessions whatever to them. Nicolson, he alleged, was too friendly to the Dictator's enemies, whereas if Mandeville had been the mediator, exemption from military service might have been conceded. Notwithstanding this flattering excuse, Rosas was much discredited in Mandeville's opinion. The South Americans, the British Minister said, not infrequently combined the "simplicity of children and the obstinacy of a mule." [24]

This unauthorized mediation of Commodore Nicolson was the only important participation in the French intervention by the agents of the United States. The Secretary of the Navy was by no means enthusiastic in his approval of the move, and cautioned Nicolson that such actions might be embarrassing if out of harmony with the policy of the Government.[25] The people of the United States, so far as there is any evidence at all, were sympathetic with Argentina in the quarrel. But there was almost nothing of criticism of France in the press, and not the slightest move of official opposition to her program.

The assertive policy which France adopted in Latin-America in 1838 excited, from the very beginning, the most violent opposition in England. The blockades of Mexico and Argentina were denounced as deliberate expressions of French antagonism to British trading interests. In the press and in Parliament, demands were raised that the Government interfere to protect the rights of British commerce. The *London Times* predicted that another Algeria was in the making in America.

[23] N. D. Captain's Letters, Nicolson to Paulding, April 22, 1839.
[24] F. O. 6, 69, M. to Strangeways, April 19, 1839. The French wrongly threw all the blame for the failure of this mediation upon the British.
[25] N. D. Officers of Ships of War, No. 27. Instructions, Paulding to Nicolson, July 8, 1839. The Secretary warned Nicolson that "such interferences . . . are delicate matters unless in accordance with express instructions, as they may, sometimes, not accord with the policy of the Government."

An "Association of Merchants trading with Mexico" was organized to bring pressure upon the Government, and similar methods were later employed with reference to the Plata situation. The most powerful financial and commercial interests in England led the chorus in the vilification of France.[26]

But there was little that the British Government could do. They could not deny the right of France to have recourse to the same coercive measure that they themselves had so frequently employed. Nor was the French press hesitant in reminding England of her sins in this respect.[27] Palmerston could interpose no actual resistance, either by diplomacy or by force, until some sort of irregularity developed. He was content to make Paris as uneasy as possible in regard to his intentions.[28]

As early as June 12, the British Ambassador at Paris, Lord Granville, was ordered to call Molé's attention to the fact that the blockades in America were a source of great inconvenience to British commerce. At Buenos Ayres, in particular, wrote Palmerston, the means of amicable arrangement had not been exhausted before coercive measures had been resorted to. To demand at the cannon's mouth, he continued, commercial privileges which were usually secured by treaty, and to use force to secure an acknowledgment of the "indisputable Principle that compensation may be claimed for injuries sustained" were, to say the least, rather novel proceedings.[29] The response of

[26] Guyot, R., *La Première Entente Cordiale.* (Paris 1926), pp. 130-136; 146-151. *London Times* for June 23, Aug. 21, 1838. The paper contains a petition from the merchants of Liverpool, and an editorial of the most sarcastic character condemning the French policy. France was charged with a desire to rob the mines of America, and to find transatlantic thrones for her Princes. *National Intelligencer,* July 14; *Niles Register,* July 21, 1838. An address was sent to Palmerston by the "Commercial Association of British Merchants trading with Mexico," which charged that the French had no right to establish the blockade.

[27] *National Intelligencer,* Oct. 19, 1838.

[28] E. D. Adams, *British Interests and Activities in Texas, 1838-1845.* (Baltimore 1910) pp. 20-24. Palmerston ordered his fleet to hover near the French squadron, but to pretend to be called away in case hostilities threatened.

[29] F. O. 27, France, 556, Palmerston to Granville, June 12, 1838. He added that some of the claims raised by Roger appeared to have been ill-founded, particularly that of Lavie. *Aff. Etr.,* Buenos Ayres, 25, p. 4, Jan. 1, 1839.

the French Minister to these representations was very encouraging. He insisted upon the reasonable character of the demands made upon Rosas, and assured Granville that he desired a prompt settlement of the difficulty. Copies of Martigny's first instructions were submitted in proof of the pacific intentions of France.[30]

Upon learning of the desire of the Paris authorities for an early settlement, Palmerston ordered his agent at Buenos Ayres to assist the French in securing the acceptance of any reasonable proposals. Mandeville should tell Rosas that it was vain for Argentina to resist a power such as France. Immediate acquiescence in her demands would be much less expensive and prejudicial to Argentine interests than would be the ultimate submission to force.[31] Palmerston also told the Argentine representative in London that he considered the French demands to be not without foundation, whereas he thought that the Argentine overtures had not been such as to admit the employment of British mediation.[32]

But the situation at Buenos Ayres did much to belie the real policy of the British Government. No sooner had Rosas broken with Leblanc than he threw himself into the arms of the already friendly Mandeville. The British annexation of the Falkland Islands was completely forgotten. The Governor went out of his way to emphasize, both in private and in public, the idea that the French operations were in reality an attack upon the privileged position of the British, and that the success of their intrigues would mean the overthrow of the party friendly to England.[33] Rosas made very tangible concessions in order to gain British good will. He exempted the nationals of that state from the legal requirement that for-

[30] F. O. 6, 62, to Mandeville, Oct. 3, 1838. F. O. 27, from Granville in Paris, Sept. 5, 19, 17 and 24, 1838.
[31] F. O. 6, 68, P. to M., Feb. 6, 1839.
[32] F. O. 6, 72, Palmerston to Moreno, April 23, 1839, Nov. 28, 1839. Palmerston referred particularly to exemption from military service.
[33] F. O. 6, 64, M. to P., Aug. 25, 1838. Rosas now told Mandeville in regard to the treaty of 1825: "I consider it as the Bulwark of our Independence."

eigners married to Argentine citizens must renounce their former allegiance. Still more welcome was Rosas' consent to conclude the slave-trade treaty which Britain had so long desired.[34] The treaty was quickly arranged by Mandeville.[35]

The French agents at Montevideo, who were, of course, not aware of the nature of the British instructions, saw only the intimacy which existed between Mandeville and Governor Rosas. They naturally assumed that the London Government was actually encouraging their enemy in his exasperating obstinacy. This conclusion was greatly reënforced by the character of later representations made by the British Ambassador in Paris. Granville was ordered to say that the French action at Montevideo "may tend to produce corresponding interference in an opposite direction by the Agents and forces of other Countries." Consul Roger, asserted Palmerston, had made the:

"complaints of France a pretext for interfering by force of arms in the internal dissensions of Political Parties of Buenos Ayres. . . . Other nations are not likely to permit their Commercial Intercourse with Buenos Ayres to be interrupted by France for such purposes as those last mentioned." [36]

It can readily be understood, therefore, why the French should refuse to trust Great Britain with the mediation of their Argentine quarrel. They were convinced that Mandeville was carrying out the threat which Palmerston had made by opposing their program.[37]

The gratifying news that British mediation had succeeded in bringing to a close the Mexican intervention, in March, 1839, only accentuated the demand at London for a similar

[34] F. O. 6, 69, M. to P., Jan. 24, 1839; *British Foreign and State Papers,* 27, pp. 713-6.

[35] F. O. 6, 69, Mandeville to Strangeways, April 21, May 23, 1839; *B. F. and S. P.,* 28, pp. 853-856; 29, pp. 521-527; 31, pp. 963, 414. Previous refusals to conclude this slave trade treaty had been based on a demand that alterations be introduced in the 1825 treaty in return for it.

[36] F. O. 6, 72, a Memorandum dated Mar. 2, 1839, giving a summary of Granville's instructions to Jan. 18, 1839.

[37] F. O. 27, 580, Granville to Palmerston, Feb. 25, 1839. Molé made, in reply, only general denials of any intention to alter the status of Martín García, or to extort a treaty by force.

development in Argentina.[38]   The *London Times* featured an extended exposition of the political intrigues of the French against Rosas, to the great annoyance of Paris.[39]   Powerful interests memorialized the Government to put an end to the blockade of Buenos Ayres and to halt the disturbance of the balance of power in South America by France.   Speaking in behalf of a petition for greater naval protection, which was signed by some three hundred of the leading merchants, shipowners, and bankers of London, Viscount Strangford was vicious in his denunciation of what he termed the:

"factious eagerness with which the most trifling and frivolous circumstances are taken up and magnified, and converted into questions of national importance to the profit, territorial, financial, political, and commercial, which France uniformly contrived to extract from all such affairs,—and the losses to which the subjects of the British Crown in that part of the world were subjected in consequence of them." [*sic*]

Lord Ashburton, whose family name was Baring, went so far as to prophesy that a continuation of such use of the blockade for commercial purposes would drive England into a breach of the peace with France.   To these attacks, Prime Minister Melbourne could only reply that, while every effort would be made to help the two parties to come to terms, he could not deny the right of France to employ a device which his own Government had recently used.[40]

The Government which Marshal Soult organized at Paris in May, 1839, had been in power only a few weeks before it was thrown upon the defensive in regard to the Plata affair.   When an appropriation bill to cover the current annual deficit and

[38] *London Times,* April 10, 1839.   Many people in France resented British mediation, however, and one paper suggested that the French Government should volunteer her good offices between Britain and Canada in the bitter quarrel which they were having at the time.   The Mexican correspondence, up to this time, was far more voluminous than that concerning Argentina. F. O. 27, 580, Granville to Palmerston, February, 1839.

[39] *Aff. Etr.*   Buenos Ayres, 24, pp. 8-13.

[40] *Parliamentary Debates,* 3d. series, 47, pp. 1396-1397; 49, p. 385 ff. House of Lords, July 16, 1839.

the cost of continuing the naval operations in America was recommended without comment to the Chamber of Deputies in early June, strenuous objections were raised by the representatives of the mercantile interests of France.[41] The feeble, halting policy of the Government, they said, had succeeded only in ruining the French trade to the Plata and in arousing increased persecution from Rosas. Three thousand troops for disembarkation should be included with the naval reënforcements, they insisted, in order that the "pitiable comedy" might be brought to a close. When an opponent protested that a direct attack on the city would be very unwise, one speaker retorted that it would at least cause the people to cease laughing at France.[42] The appropriation remained under consideration for several weeks. It was eventually approved by both Chambers, with the understanding that the Government would exert every effort, short of despatching an army, in order to bring the affair to a favorable conclusion.[43]

It was this debate which postponed the sending of the earlier instructions prepared for Martigny,[44] and many weeks passed before a new policy was formulated. Considerable difficulty

[41] *Archives Parlementaires,* 125, pp. 257-258; 126, pp. 93-95. June 1-19, 1839. This debate reveals that France had employed 195 vessels and 26,341 men in her operations against Mexico and Buenos Ayres.

[42] *Ibid.,* 126, pp. 278-281, June 24. From a side remark that the blockade itself was not legal, the debate drifted into a bitter quarrel as to whether the Government did not really intend to use the extra vessels to aid the reactionary party in Spain. The Government eventually vindicated its intentions in this respect.

[43] *Ibid.,* 127, pp. 38-39, 509, 544, 553, 581-582, 773-776. The debate was the occasion for a vigorous revival of the demand for a more powerful navy and a more aggressive support of trade in every quarter of the world. It was this attitude on the part of France, together with the newly adopted practice of subsidizing steam mail packets, which so alarmed certain quarters of British opinion. Among ultra-Tories, the panic concerning French designs became not dissimilar to that of Britain in the first decade of the nineteenth Century.

[44] See chapter II, note 124. The extended instructions which Soult prepared for Martigny, on June 24, were never sent. In this letter he emphatically reäffirmed Molé's command to take the initiative in opening direct negotiations with Rosas, while also separating himself from Rivera. Martigny, at the same time, was not denied the privilege of choosing the opportune moment for taking such action, although he was charged expressly to enter into no undertaking which would not facilitate a prompt and honorable settlement with Rosas. *Aff. Etr.,* Buenos Ayres, 25, to Martigny, June 24, 1839.

was experienced in determining what powers the commander of the reënforcements, Admiral Dupotet, was to be accorded. The Cabinet at first was of the opinion that he should take over the diplomatic as well as the military control. But some objected on the ground that it would be unwise to risk the disruption of the entire local program by displacing Martigny.[45] It was the influence of ex-consul Roger that finally decided the question. He declared emphatically that Rosas would not negotiate with a naval commander. It was agreed, therefore, that the Admiral's authority should extend only to military matters, and that final diplomatic power should continue to reside with Martigny.[46]

In the light of the limitation thus placed on the powers of the new Admiral, the instructions which he was given were rather confusing. Soult wrote that since the French Government had despaired of forcing Rosas to sue for peace by means of the blockade alone and desired to be free from all responsibility for continuing the affair, Dupotet should not wait for an offer from Rosas, but come forward himself with a definite proposition. The terms should be simply most-favored-nation treatment for French residents until the conclusion of a treaty, and the recognition in principle of the claims due the nationals who had suffered at the hands of the Argentine Government. The amount of the several claims should be determined by arbitration. The ultimate conclusion of the settlement would be left to Martigny. Care should be taken, however, not to compromise the interests of the friendly party in Uruguay nor to consent to expel Rivera's forces from Martín García.[47]

The departure of the reënforcements was delayed until October, 1839, because of the illness of Dupotet, and in the mean-

---

[45] *Aff. Etr.*, Buenos Ayres, 25, pp. 257-264. An unsigned memorandum, dated August, 1839.

[46] *Ibid.*, 25, Soult to Dupotet, August, 1839. The fact that Roger's influence was decisive, is recorded in pencil at the beginning of the document.

[47] *Ibid.* This direct order for Dupotet to treat with Rosas was apparently never repudiated. *Ibid.*, 27, p. 170 ff.

time a new orientation was given to French policy.[48]   Formal instructions were sent to Martigny on October 21.   The agent's position was now fully approved in refusing British mediation and in concluding that force alone remained to them.   But at the same time, Soult explained that no troops could be expected from France, and that Martigny should take care, while assuring Rivera of French loyalty, to reserve his right to deal separately with Rosas at any time.   Upon the arrival of Dupotet, a direct proposal should be made to Rosas to the effect that the French be placed on a par with the British. He might even agree to restore Martín García to Rosas, if that were a *sine qua non* of peace.[49]   Just how the various parts of these instructions could be harmonized was not made clear.

Additional instructions, which were sent a few days later, only increased the confusion.   The proposal of Martigny to subsidize Rivera for the transfer of 2,000 troops to Entre Rios was definitely approved.   But if the active assistance of that leader could not be secured on such terms, Martigny should consider the advisability of abandoning him.   He might also, said Soult, take advantage of the aid which Mandeville had supposedly been ordered to afford him.[50]   To make matters still worse, Admiral Dupotet was told, upon his departure, that his mission was entirely distinct from that of Martigny.   The agents should strive to reach agreement, but each should nevertheless act upon his own responsibility.[51]   It would have been surprising indeed if difficulties and misunderstandings had not been encountered in executing such a series of instructions.

But more instructions were yet to come.   A decidedly new

---

[48] *Aff. Etr.* Buenos Ayres, 25, pp. 215-217. Submitted to Soult in September, 1839. F. O. 6, 72, Domestic Letters. British merchants and shipowners were flooding the Foreign Office with petitions against the French blockade. Glasgow Ch. of Commerce, Oct. 2; Com. for relaxing Blockade, Oct. 17; from Liverpool, Nov. 7; and others. Aberdeen attacked the pacific blockade as illegal. *Parliamentary Debates* 3rd, 51, p. 572. Jan. 27, 1840.

[49] *Aff. Etr.* Buenos Ayres, 26, p. 91 ff. To Martigny, Oct. 21, 1839.

[50] *Aff. Etr.* Buenos Ayres, 26, p. 101. Soult to Martigny, Oct. 25, 1839. Soult and Palmerston had, in the meantime, resumed their co-operation in Spain. See Hall, *op. cit.,* pp. 212-218.

[51] *Ibid.,* 26, p. 68. Foreign Minister to Minister of Marine, Oct. 15, 1839.

direction was given to French policy in December, 1839, after the misconception at Paris concerning the purposes of the British agent at Buenos Ayres was finally cleared up. The difficulty came into the open when Palmerston accused the Paris authorities of using their Argentine claims as a mere pretext to overthrow Rosas and extract a treaty by force.[52] Soult immediately returned a counter-charge that Mandeville himself had encouraged the obstinacy of Rosas and had actually engineered the secret negotiations between the Governor and Rivera the previous summer.[53] Palmerston immediately demonstrated from Mandeville's own letters that these suspicions were groundless. Already alarmed, as he was, by developments in the East, Soult was overjoyed to learn that he could really count on British assistance in extricating himself from the trouble in the Plata.[54] A letter to Martigny on December 12 ordered him to disengage himself at once from all other preoccupations, regardless of attendant complications, so as "to enter into direct negotiations with the Argentine Government" and to put himself at the same time in connection with Mandeville. Soult strongly insisted that France must not fail to take advantage of her accord with the British Cabinet

"to bring that sad quarrel to a prompt and honorable conclusion by means of negotiations. I would not know how to say how much importance the Government of the King attaches to it." [55]

It may easily be imagined that Martigny regarded the in-

[52] *Aff. Etr.* Buenos Ayres, 26, pp. 145-161. Granville to Dalmatrie, Nov. 7, 1839.

[53] *Aff. Etr.* Buenos Ayres, 26, p. 189 ff. A copy of an enclosure of Palmerston to Granville, Nov. 19, 1839. The incident referred to was a three weeks' visit of Mandeville to Montevideo while negotiating a slave trade treaty with Rivera. The charge had appeared in the *Journal des Débats* in October 1839, and was later answered by an indignant denial from the British agent. Mandeville's contention was perfectly true that Rosas himself had been greatly angered by the visit in question. F. O. 6, 69, M. to P., July 8, 1839; *ibid.*, 70, from M., Dec. 24, 1839.

[54] F. O. 27, 589. Granville to Palmerston Dec. 2, 7, 1839.

[55] *Aff. Etr.* Buenos Ayres, 26, pp. 205-206. Soult to Martigny, Dec. 12, 1839. Soult was more interested in the Eastern question. See Brossard, *op. cit.*, pp. 225-226. In the debates on the Address to the King in Jan., 1840, the Government was easily able to command a vote of confidence, against an opposition demanding more drastic measures, on the ground that too great activity by France would embarrass Rivera and Lavalle. See *Le Moniteur Universel*, Jan. 7, 8, 15, 1840.

structions which he received from time to time with misgivings, for he was engaged in a program which could not be altered with the same facility that the Paris authorities displayed in changing their minds. When Dupotet arrived at the Plata river in January, the effort to interest General Rivera, by subsidies, in an invasion of Entre Rios was in full swing. Martigny was also committed irrevocably to the support of the Unitarian crusade against Rosas; a considerable portion of the fleet was in the Paraná river co-operating with Lavalle.[56]

The reënforcements brought by Dupotet immediately gave new life to the blockading activities, but in vain were all their efforts to secure the aid of Rivera. That leader demanded the supreme command for himself, and offended the patriotism of the Argentine Commission by insisting upon the detachment of the inter-river Provinces from the Confederation.[57] By the end of February, the efforts of the French had run completely aground. Lavalle's small army in Entre Rios was left alone to face the forces of Echagüe.[58]

The arrival of the instructions of December 12 at this juncture gave rise to serious disagreement between the two French agents. Martigny was thoroughly disgusted at Soult's sudden change of front. He declared that the execution of the orders to negotiate at any price would forever ruin the prestige of France in South America.[59] On the other hand, the encouragement of this letter was just what Dupotet needed to make him break away entirely from his colleague. At the invitation of Mandeville, the French Admiral consented on February 24 to confer with a representative of the Buenos Ayres Government in the harbor outside the city. It was understood that all proposals should emanate from Rosas, and that Martigny would have the final say as to their acceptability.[60]

Mandeville was apparently only too glad to embarrass the distrusted Martigny. At any rate, he planned a meeting be-

[56] Durand, *op. cit.,* pp. 82-84.
[57] Saldías, *op. cit.,* vol. 3, pp. 143-157, 169.
[58] Durand, *op. cit.,* pp. 82-84.
[59] *Aff. Etr.* Buenos Ayres, 26, pp. 253-268. Despatch of Martigny, Feb. 28, 1840.
[60] F. O. 6, 74, M. to P. Jan. 14, 17, Feb. 2, 29, 1840.

tween Dupotet and Arana deliberately for that end. He received from Rosas four definite proposals on the basis of which an armistice might be arranged: (1) All pending negotiations should be shifted to Paris, while (2) the blockade should be raised immediately and Martín García restored. (3) Rosas should agree that French aliens would be treated on the same basis as that enjoyed by foreigners in France, but (4) the French agents, on their part, should recover within a limited number of days all armament, munitions, and other war stores which they had furnished to the enemies of Rosas. Mandeville was admittedly confident that Martigny would never accept such terms, but he arranged, nevertheless, for Dupotet to take dinner with himself and Secretary Arana on board the British corvette "Action," the night of February 29. The banquet was set with copious liquid refreshments. In a note written directly before the guests arrived, the British Minister said: "When the Champaigne [sic] works, I shall see what it produces."[61]

The hilarious session on board the "Action" lasted throughout the night. A second note by Mandeville, written early the following morning, recorded that the outcome was most gratifying. There had been profuse compliments on both sides and enthusiastic agreement to the terms on the part of the Admiral.[62] In a later more extended report, the British agent explained to Palmerston that Dupotet had openly avowed that Roger alone had been the cause of the rupture. The Admiral declared, furthermore, that if he himself had not been cheated out of his diplomatic powers by that same man, he would not hesitate to accept the terms proposed. He promised to send them directly to Paris, if Martigny should refuse to accept them.[63]

The two French agents now found themselves at sword's points. Martigny was naturally indignant at the Admiral's unwarranted assumption of authority. Dupotet replied with

[61] F. O. 6, 74. Mandeville to Palmerston, Feb. 29; same to Strangeways, Feb. 29. *Aff. Etr.* Buenos Ayres, 28, p. 4.
[62] F. O. 6, 74. Mandeville to Strangeways, Feb. 29 and March 1.
[63] F. O. 6, 74. Mandeville to Palmerston, March 1, 20, 1840 and enclosures.

equal heat, vigorously defending his action.[64] On the question of restoring Martín García during the contemplated armistice, the Admiral himself felt obliged to retract what he had agreed to under the inspiration of the champagne. He informed Arana on March 12, that the island would have to be retained as a guarantee until peace was made.[65] The French diplomatic agent submitted his formal objections to the Argentine proposal on March 26. Peace must be made, he said, with the termination of the blockade. Because the Argentine law differed from that of France by including as citizens all foreigners resident two years or married to natives, the suggested reciprocal treatment of aliens, he maintained, was not satisfactory. Frenchmen must be granted, without condition, most-favored-nation treatment until a commercial treaty should be concluded and their claims settled.[66]

The "Action" incident brought all military operations to a complete standstill. So embittered was the French agent toward Mandeville that the former flatly refused to make use of British mediation, as he was instructed to do. The blockade was relaxed, and Lavalle and Echagüe remained quietly watching each other for four months with scarcely a hostile move on either side.[67]

The later instructions sent by Marshal Soult were even more insistent that the intervention should be abandoned. The pressure from the British Foreign Office had gone so far, in early 1840, as to threaten to ignore completely the ineffective blockade.[68] Soult's final letter of February 26 made Martigny himself responsible for all the accumulated blunders in the unfortunate affair. He had sacrified French interests

[64] *Aff. Etr.*, Buenos Ayres, 27, p. 102 ff. Martigny to Dupotet, March 7; Dupotet to Martigny, March 9.

[65] *Ibid.*, p. 107 ff.

[66] F. O. 6, 74. Mandeville to Palmerston, April 6, 1840. Enclosure, Martigny to Mandeville, March 26, 1840. This reply of Martigny was indeed reasonable enough, and Palmerston in June ordered Mandeville to urge its acceptance at Buenos Ayres. See F. O. 6, 73, P. to M., June 25, 1840.

[67] Page, *op. cit.*, pp. 340-342.

[68] F. O. 27, 598. Palmerston to Granville, Feb. 14, 18, 1840. The ineffectiveness of the blockade was due to the diversion of vessels to the aid of Lavalle.

and embarrassed his government both politically and finan-
cially, charged Soult, by transforming a dispute over reparations into an attempt to overturn the Government of Buenos
Ayres. The meager stake which France had in the quarrel
would never justify them in sending an army. Such a course
would occasion grave, if not alarming complications in both
Europe and America. Martigny must cease the enlistment of
French nationals in the quarrel, and seek an immediate settlement with Rosas.[69] A copy of this despatch of February 26
unfortunately fell into the hands of Rosas himself, which
fact was enough to nullify every future negotiating effort of
Martigny.[70]

The French agent eventually made his attempt to negotiate
with Rosas, in May, 1840. Through the Sardinian consul,
he requested a conference with the Governor at Buenos Ayres.
France would admit some alterations in her demands, he promised, and would be content with a private written assurance
from the Governor that her nationals would enjoy most-
favored-nation treatment. Rosas would not agree to treat on
such indefinite terms, and declared that he would give only
a verbal statement in regard to the treatment of the French
nationals.[71] Having the advantage of his knowledge of the
nature of the French instructions, the Dictator was thus gratifying his pride by keeping the great European power begging
at his gate.

This humiliating rebuff, which was quickly followed by the
news that Thiers had succeeded the cringing Soult as head of
the Paris Government, infused new life into the French program. Martigny entered into a Protocol of alliance with the

[69] *Aff. Etr.* Buenos Ayres, 26, p. 251 ff; See Pereyra *op. cit.,* pp. 80-83.
Vedia, *op. cit.,* pp. 108-109.
[70] Saldías, *op. cit.* vol. 3. 163-166. Rosas published the letter in the
Archivo Americano; Brossard, *op. cit.* pp. 225-226, says that it was pur-
loined from the French consulate.
[71] F. O. 6, 74. Mandeville to Palmerston, May 18, 1840; F. O. 6, 75.
Same to same June 19, 1840. Rosas later said that he contemplated granting privileges to Oriental citizens which "it would be neither politic nor
expedient to extend to French subjects." This statement will be clarifying
when we consider one Article of the French treaty of Oct. 29, 1840. They
both indicate that Rosas was seriously contemplating some sort of organic
connection between Uruguay and the Argentine Confederation.

Argentine Commission on June 22, and Lavalle abandoned his inactive policy.[72] But when the Unitarian army attacked Echagüe on July 15, it was driven pell-mell from the field, and did not stop until it had found protection under the guns of the French fleet on the Paraná river. A few days later, the French leaders loaded the entire army of Lavalle, without their horses, on board transports, and started down the river for an unknown destination.[73]

Important developments had meanwhile been taking place in Europe, to which we must turn our attention.

Adolphe Thiers had been entrusted with the task of forming a new French Cabinet on March 1, 1840. The previous Ministry had been obliged to retire because of a republican insurrection,[74] and there was precious little in the circumstances of the change of leaders to furnish a foundation policy for a new Government. The new leader was a resourceful politician, however, and within a short time gathered around him a considerable following. He built up his power by a shrewd program of domestic legislation, buttressing it by what he was pleased to call a "foreign policy of dignity."[75]

The foreign policy of Thiers differed not at all from that of Soult in its major premise that British friendship must be maintained. But the new Minister was much more confident than his predecessor had been concerning his ability to accomplish that end. He wrongly assumed that the natural antagonism between Russia and the Whig Government in London would make it impossible for these two nations to coördinate their policies in the Near East, where the Pasha of Egypt, encouraged by the French, was about to force Turkey to

[72] E. Quesada, *La época de Rosas, su verdadero carácter histórico.* (Buenos Ayres 1898), pp. 254-256.

[73] Durand, *op. cit.,* pp. 84-91. *Memoria de Gen. Ferré, op. cit.* Page, *op. cit.,* p. 342.

[74] François le Goff, *The Life of Louis Adolphe Thiers.* Trans. by T. Stanton. (1879), pp. 86-88.

[75] Allison, *op. cit.,* pp. 271-289.

grant him Syria as a part of his hereditary domain.[76] In all other questions, Thiers would take pains to promote his cordial relations with the British Government. He asked the French public to discontinue their incessant recrimination against England.[77] He initiated a negotiation for a new tariff arrangement with Great Britain.[78] Thiers then did Palmerston a notable service by conducting a successful mediation in a quarrel between Britain and Sicily over the sulphur monopoly.[79] In early May, he secured Palmerston's consent for the transfer of the ashes of Napoleon to the Invalides, and he exploited the incident to the limit as tangible evidence of the good will of England.[80] Such was the program into which a new policy for the Plata expedition had to be fitted.

Thiers' boast that his was to be a foreign policy of dignity called forth immediately a cry from commercial centers that he must put an end to the ruinous and disgraceful condition of affairs in the Plata river. From Chambers of Commerce at Havre, Marseilles, Cette, Montpellier, Bordeaux, Nantes, and elsewhere, these petitions poured in upon the President of the Council. "Was France to sacrifice all of her trans-Atlantic influence?" they asked; "Was her dignity to become a meaningless word because she would not protect her subjects and their commerce?" [81]

The question came up before the Chambers in late April, in connection with a special appropriation bill for more than two million francs, largely to cover the drafts of Martigny.[82] Considerable opposition to the measure was encountered from

[76] Guyot, op. cit., pp. 152-166; Rodkey, F. S., The Turkish-Egyptian Question in the Relations of England, France, and Russia, 1832-1841. University of Illinois Social Science Studies, Vol. II, No. 3-4 (1924), pp. 64-69; 78-81; See also Major J. Hall, op. cit., pp. 241-266.

[77] Le Moniteur Universel for April 15, 1840.

[78] Guyot, op. cit., pp. 166-187.

[79] F. O. 27, 599. Palmerston to Granville April 20, 23 ff., 1840.

[80] Ibid. Same to same, May 9, 1840. Le Moniteur Universel, June 27 and 28, 1840. The French press greatly emphasized the enhanced prestige which this act gave them in Turkey. With Walewski, the son of Napoleon, talking to Mehemet Ali in Egypt, the stage was now set for an ideal episode for the purpose of exciting the French imagination.

[81] Aff. Etr., Buenos Ayres, 27, p. 10 ff. April 6 and 7, 1840.

[82] Ibid., 27, p. 42. The major appropriation was for 1,500,000 francs, which was supplemented by requests for 300,000 and 540,000 respectively.

a number who disliked the practice of entrusting an agent with such large sums, in the expenditure of which no account was given.[83] Thiers immediately seized the opportunity to whip his following into line. He made the matter a question of confidence, and carried it through the two Chambers by overwhelming majorities. The Foreign Minister himself led out in the plea that Frenchmen must no longer endure a position of inferiority to the British and Americans. The French flag must be respected in American waters! He pledged all the resources of France in securing their just deserts in the war with Rosas.[84]

In the instructions which Thiers sent to Martigny directly after his parliamentary victory, the "lion of the tribune" was considerably less ferocious than he had appeared to be during the debate. Without compromising the honor of France, the agent was to seek a pacific settlement with Rosas, he wrote, on the usual terms of most-favored-nation treatment of nationals, the admission of liability by Rosas for the various claims and indemnities, and the determination of their amount by means of arbitration. Great Britain, Thiers continued, was complaining very much of their policy; all appearance that he was avoiding her good offices should therefore be carefully avoided by Martigny. The policy of seeking local allies was permissible, but neither the French Ministry nor the Chambers could longer approve a system which committed France to such large financial expenditures. As a last extremity, the Government might consent to send a force to the Plata of sufficient strength to crush the resistance of Rosas; but this would not be possible before the lapse of five or six months, when the Eastern question would have approached a solution. "I repeat it," Thiers concluded, "we are indeed far from being inclined to the employment of a measure of that gravity." [85]

[83] *London Times* for April 28, 1840.

[84] *Le Moniteur Universel,* May 14, 16, 1840. It passed the Chamber of Peers by 103 to 3 on May 13. None of the critics who demanded a more vigorous program could consistently oppose the appropriation.

[85] *Aff. Etr.,* Buenos Ayres, 27, pp. 66-73. Thiers to Martigny May 15, 1840.

Two weeks had not passed before Thiers had completely abandoned this cautious attitude. About May 20, news reached Paris concerning the Dupotet-Arana conference of February 29. With the public mind already aroused over the Plata question, the account of this incident gave rise to a veritable furor. An insistent demand was echoed from every quarter that the government settle their score with the insolent Dictator.[86] The *Revue des Deux Mondes* for May 31 made particular mention of the fact that the affair of Buenos Ayres was commanding special attention, and the editor severely criticized the interference of Dupotet.[87] Thiers decided to send a powerful expedition immediately. He wrote to Martigny early in June,[88] that the King had determined to send Admiral Baudin, the hero of San Juan d'Ulloa, with considerable reënforcements to take over the direction of the operations. In the meantime, the hostilities against Rosas should be pressed with all vigor. The letter concluded as follows:

"If there is moral certainty of arriving at a solution by means of a new subsidy, . . . you will receive immediately the authorization to furnish it to our allies. . . . But it must be thoroughly appreciated that this affair must be promptly terminated, it may be, as I desire very much, by the triumph of the auxiliaries which you have secured for France, it may be by means exclusively French." [89]

Thiers was soon to learn, however, that Palmerston's representations in regard to the policy of Martigny were not to be set aside in such a cavalier manner.[90] The British Minister had been much annoyed at the confident spirit of Thiers, and had already prepared an arrangement which would prick the

---

[86] *Correspondencia Diplomática del doctor José Longinos Ellauri, 1839-1844.* (Montevideo 1919) pp. xxi-xxii, 19-24. A letter dated May 30.

[87] *Revue des Deux Mondes,* 1840, vol. 2, p. 623.

[88] The exact date is not given on this document. Baudin's appointment was made some time before June 10, however. *Aff. Etr.* Buenos Ayres, 28, pp. 26-44.

[89] *Aff. Etr.,* Buenos Ayres, 27, pp. 247-253. Thiers to Martigny, June, 1840. It may be noted that a settlement by voluntary negotiation was not here contemplated.

[90] F. O. 27, 602. Granville to Palmerston, March 6 and 13, 1840. F. O. 27, 599. Palmerston to Granville, May 12, 26, 1840. *Aff. Etr.,* Buenos Ayres, 27, pp. 75-85. Granville to Thiers, May 15.

bubble of the French program in the Near East.[91] He did not intend to allow the Argentine intervention to get out from under his control, as it now threatened to do. The British public was even more alarmed than was the Foreign Minister at the news of the naval preparations under way in France. To the several interpolations on the subject which Palmerston encountered in Parliament, he invariably replied that no effort would be wanting from the British agents to promote a settlement of the difficulty at Buenos Ayres.[92]

Upon hearing that Baudin had been chosen to head the new expedition, Palmerston hastened to prepare an account giving an exhaustive review of the course of the French intervention in the Plata. The several documents, totaling some 134 pages of manuscript, were delivered to the Government in Paris about June 22.[93] The exposition was a scathing attack upon French sincerity. It was unanswerable in its main argument that the French agents had intermixed unnecessarily in local political affairs, and had subordinated the securing of their reparations to the purpose of overthrowing Rosas. Every detail of the intrigue of the French with the enemies of Rosas was set forth.[94] In one section of the document, a striking contrast was drawn between the various statements made by the Paris authorities, and the corresponding actions of their agents at Montevideo. A section marked *A* contained an abstract of the many assertions of the French to the effect that they desired a prompt and amicable settlement with Rosas, including extracts from instructions which had been submitted to London. Another, marked *B*, reproduced from Mandeville's reports the actual policy which the French agents had pursued, empha-

[91] Hall, *op. cit.*, pp. 241-248. It is significant that in January, 1840, the Russian Ambassador at Washington made a most ostentatious show of his sympathy for Rosas against France. See F. O. 6, 74. Mandeville to Palmerston, May 18, 1840 and enclosures. From reports of General Alvear at Washington, Jan. 10 and 15, 1840, Saldías, *op. cit.*, vol. 3, pp. 160-163. Guyot, *op. cit.*, p. 189. From F. O. Russia, 396, Palmerston to Bloomfield at St. Petersburg, Aug. 4, 1840.

[92] *London Times* for May 9, 20; *Parliamentary Debates,* 3rd series, Vol. 54, pp. 1113-1114. June 12, 1840.

[93] F. O. 27, 599. Palmerston to Granville, June 16. Later material followed on July 26. Part of it was given to Guizot in London on June 15.

[94] *Aff. Etr.* Buenos Ayres, 27, pp. 203-229.

sizing their repeated refusals to accept British mediation, and their statements that they would treat with the Argentine barbarian by means of cannon and not with paper. The numerous impolitic statements of Dupotet in his unguarded conversation of the "Action" were fully reproduced. The document contained no threat and no declaration of British policy; but it would have been a terrific thing to release to the press. It made perfectly clear that Palmerston would tolerate evasion no longer in the matter of negotiating with Rosas.[95].

The notification from London placed Thiers in a most uncomfortable dilemma. He could not repudiate the promises already made to the French public and to Martigny, and yet it was extremely important that he should avoid a break with England at this critical juncture of the Eastern question. The formal instructions which he prepared for Baudin on June 26, a copy of which was sent to London, show very clearly that the belligerent spirit of the French Minister had moderated considerably since his previous letter to Martigny. Thiers charged that Baudin's first responsibility should be to take advantage of any disposition on the part of Rosas to negotiate their difficulties. Embarrassments in regard to the blockade itself, as well as other more serious dangers, he said, made the Government's insistence upon this point extremely urgent. Only in the event that Lavalle's army should be in a position of almost sure success was the Admiral to continue the policy of supporting the Unitarian revolution. At all events, it should be made perfectly clear to the British agents and to neutrals generally that France was ready to treat with Rosas on terms of equal privileges for her nationals apart from commercial advantages, and immediate pecuniary indemnity for the usual claims. Buenos Ayres should be allowed no compensation for the rigors of the blockade. If the total amount of the reparations could not be fixed, the obligation should at least be admitted in principle. Thiers emphasized, in conclusion, that the

[95] *Aff. Etr.* Buenos Ayres, 27, pp. 162-202. At the same time, Palmerston was telling Mandeville that the demands which Martigny had presented in place of Dupotet's terms were most reasonable. F. O. 6, 73, P. to M., June 25.

King was very anxious to terminate an arrangement which was injuring commerce, compromising their friendship with other nations, and which might eventually entail strenuous exertions on the part of the government.[96]

In early July, a rumor began to circulate in Paris that Thiers had modified his earlier plans in regard to the Plata expedition. It was reported in the press that the military contingent intended for Baudin had been cut to a mere 500 marines and sixty engineers.[97] Just what the circumstances actually were cannot be definitely determined; but it is known that the commander himself protested vigorously to the Cabinet, saying that he would not consent to head the expedition unless the inclusion of a considerable force for disembarkation would allow him to avoid the unthinkable alternative of bombarding the city of Buenos Ayres.[98] After several days of delay, the Government decided to include 1500 troops, together with a battery and engineers.[99]

But when the time of Baudin's departure drew near, Louis Philippe lost heart. He feared above all that Great Britain might be offended. Only a few hours before the scheduled sailing of the squadron from Cherbourg, a telegram was sent from Paris informing the commander that his military force had been cut to five hundred marines. The Admiral's reply apparently lacked something of the proper respect, for on July 9 he was abruptly deprived of his command.[100]

The French Government declared emphatically through its official organs that there had been no change in Baudin's instructions and no diminution of the military force which was to accompany him. It was pretended that a difference of opinion had arisen in regard to the transfer of a consul

[96] *Aff. Etr.*, Buenos Ayres, 28, pp. 46-57. Palmerston wrote Mandeville: "A rejection of these terms would place the Buenos Ayres Government so much in the wrong in the judgment of the World, that the French would be supported by public opinion in any measures which they might resort to against Buenos Ayres." See F. O. 6, 73, Palmerston to Mandeville, July 3, 1840.

[97] *London Times,* July 1 and 4, 1840.

[98] Brossard, *op. cit.*, pp. 226-228.

[99] *London Times* for July 9, quoting from the *Courrier Français* of July 7. Durand, *op. cit.*, pp. 93-94.

[100] Brossard, *op. cit.*, pp. 228-229; Durand, *op. cit.*, p. 94.

from the West Indies to the Plata.[101]   But the same authorities were careful to inform the British agents in Paris differently. Henry Bulwer reported a conversation with the French King, held on the very day of Baudin's retirement, in part as follows:

"His Majesty . . . spoke of his earnest desire that the affairs of Buenos Ayres might be promptly arranged, and [said] . . . that he had interfered to diminish the Armament which it had been intended to send there." [102]

Baron Mackau, a naval officer of considerable experience in the West Indies, was chosen to command the expedition. The departure was delayed for approximately two weeks.[103]

Into this very delicate adjustment, where the French were exercising great care to avoid offending the British Government, the announcement made from London on July 15 that a Convention had been signed between England, Russia, Prussia, and Austria in regard to the Turko-Egyptian question dropped like a bomb-shell.[104]   By a threat of resignation from the Cabinet, Palmerston had finally forced his hesitant colleagues to accept the arrangement which he had made.   Liberal England was therefore lined up with reactionary Europe in declaring that Mehemet Ali must renounce his hereditary claim to Syria, and return the northernmost provinces to the Sultan.[105]   France had not even been consulted.   Thiers might talk loudly of war and the French press writhe with anger, but the masterful British Secretary demonstrated in the end that he was right

[101] *Revue des Deux Mondes* 1840, vol. 3, p. 141. *Chronique de la Quinzaine*, dated July 14, 1840. The article asserts that 1500 marines had been agreed upon.
[102] F. O. 27, 604. Bulwer to Palmerston, July 10, 1840. Bulwer was confident that this was the cause of the change of Commanders.
[103] *London Times*, July 13, 14, 15, 1840. Paris papers reported the change on July 11, and it was officially announced on July 12 in the *Moniteur*. Opposition papers bitterly attacked the vacillating policy of the Foreign Minister.
[104] Rodkey, *op. cit.*, p. 150 ff. Guyot, *op. cit.*, pp. 166-187. The French Chambers adjourned on the 15th also. See *Le Moniteur*, July 16, 1840. It may here be noted that the *London Times* of July 15 and 20 severely criticized this Whig betrayal of the sincere friendship of Thiers.
[105] Rodkey, *op. cit.*, p. 150 ff. Algernon Cecil, *British Foreign Secretaries* (London, 1927), pp. 154-156. Hall, *op. cit.*, pp. 275-278.

in his calculation that the government of Louis Philippe would not dare fight all of Europe.[106]

The crisis which was precipitated by the declaration of July 15 could not have failed to have had some effect on the large naval expedition which was about to leave France for the Plata. The situation with which the Paris government was confronted surpassed the worst fears of Louis Philippe, and there was now every conceivable reason for them to disentangle themselves from the Argentine affair. But to have abandoned the Mackau expedition abruptly would only have made conditions worse. It would either be interpreted as an act of cowardice at home, or would constitute a defiant answer to a European challenge that France could ill afford to accept. On the other hand, if the government should eventually find it necessary to accept defeat in the Near East, a vigorous enterprise conducted in South America might serve to compensate somewhat and save the face of the Paris authorities. It is significant to learn, therefore, that a British agent in Paris was approached by a high officer of the Admiralty, on July 17, with "the most earnest request" that Mackau might enjoy the services of the good offices of the British Government in coming to terms with Rosas. Martigny would have no part in the negotiation, the Britisher was assured, and the new orders were most pacific in character. Palmerston immediately replied that Mandeville would render every aid.[107] The *London Times* observed on July 20, in connection with a discussion of the attitude of the French press, that "there seems to be less bounce about the [Mackau] expedition than when it was first planned." [108]

Neither Mackau's force nor his instructions differed greatly from those which had been intended for Baudin. Three war

[106] Guyot, *op. cit.,* pp. 190-211; Rodkey, *op. cit.,* p. 170 ff.; Hall, *op. cit.* p. 279-286. It was during this furor that Louis Napoleon's *coup* at Boulogne took place.

[107] F. O. 27, 604, Bulwer to Palmerston, July 17, 1840. *Ibid.,* 600, Palmerston to Bulwer, July 20. *London Times,* July 23.

[108] The *Revue des Deux Mondes* of July 31 asserted that Palmerston had deliberately taken advantage of the embarrassment of France. [1840, vol. 3, p. 284.] *London Times,* July 20, 1840. The British assumption that France originally intended occupation or conquest had very little, if any, foundation.

vessels equipped for the expedition were ordered to remain at Toulon,[109] but the squadron still included thirty-six vessels with 6,000 seamen on board.[110] Baudin's instructions were given to Mackau *in toto*, with the date simply changed to July 21. In several supplementary observations, Thiers explained to the new leader that the blockade could not be raised if the negotiations should be transferred to Paris. Their financial support to Lavalle and Rivera must be discontinued, and Mackau should not hesitate to make peace apart from these leaders. The idea that France was under binding obligation to these local parties as allies, he definitely repudiated. Wrote Thiers:

"They cannot demand that you pursue indefinitely . . . a struggle in which we have not engaged them, in which they have spontaneously and voluntarily engaged themselves, and for the success of which they have asked and obtained our aid, without rendering us anything like the assistance which they have received from us." [111]

If it should become necessary to renew hostilities, the Admiral might agree to assist their local associates to the extent of 500,000 francs. He would no longer be limited, as heretofore, to the employment of naval measures only.[112]

The squadron departed for the Plata on July 24, which was just about the time that the defeated army of Lavalle began its journey on the transports down the Paraná.

Events in the Plata moved rapidly from July to September, 1840. A small band from Lavalle's force was fortunate enough, in early August, to capture a large number of horses near San Pedro in the Province of Buenos Ayres. The French then prevailed upon the Unitarian leader to disembark his entire force of 3,300 men, with their six cannon, on the right

[109] *London Times* of July 21, quoting the Paris *Commerce* of July 19. *Aff. Etr.* Buenos Ayres, 28, pp. 59-60. Mackau to Thiers, July 21, protesting against the diminution of his force.

[110] *Le Moniteur Universel,* July 25, 1840.

[111] It should be noted that the major premise of M. Thiers is not quite true. France had actively sought allies.

[112] *Aff. Etr.,* Buenos Ayres, 28, pp. 51-57. Instructions to Mackau, July 21, 1840.

bank of the Paraná. While the fleet vigorously blockaded the Argentine capital, the army moved directly upon it.[113] By a vigorous thrust, Lavalle might easily have gained control of Buenos Ayres, for Rosas was entirely unprepared. Excessive caution permitted this opportunity to escape. But the army of 5,000 men whom Rosas managed to gather together by August 23, were a heterogeneous lot, and presented no formidable appearance. The first news of Baudin's expedition, which reached the river on August 12, had meanwhile stirred Martigny to new efforts. By the end of August, he had succeeded in reviving the alliance between Uruguay and Corrientes.[114] It seemed that the Dictator must surely succumb to this combination.

But just as quickly, the outlook changed. Lavalle was greatly disappointed because no sympathetic demonstration raised its head within the city.[115] Lacking confidence in his own army, and perhaps in the loyalty of Dupotet, he informed the French leader that he would not attack the forces of Rosas unless all the available marines from the fleet were placed at his disposal. Dupotet must also promise that the forces accompanying the new expedition could be similarly employed. The French Admiral refused to accede to these requests. The later news that Baudin had been superseded, accompanied by a slight relaxation of the blockade, apparently confirmed all the fears of Lavalle. At any rate, he suddenly gave the order on September 6 for a general retreat, without having struck a single blow at his adversary.[116]

This retirement of Lavalle was disastrous to the Unitarian cause. The covert opposition to Rosas within the city, which

---

[113] Durand, *op. cit.*, pp. 91-93.

[114] F. O. 6, 75, Mandeville to Palmerston, Aug. 25; Durand, pp. 94-96; Saldías, vol. 3, pp. 186-197. *Colección de tratados, etc. de Uruguay*, vol. 1, pp. 89-92. The alliance was consummated on Aug. 27.

[115] F. O., 6, 75, M. to P., Sept. 23; Saldías, vol. 3, pp. 186-197. Saldías thinks that Lavalle's French backing made real popular support for him impossible.

[116] Page, *op. cit.*, p. 345; Saldías, vol. 3, pp. 186-197; Durand, *op. cit.*, pp. 94-97; Brossard, *op. cit.*, pp. 229-230; José María Paz, *Memorias póstumas del general José María Paz*, 3 vols. (La Plata, 1892) vol. 3, pp. 5-6. This incident has never been satisfactorily explained. Some say that Lavalle was deceived by a ruse of Rosas; others say that he expected an attack upon his rear.

had been gaining considerable headway, was ruthlessly crushed. A reign of terror ensued for several days, in which neither the lives nor the property of those suspected of Unitarian sympathies were safe. Assassinations occurred every day; hundreds were imprisoned; the property of all suspects was made liable for confiscation in restoration of the considerable damage done by Lavalle.[117]

The outlook for the pending French negotiation was dark indeed. Mandeville at first could get no encouragement from Rosas, in reply to his insistence that Martigny's terms of the previous March should be accepted.[118] With the nearer approach of Mackau's squadron, however, and redoubled pressure from Mandeville, the Buenos Ayres authorities became considerably more tractable.[119]

When Admiral Mackau arrived at Montevideo on September 23, he found himself between two fires. On one side was Dupotet, who was intimate with Mandeville and entirely out of sympathy with the attack upon Rosas.[120] Dupotet assured Mackau that the former French agents had been largely to blame, and that Martigny, even then, was under the influence of parties within Montevideo who were interested for financial reasons in the continuation of the blockade.[121] On the other side, Martigny insisted that they must act decisively, in order to prevent the defeat of all that the French and their allies had so long striven for. It would be worse than useless, he said, to treat with the faithless Dictator, and France certainly could not approach him at that time without serious damage to her dignity. But if the Admiral must negotiate, Martigny insisted that it should be only in conjunction with those local parties

[117] F. O. 6, 75, Mandeville to Palmerston, Sept. 23 and Oct. 14. A. M. Cervantes, *Estudios históricos políticos y sociales sobre el Río de la Plata* (Paris, 1854), pp. 154-167; Durand, *op. cit.*, pp. 96-97. *National Intelligencer,* Jan. 7, 1841, reported that assassinations had risen to fifteen a day.

[118] F. O. 6, 75, Mandeville to Palmerston, Aug. 25 and Sept. 12, 1840, and enclosures.

[119] *Aff. Etr.*, Buenos Ayres, 27, p. 328.

[120] F. O. 6, 75, Mandeville to Palmerston, Oct. 10, 1840.

[121] F. O. 6, 75, Mandeville to Palmerston, Oct. 28—a report of a conversation between Mackau and Mandeville on Oct. 13. *Aff. Etr.,* Buenos Ayres, 28, pp. 138-140. Memorandum of Mackau.

who had been associated with the intervention from the beginning, and with whom they had entered into formal engagements.

There was really little choice as far as Mackau was concerned between these two alternatives. Lavalle was certainly in no position of sure success, and Rivera had frequently proved untrustworthy. It seemed, moreover, that only a madman would now decline to consider a reasonable peace proposal, for Rosas realized that no sympathy could be expected from Great Britain if he now refused to come to a settlement. Mackau had also to consider the fact that any vessel might bring news of the outbreak of a general war in Europe.[122] To the insistence of the Montevidean authorities that they be included in the peace negotiation, Mackau replied as follows:

"France . . . has considered neither the Oriental Republic nor the troops which are under the command of General Lavelle as her allies; she has seen in them only auxiliaries which events unforeseen had brought to her. The rest have been personal acts of her agents." [123]

On September 25, Mandeville received a note from Dupotet asking for an expression from the Buenos Ayres Government concerning the basis on which they would treat with the French. A statement from Arana giving assurances of proper respect for the rights of Frenchmen was in the hands of Mackau by September 29. The admiral addressed a most flattering and conciliatory reply to the Argentine Foreign Minister on October 3, requesting that they arrange for a meeting on a vessel carrying both flags. The proposal was readily agreed to, and Mackau appeared in the outer roads of Buenos Ayres on October 12.[124]

The first meeting with Secretary Arana, who had full charge of the negotiation while Rosas was absent with the army, was on the 14th. During the first week they made little progress, the Argentine negotiator being most unreasonable in his demands. Mandeville was obliged to exert strong pressure, and

---

[122] Durand, op. cit., pp. 97-99. Brossard, op. cit., pp. 229-232. Page, op. cit., pp. 364-366.
[123] Vedia, op. cit., pp. 122-127.
[124] F. O. 6, 75, Mandeville to Palmerston, Oct. 10, 1840.

Rosas himself finally intervened to grant the particular indemnity article which the French required.[125]   At one point in the parley, the murder of an alleged French subject on shore almost wrecked the negotiation.   Arana was a master in the art of delay, however, and time was on his side.   The anxious Mackau surrendered point after point to his patient opponent. The Convention was finally signed on October 29.[126]

As far as French interests were concerned, the Mackau treaty was equitable enough; but it completely abandoned the local allies of France, and left a most unfortunate heritage for the entire river country.   The French claims were acknowledged, and were to be entrusted to an arbitration court for adjudication.   Martín García and the captured war vessels should be restored to Buenos Ayres, and the blockade be raised within eight days after the ratification of the Convention by Rosas.   Proscribed Argentines who would lay down their arms within that same period of time would be granted amnesty by Rosas; but this privilege did not extend to the leaders or to any whose presence in Argentina was "incompatible with law and order."   Each state should accord to the nationals of the other most-favored-nation treatment, with an interesting exception specified in Article VI that special civil and political rights which might in the future be extended to the nationals of other South American states were not to be claimed by France.   Article IV was the most objectionable of all.   Rosas agreed to respect the independence of Uruguay only "so long as the rights, honor, and security of the Argentine Confederation" were not endangered.[127]

Although Mackau was enthusiastic over his accomplishment,[128] it is perfectly evident that the settlement was a victory for Rosas.   The Governor had defied a European power for more than two years, and had made peace voluntarily on terms

[125] F. O. 6, 75, Mandeville to Palmerston, Oct. 28.   Mackau's aid was Thomas Page, who later defended the mission in the *Revue des Deux Mondes*.

[126] Durand, *op. cit.,* pp. 99-102.

[127] The original is found in *Aff. Etr., ibid.,* 28, pp. 171-175; *British Foreign and State Papers* 29, pp. 1089-1091; Pereyra, *op. cit.,* pp. 98-100. Minor points covered the exchange of salutes, and the restoration of merchant vessels. Vedia, *op. cit.,* pp. 121-122. Rosas ratified the treaty on Oct. 31.

[128] *Aff. Etr., ibid.* 28, p. 177-182.

considerably less unfavorable than Roger's original demands. His local enemies were hopelessly discredited by their connection with the foreigner, and he was left free to determine when and to what extent he should interfere in the affairs of Uruguay. The sixth article suggested a definite intention on his part to bring that state into a more or less direct political connection with the Argentine Confederation. So great was the jubilation of the Federalist party at Buenos Ayres over the treaty, that Mackau's party was fêted in the old palace of the viceroys for more than two weeks as the guests of Rosas and his daughter, Manuelita.[129] A lasting friendship was here formed between Rosas and Mackau, which became an important factor in the later relations between their respective countries.[130]

The rejoicing at Buenos Ayres was more than balanced by the extreme bitterness of the parties at Montevideo. The alliance between Rosas and Oribe, which the intervention had so firmly cemented, loomed up as an inevitable menace to the independence of Uruguay. The Orientals were particularly offended by the return of Martín García to Rosas, in the capture of which they had shared.[131] Among the vicious attacks emanating from the Montevidean press, there appeared a measured and well-documented pamphlet written by Florencio Varela. It went not a little way in establishing its contention that France had violated some very definite legal obligations toward her former associates when she abandoned them.[132] Varela's attack was considered important enough to merit an extended reply in the form of an anonymous pamphlet printed at Buenos Ayres a few months later, from the pen of someone who had access to the official French correspondence.[133] The British also came in for a share of this abuse. It was

[129] Rosas' wife had died a year before. Durand, *op. cit.*, pp. 102-107. Brossard, *op. cit.*, pp. 233-234. Rosas released 600 political prisoners. F. O. 6, 75, Mandeville to Palmerston, Nov. 5, 1840.

[130] *Aff. Etr., ibid.* 29, pp. 253-255. Feb. 25, 1842.

[131] Vedia, *op. cit.*, pp. 122-127. The attack was led by a Montevidean paper, *El Nacional.*

[132] F. Varela, *Sobre la convención de 29 de Octubre de 1840.* (Montevideo 1840) 79 pages and 440 documents.

[133] *Quelques Réflexions en réponse à la Brochure publiée à Montevideo par D. Florencio Varela.* In F. O. 6, 78. Enclosures of Mandeville, March 20, 1841.

charged that they had been bought off by Rosas at the price of the Falkland Islands. One paper declared that the United States alone was qualified to mediate in American affairs.[134]

The local warfare in Argentina was resumed so enthusiastically, after the withdrawal of the French, that observers doubted if peace would ever be restored. Mandeville wrote despairingly in February, 1841:

"Until one of the contending parties is annihilated, there is no prospect of repose or tranquillity." [135]

Rosas decreed the blockade of the ports of Uruguay in January, 1841, and successfully resisted Rivera's attempt to wrest the control of the river from him in May.[136] Lavalle had just been successful in capturing Santa Fé in November, 1840, when he learned that the French had abandoned him. He bravely refused Mackau's offer of an asylum and a pension in France.[137] With his back to the wall, the Unitarian leader shook off his previous lethargy, and for a year gave an excellent account of himself against heavy odds. In October, 1841, his army was finally crushed by a superior force under Manuel Oribe. Lavalle himself was mortally wounded soon after the battle.[138] Oribe's Argentine army then turned its attention to the forces of Uruguay and Corrientes.[139] The failure to include Rivera's Government in the negotiations of 1840 left the door open for Rosas now to deny the legal status of the Montevidean authorities.[140]

Rosas had by this time raised himself to the unchallenged leadership of the Federalist party in Argentina. The dictatorship which had been extended to him for six months in April, 1840, was again accepted by him, under some protest,

[134] F. O. 6, 78. Mandeville to Palmerston, Jan. 18, 1841. *El Nacional* for Jan. 8, 1841, sent as an enclosure by Mandeville.
[135] F. O. 6, 78. Mandeville to Palmerston, Feb. 17, 1841. Arana at this time refused to accept the British principle on neutral goods, but adopted that of the United States,—that the flag determined the nationality of the cargo.
[136] F. O. 6, 78. Mandeville to Palmerston, May 31, 1841.
[137] *Aff. Etr.* Buenos Ayres, 29, pp. 72-85. The report of M. Halley, whom Mackau had sent to Lavalle. Saldías, *op. cit.*, 3, pp. 212-213.
[138] Durand, *op. cit.*, pp. 110-115. Brossard, *op. cit.*, p. 249 ff. Quesada, E., *La guerra civil de 1841 y la tragedia de Acha.* (Córdoba 1916).
[139] Vedia, *op. cit.*, pp. 127-128.
[140] Durand, *op. cit.*, pp. 107-110. Brossard, *op. cit.*, pp. 240-248.

for a similar term in December. The duties of the office had come to be very burdensome to Rosas, and there was probably a measure of sincerity in his repeated requests that he be allowed to resign.[141]   But he knew, as did everyone else, that there was no one to take his place, now that his party extended throughout the Confederation.[142]   An attempt to assassinate the Dictator in March, 1841, reacted powerfully in his favor,[143] and the popularity of his able daughter was one of his greatest assets.[144]

On the very day that the Mackau Convention was signed, a new French Government under the leadership of Guizot and Soult came into power. When the Eastern crisis had come to a head, the French King had refused to follow Thiers into war.   Born under such auspices, the new Government was particularly open to attack on any issue which smacked of a weak foreign policy. The Mackau Convention came in for its due share of attention.

The Argentine question was brought up in the Chambers in February, 1841. The treaty was criticized severely by the Peers for its abandonment of the allies of France, for the surrender of Martín García, and for the failure to secure most-favored-nation treatment without the vague qualifications attached.   Guizot replied that since the treaty had been negotiated in accordance with instructions, international comity demanded that it should be ratified. The essential demands of the French had been secured, and in the light of previous difficulties, the negotiator had done well to treat with Rosas

[141] F. O. 78, Mandeville to Palmerston, Dec. 14, 1840. This arduous manner of life of Rosas was not a myth. The Dictator never left his house, and had no regular hours for sleep. He ate voraciously, only once a day, usually between one and four in the morning. Mandeville wondered that even Rosas' wonderful physique could withstand his habits. See F. O. 6, 83. Mandeville to Aberdeen, Jan. 15, 1842.

[142] Brossard, *op. cit.*, p. 249 ff.

[143] F. O. 6, 78. Mandeville to Palmerston, April 1, 1841; Brossard, *op. cit.*, p. 431. One cannot but suspect that the infernal machine episode was staged by Rosas himself, although there appears to be no evidence to support it.

[144] Saldías, *op. cit.*, vol. 3, pp. 280-287. The author tells of a plan to make the Government pass to Manuelita by hereditary right.

at all. It was extremely desirable, he concluded, that France should disengage herself from the interminable disorders of those countries. The real strength of Guizot's defense was demonstrated a few days later, when the same question came up in the Chamber of Deputies. The fact that Thiers himself, the leader of the opposition, had been responsible for the instructions given to Mackau prevented any serious attack.[145] This same consideration assumes great importance later, when a demand for a new intervention is raised.

The responsible press of Paris quickly rallied to the support of the Government. The following quotation is taken from the *Revue des Deux Mondes,* the organ which had so praised the American policy of Molé in 1838:

"What would have happened if the war had broken out in Europe. One portion of our naval force would have been found adventuring in the South Seas, and six thousand of our marines, instead of fighting in the Mediterranean, would have been miserably engaged in the Plata, in order to determine whether Buenos Ayres would be badly governed by Rosas, by Lavalle, or by some other chief. . . .

"The millions which we have spent in the Plata and in the *Banda Oriental,* we could have spent with profit in more than one French *department*; and if we wished at any price to cast them at a distance, it would be better to use them in our colonies, in the Antilles, even in Algeria." [146]

The editor had at least learned that an ill-considered foreign policy was an expensive form of public entertainment.

---

[145] *Le Moniteur Universel,* Feb. 9 and 21, 1841. One speaker praised the vigorous measures of Captain Venancourt at Buenos Ayres in 1829.

[146] *Revue des Deux Mondes,* 1841, vol. I, pp. 124-125. See chapter II, note 16.

CHAPTER IV

FRANCO-BRITISH POLICY IN THE ARGENTINE, 1841–1844

However necessary the ratification of the Mackau Convention may have been for the European policy of France, it soon became apparent that the treaty left much to be desired as far as her interests in the Plata countries were concerned. The French Government was left with no standing or prestige on either side of the river. All parties at Montevideo, including the rapidly increasing French immigrant population, were disgusted with "the shameful capitulation of Mackau." [1] France was both hated and despised in the Argentine Provinces. The French claims which had been specifically acknowledged in the Convention itself were promptly adjudicated;[2] but Rosas gave the new French Chargé-consul, Lefèbre de Bécourt, no satisfaction whatever in regard to the several hundred additional claims for sequestered property, which had accumulated during the hostilities. As long as the local disorder continued, the Governor could always plead the exigencies of circumstances as an excuse for delay. Bécourt made no secret of his convictions in regard to the unsatisfactory character of the treaty of October 29.[3] Less than a year after it was signed, the French Admiral was suggesting a Franco-British intervention to put an end to the interminable strife and safeguard their interests.[4]

[1] F. O. 6, 83, *El Nacional* of Montevideo for Mar. 18, 1842. Enclosure of Mandeville, Mar. 25, 1842. F. O. 27, 626, Bulwer to Palmerston from Paris, July 5, 1841. Mandeville reported June 14, 1841 that 2000 French Basques had reached Montevideo within six weeks. See F. O. 6, 78.

[2] F. O. 6, 78, Mandeville to Palmerston, Apr. 23, 1841. $160,000 was the total award to France. $25,000 was to be paid immediately and $4,000 a month beginning with May, 1841.

[3] F. O. 6, 78, Mandeville to Palmerston, Mar. 20, 1841, Apr. 23, 1841.

[4] F. O. 6, 89, Mandeville to Palmerston, Sept. 17, 1841; Oct. 29, 1841. Guizot had authorized the Chargé on July 2, 1841, to co-operate with the British Minister in the mediation which the latter was attempting. *Aff. Etr.*, Buenos Ayres, 29, p. 131.

Notwithstanding the complaints of the French agents in Argentina, Guizot was determined not to entangle his Government again in the political affairs of that country. He informed Bécourt in February, 1841, that there was nothing in the objectionable circumstances connected with the policy of Rosas which would justify France in the adoption of new coercive measures. Guizot did not deny that it was probable that Rosas would support the cause of Oribe in Uruguay, and he admitted that the overthrow of Rivera's Government by such a combination would both endanger French nationals in Uruguay and constitute a violation of the recent treaty. In order to avoid all possible embarrassment in this respect, he directed Admiral de Clerval to use force, if necessary, in order to secure the release of all French nationals from the army of Rivera.[5]

In spite of the pacific nature of the instructions of Guizot, the relations between the French agents at Buenos Ayres and Rosas became steadily more unfriendly. The irritating correspondence over claims developed into an angry quarrel in April, 1842. Several French citizens suffered physical violence during an outbreak of popular fanaticism directed against all who were suspected of Unitarian sympathies. The French agent, wrote Mandeville, "expressed himself in hasty, but perhaps not very inexact Animadversions on the distribution of justice in the Town," while Arana charged with equal right that the French war vessels were providing asylum for all fugitives from justice.[6] The relations became even more strained later in the same year when the prospect of Oribe's invasion of Uruguay threw the French immigrant population of that state into a panic.

While the prestige of France was thus at its nadir, Great Britain was enjoying a position of unchallenged dominance in the Plata. Her friendship was courted by both parties. When Mandeville was authorized in 1841 to accept the invitation of Montevideo to attempt a mediation with Rosas,[7] he was

---

[5] *Aff. Etr.,* Buenos Ayres, 29, p. 230. To Bécourt, Feb. 17, 1842.
[6] F. O. 6, 83, Mandeville to Aberdeen, Apr. 23, 1842. Guizot approved of this giving of asylum, and suggested that Arana himself might need it some day. *Aff. Etr.,* Buenos Ayres, 30, pp. 66-67. To Lurde, July 26.
[7] F. O. 6, 78, Palmerston to Mandeville, May 5, 1841; *Parliamentary Debates,* 3rd Series, 58, pp. 706-707. Commons, May 24, 1841.

able to exact as the price of his admittedly hopeless effort the discharge of all unsatisfied claims of British subjects against the Oriental Government.[8] The Argentine reply to the tender of the good offices of the British Government in July, 1841, afforded abundant evidence of the fact that a settlement between Rosas and Rivera was impossible. The conditions of peace which Rosas laid down were as follows: (1) the reinstatement at Montevideo of the legal Government of Oribe; (2) the exile of Rivera to Europe, to return only by permission of Oribe; (3) the expulsion of Argentine emigrés from Uruguay; and (4) an acknowledgment of the claims of the Argentine Government in payment for the assistance which they had afforded the legal President of the Oriental Republic. Mandeville could not, of course, transmit such terms to a government recognized by Great Britain. Arana himself admitted privately the correctness of the British contention that it was ridiculous to regard the commander of the Argentine army then attacking Lavalle as the President of Uruguay.[9]

The Oriental Government had other reasons, however, for encouraging the friendship of England. The idea had gained considerable headway in Montevideo that Her Majesty's Government should be invited to assume a protectorate over the state. Consul Hood had been approached repeatedly on the question early in 1841.[10] Palmerston regarded it with little enthusiasm. The British Government, he replied on July 7, 1841, was not willing to undertake the embarrassing responsibilities of such an arrangement unless they were granted full control over both the domestic and foreign affairs of the state. This, he thought, was hardly to be expected. He concluded as follows:

"I have, therefore, to instruct you to say nothing, either to encourage or discourage any such plan, but . . . you will confine

[8] F. O. 6, 79, Mandeville to Palmerston, July 19, Aug. 8, 10 and enclosures. For these claims, $15,228 were turned over to consul Dale at Montevideo on July 22. Bécourt attempted to aid Mandeville, but early desisted for fear of prejudicing Rosas further.

[9] F. O. 6, 79, Mandeville to Palmerston, Sept. 15, 1841. Approved by Aberdeen, Dec. 8, 1841.

[10] F. O. 6, 78, Mandeville to Palmerston, Mar. 17, 1841.

yourself to agreeing to transmit that communication to Her Majesty's Government." [11]

Mandeville was approached officially on the same matter in December, 1841, during his visit to Montevideo for the purpose of ratifying a slave-trade treaty recently concluded. Señor Vidal, the Foreign Minister, expressed his willingness at this time to enter into a treaty which would grant to Great Britain "great and exclusive advantages," among which would be "a Post on the River Uruguay to be assigned as a Depot of the productions, natural and manufactured, of the British Empire," if England would only put an end to the war with Rosas and promise to protect Uruguay. This offer was put into the form of a treaty on December 5. Since the concessions given to the British would be derived from special services, Vidal explained that "they could not be asked or claimed by other Powers with whom Treaties may exist." That this proposition was no idle or even secret project is demonstrated by the fact that a petition supporting it, signed by sixty-four resident British merchants, was presented to Mandeville on December 24.

The British Minister gave Vidal little encouragement on the question. The responsibilities of protection were too great, he said, and the special privileges to be enjoyed would lead to endless friction with other powers. [12] Mandeville suggested that they should conclude, instead, a regular treaty of commerce. But Vidal said that he must first know the reaction of the London Cabinet to his own proposition. Mandeville departed for Buenos Ayres on December 26, and immediately informed his government of the offer. [13] It was not until June, 1842, that Montevideo was notified that their proposition had not

[11] F. O. 6, 79, Palmerston to Mandeville, July 7, 1841. A similar offer was reported to have been made to Brazil by Rivera, who volunteered to be the viceroy of the Emperor. F. O. 6, 79, Mandeville to Palmerston, Sept. 16, 1841. It may well be possible that such a proposal was also behind a persistent rumor in 1843 that Spain was about to aid Montevideo. See F. O. 6, 90, Mandeville to Aberdeen, Aug. 10, 1843.

[12] F. O. 6, 79, Mandeville to Palmerston, Nov. 27, Dec. 6, Dec. 24, 1841. In January, 1842, the Montevidean Government asked for the removal of Consul-General Hood of Great Britain because of his intimacy with Oribe. F. O. 6, 83.

[13] F. O. 6, 83, Mandeville to Aberdeen, June 17, 1842 and enclosures.

been acceptable to London. The regular treaty of commerce between them was immediately negotiated. The relations between Mandeville and the Oriental Minister were by this time quite cordial. The negotiations had also considerably strengthened the international status of the Montevidean Government, which Rosas was refusing to recognize.[14]

Other considerations contributed to the shifting of British sympathy to Montevideo. Prominent among them was the general feeling of disgust in Europe with regard to the system of terrorism practiced by the Federalist party in Argentina. In Buenos Ayres, it took the form of periodic popular outbreaks engineered by a patriotic organization known as the Mazorca Society. The responsibility for the horrible orgy of violence in the city in April, 1842, was attributed by Aberdeen directly to Rosas himself. The Dictator made, indeed, no attempt to restore order until the party spirit had been allowed ample expression.[15] Had it not been for the fact that British subjects were surprisingly immune from these attacks, Her Majesty's naval force would undoubtedly have interfered. Another grievance which the British had against Rosas was that he forbade any communication through Argentine territory with the state of Paraguay,—for since the death of the old Dictator, Francia, in 1840, the authorities at Asunción had abandoned the former policy of isolation.[16] But the most serious quarrel which Great Britain entertained with the Governor concerned his utterly irresponsible financial policy. The recurring annual deficit of the Buenos Ayres Government worried

[14] F. O. 6, 83, Vidal to Mandeville, June 18, 1842. F. O. 6, 84, Mandeville to Aberdeen, July 26. See *Colección de tratados, op. cit.*, 1, pp. 139-156. The treaty here dated Aug. 26 was arranged in London. In 1844, some of Mandeville's confidential letters to Vidal were published by the Montevidean authorities to the very considerable embarrassment of the British Government. See F. O. 6, 94, Aberdeen to Mandeville, July 3, 1844.

[15] F. O. 6, 82, Aberdeen to Mandeville, Aug. 3, 1842. F. O. 6, 83, Mandeville to Aberdeen and to Canning, April 18, 19, 24, 1840. Saldías, *op. cit.*, 3, pp. 384-390, differs markedly from the usual account by trying to rehabilitate the Society of the Mazorca. *Niles Register* 63, p. 51, Sept. 24, 1842, commented: "Humanity calls aloud for the interference of higher powers, that there may be a termination to such revolting and bloody scenes."

[16] F. O. 6, 83, M. to A., June 20, 1842. Dr. Francia died in September, 1840. A British merchant, in June, 1841, had been allowed to proceed

him not the least bit, and no attempt was made to meet the obligations on the public debt, which were largely to British creditors. The rapidly depreciating paper currency, moreover, demoralized trade. A great number of merchants who had speculated on the return of peace in 1841 were in embarrassing circumstances.[17] As long as the ruinous and purposeless turmoil continued, there seemed precious little prospect for any improvement of these conditions.

The local warfare showed no signs of abating. While Lavalle was being run down by the Federalist forces, a combined army under Paz, Ferré, and Rivera seized control of Entre Rios and gave promise for a time of defending the line of the Paraná river against the Federalist forces.[18] But this alliance broke up in late 1841 in a quarrel over Rivera's schemes. In April of the following year, Oribe was therefore able to transfer his entire army into Entre Rios. In the face of this danger, the coalition was revived for a time. Rivera's army again crossed the Uruguay river, and the allies confronted their old enemy. During the succeeding months, in which the forces were entirely inactive, Paz fell out with his associates, however, and returned to Montevideo.[19] We must leave the two armies in this position while we return to Europe.

The humiliation which France had suffered at the hands of Palmerston in 1840 made impossible any relations of intimacy between the two countries as long as the Whigs remained in

---

to Paraguay in an Argentine vessel (F. O. 6, 78, M. to P., June 14, 1841), but it was only by the help of Rivera that an official agent later reached Asunción. F. O. 6, 82, A. to M., Nov. 2, 1842. The agent accomplished nothing and was finally expelled by the authorities. S. D., Buenos Ayres, Despatches, Consular, 6, A. Edwards to Secretary of State, June 17, 1843. Enclosure of Annual Message of Lopez, Nov. 24, 1842. See also F. O. 51, Montevideo, E. J. Phillips to T. S. Hood, Feb. 14, 1843.

[17] F. O. 6, 83, M. to A., Jan. 14, 1842 and enclosures. The deficit was 13 million dollars in 1841, and 25 million in 1842—F. O. 6, 88, M. to A., Jan. 2, 1843. The interests of Baring Bros. received frequent support from Mandeville. See F. O. 6, 82, A. to M., Mar. 31, 1842; ibid., 84, Mar. 31, 1843; Sept. 23, 1843.

[18] Pereyra, op. cit., pp. 113-115. Durand, op. cit., pp. 116-120.

[19] Brossard, op. cit., p. 249 ff. Durand, op. cit., pp. 120-123. Saldías, op. cit., vol. 3, pp. 347-380.

office. Guizot refused to name an Ambassador to London, and declined to resume the negotiations begun by Thiers concerning the tariff and the slave-trade treaties. Not until after Melbourne's Government had been overwhelmingly defeated in a general election was a settlement of the Eastern question made, in July, 1841.[20]

The relations between France and England took a decided turn for the better after the Government of Sir Robert Peel came into power in September, 1841. The new Premier and his Foreign Minister, Lord Aberdeen, were men of peaceful convictions and were perfectly ready to co-operate with Guizot, in spite of the fact that the Tory tradition of hostility to France was present in their Cabinet in the person of the Duke of Wellington. The French Minister reciprocated most heartily this friendly attitude of his British colleagues. The persistent effort of these three men to find a basis for the renewal of the *entente* between the two Governments was to be an outstanding feature of their relations.[21]

It was not easy for Paris and London to bring their policies into harmony. Guizot clearly over-reached himself in December, 1840, when he signed a new slave-trade treaty with the British authorities, granting to their cruisers the right to search French vessels. A storm arose in the Chambers over the question, which threatened to overwhelm the Paris Government, already embarrassed, as it was, by the death of the heir to the throne. Guizot was obliged to withdraw his signature from the treaty in the following November, to the great disgust of England.[22] After the failure of the slave-trade treaty the two governments encountered further obstacles over supposedly conflicting interests in Spain.[23] One of the few

[20] Guyot, *La Première Entente Cordiale*, pp. 211-228, 242-243; M. O. d'Haussonville, *Histoire de la Politique Extérieure du Gouvernement Francais, 1830-1848*, 2 vols. (Paris 1850) Vol. 2, pp. 1-6.

[21] Guyot, *op. cit.*, pp. 242-244. *The Opinions of the Right Hon. Sir Robert Peel, expressed in Parliament and in Public.* (London 1850), pp. 26, 238-239. Hall, *op. cit.*, pp. 331-332. F. P. G. Guizot, *Memoirs of Sir Robert Peel.* (London 1857), pp. 142-149.

[22] Guyot, *op. cit.*, pp. 245-46; Hall, *op. cit.*, pp. 333-334. This was the Quintuple treaty on the slave trade. Allison, *op. cit.*, pp. 292-309.

[23] Hall, *op. cit.*, pp. 335-346.

places where the prospect for an agreement was really favorable was in the Plata.

The fact that France and England had a definite common interest in bringing the turmoil in Argentina to an end was early recognized by the British Foreign Office. In February, 1842, Aberdeen informed Guizot, through the British Ambassador in Paris, Lord Cowley, concerning the offer of special commercial privileges which England had received from Montevideo, and had refused. Cowley was directed to suggest that no action was better calculated to safeguard their common interests in Uruguay than was a united intervention. The letter continued:

"Her Majesty's Government earnestly hope that the French Government will be willing to join with them in making such representations to the contending parties, as may, by securing the territory of Uruguay from further violation, put an immediate stop to hostilities and lead . . . to the establishment of permanent peace." [24]

Guizot readily assented to this proposal, although the letters sent to his own agent at the very time were refusing the plea for a more active policy.[25]

The instructions which went out from London and Paris in regard to the proposed joint mediation reveal a wide divergence in the attitudes of the two Governments. Aberdeen informed Mandeville of the intended action in a letter of March 12. It contained the following threatening sentence:

"If, notwithstanding all your efforts, the Buenos Ayres Government should still refuse our mediation, and to persist in a war not justified by any National objects and carried on solely from personal animosity, you will inform the Argentine Minister that a just regard for the Commercial interests of Her M's Subjects in the River Plata will impose on Her M's Government the duty of resorting to other measures for the purpose of removing the obstacles which at present interrupt the peaceful navigation of those waters." [26]

Since it said nothing concerning the policy of France, Guizot could not object to such a statement. The French Minister

[24] *Aff. Etr.*, Buenos Ayres, 29, p. 222. Aberdeen to Cowley, Feb. 8, 1842.
[25] *Ibid.*, pp. 224-227.
[26] F. O. 6, 82, A. to M., Mar. 12, 1842.

was so cautious, however, that he would not trust the belligerently inclined Bécourt with the mediation. He requested that no action should be taken by Mandeville until the arrival of Baron de Lurde, the new French agent who was about to depart for Buenos Ayres.[27]

Lurde's instructions were not prepared until May 23. They gave evidence from beginning to end of the strong desire of the French Government to develop more cordial relations with Rosas. The new Minister was directed to avoid the support of all ill-founded claims, especially those arising from the unfortunate tendency of French residents to intermix in political affairs. He should leave the reclamations, as far as possible, to the local courts and administrative agencies. Every effort should be exerted to soften the hostility of the people toward France and to prepare the way for a treaty of commerce. At the very end of the despatch, Guizot stated that France had agreed to mediate between Buenos Ayres and Uruguay in concert with Great Britain. While the French Government did not wish to deny that Rosas had a right to make war on Uruguay, they were greatly interested for the sake of their resident nationals and their trade, he said, that the independence of that state should be preserved.[28]

The threatening attitude which Aberdeen had portrayed was probably the result of the heavy pressure which was being exerted upon him. The Foreign Office was being bombarded with letters, memorials, and petitions declaring that, for the sake of British trade and the cause of civilization in South America (ends which never seemed to conflict), the independence of the Oriental state must be maintained. Above all, the control of the navigation of the rivers should be wrested from the blighting hand of Rosas.[29] The terrible Mazorca massacre of April, 1842, which had so horrified Aberdeen,

[27] F. O. 6, 82, A. to M., Mar. 29, 1842.
[28] *Aff. Etr.*, Buenos Ayres, 30, pp. 32-44. French Basques were swarming to Montevideo. See F. O. 6, 83, M. to A., Feb. 12, 1842. About 19,000 had arrived in the river in six years; perhaps one-third of these came in 1841.
[29] Brossard, *op. cit.*, pp. 265-274. F. O. 6, 86, Domestic Letters, Various. February to August, 1842. For trade conditions in England in 1842, see G. M. Trevelyan, *Life of John Bright.* (Boston 1925), pp. 70-83.

was brought forward as another powerful argument to justify an intervention.[30]

It is an interesting fact that the relative hostility which the French and British agents in the Plata displayed toward Rosas was almost the exact reverse of that shown by their respective governments. Both of the French agents were bitter toward the insolent Dictator. Admiral Clerval had repeatedly expressed his willingness to undertake measures designed to force him to cease his ruinous and selfish war.[31] Mandeville, on the other hand, was an intimate friend of Rosas and his daughter and a frequent visitor at their home.[32] There was much, of course, in the policy of Rosas which displeased the British Minister; but the latter was nevertheless convinced that the strong hand of the Governor was absolutely indispensable if there was to be any government at all at Buenos Ayres.[33]

The British agent received his instructions in regard to the joint mediation, in June, 1842,[34] and immediately urged Rosas in private to accept their good offices. The Governor was surprisingly frank in his reply. His obligations to Oribe and to his party, he said, committed him inevitably to the war against Rivera. If he should ever lose his influence with the people, the life of no foreigner in the country would be safe. Britain and France could easily capture the city, he said, but the people would support him and he could starve out the invaders. The Dictator concluded as follows:

"There is no aristocracy here to support a Government. Public opinion and the masses govern, and if I do not in some thing, for instance war with Rivera, give way, I am lost." [35]

As soon as Lurde reached the Plata, on August 2, the agents turned their attention to the task of mediation. Three days

[30] *Aff. Etr.*, Buenos Ayres, 30, pp. 66-67. Guizot to Lurde, July 26, 1842. F. O. 6, 82, A. to M., Aug. 3, 1842. Aberdeen's language was unusually severe in this expression of his horror and disgust.
[31] Brossard, *op. cit.*, p. 270. From Massieu de Clerval, Dec. 12, 1842.
[32] F. O. 6, 84, M. to A., Aug. 3, 13 and 16, 1842. Some popular feeling against Mandeville had been aroused by his negotiations with Vidal.
[33] F. O. 6, 84, M. to A., July 7, 1842.
[34] F. O. 6, 83, M. to A., June 10, 17, 1842.
[35] F. O. 6, 84, Mandeville to Aberdeen, July 7, 1842.

later, they received from Foreign Minister Vidal of Uruguay a statement outlining his minimum requirements. That state must be freed from the interference of Rosas, and amnesty be granted to all political offenders. Vidal requested in vain that Corrientes also be included in the mediation, and that the Europeans should declare that in case Rosas refused to accept their terms, they would garrison Montevideo, permit the arming of foreigners, and disallow any Argentine blockade of the ports of Uruguay.[36] The mediators tendered their good offices to Secretary Arana on August 24. Their first oral explanation that they were authorized by Montevideo to propose most reasonable terms of peace was later reduced to writing at the request of Rosas.[37]

It was not until October 18 that Rosas submitted his reply. He informed the agents on that date that their mediation could not be accepted because it was impossible for him to treat with the Oriental Government while Rivera was at its head. He would not insist that any particular candidate should take Rivera's place, however. With a pretense of deference to the popular will, Rosas nevertheless agreed to place the mediation question before his Assembly.[38] The introduction of the proposal in this body was the occasion for an organized patriotic demonstration at Buenos Ayres. The measure was, of course, emphatically rejected by the Assembly.[39] The one unusual thing about this episode was perhaps the fact that Rosas did not pretend, as heretofore, that General Oribe was already the President of Uruguay.

Before the reply of the Governor was received, other British instructions were on the way. Lord Aberdeen had suggested to

[36] Saldías, *op. cit.*, vol. 3, p. 403. F. O. 6, 82, A. to M., Nov. 2, 1842; F. O. 6, 84, M. to A., July 16, Aug. 8, 16, 1842. Pereyra, *op. cit.*, pp. 127-130.

[37] F. O. 6, 84, M. to A., Aug. 25, 26. Had Rosas accepted the mediation, the terms would have been (1) an armistice until Mar. 15, 1843, the expiration of Rivera's term of Presidency, to which office he was not Constitutionally eligible for re-election; (2) the return of the troops of both republics within their respective territories; (3) as general an amnesty as possible. Thus Rosas would not have to treat with Rivera, and Oribe's party would have an opportunity to show its strength in an election.

[38] F. O. 6, 84, M. to A. Oct. 24, 1842, and enclosures.

[39] *Ibid.*, Nov. 15, 1842.

Paris in late August that it would be advisable to adopt a more vigorous policy at Buenos Ayres. It was evident, he said, that Rosas had no intention of accepting their mediation. Lord Cowley was therefore to impress upon Guizot:

"the urgent necessity of some immediate and energetic steps to putting [sic] a stop to the evils which are inflicted upon the Countries in question, and by which the interests and personal Security of the Subjects of Neutral Nations are seriously affected. You will invite Monr. Guizot to unite the efforts of France with those of Great Britain in such a manner as both Governments may agree upon as leading to that cessation of hostilities which the offer of their joint mediation has hitherto failed of affecting." [40]

The French Minister, who wished always to be agreeable to Aberdeen, again indicated his general assent. Without any further conversations on the question, the British Minister informed Mandeville that additional measures had been agreed upon with France.[41] A subsequent letter of October 5 said that the prospective undertaking would be executed without delay. The agents should, accordingly, base their representations:

"on the intentions of the two Governments to adopt such measures as may be considered necessary for bringing the hostilities between the two Republics to a close." [42]

Would it be an unwarranted conclusion for Mandeville to draw from these instructions that a considerable naval force was about to leave for the Plata?

These later instructions reached Mandeville in early December, on the eve of a decisive battle between Rivera and Oribe in Entre Rios. On December 6, Rivera attempted a rash attack upon the position of his enemy at *Arroyo Grande*,[43] and suffered a disastrous defeat in consequence. The Oriental

[40] *Aff. Etr.*, Buenos Ayres, 30, pp. 112-114. Aberdeen to Cowley, Aug. 23, 1842.

[41] F. O. 6, 82, A. to M., Sept. 7, 1842. Enclosure, Cowley to Aberdeen, Aug. 26.

[42] F. O. 6, 82, A. to M., Oct. 5, 1840.

[43] Saldías, *op. cit.*, 3, pp. 407-412. The author claims that Rosas staged a scene before Mandeville on Nov. 26, in which he represented Oribe's position as almost entirely defenseless. Rivera's rash attack was due to the resulting false tip from Mandeville, he says.

President escaped across the Uruguay river with but a small fraction of his army. The road to Montevideo lay unobstructed, and the city was almost entirely without defenses. If Oribe had not tarried so long to take vengeance on the scattered enemy, he could easily have entered the city. Under the direction of General Paz, a small group of Argentine *émigrés, Corrientinos,* and freed negroes [44] set to work feverishly to improvise some fortifications for Montevideo. General Rivera, as was always his custom, kept to the open country.[45]

Mandeville and Lurde assumed that the time had come for them to act. On December 16, they issued a formal public declaration to the effect that the belligerent parties must agree to an immediate armistice and must hold their troops within their respective borders.[46] On the following day, the commanders of the British and French naval forces on the river were ordered to take all precautionary measures necessary for the safety of their fellow-nationals at Montevideo, especially in case of an attempted assault upon the city.[47] But Buenos Ayres paid no attention to the summons of December 16, and when the expected European forces did not arrive, the two Ministers found themselves in a most embarrassing situation. Mandeville was reminded by Montevideo, on January 2, that several thousand Argentine troops had already crossed the Uruguay river, but he could only reply as follows:

"His Excellency [Lurde], as well as myself, are at a loss to comprehend and deeply regret whatever has prevented the British and French Naval Forces, which were to have left Europe in the early part of October, but certainly during that month, from not having made their appearance in the River Plata before this time:—because until it comes, we have authority neither to land Troops nor to furnish assistance,—nor any [assistance] to give nor Troops to land, if we had the Power to do so."

[44] On Dec. 12, 1842, all negro slaves were declared free by the Oriental Government; they were forced into the army on Dec. 13. See *Bentley's Miscellany,* 55 (London 1864), pp. 502-511.

[45] Durand, *op. cit.,* pp. 123-128.

[46] F. O. 6, 184, Mandeville to Arana, Dec. 16. See *National Intelligencer* for March 1, 1843.

[47] F. O. 6, 84, M. to A., Dec. 18, 1842, and enclosures. The British order of Dec. 17 was sent to Capt. P. G. Haynes, who was directed to inform Commodore Purvis of it.

They would surely arrive, he thought, within the three weeks interval which would elapse before Oribe could reach Montevideo.[48]

It is a curious fact that this new policy on the part of the European agents, for which the instructions of Aberdeen were exclusively responsible, was interpreted much more severely by Lurde than by the Britisher himself. Indeed, so arrogant did the French agent become toward Rosas that Mandeville was led to suspect that the Paris government had decided to extract a new treaty by force.

But no amount of mere talk would relieve the desperate situation at Montevideo, and the agents could not even give their consent to the arming of their nationals within the city.[49] The most that they could do was to authorize some precautionary measures for self-defense. Before beginning the story of the siege of Montevideo, however, we must determine why the reënforcements from Europe had failed to appear.

When the question of a joint naval expedition to the Plata came up for final decision, the French Cabinet declined to approve Aberdeen's suggestion.[50] The influence of Baron Mackau, who was now Minister of Marine, appears to have been the decisive factor. Guizot asked his colleague, in late September, concerning the possibility of saving Montevideo from capture and the nature of the effort required, and, finally, whether the security of the French population within the city and the development of French interests established there would be "seriously compromised if one were to abandon events to their course." [51] Mackau replied emphatically that neither the independence of Uruguay nor the persons and property of the many French residents of that state would be endangered in the least by the triumph of Oribe. He suspected that there were ulterior motives back of Aberdeen's request. He recalled the fact that the custom's receipts of Montevideo had been

---

[48] F. O. 6, 88, M. to A. and enclosures, Jan. 7, 1843.
[49] *Ibid.*, Jan. 4, 1843. Enclosure, Lurde to Arana, Dec. 12, 1842. Also *ibid.*, Jan. 24, Feb. 2, and Feb. 10, 1843.
[50] Guyot, *op. cit.*, pp. 247-252.
[51] *Aff. Etr.*, Buenos Ayres, 30, pp. 151-152. Guizot to Mackau, Sept. 30, 1842.

sold to a British firm for a term of six months, and that there
was much talk of the place going over entirely to British control. It would therefore be exceedingly imprudent for France
to become again enmeshed in the quarrel, especially before the
results of the impending military action gave them a basis on
which to choose the party which would best serve their interests.[52]

It was not until the end of November that the decision of the
French Government was finally sent to Lurde. Previous despatches from London, wrote Guizot, had clearly suggested
the desirability of joint interference by force. It seemed now,
however, that Aberdeen fully concurred in the French decision
not to embark upon such an enterprise, for the British Minister even denied having entertained the intentions attributed to
him. The interests which the French had in the river country,
continued Guizot, would not justify a more active policy, especially in view of the fact that other considerations of importance would thereby be compromised.[53]

The sincerity of Aberdeen's concurrence with the French
attitude is open to serious doubt. On December 7, he wrote
to Mandeville that the acceptance at Buenos Ayres of the
offer made by Montevideo:

"will spare the Gov'ts. of Great Britain and France the disagreeable alternative of resorting to any ulterior measures should such
be thought necessary for the purpose of rendering their mediation
more effective. I have at the same time to inform you that the
possible adoption of such measures is still under the consideration
of the two Governments." [54]

When the European authorities finally learned, in March,
1843, concerning the summons which their agents had issued on
December 16, it was necessary that they should reach a definite understanding on the question. Aberdeen took the initiative. He prepared a letter for Cowley in Paris, the original
draft of which reveals that not until this time had he aban-

[52] *Aff. Etr.*, Buenos Ayres, 30, pp. 153-161. Mackau to Guizot, Oct. 6,
1842. The friend of Rosas is here speaking. F. O. 6, 86, M. to A., Mar.
31, 1843.
[53] *Aff. Etr.*, Buenos Ayres, 30, pp. 218-221. Guizot to Lurde, Nov. 30,
1842.
[54] F. O. 6, 82, A. to M., Dec. 7, 1842.

doned the idea of forcible intervention. The declaration made by their agents, he wrote, had scarcely been warranted by their instructions, but he was not inclined to disapprove it in the absence of more detailed information. Since it was very probable that the summons had been ignored, Guizot should be presented with the following statement in regard to British policy on the subject:

"It is the earnest wish of Her Majesty's Government to arrest the fruitless and ferocious warfare which is desolating the States of Buenos Ayres and Montevideo; but they desire to avoid

(first draft, not sent)	(the corrected draft)
all interference with either of those states beyond that which they may deem necessary for the accomplishment of so humane and desirable an object, and which may also	all forcible interference for the accomplishment of so humane and desirable an object, and which should not

be required for the protection of the Lives and Properties of British and French Subjects established in either of those Countries." [55]

The original statement clearly contemplated forcible interference to stop the war; the second definitely repudiated it.

Guizot, of course, could heartily approve the policy of the London government as explained, but his own reaction to the declaration under consideration contrasted sharply with the calm view of Aberdeen. The French Minister could not understand why an agent should have made himself a party to such an action without any authorization whatever from his Government. To Lurde's explanation that he had assumed that all of Mandeville's instructions had been approved at Paris,[56] Guizot replied that he had no knowledge of any letters from London which could have suggested such a course. Aberdeen had explicitly denied that he had entertained any intention to intervene. The amicable relations of France with Argentina should not have been compromised merely to bring to a close the unfortunate war. France would have no grounds to protest, he asserted, if Oribe replaced Rivera as President of Uruguay. French nationals must learn to live at peace with

[55] F. O. 27, 663, Aberdeen to Cowley, Mar. 17, 1843.
[56] Aff. Etr., Buenos Ayres, 30, pp. 221-22. From Lurde, Dec. 6.

any government in control at Montevideo, so long as their rights were respected. In the future, Guizot concluded, Lurde should not be guided by British instructions.[57]

Aberdeen's repudiation of the idea of forcible intervention at Montevideo did not appear in his own instructions until April. The British Minister became much more emphatic in asserting his new policy when he learned, several weeks later, of Mandeville's January statement to Vidal concerning the expected arrival of a force from Europe. The agent was sent the following stinging rebuke by Aberdeen:

> "I have no knowledge of the authority on which you entertained any such expectation; and I am compelled to observe that, in the absence of any information or instructions on the subject from this Office, you did wrong in making that Expectation the ground of an assurance to the Montevidean Government." [58]

But the damage had already been done. Aberdeen's ill-considered and not altogether straight-forward instructions had virtually involved the honor of both countries in the defense of Montevideo. Guizot had been definitely betrayed into a situation which he would have avoided at almost any cost.

When the army of Oribe finally reached Montevideo on February 16, 1843, all was confusion within the place. The defenders of the crude earth-works which Paz had hastily constructed across the land approach to the city were few in number, poorly armed, and badly organized. The town was crowded with refugees, many of them French Basque immigrants, who had fled before the invading army. Between the nearly twenty thousand foreigners within the city and the somewhat larger native population, there was little or no arrangement for co-operation. The French consul, M. Pichon, who was responsible for the safety of his nationals, had taken some precautionary measures for their self-defense in case the place should be

---

[57] *Aff. Etr.*, Buenos Ayres, 31, pp. 43-45. Guizot to Lurde, Mar. 30, 1843.
[58] F. O. 27, 666, Cowley to Aberdeen, Mar. 20, 1843. F. O. 6, 87, A. to M., April 5, May 3, 1843.

captured. But this did little to strengthen the outer lines. British and French marines had been sent ashore to protect the customs house and the property of foreigners.[59] Commodore Purvis, the British commander, went so far as to forbid Admiral Brown's Argentine fleet to bombard the city and thereby endanger British property.[60] The same officer then sought to deprive the Argentine vessels of their non-descript crews, predominantly British and Irish, by issuing a declaration forbidding his nationals from serving with either belligerent.[61]

Viewed from outside Montevideo, the very confusion of this inco-ordinated feverish activity, in which the British and French were taking such an active part, seemed ominous. Rather than risk the consequences of an attack upon the fortifications, which in fact could hardly have failed to succeed, Oribe retired to a small knob called Cerrito, a few miles from the capital, and began the construction of a defensive system of his own. After a month more of preparation, Montevideo had placed itself in a relatively secure position.[62]

The fact that Rivera's term as President would expire on March 15, 1843, gave rise to some hope that a settlement might be arranged on the basis of a new election. Rivera himself would not be eligible for reëlection. When Mandeville visited the Uruguayan capital in the middle of that month, to conclude the ratification of a commercial treaty, he suggested to the acting executive, Señor Vasquez, that an armistice and a new election might readily solve their difficulties. The Oriental leader at first regarded the proposition favorably. Rivera would resign his position as head of the army and leave the country, as would the Argentine troops. A new election could then be held with Oribe as a candidate.

[59] *Parliamentary Debates,* 3rd Series, vol. 69, p. 244; *Niles Register* 64, p. 162, May 13, 1843, says that American marines too were landed; F. O. 6, 88, M. to A., Mar. 12, 1843.
[60] F. O. 6, 88, M. to A., Feb. 20, 1843.
[61] *Niles Register,* May 13, 1843. Vol. 64, p. 162.
[62] F. O. 6, 88, M. to A., Mar. 12, 1843. Brossard, *op. cit.,* pp. 277-282. Durand, *op. cit.,* pp. 128-131. Giuseppe Garibaldi, in his *Autobiography* 3 vols. (London 1889) vol. 1, p. 126 ff., tells of the disorder within the city, and marvels that Oribe did not make a resolute attack against it.

But this easy settlement of the problem was not to be achieved. Whether from the pressure of his colleagues or from the conviction that the absent Rivera would not accept the arrangement, Vasquez altered the proposal considerably when he submitted it in writing a few days later. During the four months' armistice to be observed for the holding of the election, Montevideo would require that Oribe's force should retire across the river. On the other hand, Rivera would resign from the Oriental army and absent himself from Montevideo only directly before and during the election. Mandeville and Lurde immediately agreed that it was useless to submit the Montevidean proposition to Rosas.[63] All that they could suggest was a curious proposal for a sort of perpetual deadlock, each side promising not to attack the other. Under these conditions, they said that the European marines would leave Montevideo.[64] This idea was, of course, also rejected. The Buenos Ayres Government announced on March 19 that Montevideo would be subjected to a strict blockade of both munitions and provisions after April 1.

The diplomatic agents were obliged to retire from the center of the stage after the later French instructions arrived, protesting that their nationals must not be harmed.[65] But the naval officers were not limited in the same way. Commodore Purvis conceived that the surest way for him to discharge his responsibility for the safety of British interests, under Mandeville's order of December 17, was to prevent an attack upon the city. At first he threatened so to act if Rosas refused to accept the election offer of Vasquez.[66] When this project was abandoned, he found another pretext. He declared that the British officers and crews of the three Argentine war ves-

[63] F. O. 6, 88, M. to A., Mar. 16, 1843. Joacquin Suarez, head of the Montevidean Senate, assumed the Presidency in lieu of an elected successor, with an appointed Chamber of Notables to assist his Cabinet. Brossard, *op. cit.*, pp. 277-282.

[64] F. O. 6, 88, M. to A., Mar. 16, 1843.

[65] *Ibid.*, Mar. 22. Enclosure, Arana to Mandeville, Mar. 19 and 20; S. D. Argentine Republic, Despatches, 5, Brent to Buchanan, July 1, 1845. F. O. 6, 88, M. to A., Mar. 31, 1843. It was Lurde who, after receiving his November instructions, refused to join Mandeville in preventing the blockade. Instructions soon to arrive confirmed him in this position.

[66] F. O. 6, 88, M. to A., Mar. 18.

sels disqualified the latter as "duly Commissioned Men of war," and consequently rendered them incapable of instituting a legal blockade.[67] On this ground he refused to allow Admiral Brown to occupy an island in the harbor of Montevideo, and declared that he would not suffer British vessels to be searched by the blockade. When Mandeville protested against such a high-handed policy, Purvis reproached the diplomatic agent for not carrying out his solemn declaration of December 16.[68]

In an effort to find some basis on which the Argentine naval operations against Montevideo might escape the interference of the British and French fleets, Rosas agreed on March 28 that merchant vessels arriving from the high seas should be exempt from the blockade. But this privilege was conceded only on the express condition that the consuls and naval commanders of the two European powers should see to it that such vessels did not engage in the coastwise trade or contribute to the arming and provisioning of the city.[69] Because of the attitude of Purvis, no attempt was made to establish even this partial blockade until six months later.

A bitter quarrel developed in early April between Purvis and the self-styled "President of Uruguay" who was besieging the capital. The occasion was a decree of Oribe that all foreigners found opposing him would suffer the same penalty as the Unitarians, which meant death. The British commander peremptorily demanded the withdrawal of this decree, and held the Argentine squadron in complete restraint awaiting compliance. Lurde, who had just received fresh word from Paris, would have nothing to do with this action. Mandeville himself felt obliged to protest against it on the ground that British interests in Argentina were endangered by such unneutral conduct.[70] To these representations Purvis paid

[67] F. O. 6, 88, Purvis to Mandeville, Mar. 25, 1843. S. D. Argentine Republic, Despatches, 5, Brent to Buchanan, July 29, 1845. "I yield to no man in our Service," declared Purvis, "a better knowledge of Blockade."

[68] S. D. Argentine Republic, Despatches, 5, Brent to Buchanan, July 29, 1845. F. O. 6, 88, M. to A., April 5, 1843. See the *National Intelligencer* for July 13, 1843.

[69] S. D. Argentine Republic, Desp., 5, Brent to Buchanan, July 29, 1845.

[70] F. O. 6, 89, M. to A., April 20 and enclosures. *Aff. Etr.*, Buenos Ayres, 31, pp. 170-171. To Lurde June 26, 1843.

not the slightest heed. After Oribe had recalled his decree some weeks later, the British commander wrote to Mandeville as follows:

"Sir, I confine myself to the protection of British life and property, and when I go beyond that, the time will arrive for yourself and the French Minister to animadvert on my conduct." [71]

The most important result of this foolish attempt of Oribe to frighten the foreigners into neutrality was that it provided the occasion for the organization of the Foreign Legion within Montevideo. Previous measures had been, theoretically, only for their self-defense; now all pretense of neutrality was abandoned by the foreign population. With the connivance, if not with the positive co-operation of the British and French naval commanders, the volunteers were fully armed and their military organization perfected. The Legion was composed of some three thousand French Basque militiamen, together with a smaller group of seven hundred or less of other nationalities, many of them Italians. The French had their own commander, and the smaller group was led by Giuseppe Garibaldi, who had but recently abandoned a wild career in the service of the republican rebels of Rio Grande do Sul.[72] The foreigners, of course, remained under arms after Oribe's decree against them had been withdrawn. They formed, from this time forward, the principal factor in the defense of the city.

The official attitude which the British Government assumed toward the strife at Montevideo was one of strict neutrality. Parliament was told that the Cabinet had no intention of resorting to coercive measures on behalf of the city. The demands received from Montevideo that Mandeville's promises of the last December be fulfilled fell on deaf ears.[73] Aberdeen's instructions regularly enjoined a neutral policy, although Purvis was commended for securing the repeal of Oribe's anti-foreigner

[71] F. O. 6, 89, Purvis to Mandeville, April 21, 1843.

[72] Brossard, op. cit., pp. 277-82: Durand, op. cit., pp. 130-132. Garibaldi, Recollections, Literature of Italy, vol. 12 (1907), pp. 331-375.

[73] Parliamentary Debates, 3rd Series, 69, p. 1250. June 2, 1843. F. O. 51, Montevideo, 24, Rodriguez to Aberdeen, Mar. 30, 1843; Vasquez to same, April 26, 1843. A later letter from Vasquez, June 9, 1843, expressed appreciation for the aid of Capt. Purvis. F. O. 51, 24, Aberdeen to Ellauri in Paris, July 18, 1843; same to Vasquez, Aug. 31, 1843.

decree.[74] The definitive statement of the British position was set forth as follows in a letter of August 1, 1843:

"It is the right of a belligerent to impose upon the ports of its enemy, either a strict blockade, . . . or to modify such blockade . . . [sic], and this right, whilst exercised in a legal manner, cannot be interfered with or contested by any third state, professing neutrality between the contending parties.

"The Queen's Advocate, therefore, assuming as he correctly does that H. My's Gov't. is not prepared to take part in the contest, is of the opinion that the naval forces of Great Britain would not be justified in forcibly putting an end to the modified blockade of Montevideo." [75]

But in these same instructions, Aberdeen left a convenient loop-hole for evading the responsibility of the British forces for enforcing the modified blockade. He said that the conditions on which the modification had been secured, namely, that the European agents should employ all the power at their command to prevent the arming and provisioning of the city by their national vessels, was of doubtful legality. But instead of making a clean breast of the matter to Buenos Ayres, to the end that a legal and effective blockade might be substituted for that of the agreement of March 28, Aberdeen merely directed that the British officers might discourage their vessels from engaging in the forbidden coastwise trade, but that they should not forcibly prevent them.[76] With such an opinion to support the natural disinclination of Purvis to co-operate with the Argentine fleet, it is not surprising that he made no attempt to fulfill the conditions agreed to. The French commander would do no more in this respect than the British. At the same time, they jealously insisted on the exemption of their merchant vessels from all Argentine interference.[77] The blockades of Montevideo and Maldonado, which were established by Rosas

[74] F. O. 6, 87, A. to M., July 5, Aug. 27, 1843 and enclosure. Later instructions threatened intervention if Oribe continued to murder his prisoners. F. O. 6, 87, A. to M., Nov. 8, 1843.

[75] F. O. 6, 87, A. to M., Aug. 1, 1843. S. D. Argentine Rep., Desp. 5, Brent to Buchanan, July 29, 1845.

[76] F. O. 6, 87, A. to M., Aug. 1, 1845.

[77] F. O. 6, 90, M. to A., Dec. 27, 1843. F. O. 6, 96, M. to A., June 20, 1844. S. D. Arg. Rep., Desp., 5, Brent to Buchanan, July 29, 1845.

in September, 1843, were, therefore, almost worthless as measures of coercion.[78]

The contradictory policies which Mandeville and Purvis were allowed to pursue for more than a year, the one pro-Rosas the other pro-Montevidean, were at least well-calculated to safeguard British interests. Purvis did not forego his opposition to the September blockades until Mandeville had explicitly recalled the order of December 17. The commander then exacted from Oribe assurances for the safety of British citizens, guarantees that no Argentine troops should enter Montevideo, and a promise that the prospective victor would accept the recently ratified commercial treaty.[79] At Buenos Ayres, the British diplomatic agent jealously defended the rights of England as a *bona fide* neutral. When Rosas tried to disclaim all responsibility in case popular anger over the actions of Purvis should result in violence to British citizens within the city, Mandeville immediately obliged him to admit his absolute responsbility in this respect under the treaty of 1825.[80] Neutral observers were inclined to regard the arrangement in the Plata as a "master stroke of policy" on the part of Aberdeen.[81] Downing Street was in receipt of the Argentine demand for the recall of Purvis for seven months before steps were taken toward that end, in April, 1844.[82] By the time the measure was executed, the feeling toward the European residents at Buenos Ayres was so bitterly hostile that Mandeville was convinced that only the restraining hand of Rosas protected them from indiscriminate massacre and pillage.[83]

It was one of the ironies of fate that the timid French Government, so concerned to avoid entanglements and to improve

[78] F. O. 6, 90, M. to A., Sept. 8, 1843.
[79] F. O. 6, 87. The cancellation of the previous order was approved by Aberdeen, Jan. 3, 1844. F. O. 6, 90, M. to A., Sept. 9, Nov. 18, 1843. These demands of Purvis were made on pain of the raising of Brown's blockade if they were not promptly agreed to.
[80] F. O. 6, 89, M. to A., June 2, Dec. 27, 1843, and enclosures.
[81] F. O. 6, 96. Note to Ouseley from Rio de Janeiro, Dec. 12, 1844.
[82] F. O. 6, 94, A. to M., April 3, 1844. F. O. 6, 94, A. to M., Oct. 30, 1844.
[83] F. O. 6, 96, M. to A., June 20, 1844 and enclosure of *Gaceta Mercantil* for June 1; *ibid.,* Nov. 15, 1844 and enclosures. F. O. 6, 89, Arana to Mandeville, May 8, 20, June 2, 1843. M. to A., June 28; F. O. 6, 84, Aberdeen to Mandeville, Aug. 27; vol. 90, M. to A., Dec. 27, 1843.

their peaceful relations with Rosas, should have suffered the greater part of the odium for the European interference at Montevideo. The presence of several thousand Frenchmen in the Foreign Legion was a far more serious embarrassment to Guizot than was the less justifiable action of the British Commodore to Aberdeen. The Legion could be neither removed nor recalled. The French Minister was particularly exasperated because Rosas seemed determined to foment that very hatred for the French which he himself so much desired to dissipate.

Along with the severe criticism which Guizot directed toward his own agents for their unneutral conduct in following the British, he took sharp issue with some of the *bravado* of Rosas. The French Minister was particularly irritated in June, 1843, over the Dictator's assertion, apparently in imitation of a recent utterance of President Tyler, that America must be kept free from all European interference. Recalling the fact in his instructions that the statement made at Washington had elicited a protest from the French agent, Guizot wrote as follows to Lurde:

"General Rosas will deceive himself if he believes that the powers of Europe will, on our part, refrain from it on any account, if circumstances create for us a duty of interfering in America. . . . We do not think at all of mixing ourselves in the internal affairs of the new American Republics. But to wish to prohibit European Governments from intervening . . . in some questions of international right and foreign policy would be an unjustifiable pretention and one to which certainly no Cabinet could adhere." [84]

Guizot also objected to the inclusion of food products by Rosas among the prohibited articles in the Montevidean blockade.[85] The realization that, in spite of all his efforts, France was sinking steadily into greater disrepute in the Plata countries, created a mental hazard for Guizot which made him exceedingly irritable and robbed his more neutral policy of the dignity and strength which London managed always to maintain.

[84] *Aff. Etr.,* Buenos Ayres, 31, pp. 170-171. Guizot to Lurde, June 26, 1843. The reference here is to Tyler's message of Aug. 11, 1842.

[85] *Aff. Etr.,* Buenos Ayres, 31, p. 184 ff. Guizot to Lurde, July 29, 1843.

The French Government started out resolutely to extricate itself from the difficulties at Montevideo. Guizot sent the consul there a peremptory order to disarm all French nationals. But Admiral Clerval, the French commander, flatly refused to support the consul in such a course. The Admiral endeavored, instead, to force the two parties to come to terms. His efforts were in vain, for the city preferred now to delay the question and to await the outcome of Rivera's activities in the country.[86] Lurde and Clerval had meanwhile become hopelessly embittered against Oribe because of his execution of two captured Frenchmen. Consul Pichon nevertheless continued his efforts to carry out Guizot's instructions. He demanded, without effect, that the Montevidean Government disarm all Frenchmen, and then threatened to withdraw his protection from those who refused to lay down their arms. He also secured a pledge from Oribe, on August 5, that French nationals should not suffer violence when the besiegers entered the city.[87]

The failure of Guizot's first move only led to a more determined effort on his part to regain a position of neutrality. Late in 1843, he despatched a new naval commander, Admiral Lainé, with express orders to disarm the Foreign Legion by force, in case the Montevidean Government should refuse to do so.[88] In reference to the murder of the captured Frenchmen by Oribe, he insisted that, although the men might have forfeited their status as French citizens, there was still a question of national dignity and humanity involved which would make it the duty of the French agents to protest against all such barbarities.[89]

The quarrel of the French consul with the Montevidean Government reached a crisis several weeks before the arrival of Lainé. On January 1, 1844, Pichon hauled down the flag

[86] F. O. 6, 90, M. to A., Oct. 18, 1843 and enclosures. Mandeville refused to aid Clerval and in this he was upheld by Aberdeen. F. O. 6, 94, Feb. 1, 1844.

[87] F. O. 6, 90, M. to A., Aug. 20, 1843. Pichon to Oribe, Aug. 3; Oribe to Pichon, Aug. 5.

[88] *Aff. Etr.*, Buenos Ayres, 31, pp. 245-247. September, 1843. Guizot regretted also the growing hostility between Brazil and Argentina. *Ibid.*, 32, p. 40. To Lurde, Jan. 23, 1844.

[89] *Aff. Etr.*, Buenos Ayres, 31, pp. 302-303. Guizot to Lurde, Nov. 28, 1843.

of his consulate and retired to a French war vessel because French citizens were not dismissed from the army.[90] Lainé arrived in late February.[91] His instructions in regard to disarming the French Legion were perfectly explicit, and he eventually secured compliance with Guizot's wishes by a twenty-four hour ultimatum delivered on April 10. The futility of the measure became apparent, however, when the Basques immediately came together in another place, renounced their French allegiance, and became the 2nd. and 3rd. battalions of the Montevidean national guard.[92]

The cause of Montevideo both gained and lost by the absorption of the Foreign Legion. The city gained some determined defenders, for the French nationals would certainly not surrender themselves to the mercies of Oribe, now that they had cut loose from the protection of their own flag.[93] On the other hand, the dominance of the foreign element within the city and the prolonged inactivity of the siege caused an alarming depletion of the native garrison. The Orientals either departed to join Rivera, or, as was not infrequently the case, actually deserted to the camp of Oribe.[94] Among those who departed was General Paz, who returned by way of Brazil to Corrientes, where he will figure later in the story.[95] The number of those who were alienated from the cause of Montevideo because of the foreign connection increased with the passage of time, until the war became quite as much an Oriental civil struggle as one between Argentina and Uruguay. The Foreign Legion was destined to make it immeasurably more

[90] F. O. 6, 96, M. to A., Jan. 20, 1844. Guizot did not think Pichon justified in leaving his post. He was recalled soon after. *Aff. Etr.*, Buenos Ayres, 32, p. 110. Guizot to Lurde, May 3, 1844.

[91] *National Intelligencer*, May 7, 1844. N. D. Brazilian Squadron, Com. Daniel Turner to Secr. Mason, July 12, 1844.

[92] S. D. Arg. Rep., Desp., 5, Watterson to Secretary of State, April 27, 1844. Durand, *op. cit.*, pp. 132-135. *National Intelligencer.* July 10, 1844. D. F. Sarmiento, *Política Arjentina, 1841-1851.* (Santiago de Chile 1887), p. 99 ff. Sarmiento has extravagant praise for the French Legion because of this action.

[93] S. D. Arg. Rep., Desp., Sept. 8, 1844. From Watterson. He thought that Oribe would murder the foreigners "with as little hesitation as he would *lazo* and slaughter so many wild cattle."

[94] Saldías, *op. cit.*, 4, p. 76 ff.

[95] F. O. 6, 96, M. to A., June 21, 1844; July 19, 1844; Dec. 14, 1844. Durand, *op. cit.*, pp. 136-140. See *National Intelligencer*, Jan. 25, 1845.

difficult to settle the local quarrel than it would otherwise have been.

With all military activity at a standstill, the contest in the Plata became, for a time, a war of propaganda. The three publications of Rosas, *La Gaceta Mercantil, The British Packet*, and the *Archivo Americano*, provided him with a most effective means of presenting the Argentine side of the case to all interested parties. The first paper was for local consumption; the second enjoyed a wide circulation among British and North American trading interests;[96] the third presented propaganda, largely documentary, in Spanish, French, and English. From Montevideo and elsewhere, the Argentine *émigrés* kept up a continuous attack upon the Dictator. Some of their writings were of a scurrilous nature,[97] similar to that of the *Gaceta Mercantil;* but much was of a different quality. The material which came from the pen of Florencio Varela was invariably of a high order, and it had great influence outside South America. The unceasing propaganda of such men as Sarmiento and Alberdi is abundantly illustrated in their published works.[98] But the fact that these Unitarian leaders were obliged to rely on European support for the realization of their patriotic purposes enabled Rosas to neutralize all of their endeavors to organize the wide-spread discontent against his tyranny within the Argentine provinces themselves.[99]

[96] Brossard, *op. cit.,* pp. 459-460. Not infrequently these organs reproduce some of the same material. The principal editor was an Italian, Pedro Angelis. See Antonio Zinny, *La Gaceta Mercantil de Buenos Aires, 1823-52,* 3 vols. (Buenos Ayres 1912.) One of the most effective apologies for the régime of Rosas appeared in the *Archivo,* over the name of Alfred Mallalieu, in the form of letters to Lord Aberdeen early in 1845. They are attributed to Manuel Moreno, an Argentine agent in London. See Zinny, *op. cit.,* vol. 3, p. 82; *La Gaceta Mercantil* for Mar. 8, 1845. For the *Archivo Americano,* see note in the bibliography.

[97] José Rivera Indarte, *Rosas y sus opositores.* (Buenos Ayres 1858.) Published originally in Montevideo in 1843. Other writers of a similarly extreme character were Lamas, Cané and Alsina. See Mariano A. Pelliza, *Historia Argentina desde su origin hasta la organización nacional,* 2 vols., (Buenos Ayres 1910) vol. 2, pp. 307-8. Saldías, *op. cit.,* vol. 4, chap. 46 and vol. 5, chap. 58 contain excellent treatments of this press propaganda.

[98] Sarmiento, *op. cit.,* pp. 103-131; J. B. Alberdi, *Obras selectas, nueva edición,* vol. 6, p. 275 ff; *ibid. Escritos póstumos,* 16 vols. (Buenos Ayres 1895) vol. 3, 14, 15. Varela was the editor of the Montevidean paper, *El Comercio del Plata.*

[99] S. D. Arg. Republic, Despatches, 5, Watterson to Calhoun, Sept. 8, 1844.

The financial bankruptcy which eventually threatened the Montevidean Government made it imperative that the city find some outside assistance. Trade was reduced to almost nothing; the custom's revenue was 6 per cent of the amount collected in 1842.[100] At the suggestion of Purvis, the city decided to send a Commissioner to visit England and France. The person selected was Florencio Varela, who had just produced an able exposition of the Oriental case in reference to the unredeemed promises of Lurde and Mandeville.[101] Varela departed for England in August, 1843, arriving at London in late October. A number of conferences with Aberdeen convinced him that no aid could be expected from Great Britain. He was definitely notified to that effect on January 2, 1844, and was unable after that date to secure an audience with the Foreign Minister. The Commissioner then made a brief visit to Paris, where he talked with Thiers and other leaders of the opposition. He returned to Rio de Janeiro at the end of Spring, and here, as it will soon appear, he secured a more sympathetic hearing.[102]

Montevideo later sent another agent to Europe, in the person of one General O'Brien, a British subject and a former comrade of San Martín. He left the Plata in July, 1844, to become the Montevidean consul at London, where he exercised great influence later in the same year.[103]

[100] Durand, *op. cit.*, pp. 136-140. John MacGregor, *Commercial Tariffs and Treaties*, Part 19, pp. 396-397, *Parliamentary Papers*, King Collection, vol. 40. (London 1847); *Accounts and Papers*, 1847, LXIV.

[101] F. Varela, *Observations on the Occurrences in the River Plate as connected with the Foreign Agents and the Anglo-French Intervention*. (Montevideo 1843). It was printed in French and Spanish also.

[102] *Autobiografía de D. Florencio Varela*, pp. 17-35. See a news item in the *National Intelligencer* of April 15, 1844; F. O. 51, 24 and 32. "After full and mature deliberation," wrote Aberdeen on Jan. 2, ". . . Her M's Gov't. cannot depart from the neutrality which they have hitherto observed throughout the war." Varela requested an audience as late as Feb. 13, 1844.

[103] Wm. Hadfield, *Brazil, the River Plate, and the Falkland Islands*. (London 1854), p. 19. F. O. 51, 32, Vasquez to Aberdeen July 25, 1844. O'Brien served as consul in London until May, 1848. See *Correspondencia diplomática del doctor don Manuel Herrera y Obes . . . de 1847 á 1852*. (Montevideo 1901), pp. 112-113.

As a result of Varela's visit to Paris, the policy which the French Government was pursuing at Montevideo became a question of serious concern to the French Chambers in May, 1844.[104] Thiers celebrated his return to political activity, after an extended vacation, by making the situation in the Plata one of the principal topics of his attack upon Guizot's foreign policy. From information furnished by Varela, he related the entire story of the abortive mediatory efforts of England and France which had culminated in the declaration of December 16, 1842. This action, he insisted, must surely have had some authorization. And yet in the face of the dire distress of their own nationals, Guizot had not only repudiated the summons of his agent, but had disowned his countrymen as denationalized adventurers. The French consul had retired from Montevideo because that government would not take the suicidal step of disarming the Foreign Legion. The French Admiral, he continued, had displayed nothing of the firmness of Purvis. Where were the forgotten guarantees of the Mackau Convention? Why had the joint intervention with England been abandoned? Why were not their nationals given adequate protection? Thiers concluded his address with a stirring appeal demanding that the Government give some practical demonstration of their boasted alliance with England by forcing Rosas to accept the joint mediation of the two powers, or at least by relieving the existing threat to the independence of Montevideo.[105]

Other speakers joined in the attack. Some ridiculed the pretention of Rosas that Oribe was the legal President of Uruguay. They quoted with effect from the earlier despatches of Lurde to prove that the prospective overthrow of Rivera by Oribe's army had previously been recognized by Guizot himself as a violation of the independence of the Oriental Republic.[106] The outlook for the Government was not encouraging. Baron Mackau made a feeble attempt to reply to these

---

[104] A slight reference had been made to the subject in the January debates. *Le Moniteur Universel,* Jan. 13, 25, 1844.

[105] *Ibid.,* May 30, 1844. So great was the commotion at the close of the speech that a recess of 15 minutes was necessary.

[106] *Ibid.,* Speech of M. Corne.

attacks by denying the accuracy of Varela's representations. He assured the Chambers that even their denationalized compatriots were protected by the "affection and sympathy of our officers." [107]

It remained for the President of the Council, on the following day, to give an effective answer to Thiers. Guizot recognized immediately the vulnerable point in the argument of his opponent, and he prefaced his defense with a careful analysis of the instructions which Thiers had presented to Mackau on July 21, 1840. He demonstrated conclusively that Montevideo had been abandoned by France in accordance with express orders from Thiers himself. France, therefore, had no obligation under the Mackau treaty to assist Montevideo in its war with Rosas, so long as the independence of Uruguay was not in danger. Thiers winced and made vigorous objections to his adversary's interpretation. But Guizot knew that he had found the heel of Achilles, and he pressed his point relentlessly home.

The Prime Minister then proceeded to the defense of his policy. The declaration of December 16, he said, had been entirely unauthorized. The earlier unhappy experiences of France in the Plata were certainly enough to make them pause before embarking upon the program suggested by Lurde, especially when they had no grievance of their own against Rosas. Great Britain, he pointed out, had just recalled Purvis because of the very activities which Thiers had so eloquently praised.[108] The French Government was fully justified by Article 21 of the Civil code in denationalizing what Guizot described as that minority of French residents of the Plata, who were being exploited within the Foreign Legion. But even these, he said, were assured of safety by the arrangement which Pichon had made with Oribe on August 5, 1843. No matter what obligations France might still have toward them, the Cabinet could not afford to allow such a group to dictate their entire policy in the Plata, where broader interests were at stake. Guizot

---

[107] *Ibid.*

[108] *Ibid.*, May 31 and June 1, 1844. At this point a voice reminded the speaker that there were not 18,000 British living at Montevideo.

suggested, in conclusion, that before M. Thiers should again advocate entangling France in the two civil wars of the Plata, he should again exercise some of the political sagacity which he had exhibited in his former instructions to Mackau.[109]

Thiers made a frantic effort to reply. Balked by his own policy of 1840 in his appeal that France was honor-bound to protect Montevideo, he embarked upon an impassioned plea on behalf of their own nationals. So vehement did he become that he was openly accused of appealing to the emotions of the Chambers. In the end, he could only reiterate his earlier demand for a joint effort with Great Britain to relieve the unhappy situation. Guizot closed the debate, easily the victor, by declaring that all means would be taken to protect French subjects at Montevideo, which were consistent with the general interests of French policy in the Plata.[110]

During the same early months of 1844, forces were gathering in London which were soon to drive Peel's Government relentlessly in the direction of a joint intervention with France in the Plata. The most powerful pressure came from a number of commercial houses trading in the river. The long paralysis of trade in that quarter had raised the price of hides in Europe to a relatively high point. With the cessation of hostilities in the Argentine provinces in 1843, and the simultaneous closing of Montevideo, speculation in this commodity became rampant at Buenos Ayres. Money was so greatly in demand that interest rates jumped to $2\frac{1}{2}$ per cent a month, and as high as 40 per cent a year. Great quantities of goods were advanced by English merchants in anticipation of the revival of trade.[111] But the speculators had not calculated on developments elsewhere. In Rio Grande do Sul two score establishments for salting beef and hides had sprung up like mushrooms in the meantime to care for the thousands of head of cattle that Rivera's men were collecting in Uruguay and selling across the Brazilian

---

[109] *Le Moniteur Universel*, June 1, 1844.

[110] *Ibid.*, Pereyra's account of this debate (*op. cit.*, pp. 41-42, 196-197, 207-211) is entirely overdrawn.

[111] *Parliamentary Papers*, King Collection, vol. 40, John MacGregor, *Commercial Tariffs and Treaties*, Part 19, pp. 396-397;—*Accounts and Papers*, 1847, LXIV.

border in order to get some ready money.[112] The news of the shipments of these cheap hides from Rio Grande caused the market price in England suddenly to collapse. The result was a severe panic at Buenos Ayres. Five of the principal commercial houses in the city went bankrupt, and within a short time, the liabilities amounted to almost half of the total amount of the paper money in circulation. The immediate loss fell most heavily upon the native establishments, but many British merchants were also caught in the crash with goods on their hands of which they could not dispose.[113]

As a result of this situation, Peel was faced with a most insistent demand in 1844, from such places as Liverpool and Manchester, that the British Government should take steps in conjunction with France to relieve the trade restrictions in the Plata. The turmoil in Uruguay must be ended, and access secured for them to the markets of Paraguay and the interior regions.[114] Peel at first displayed no enthusiasm for the idea. He said in Parliament that all means short of armed intervention had already been tried. Although he appreciated the importance of the commercial interests at stake, he could not, he affirmed, as a Minister of peace, undertake to impose any arrangement upon the states in question. Recent news, he added, held out the prospect of an early peace, probably in the victory of the Buenos Ayres party. He concluded as follows:

"If any armed intervention could be justified, it could only be so by the concurrence in it of the three powers most deeply interested in the termination of the war,—Britain, France, and the Brazils." [115]

Before the close of the year, these commercial interests found in General O'Brien an indefatigable promoter, who organized their pressure to almost irresistible proportions.[116]

[112] F. O. 6, 96, M. to A., June 21, 1844.
[113] MacGregor, *op. cit.*, pp. 396-7.
[114] *Ibid.*, pp. 406-410. *Parliamentary Debates*, 3rd series, vol. 73, p. 755 ff. An interpellation by Mr. Ewart, March 8, 1844.
[115] *Ibid.*, 73, p. 757; 74, pp. 1257-1259.
[116] *Aff. Etr.*, Buenos Ayres, 33, pp. 17-31. O'Brien later said that he secured ten petitions from the manufacturing districts of Yorkshire, Liverpool, Manchester, Leeds, Halifax, and Bradford, signed by some 1500 of

Another type of propaganda against Rosas in England found its basis of appeal in the prevailing disgust in religious and humanitarian circles at the excesses of the despotism at Buenos Ayres. A pamphlet, supposedly written by a British clergyman residing in Montevideo, which was circulated in Great Britain, presented a most revolting picture of the cruelty and sacrilege of the Dictator. The clergy of the entire United Kingdom were called upon to raise their "irresistible voices" in behalf of justice, civilization, and Christianity in South America. The British and French Governments must not, it declared, permit such a tyrant to "extend his dominion on earth." [117]

The relations existing between the two European governments in 1844 did not easily lend themselves to a new co-operative policy in the Plata. They had drifted steadily apart since 1842. Their interests clashed in Africa, in the Far East, New Zealand, and the Pacific. Their agreement in regard to Spain was very precarious.[118] Guizot had recently been obliged by the Chambers to request at London an alteration of their old slave-trade treaties of 1831 and 1833.[119] The Duke of Wellington and his followers were, at the same time, convinced that France was plotting to invade the island. The Foreign Ministers had made a desperate attempt, early in the year, to revive their *entente* by an agreement to co-operate in preventing the annexation of Texas by the United States.[120] But France had little material interest in the Texas question, and

---

the Bankers, Merchants, and Manufacturers in each place. See *General Index, Public Petitions,* House of Commons, 1833-1852, p. 47.

[117] A British Resident of Montevideo, *Rosas and Some of the Atrocities of his Dictatorship.* (London 1844), pp. 1-32. Just how wide a hearing this appeal received it is not possible to say.

[118] Guyot, *op. cit.,* pp. 231-242, 256-260.

[119] *Le Moniteur Universel,* Jan. 25, Feb. 2, 3, 1843; Jan. 9, 17, 1844. Especially after the Webster-Asburton treaty failed to incorporate the right of search, this charge of Guizot's subservience to England on this question became irresistible. The influence of Louis Cass in this respect has been greatly overemphasized.

[120] Antonio de Peña y Reyes, *Lord Aberdeen, Texas y California—Archivo Histórico Diplomático Mexicano,* no. 15. (Mexico City 1925), pp. xx-xxii, 13-15. With no thought of a possible common policy with England, Guizot expressed gratification that he did not have Purvis' actions to account for. *Aff. Etr.,* Buenos Ayres, 32, p. 101. To Lurde, Mar. 28, 1844.

Guizot would not go to war with America in order to promote the trading interests of Great Britain.[121]

The *entente* was practically destroyed in the summer of 1844. Simultaneous friction over Morocco and the Pacific island of Tahiti brought them to the verge of war.[122] The trouble over Morocco began when a French army invaded the country from Algeria in June, 1844. The initial nervousness of the British Cabinet grew into alarm in early August, especially when the Prince de Joinville, a noted advocate of the annexation of Morocco by France, appeared before Tangiers with a war fleet.[123] In the meantime, British hostility toward France had been raised to fever heat by the arrival in England, on July 31, of a Mr. Pritchard, an ex-missionary and British consul on the island of Tahiti, in the Society group, a place which had recently been taken under the sovereignty of the French Crown.[124] Pritchard had been arrested by the French commander, imprisoned for a time on a war vessel, and then expelled from the island. The fact that he had been actively engaged in stirring up native resistance to French control was overlooked at London, and the British public saw only the fact that Catholic France had roughly handled a Protestant missionary and a British official. All the instinctive national and religious jealousies came to the surface, and war was in the air. Neither government was in a mood to conciliate. Guizot made no move toward accommodation, even when Aberdeen threatened to present a formal demand for an indemnity

---

[121] Justin H. Smith, *The Annexation of Texas.* (New York 1911), pp. 392-400. For an attempt to influence French opinion toward the acceptance of the policy of co-operation with Britain in Texas, see *Revue des Deux Mondes* 1844, vol. 3, pp. 59-94; "Le Texas y les Etats-Unis," by A. Cucheval. *Niles Register,* for June 12, 1845.

[122] F. P. G. Guizot, *Memoires pour servir à l'histoire de mon Temps.* (Paris 1865) vol. 7, pp. 40-129. T. MacKnight, *Thirty Years of Foreign Policy.* (London 1855), pp. 348-357. Russia was endeavoring to pry Britain and France apart in 1844 for the sake of the Tzar's Near Eastern policy.

[123] C. F. M. Rousset, *La Conquête de l'Algérie, 1841-1857,* 2 vols. (Paris 1904) vol. 1, p. 301-328.

[124] Guizot, *Memoires,* Vol. 7, pp. 40-129, 150-183. The action of the French Commander at Tahiti in this case was entirely unauthorized. See Taschereau, *Revue Rétrospective ou Archives secrètes du dernier gouvernement, 1830-1848.* (Paris 1848), pp. 479-480. The British seized and held the Sandwich Islands for a time in retaliation. See S. F. Bemis, *American Secretaries of State,* V, p. 223.

if it were not volunteered. The French Ambassador in London finally exceeded his instructions in granting the necessary concession only one day before the proroguing of Parliament, on September 5, would have caused a break in relations. The Morocco settlement followed a few days later.[125]

The crisis of the summer had been exceedingly uncomfortable for the two Foreign Ministers. Both of them were staking their policies on a continuation of friendly relations.[126] The reaction after the release of the tension made them more desirous than ever to reach a more satisfactory accord. A dramatic step in this direction was made in the visit of Louis Philippe to Windsor Castle in October.[127] It was in connection with this effort to rebuild the faltering *entente* that the attention of Paris and London came to be focused again on the affairs of the Rio de la Plata.

[125] Hall, *op. cit.*, pp. 346-368. Guyot, *op. cit.*, pp. 261-266. B. Willson, *The Paris Embassy.* (London 1927), pp. 184-186. *Cambridge History of British Foreign Policy*, II, pp. 182-5, 263-4, 641-2.

[126] Rousset, *op. cit.*, pp. 366-67. Chas. S. Parker, *Sir Robert Peel.* 3 vols. (London 1899) v. 3, pp. 392-395.

[127] Taschereau, *Revue Rétrospective, op. cit.* No less than five personal letters between the French and British sovereigns are here given, between the dates of Oct. 15 and Oct. 30, 1844.

CHAPTER V

JOINT INTERVENTION

The failure of President Rivera to redeem his promises of 1838 to aid Brazil in suppressing the rebels of Rio Grande do Sul made him the enemy of the Imperial authorities quite as much as that of Rosas.[1] In 1841, the Brazilian agent at Buenos Ayres had approached Rosas with the suggestion that their governments should assist each other in suppressing domestic disorder. The reaction of Rosas to this idea was very encouraging. He assured the agent that he had no designs upon Uruguay and that a primary objective of his foreign policy was to maintain an alliance with the Imperial Government against the rebel anarchists threatening them.[2] No formal commitments were entered into, but relations became very cordial. Brazil's friendship was clearly demonstrated in May, 1842, when she offered Rosas the service of her fleet, at a time when rumor made it appear that Admiral Brown was about to desert to Rivera.[3]

Oribe's invasion of Uruguay, in 1843, influenced Brazil to propose again an arrangement similar to that which Rosas had suggested two years before. The Imperial Government succeeded in negotiating, in March, a treaty with the Argentine representative at Rio de Janeiro, which established an offensive and defensive alliance between the two major states directed against Rivera's party in Uruguay and the insurrec-

[1] Vicente G. Quesada, *Historia diplomática latino-americana,* 3 vols. (Buenos Ayres 1919), vol. 2, *La Política del Brasil con las Repúblicas del Río de la Plata,* pp. 152-156. Palomeque, *Estudios Históricos,* vol. 1, *op. cit.,* pp. 5-9.
[2] F. O. 6, 78, Mandeville to Palmerston, Mar. 20 and enclosure, May 31, Sept. 13, 1841.
[3] F. O. 6, 83, M. to A., May 21, 1842 and enclosures. Rivera and Ferré had been intimate, in 1842, with Don Benito Gonzalvez, chief of Rio Grande. F. O. 6, 84, Mandeville to Aberdeen, Nov. 26, 1842. See Zinny *La Gaceta Mercantil* 3, pp. 103 for their treaty.

tionary group in Rio Grande.[4]   The advantages which Brazil
would derive from this arrangement were obvious.   She would
not only be better able to crush the illusive disaffection in her
southern province, but would also score a distinct gain by
making the victorious lieutenant of Rosas her debtor, and by
securing a right to participate in the pacification of Uruguay.
For similar reasons, the government at Buenos Ayres showed
little enthusiasm for the treaty when it was presented for
their approval.   The aid of Brazil could not be decisive against
the resistance of the Europeans at Montevideo.   The treaty
was therefore rejected by Rosas, on the ground that it had
not been authorized.   The Dictator cleverly suggested, at the
same time, that the proposal concerned matters upon which
Oribe himself, as legal President of Uruguay, was fully competent to treat.[5]

The rejection of this treaty of 1843 produced a definite
change in the attitude of the Imperial authorities toward
Rosas.   Suspicion revived that the Dictator intended to extend
his control over Uruguay, and the two states resumed their
traditional attitude of hostility.   A quarrel between Rosas and
the Brazilian agent at Buenos Ayres, in connection with the
blockade of Montevideo, late in 1843, caused a temporary suspension of diplomatic relations, and greatly contributed to the
growing estrangement between the two governments.[6]   The
Brazilian authorities turned deliberately to their project of
cementing an alliance with the state of Paraguay, whose declaration of independence on November 27, 1842, had been
flouted by Rosas.   This state was being denied communication
through Argentine territory.   Brazil and Paraguay were not
in a position as yet to challenge the Argentine Dictator alone.
But they felt confident that they might count on the support
of Great Britain, and perhaps of France, in any legitimate en-

[4] Palomeque, *op. cit.*, 1, pp. 23-26, 64, 108.   Brazil's Chargé barely escaped
a bodily assault at Montevideo from Garibaldi in July, 1843.   F. O. 6, 89,
Mandeville to Aberdeen, July 16, 1843.

[5] F. O. 6, 90, M. to A., Aug. 14, 1843.   Written after a conversation with
Rosas on the treaty.

[6] F. O. 6, 90, M. to A., Sept. 15, 21, Oct. 24, Nov. 19, 1843.

deavor to restore peace in Uruguay and to secure the free navigation of the rivers.[7]

The plans of Brazil were hastily matured in 1844, when she learned, probably through Varela, that France and England were about to discontinue their interference at Montevideo. General Paz was encouraged to revive the latent hostility toward Rosas in Corrientes.[8] Brazilian officers were sent to reorganize the army of Paraguay, and engineers assisted in the building of her military roads. After the recognition of the new state by Brazil in September, 1844, the counsels of the Imperial Government became dominant at Asunción.[9] A commercial treaty between Paraguay and Corrientes was concluded in the same year, and the alignment of the local parties was later completed when Montevideo recognized the interior state in May, 1845.[10] The rumor was generally current that Brazil had some large scheme of intervention on foot.[11]

In August, 1844, one Viscount Abrantes left Rio de Janeiro for Europe. His mission, ostensibly, was to settle some commercial questions with England and Prussia; but in reality, he was sent to secure the assistance of the British Government for Brazil's policy in the Argentine.[12] This attempt was being made in spite of the fact that a quarrel was then raging between Rio de Janeiro and London over the renewal of their

[7] Brossard, op. cit., pp. 304-314. Rosas refused to open the rivers at Lopez's demand in December, 1844, and all communication came to an end in July, 1845. B. Poucel, Le Paraguay Moderne. (Marseille 1867) Appendix, ix-xxvi. Paraguay was reputed to have had a population of 400,000—equal to the total of Buenos Ayres, Entre Rios, Corrientes, and Uruguay. See McGregor, Commercial Tariffs, op. cit., pp. 284-302.

[8] S. D. Brazil, Desp., vol. 12, Profit to Upshur, Feb. 10, 1844; vol. 13, Wise to Calhoun, Aug. 14, 1844.

[9] Carles Oneta y Viana, La Diplomacia del Brazil en el Rio de la Plata, pp. 18-24; Ernesto Quesada, Historia diplomática nacional. La política argentino-paraguaya. (Buenos Aires 1902), pp. 11-15. See decree of Governor of Corrientes, Oct. 7, 1844. British Foreign and State Papers, 33, p. 760.

[10] Oneta y Viana, ibid. Brossard, op. cit., pp. 293-4. Zinny, op. cit., vol. 3, pp. 78-79. In February, 1845, peace was restored in Rio Grande do Sul. See Robertson "Emperor Dom Pedro II," pp. 245-6. Palomeque, op. cit., pp. 9-15.

[11] National Intelligencer, Oct. 24, 1844; Niles Register, 67, pp. 208-209, Dec. 7, 1844. S. D. Brazil, Desp. 13, Wise to Calhoun, Aug. 14, 1844; N. D. Brazil Squadron, Com. Turner to Mason, July 12, 1844 and enclosures.

[12] F. Durand, op. cit., pp. 144-147; Carlos Calvo, Le Droit International, vol. 1, pp. 230-232.

commercial and slave-trade treaties. These were about to
expire, the first on November 10, 1844, the second on March
13, 1845.[13]

Negotiations in regard to the new commercial treaty had
been in progress for more than two years. Brazil had no
desire to renew the tariff arrangement of 1825, which had been
granted to Britain in return for services rendered in securing
her independence from Portugal. It limited Brazilian duties
on English produce to 15%,[14] and left the London government
free to raise prohibitory tariffs against the sugar and coffee
of the South American state. Peel's concern for the welfare
of the British West Indian planters, so hard hit by negro
emancipation,[15] had led him to lay down the condition that
no concession on the question of British sugar duties could be
expected as long as negro slavery remained legal in Brazil.
The sop of a reduction of 2d. per pound in the coffee tariff,
which Peel held out as a compensation for Brazil's renewal of
the 15% provision,[16] had only elicited some embarrassing questions as to why England should lose her scruples in regard to
slave labor when coffee rather than sugar was produced by it.[17]
In order to bring additional pressure to bear on the hesitant

[13] British Foreign and State Papers, 14, pp. 1008-1025. This date included a two-year extension for the treaty of commerce. Pereira Pinto, A.,
Apontamentos para o direito internacional, ou Collecção completa dos
tratados celebrados pelo Brazil. (Rio de Janeiro 1864) pp. 128-136, 155-
186, 273-292, 404-407, 419-425, 462-486. Also Jane E. Adams "Abolition of
the Brazilian Slave Trade" Journal of Negro History (Oct. 1925) 10, pp.
609-17, 627-30. Article I of the 1826 treaty, defining the slave trade as
piracy under Brazilian law, was not revokable; F. O. 84, Slave Trade, 697,
Palmerston to Howden, June 4, 1847.

[14] This 15 per cent provision had not been very loyally enforced by
Brazil, however. See S. D. Brazil, Desp. 11, Hunter to Forsyth, Sept. 12,
1838.

[15] The Melbourne Ministry had been defeated in May, 1841, on the question of slave trade and sugar duties. Hansard's Debates, 3rd Series, 58,
pp. 1-709, intermittently. See p. 667 in particular. S. J. Reid, Lord John
Russell. (London 1895), pp. 121-125.

[16] F. O. 13, 178, Aberdeen to Hamilton, Feb. 1, July 6, 1842.

[17] F. O. 13, 219, Aberdeen to Aranjo Ribeiro in London, Jan. 9, 1844.
The British Minister explained the difference in his attitude toward slave-
labor coffee, not by the obvious fact that coffee was not grown in the
British West Indies, but on the ground that coffee culture was less dependent on the slave trade than was sugar production, the former being
less strenuous and giving employment to women and children. This argument would have sounded more plausible had the lowering of British sugar
duties been conditioned on the abolition of the slave trade, and not on
slavery itself in Brazil.

Rio Government,[18] an Act of Parliament had been pushed through in June, 1844, which reduced the duty on foreign free-labor sugar, grown in the East Indies, from the prevailing 64 shillings to 34 per cwt. The tariff on British colonial sugar remained at 24 shillings.[19] If Brazil should now allow the old treaty of 1825, with its most-favored-nation clause, to lapse, the new discriminatory law would automatically become operative to the great disadvantage of her produce in British markets.

The South American state quite naturally resented such commercial dictation. They had no respect for what they termed England's "grotesque jumbling of profit and philanthropy." Encouraged by the powerful financial and agricultural interests who were entrenched behind the illegal but unhampered slave-trade,[20] the Imperial Government decided to reject the British commercial proposal and to refuse outright to negotiate a new slave-trade treaty to replace the one which they had inherited from Portugal.[21] The two questions were thus deadlocked when Abrantes arrived at London in early November, 1844.[22]

The representations advanced by Abrantes suggesting the desirability of a joint intervention in the Plata received a sympathetic hearing from Lord Aberdeen. A similar policy was being urged upon the London Foreign Office by parties nearer home. After a conference between the two men on November 18, the British Minister indicated his hearty approval of the general purposes of the offer held out by Brazil, and prom-

[18] F. O. 12, 209, Aberdeen to Hamilton, April 3, 1844.
[19] William Page, *Commerce and Industry, Historical Review.* (London 1919), pp. 149-151.
[20] S. D. Brazil, Desp. 11, Hunter to Forsyth, Nov. 25, 1839; vol. 12, same to Webster, Nov. 8, 1842.
[21] S. D. Brazil, Desp. 12, Hunter to Webster, Nov. 8, 1842. Brazilians declared that Britain left them only the alternative of abolishing slavery "for the privilege of exporting at somewhat relaxed duties, commodities they could no longer furnish" without slaves. England also took action, however, against the employment of British capital in the slave trade or in the slave-labor production of sugar. See *Parliamentary Debates,* 3rd Series, 71, pp. 930-952.
[22] F. O. 13, 214, Hamilton to Aberdeen, Oct. 2 and Nov. 25, 1844; F. O. 13, 221, Aberdeen to Hamilton, Jan. 24, 1845. Friction had also arisen over the enjoyment of extraterritorial court privileges by British subjects in Brazil under the old treaty.

ised that he would prepare appropriate instructions. It is a significant fact that, up to this point in the negotiation, the idea of French co-operation had been suggested by neither party, so far as the records reveal. As late as November 22, the French Ambassador in London was certainly not aware of the real purpose of the Abrantes mission.[23] The dates become important. On the 26th, a written statement was sent by Aberdeen to the Brazilian agent to the effect that two requirements would have to be met before Britain could co-operate in the desired intervention. In the first place, France must also be persuaded to become a party to the coercive measures; second, for the sake of the harmony necessary in such an enterprise, all grounds of difference between Great Britain and Brazil would have to be removed.[24]

The reasons behind Aberdeen's second condition are clearly explained by the Foreign Minister's own statement to his agent at Rio de Janeiro. Because of the commercial interests at stake, he wrote, England was not indisposed to co-operate with Brazil in putting an end to the intolerable state of affairs in the Plata. He continued as follows:

"You will perceive, however, that I have stated the necessity, before entering into any intimate concert with the Brazilian Government, of removing all causes of misunderstanding between Great Britain and Brazil. In saying this I had reference to the position in which we stand with respect to the Commercial Treaty and to the Treaty for the abolition of the Slave Trade."

A refusal to sign the commercial treaty, continued Aberdeen, would be "little short of actual hostility." [25] The desired alterations in the slave-trade treaty might be foregone, but Britain had a right to demand a continuation of the old one, he insisted, and "the present moment is obviously appropriate for procuring from the Brazilian Government an acquiescence

[23] F. O. 13, 219, Abrantes to Aberdeen, Nov. 9 and Nov. 19. In reporting a conversation with Abrantes on Nov. 22, Aulaire spoke only of the Commercial treaty as the purpose of his mission, and said not a word of interference in the Plata. See *Aff. Etr., Brésil* 23, p. 161; Aulaire to Guizot, from London, Nov. 22, 1844.

[24] F. O. 13, 219, Aberdeen to Abrantes, Nov. 26, 1844.

[25] F. O. 13, 209, Aberdeen to Hamilton, Dec. 4, 1844.

in our proposal." [26] Aberdeen said that he did not believe that a mere exhortation would be sufficient to secure the submission of Rosas, and he also acknowledged the undesirable possibility that Montevideo might fall into the hands of Brazil. He was not interested in the recognition of Paraguay, however. Little harm would result, he said, if the inhospitable government at Asunción were made to wait for the recognition of its independence.[27]

The explanation of the desire on the part of Aberdeen that France should also be associated in the intervention involves a general consideration of the relations between the two European states. In the first place, it was obvious that the exclusion of France in this instance would have been productive of friction and suspicion. Furthermore, the requirements for the success of the recently inaugurated movement toward the renewal of the Franco-British *entente* provided a powerful argument for her active co-operation.[28] A lasting friendship between the two powers must have a foundation more substantial than the smiles of their sovereigns at Windsor and the assuring notes of the Foreign Ministers. A common objective enterprise was sorely needed, one which would lend to their *rapprochement* an element of permanence and would demonstrate before their own people and the European community at large that the boasted *entente* was a reality. A joint expedition to the Plata was already being called for, as we have seen, by commercial interests in England and by the troublesome opposition in the French Chambers.[29]

The previous plan for the co-operation of the two Governments in behalf of an independent Texas had, moreover, just run aground. The limitations of that project had been appre-

[26] F. O. 84, 525, Slave trade, Aberdeen to Hamilton, Dec. 4, 1844.
[27] F. O. 13, 209, Aberdeen to Hamilton, Dec. 4, 1844.
[28] See chap. IV, note 119. Aberdeen was prepared to sacrifice the British right to search French slavers in return for joint surveillance of the coast. Palmerston was disgusted at this concession. G. P. Gooch, *The Later Correspondence of Lord John Russell*, 2 vols. (N. Y. 1925) Vol. 1, p. 78. Letter to Russell, Jan. 9, 1845.
[29] Emile Bourgeois, *Manuel Historique et Politique Etrangère*, 4 vols. (Paris 1919-20, 1927) Vol. 3, pp. 256-57. Russia was urging Britain to aid her in hastening the demise of Turkey, and trying to pry France and England apart. Brossard, *op. cit.*, pp. 294-298.

ciated by the Foreign Ministers in the preceding July, and it had been held in abeyance awaiting the outcome of the Presidential election in the United States. The news of Polk's victory, which appeared in the London papers on November 25, was the *coup de grâce* to the Texas program.[30] Guizot's announcement a week later that no decisive action could be expected from France on that question merely asserted what was clearly apparent. Aberdeen had already withdrawn his own promises to Mexico and had determined to avoid a clash with the United States unless forced to act in defense of the legitimate claims of Britain in the Oregon country.[31] The fact that French participation was suggested by Aberdeen immediately after the news of Polk's election reached London would be sufficient to make one suspect that the South American enterprise was to be substituted for the one in North America, as an objective expression of their *entente*. This conclusion is fully supported by a statement which the British Minister made to the French Ambassador at London in October, 1845, which the latter reported as follows:

"We could hardly hope to have success in the affair of Texas, . . . and we have run aground in spite of the excellent intelligence of our guests. But here [in the Plata] a complete success appears to me indispensable for our general policy, and I have all confidence that we will obtain it."[32]

The eagerness with which Aberdeen seized upon this new opportunity to co-ordinate British-French policy is more easily understood when the situation within the British Cabinet is

[30] J. H. Smith, *Annexation of Texas.* (N. Y. 1911) pp. 402-404, 414-419. Peña y Reyes, *Lord Aberdeen, Texas, y California, op. cit.,* pp. 3-12. From Murphy, Dec. 1, 1844, Jan. 1, 1845. Latané, J. H., *American Foreign Policy.* (New York 1927) pp. 255-258. Guizot's Texas policy was a wide departure from the traditional French attitude, and he himself declared that his country would never forgive him. G. P. Gooch, *op. cit.,* 1, p. 91.

[31] Smith, *op. cit.,* pp. 402-413. E. D. Adams, *British Interests and Activities in Texas.* (Baltimore 1910), pp. 190-191, 203-7. Peña y Reyes, *op. cit.,* pp. 16-18, 20-23. The likely possibility suggests itself that Aberdeen had in the back of his mind the advantage of having a section of the British fleet in the Plata river, already half way to Oregon. Aberdeen was thoroughly alarmed over Oregon in March and April, 1845. See F. O. 5, America, 423, to Pakenham, Mar. 3 and Apr. 6, 1845.

[32] *Aff. Etr.,* Buenos Ayres, 34, pp. 278-280. Jarnac, from London, to Guizot, Oct. 9, 1845.

taken into consideration. The Duke of Wellington was entirely out of sympathy with the Foreign Minister's trustful policy toward France. He expected, almost any moment, to see an invasion of defenseless England by means of the new steam vessels which the Paris government had been subsidizing.[33] Even those who were less alarmed than he concerning French designs doubted the wisdom of staking too much on the precarious tenure of Guizot.[34] With this alarmist agitation of the Duke, Aberdeen had no patience. He wrote to Peel on December 31, 1844, as follows:

"It is impossible for me to approve of a system which would virtually stultify our whole policy for the last three years. . . . Why incur an enormous expense, and create general distrust at a moment when there is no reason to apprehend any danger?" [35]

The astute Prime Minister reconciled Wellington to a more moderate program of defense by suggesting that the panicky effort advocated by the Duke would only demonstrate more clearly the weakness of England, and might precipitate an immediate attack from France.[36]

Relations with France were therefore a matter of primary concern to the London Cabinet. Peel was already considering the advisability of altering their slave-trade treaties in accordance with the demands of the French Chambers, in order to give Guizot some ground on which to defend his policy of friendship for England.[37] It is highly significant, in this con-

---

[33] Thiers had done much to start this subsidizing practice, which was in general use among Governments. See the *London Times,* May 18, 1840.

[34] C. S. Parker, *Sir Robert Peel from his private papers,* 3 vols. (London 1899) 3, pp. 206, 399. F. P. G. Guizot, *Memoirs of Sir Robert Peel.* (London 1857), pp. 157-158. Guizot to Aberdeen, Dec. 3, 1844, commenting on the fact of the jealousy between their agents everywhere.

[35] *Ibid.,* pp. 396-7.

[36] Parker, *op. cit.,* vol. 3, pp. 198-200. Wellington to Peel, Dec. 27, 1844.

[37] Allison, *op. cit.,* p. 309 ff. Guizot had very narrow escapes in the Chambers in May, 1845 and January, 1846. The Mexican Minister to England reported in October, 1845, that French opinion was so hostile to Britain that Her Majesty's Government would not dare expose themselves to a war with the United States without a perfect understanding with France, who might easily make common cause against England. See J. H. Smith, *War with Mexico,* 2 vols. (N. Y. 1919) vol. 2, p. 506. E. D. Adams, *op. cit.,* pp. 236-253. G. P. Gooch, *op. cit.,* 1, p. 78. Letter to Russell, Jan. 9, 1845. A new slave-trade treaty in May, 1845, provided for joint surveillance of the African coast.

nection, to note that Peel later took occasion to emphasize before Parliament, in February, 1845, that there was no better evidence of the cordial relations existing between France and England than the agreement recently arrived at in regard to the Plata war.[38]

Another proof of the important part which ulterior considerations played in determining Aberdeen's Argentine policy is found in the fact that he never developed any clear idea of just what he purposed to accomplish. Brazil's share in the intervention was manifestly regarded in London as a question incidental to the securing of their treaties. Although the British Minister realized that coercion would be necessary to secure the acquiescence of Rosas, he made no calculation of the probable nature or extent of it. He came to no definite understanding with Paris, moreover, as to the place which the river navigation question was to occupy in the intervention, and he was equally vague in regard to the status of General Oribe.[39]

Guizot was entirely unprepared for the proposal which Aberdeen and Abrantes presented to him in early December, 1844.[40] To reverse the policy which he had pursued with so much patience and sacrifice for the preceding two years was not an easy thing for him to contemplate. Only a few months before, he had gone out of his way to discourage the growing hostility between Brazil and Argentina.[41] The British Ambassador reported from Paris, on December 12, that Guizot showed no enthusiasm for the enterprise. The French Government, he said, was not in favor of the adoption of any military measures of a coercive nature against Buenos Ayres, and was equally opposed to any interference with the political institutions or the governments of any of the Plata countries. Guizot

[38] *Parliamentary Debates* 3d Series, 77, pp. 169-170.
[39] F. O. 6, 96, Ouseley's notes, dated Dec. 12, 1844.
[40] *Aff. Etr., Brésil,* 23, pp. 165-166, 237. The Nov. 26 note from Aberdeen to Abrantes was transmitted to Paris when Abrantes wrote directly to Guizot, on Dec. 9.
[41] *Aff. Etr.,* Buenos Ayres, 31, pp. 317-318. Guizot to Lurde, Dec. 23, 1843.

would also require that no one should "derive or claim any separate advantage for the intervention." [42] Aberdeen immediately replied that his idea was merely that of a

"combined Naval demonstration, which, if disregarded, would be extended to a blockade and an occupation of the various rivers passing through the territories. It might, however, be necessary for Brazil to act with a military as well as a naval force. It would be against Buenos Ayres alone that the measures of compulsion would be required." [43]

It proved to be no easy task to persuade Guizot and Mackau to give their consent to the intervention. Paris was besieged throughout December and January by three enthusiastic promoters, in the persons of Abrantes, O'Brien, and Mr. Gore Ouseley, the latter being the newly selected British Minister to the Plata.[44] The French Government made it clear that they considered Rosas more capable and dependable than any of his rivals; above all, they had no desire to convert him into a second Abdel Kadr, one at a time being sufficient.[45] As late as January 14, the Brazilian agent expressed his dissatisfaction with the verbal statements previously issued by Guizot, and requested that the final decision of the French Government be submitted to him in writing.[46] Baron de Lurde arrived in Paris during this same month, and threw his powerful influence on the side of the interventionists.[47]

Politics also played a part in determining the French decision. During the latter half of January, the French Government was shaken to its very foundation in the debates on the address to the King. Guizot was pilloried unmercifully for his surrender to England in regard to Morocco and the Pritch-

[42] F. O. 27, 691, Aberdeen to Cowley, Dec. 17, 1844, referring to a letter from Cowley of Dec. 12.
[43] Ibid.
[44] Aff. Etr., Buenos Ayres, 33, pp. 17-41. From a copy of a pamphlet on the subject prepared by O'Brien. This agent even secured an interview with Louis Philippe on the matter.
[45] F. O. 6, 103, Ouseley to Aberdeen from Paris, Jan. 10, 1845. Guizot had been talking to Mackau.
[46] Aff. Etr., Brésil, 23, pp. 216-217. Abrantes to Guizot, Jan. 14, 1845. Guizot had expressed his "substantial agreement" in previous conferences of December 22 and January 13.
[47] Aff. Etr., Buenos Ayres, 34, pp. 4-5. Guizot to St. Aulaire in London, Jan. 21, 1845.

ard indemnity in the previous September. He was summoned by an overwhelming vote to cease his talk of a British *entente* until the existing slave-trade treaties had been altered.[48] Thiers was on hand to reiterate his demand for a practical demonstration of the value of the British alliance by means of a joint expedition to the Plata.[49] So uncontrollable was the uproar in the Chamber of Deputies on January 25, following a doubtful vote on a resolution condemning the Pritchard indemnity, that the President was obliged to dismiss the session in the midst of the tumult. The Ministry saved itself two days later by the narrow margin of eight votes on a motion commending the Government for keeping the peace.[50] With Guizot in such dire straits for some means to defend the British *entente*, it would have been no light matter for him to have refused the invitation of Aberdeen to co-operate in the expedition to the Plata.

With several qualifications, therefore, Guizot consented, on January 21, to participate in the enterprise. France would take part in a blockade, he said, to relieve Montevideo and to convince Rosas of the futility of interfering in Uruguay. The opening of a way to Paraguay might also be attempted. But Guizot insisted that in no event should they deny the right claimed by Rosas to prohibit his enemies from participating in governmental affairs in Uruguay and from securing asylum there.[51]

Aberdeen's vague reply betrays his great desire to secure the co-operation of France. He agreed with Guizot that no gratuitous aggression against Rosas should be undertaken. Neither should access to Paraguay or freedom of river navigation be too vigorously pressed. He even suggested that the mere severance of Oribe's communications might oblige the Argentine troops in Uruguay to withdraw. For reasons which were unknown to the French Ambassador, Aberdeen seemed

[48] *Le Moniteur Universel*, Jan. 16, 17, 18, 1845. The Marquis de Boissy led the attack.
[49] *Ibid.*, Jan. 22, 1844.
[50] *Ibid.*, Jan. 26 and 28, 1845.
[51] *Aff. Etr.*, Buenos Ayres, 34, pp. 4-5. Guizot to St. Aulaire in London, Jan. 21, 1845.

now to attach much less importance to the participation of Brazil.[52] (The French knew nothing concerning the details of England's difficulties with Brazil.) Aberdeen's reply was satisfactory to Guizot, and the latter informed the Brazilian agent, in a letter of January 31, that France had decided to cooperate with the other two powers in the Argentine project.[53]

Guizot still gave evidence of great anxiety over the decision. The French Ambassador in London was advised on February 11, that his government did not "know how to insist too strongly" that their intervention should partake only of the character of a neutral armed mediation, and should not be directed against Rosas further than to employ naval pressure upon the party refusing to treat for peace. The question of river navigation should be raised by them only incidentally, if at all. In view of the inevitable complications which would attend Brazil's participation, Guizot said that he would much prefer that the Imperial Government occupy only a secondary position in the operations. He admitted, however, that it would be embarrassing at that late date to make such a demand.[54]

Guizot's suggestion concerning the elimination of Brazil provided Aberdeen with an opportunity for which he had been seeking. The British Minister was thus spared the inconvenience of explaining the discreditable bargain which he had tried to make with Brazil in regard to the two treaties.[55] He immediately agreed that it would probably be better to leave the South American state out altogether—a move which was fool-

[52] *Aff. Etr.*, Buenos Ayres, 34, pp. 6-7. Aulaire, from London, to Guizot, Jan. 28, 1845. Aulaire gave as his own opinion that Rosas would be more likely to accede voluntarily to their requirements if Brazil were not included.

[53] *Ibid., Brésil* 23, p. 237. To Abrantes in Paris, Jan. 31, 1845. It is a significant commentary on French opinion to know that the unofficial French press suspected a collusion between Britain and Brazil for mutual aggrandisement to the exclusion of France. See Pereyra, *op. cit.*, pp. 149-150. *La Presse*, Feb. 9, 1845. Peel announced in Parliament as late as Feb. 6, that they hoped to enjoy the aid of Brazil in the intervention. Hansard, 3d Series, 77, pp. 169-170.

[54] *Aff. Etr.*, Buenos Ayres, 24, p. 8. To St. Aulaire in London, Feb. 11, 1845. "At the instant that France and England are in agreement," Guizot said, "their action should be independent."

[55] F. O. 13, 221, Aberdeen to Hamilton, Feb. 21, 1845. Brossard, *op. cit.*, pp. 300-303. It has been erroneously assumed in other treatments of this episode that England alone was responsible for excluding Brazil.

ish indeed, if they really intended to coerce Rosas.[56] It was decided, then, to exclude Brazil. Aberdeen instructed Ouseley not
to communicate at all with the Imperial authorities in regard
to the European plans if they had not accepted the British
treaties before he arrived at Rio de Janeiro. If Brazil had
taken favorable action, Ouseley might condescend to discuss
the project; but on no account was the South American state
to be allowed to participate actively in the enterprise.[57] The
new Argentine policy was of great importance, apparently, in
the general scheme of Franco-British relations; but neither
Paris nor London cared enough about the objectives of their
enterprise to provide the force necessary for achieving them.[58]

The British agent was to precede his French associate to
Buenos Ayres by about a month. His instructions were quite
belligerent in character. Ouseley was ordered to inform Rosas
that the latter would be compelled by force to comply with their
demands if he did not, in a dignified and voluntary way, cease
his unjustifiable interference in Uruguay.[59] Aberdeen wrote:

"The time has come when the rejection of this advice will involve him in dangers and difficulties from which he cannot hope
to escape without serious injury to his power."

If Rosas gave heed to this "friendly advice," continued Aberdeen, the agents should see to it that the Argentine émigrés, together with Rivera and perhaps Oribe, withdrew from Oriental
territory. The European Commissioners should then arrange
a settlement upon an impartial examination of the claims of
the rival governments. On the other hand, if Rosas should be
foolhardy enough to ignore their representations, Aberdeen
directed as follows:

[56] Durand, op. cit., pp. 147-149.
[57] F. O. 13, 221, Aberdeen to Hamilton, Feb. 21, 1845. F. O. 6, 102,
Aberdeen to Ouseley, Feb. 20, 1845.
[58] Aff. Etr., Buenos Ayres, 32, p. 270. Guizot to Jarnac in London, Aug.
18, 1845: "The views which Mr. França [Brazilian Foreign Minister] has
allowed to come to light . . . prove how far we were right in avoiding the
co-operation of Brazil. It is evident that the Cabinet of the King
[Brazilian] would have profited from our intervention in order to pursue
some private projects, and to implicate ourselves in some affairs where
we do not have any interest."
[59] Ouseley was ordered to ignore Mareuil, the French Chargé at Buenos
Ayres, in getting this first word with Rosas. Mareuil's suspicion must not
be aroused however. F. O. 6, 102, Canning to Ouseley, Mar. 5, 1845.

"You will invite your colleague to join with you in declaring that, if by a certain day the support of the Argentine Troops is not withdrawn from the besieging Army, and the Blockade of the City raised, the Commanders of the English and French Squadrons will be directed to effect these objects by force. It is needless to say that this declaration, when once made, must be adhered to." [60]

In outlining the forcible measures which were to be employed, Aberdeen's instructions left much to be desired. The naval forces of the two powers might establish a blockade of Buenos Ayres, and perhaps interfere at Montevideo if they should find the Argentine troops already in possession of it. But Ouseley was cautioned as follows:

"You will bear in mind that H. M.'s Government have no intention of carrying on any operation whatever by land; and you will not Consent to the disembarkation of any men from Her Majesty's Vessels beyond what may be requisite for the occupation of Martín García, or any other spot, of which, for the security of the Combined forces or to make their operations effective, it may be necessary to take temporary possession." [61]

The occupation of the tributaries of the Plata, he continued, was not to be attempted merely in the event that Rosas should refuse the free navigation of them. The one great purpose of securing peace should be left unencumbered by such extraneous considerations. Nevertheless, he added:

"If the opportunity of furthering any collateral object of importance should offer itself,—such as for instance, the opening of the Navigation of their Rivers, or the restoration of peace to the Governments of Corrientes and Entre Rios . . . , I need hardly tell you that it will be your duty to use it to the best of your ability. . . . [Should it be found that peace cannot be restored without resort to force,] I shall be prepared to give you instructions to unite with the French Minister in an endeavor to place the free navigation of the River Plate and its tributaries on a secure footing." [62]

[60] F. O. 6, 102, Aberdeen to Ouseley, Feb. 20, 1845.
[61] Ibid.
[62] Ibid. In the light of these instructions, Aberdeen's later assertion before Parliament on June 27, 1845, that a petition for forcing such free navigation could not be heeded because "we are bound to respect the rights of independent nations, be they weak or be they strong," sounds hypocritical. He was more considerate of British trading interests than he pretended to be. See Parliamentary Debates, 3rd Series, vol. 81, pp. 1306-1307.

There were two obvious defects in Aberdeen's instructions. In the first place, no provision was made for the solution of the central problem of forcing Rosas to withdraw his troops from Uruguay. Next, the agents were not told what means they should employ to secure the free navigation of the streams and the suggested pacification of the inter-river provinces. Certainly they would have to go beyond a mere blockade of Buenos Ayres. Did the British Minister intend that his forces should seek military assistance from the enemies of Rosas? Such an interpretation would not do violence to the spirit of the instructions, although no explicit statement was made to that effect. Aberdeen was mistaken if he thought that the European naval forces could accomplish the objectives mentioned by striking an imposing attitude.

The instructions which Guizot prepared for his agent, Baron Deffaudis, reveal the strong desire of the French Government to avoid giving offense to any South American party. Deffaudis was directed to explain, during his stop at Rio de Janeiro, that France and England had decided to assume the full responsibility of the enterprise not from interested motives, but in order to avoid embroiling two neighboring states.[63] Rosas was to be approached, not with an ultimatum, but with a reminder of the honest efforts of the French Government to observe a strict neutrality at Montevideo. The Dictator should be assured, wrote Guizot, that France had no intention to begin again a quarrel which had been happily terminated in 1840. The dignity of the Argentine state would be respected in every particular, except as the European powers were bound to protect the independence of Uruguay. Their efforts to secure the release of the French nationals from the Foreign Legion would continue as before. Under these conditions, it was probable, thought Guizot, that Rosas would agree voluntarily to recall Oribe. In that event, he cautioned that Deffaudis must be ready to oppose the unwarranted pretentions of the Montevidean party, and to insist that the Argentine Unitarians be

[63] The instructions to the French agent at Rio also authorized the most friendly representations. *Aff. Etr., Brésil* 23, p. 266. To Mr. Ney, May 1, 1845.

expelled from Uruguay. The instructions continued as follows:

"You will declare that the two great powers have not intervened to satisfy local hatred, the rivalries of the émigrés [*sic*], but rather for the purposes of establishing peace on some solid bases . . .; you will say proudly but firmly that, far from taking the part of one or the other of the two Republics, the two Cabinets are determined to guarantee the security of each of them for the future, that of Buenos Ayres as much as Montevideo." [64]

Guizot authorized no coercive measures beyond the establishment of a blockade in the Plata and the seizure of Martín García. The objective of free river navigation was to be pursued only in case it should arise apart from compulsion and after the other difficulties had been settled. But much of Guizot's studied moderation was nullified by the final order that Deffaudis was to act in absolute accord with Mr. Ouseley. [65]

In order to make doubly sure, however, that Rosas would not misunderstand the friendly disposition of France, the Paris Government took another precaution. At the request of Mackau, a special agent was sent several weeks in advance of Deffaudis, bearing private and confidential assurances to Rosas. The messenger was Captain Page, Mackau's own assistant in 1840, and therefore personally known to the Dictator. [66] Guizot was pleased with the idea. He wrote Mackau on March 4:

"No one is more fitted to explain our true intentions there. . . . We have not had, nay, not for a moment, the least idea of impairing his [Rosas'] rights or power, nor of interfering in the internal affairs of the country. . . . Let M. Page not fail to remove every doubt which he [Rosas] may have in this respect; he will be the faithful interpreter of our policy, and will render a service . . . to President Rosas himself." [67]

[64] *Aff. Etr.*, Buenos Ayres, 34, p. 28 ff. To Deffaudis, Mar. 22, 1845. Deffaudis had been the French agent to Mexico in 1838-39.
[65] *Ibid.*
[66] *Aff. Etr.*, Buenos Ayres, 33, p. 118. Guizot to Mareuil, Mar. 1, 1845.
[67] S. D. Brazil, Desp. 14, *Colección de documentos oficiales, Archivo Americano.* (Buenos Ayres 1845) p. 80. It is clear that this was not calculated to help Mr. Ouseley. The British agent was made very suspicious of Page; Mareuil was offended. F. O. 6, 103, O. to A., May 25, 1845; Pelliza, *Historia argentina*, 2, pp. 298-301.

It is difficult to understand why two governments should embark upon a joint enterprise of the magnitude of the Plata intervention without a more definite understanding than that which existed at this time between Guizot and Aberdeen. About the only point on which they were agreed was the fact that a brilliant success in the endeavor would be of great assistance to them in their general policies.[68] Aberdeen was setting out to assert in Argentina, as he had recently done in China, the sacred British dogma of the divine right to trade. Guizot, on the other hand, entertained only fears and misgivings over entangling himself in Argentine affairs. Yet the French Government needed every possible resource to enable it to defend its foreign policy before the Chambers. Even with the new British slave-trade treaty[69] and the Plata expedition to aid him, Guizot had great difficulty in doing so. In June, 1845, he was obliged to take refuge behind the principle of the balance-of-power in America in order to avoid the charge of subservience to England on the Texas question.[70]

The actions of Mr. Ouseley, during his short stay at Rio de Janeiro in April, 1845, augured nothing of good for the success of the joint intervention. He found that a favorable decision had not been made in regard to the British treaties. The haughty manner in which he held aloof from the Brazilian Government increased the estrangement developing between them. At the same time, Ouseley was most unwisely intimate with General Guido, the Argentine agent, to whom he entirely

[68] Parker, *op. cit.*, 4, pp. 398-402. *Aff. Etr.*, Buenos Ayres, 34, pp. 278-280. Jarnac, from London, to Guizot, Oct. 9, 1845. Peña y Reyes, *op. cit.*, pp. 49-51. Murphy from London, Nov. 1, 1845.

[69] Hall, *op. cit.*, p. 334. *Niles National Register*, 69, pp. 301; 68, 389, July 12, 1845.

[70] *Le Moniteur Universel*, June 11, 1845. *Niles Register*, 68, p. 389, July 12, 1845. The principle here stated could have had no intelligible application to the Argentine affair, and Guizot, of course, needed no such make-shift principle as this on which to justify his South American policy. It is hardly probable that Guizot really entertained any hostile intentions toward the United States, although the *London Times* was making a strong bid for French support because of "the dangers which threaten Europe from the indefinite expansion of the United States." See *Niles Register*, June 14, 1845.

misrepresented the nature of the joint effort of the two European powers. Guido wrote to Rosas on April 15, that from what the British agent told him, England's consent to co-operate in the mediation had apparently been secured by pressure from the Paris authorities. For the latter government, he said, the action was a "game calculated to hush the opposition in the Chambers, . . . and prolong by this measure the existence of the Cabinet." It was evident, continued Guido, that Ouseley distrusted the colonial designs of the French. England would therefore prefer a direct settlement with Buenos Ayres, and stood ready to oppose the designs of either France or Brazil.[71] Rosas would not be slow to grasp the possibilities of this situation.

The exclusion of Brazil from the intervention undoubtedly produced a slackening up of the general war preparations against Rosas which had been going on in the interior states. Foreign Minister França of Brazil was greatly embarrassed over the outcome of the Abrantes mission. To General Guido he was obliged to perjure himself in regard to it, and the month of June, 1845, saw him displaced by a Minister more friendly to Argentina.[72] The enmity between Brazil and England was greatly intensified during the year on account of the outrageous Aberdeen slave-trade bill of August 8, 1845.[73] Any co-opera-

[71] *Colección de documentos oficiales, Archivo Americano,* (1845) pp. 7, 8-11. A letter from Moreno in London dated Feb. 21, strengthened this allegation of jealousy between the two powers. S. D. Argentine Republic, Desp. 5; Brazil, Desp. 14, and enclosures.

[72] F. O. 6, 103, Ouseley to Aberdeen from Rio de Janeiro, April 10, 1845; Palomeque, *op. cit.,* pp. 9-15; *Niles Register* 68, p. 389. For a thorough-going arraignment of the policy of Brazil, see Saldías, *op. cit.,* vol. 4, p. 322 ff. Brazil had been overjoyed with the earlier reports of the success of Abrantes. *Aff. Etr., Brésil* 23, pp. 39-40. Jan. 13, 1845. S. D. Brazil, Desp. 14, Wise to Buchanan, June 30, 1845. *National Intelligencer,* Oct. 2, 1845.

[73] The Aberdeen Bill (8th and 9th Victoria, cap. 122) gave to British Admiralty Courts the authority to adjudicate Brazilian vessels taken in the slave trade by British cruisers. It amounted to a unilateral assertion of the right of search, and an interpretation of one Article of the treaty of 1826 as equivalent to defining the slave trade as piracy under International Law. See Jane Adams, *op. cit., Journal of Negro History 10,* p. 618 ff. The British duty on foreign free-labor refined sugar, for instance, was reduced to 28s. per cwt., as against 104s for that on slave-labor sugar; the former was further decreased in 1846, until the fall of Peel's Ministry brought a change of policy. W. Page, *Commerce and Industry,* pp. 156,

tion on the part of these two countries subsequent to this measure was out of the question.

In the meantime, affairs at Montevideo had reached a crisis. Rosas had attempted to force the matter to an issue by announcing in January, 1845, that all communication would be prohibited with Montevideo and Maldonado after February 20.[74] So accustomed were the European commanders to oppose the measures of Rosas, that they replied that the application of the blockade to British and French vessels would be suspended until they decided whether such a measure could be permitted. The British commander, Commodore Pasley, later made his claim to exemption conditional on the rejection of the measure by the French Admiral, Lainé.[75]

By the end of March, the French Chargé at Buenos Ayres finally decided that Rosas was under no obligation to refrain from altering the partial blockade which had been agreed upon two years before. He informed Arana accordingly, on March 27, that the new blockade would be acknowledged by the French forces.[76] But when the Buenos Ayres authorities served notice, two weeks later, of their purpose to execute the orders of the previous January, the European admirals declared that the matter would have to be deferred until April 30, in order to allow their nationals time to leave Montevideo. The commanders also reserved their right to communicate freely with Montevideo or other ports of Uruguay whenever it served their purpose to do so. Lainé announced that he would freely receive on his vessels "all who should claim the protection of the French flag." [77]

---

162. Moore, *op. cit.*, 6, p. 408. The decision in the Antelope Case (10 Wheaton, 66) in 1825 would give this Aberdeen bill no legal justification in International Law.

[74] S. D. Argentine Republic, Desp. 5, Arana to Mr. Brent, Jan 11, 1845. Enclosure of Brent, July 29, 30, 1845.

[75] S. D. Arg. Rep., Desp. 6. Brent to Buchanan, July 29, 30, Sept. 23, 1845. Mandeville argued powerfully for recognizing it. On Feb. 13, Rosas declared all communication between Buenos Ayres and Montevideo closed after Mar. 1. Pasley's action was approved, F. O. 6, 100, Aberdeen to Mandeville, May 27, 1845.

[76] *Colección de documentos, op. cit.*, p. 38. S. D. Brazil, Desp. 14. Mareuil to Arana, Mar. 27, 1845.

[77] *Ibid.*, pp. 39, 51-52.

The cause of Montevideo seemed hopelessly lost. Rivera's army had just been completely crushed in the battle of *India Muerte*, on March 27. That leader himself and those of his followers who had not deserted to Oribe suffered detention by the Brazilian officials in Rio Grande, where the prolonged rebellion had finally been put down.[78] Oribe's control of Uruguay outside of the two port cities was unchallenged. He had now 6,000 Orientals under his command, along with his 8,000 Argentine troops. Of the 3500 men defending Montevideo, perhaps less than 400 were natives of Uruguay.[79] The United States Chargé at Buenos Ayres, Mr. Brent, tried to assist Rosas by offering to mediate, on April 11, on the basis of the surrender of Montevideo to Oribe without violence or bloodshed. Rosas immediately accepted the proposal, but the news of the imminent arrival of the new British Commissioner caused the matter to be postponed.[80]

Mr. Ouseley reached Montevideo on April 27, just three days before the rigorous blockade was to have become effective. The coincidence seems hardly accidental. He immediately became alarmed, and ordered that steps be taken to prevent an attack upon the city. He wrote Mandeville that "Montevideo must not be taken." [81] On May 10, the British Commissioner submitted a memorandum to Arana, in which the arrogant threats of Lord Aberdeen lost nothing of their sting. Rosas was peremptorily summoned, on penalty of coercive measures which would seriously injure his moral and political power, to desist in his attempt to displace the regularly elected Government of Montevideo.[82] The very wording of this demand of Ouseley

---

[78] *La Gaceta Mercantil*, April 8, 1845. See Zinny, *op. cit.*, 3, p. 84. *National Intelligencer*, May 24, 1845. Durand, *op. cit.*, pp. 140-144.

[79] S. D. Argentine Republic, Desp. 5, Brent to Buchanan, July 30, 1845; *Aff. Etr.*, Buenos Ayres, 34, p. 97. Page to the Ministry, June 24, 1845. Brent said 211 were Orientals; Page said 420; there were also 600 armed negro freedmen in the city.

[80] S. D. Argentine Rep., Desp. 5, Brent to Buchanan, Aug. 2, 1845. This move of Brent was not authorized in his instructions, but was apparently made in good faith.

[81] F. O. 6, 103, O. to A., April 27, 1845. From off Montevideo.

[82] F. O. 6, 103, O. to A., May 21, 1845. *National Intelligencer*, Jan. 1, 1846.

was ill-advised, because there had been no regular election in Uruguay since the retirement of Rivera.

The first angry reaction of the Buenos Ayres Government to this summons quickly gave way to a more tactful policy. On May 24, Rosas submitted a number of counter-proposals. Argentina would repudiate, in the first place, he said, all right to interfere in the domestic affairs of Uruguay on the same grounds that would lead her to resist vigorously any foreign intervention. Second, his troops would return when Oribe, as legal President of the Oriental Republic, declared that he no longer required their services. But Rosas added that the recognition of the blockade of Montevideo without delay "must be the first step in any negotiation." A final statement of the Dictator declared that the mediation of Brent, which had already been accepted, must take precedence over the proceedings of Ouseley.[83]

These terms were, of course, unacceptable to the British agent. The intrusiveness of Brent was particularly irritating to him. Ouseley had already been annoyed by the sending of similar notes from the legations of Portugal, Bolivia, and the United States, requesting that he attend a conference and furnish explanations concerning the activities of the British cruisers at Montevideo.[84] Ouseley forwarded a vigorous complaint to London against the attitude displayed by the North American agent. He said in part:

"The fact is that Mr. Brent, young in diplomacy, although of advanced age,—anxious to render himself conspicuous in this his first diplomatic appointment, and ambitious of placing the United States before the world as exclusively the Champion of all America, and especially of these Republics,—is a ready tool in the hands of General Rosas. The Governor, working on his senile vanity, and flattering his personal and strong National prejudices and hostility to England, causes him to write Notes, call diplomatic meetings, make Protests, etc., just as His Excellency pleases." [85]

[83] F. O. 6, 103, O. to A., June 20, and enclosures.
[84] F. O. 6, 103, O. to A., May 29, and enclosures; S. D. Arg. Rep., Desp. 5, *Archivo Americano, op. cit.*, (1845), pp. 53-56. These requests were repeatedly renewed, and as many times refused.
[85] F. O. 6, 103, O. to A., May 21, 1845.

Ouseley transmitted his refusal of the Argentine terms to Rosas on May 28, just one day before Deffaudis arrived at Montevideo.[86] The French agents as yet had taken no part in the negotiation.

The shrewd policy which Rosas now adopted in order to drive a wedge between England and France is illustrative of his unscrupulous political tactics. In spite of the contrast between the previous neutrality of the French agents at Montevideo and the bitterly maligned policy of Purvis, and notwithstanding the variation between the present hostile ultimatum of Ouseley and the extremely amicable representations of Capt. Page, Rosas deliberately set himself to court the friendship of the British and to blacken the character and purposes of France. On the same day that Arana had sent his unacceptable terms to Ouseley, May 24, the following paragraph appeared in the *British Packet* of Buenos Ayres, purporting to express the sentiments of the British community:

"Let the foreigners who sustain that phantom of a government which holds a precarious sway only within the wall of the beleagured town of Montevideo be at once undeceived,—let them know that England neither winks at French colonization nor countenances Brazilian ambition, and all the monstrous system of iniquity by which the war has been so long prolonged will immediately give place to the restoration of legal order and general tranquillity on both banks of La Plata. Honor, justice, humanity demand it with no less urgency than the interest of our country, to win back the forfeited affections of a people once so warmly attached to everything that was British." [87]

By means of such misrepresentation, any subsequent action of the French squadron at Montevideo could be stigmatized to the British residents in Argentina as an attempt to create a French colony in Uruguay. Ouseley's interference and his arrogant memorandum would be connived at by Rosas. Perhaps the British Commissioner himself might be won over to

[86] F. O. 6, 103, O. to A., June 20, 1845; *Archivo Americano,* 1845, pp. 67-71. The *Archivo* contains an account of a secret Conference on June 2, at which Ouseley accepted these terms of Arana; but this story cannot be corroborated at London or at Washington. One suspects that it was a forgery of Rosas, and a part of his disreputable scheme of casting all the blame for the intervention on the French.

[87] S. D. Arg. Rep., Desp. 5. Enclosure of Brent, July 1, 1845.

the point of view of his own nationals.[88] The truly conciliatory
policy of the French Government had no chance to vindicate
itself in such a situation. Capt. Page departed from Buenos
Ayres at the end of July, thoroughly disgusted at what he
called the chicanery, bad faith, and calumny of which France
had been made the victim by the Argentine Government.[89]

Immediately upon his arrival at Montevideo, Deffaudis became alarmed, as had Ouseley, over the probability of an early
capitulation of the city. At the suggestion of the British Commissioner, they issued identical orders to their naval commanders to take whatever precautions might be necessary to
forestall an attack.[90] Deffaudis entertained not a little resentment because of the previous actions of his British associate, but an adjustment between them was finally made.[91]
They were perfectly agreed, however, in rejecting the terms
proposed by Rosas. Brent's mediation, they declared, could
not be admitted, nor could the recognition of the blockade of
Montevideo be allowed as a preliminary to the negotiation.
They demanded, instead, an immediate armistice, during which
even the partial blockade of the Uruguayan capital should be
suspended. To refuse this, they asserted, would amount to the
rejection of all their overtures.[92]

The attempted mediation immediately ran aground.[93] A
memorandum written by Ouseley in early July, but not immediately sent to London, recorded his not over-optimistic view
of the situation. The commerce of Montevideo would be of little benefit to British trade, he mused, without communication
with the country behind the city. It could never balance the
loss which would be occasioned by a blockade of Buenos Ayres.
He continued as follows:

[88] Brossard, op. cit., pp. 460-462.
[89] Pelliza, op. cit., 2, pp. 298-301. See Brossard, op. cit., pp. 328-338,
Page to Lainé, July 30, 1845. Durand, op. cit., p. 150.
[90] F. O. 6, 103, O. to A., June 28, 1845. National Intelligencer, Sept.
24, 1845. They threatened to sink Brown's fleet if he attacked the city.
[91] F. O. 6, 103, O. to A., June 20, 1845.
[92] Ibid., June 28, 1845. S. D. Arg. Rep., Desp. 5, Brent to Buchanan,
Aug. 2, 1845.
[93] For a good Argentine account of these negotiations, see Saldías, op.
cit., vol. 4, chap. 54, p. 174 ff.

"The only material advantage, therefore, to be gained by hostilities will be the opening of the Rivers to our Commerce. . . . As to the end, ostensibly in view, vizt., inducing Governor Rosas to yield the objects of the negotiation, I look upon it that if once he decides on resistance, it will be hopeless to attempt to force him by means of a Blockade."

The French agent had refused to reinstate Oribe at Montevideo, he continued, on condition that Rosas acknowledge the independence of Uruguay. The bitterness felt by the parties within the city, as well as the terms of their own instructions forbade such a move.[94] They had therefore no alternative, Ouseley concluded, but to proceed to coercive measures. They could open the rivers to Paraguay, perhaps to Bolivia, furnish aid to General Paz, and encourage the detachment of Corrientes and Entre Rios from the Confederation. Preparations would begin immediately, but actual operations should be delayed until perhaps the end of August, it being impossible for Paz to act during the rainy season.[95]

The Commissioners issued a public statement on July 8 that "no election or reinstallation of General Oribe in the presence of Argentine Forces could be admitted as legal or [be] recognized by their respective Governments." [96]

A break was precipitated earlier than the agents had planned. A despatch from London approving the postponement of the Montevidean blockade in the previous January reached Ouseley on July 19. He immediately closed the conversations with Arana on that question.[97] The Argentine Minister insisted in vain that Pasley's decision had been expressly conditioned on the action of Lainé, and that the French Admiral had later agreed to recognize the blockade.[98] Preparations

[94] F. O. 6, 104. A memorandum of Ouseley dated July 5, 1845. Deffaudis said he would "cut off his right hand" before he would admit Oribe into Montevideo.

[95] Ibid. Another despatch to Aberdeen, on the same date, charges that Page was bribed by Rosas to delay hostilities under express orders from his king. Ouseley was still bitter against Brent for his opposition.

[96] Archivo Americano, 1845, pp. 56-65.

[97] F. O. 6, 104, O. to A., July 20, 1845. F. O. 6, 100, Aberdeen to Mandeville, April 21, 1845.

[98] Archivo Americano, op. cit., pp. 62-63. On July 14, 1845, Peel announced that this very blockade had been assented to by Britain. Parliamentary Debates, 3rd series, 82, pp. 476-477.

on the part of Oribe were at once begun for an attack on Montevideo. The Allied agents sent an ultimatum to Rosas on the 21st, allowing the Governor ten days to withdraw his troops from Uruguay. They also informed Oribe that all of his ports would be blockaded if his attacking preparations were not discontinued. Brown's fleet was detained at Montevideo because he refused to discharge the French and British nationals from his crew.[99]

Several efforts to avoid the break were futile. Deffaudis made one conciliatory move by securing a promise from Montevideo to disarm all Frenchmen, if the Argentine troops, officers, and artillery should be withdrawn from Uruguay. Mr. Brent eliminated another cause of friction by withdrawing his own mediatory offer.[100] But the matter had gone too far. Rosas rejected the European ultimatum, and Oribe defied the threats of the Europeans. Rosas also took advantage of the numerous visits of Ouseley with Manuelita by attempting to dissuade the British agent from co-operating with the French forces in the coercive measures. The European Commissioners received their passports on July 30, and departed from Buenos Ayres.

But friendly relations were, technically speaking, not broken. The old diplomatic agents, Mareuil for the French and Ball for the British, still remained at Buenos Ayres.[101] The interventionist forces contented themselves, for the time being, with blockading the Oriental ports held by Oribe. They announced that they would safeguard the independence of Uruguay until the Argentine troops had been withdrawn.[102]

The European agents fully realized that they faced a difficult task. Ouseley wrote to Aberdeen that nothing could be

[99] *Archivo Americano,* 1845, p. 98 ff. F. O. 6, 104, Ouseley to Aberdeen, August 2. S. D. Arg. Rep., Desp. 5, Brent to Buchanan, Nov. 14, 1845.
[100] F. O. 6, 104, O. to A., July 26. S. D. Arg. Rep., Desp. 5, Brent to Buchanan, Aug. 2, 1845.
[101] F. O. 6, 104, O. to A., Aug. 2, 1845.
[102] S. D. Arg. Rep., Desp. 5, Brent to Buchanan, Nov. 14, 1845 and enclosures. F. O. 6, 104, O. to A., Aug. 5, and enclosures. The government which Oribe had set up at Buceo with a representative Assembly and the custom house was, of course, completely ignored. See S. D. Arg. Rep., Desp. 5, Brent to Buchanan, Nov. 14, 1845. Brown's fleet was captured.

more "fatally erroneous" than the idea that a mere demonstration of force, accompanied by diplomatic pronouncements would be sufficient to coerce the Dictator. The exclusion of Brazil from the intervention had been a sad mistake, he said. Paris and London must each send one thousand troops at once, together with a number of small vessels capable of navigating the shallow portions of the river.[103] Meanwhile the agents managed to fit out, at considerable expense, a score of small vessels to aid them in the blockade and in the capture of Martín García. But such measures, of course, left the situation in Uruguay entirely unchanged.[104]

It was with considerable reluctance that the agents finally proceeded to the extreme measure of blockading Buenos Ayres. The many British and French nationals living at the Argentine capital were unanimously opposed to that measure.[105] It could not be decisive against Rosas and would only ruin their trade. But the blockade was the only device by which pressure could be brought to bear by the European forces. It would also serve to relieve the desperate financial situation of the government at Montevideo by forcing all Plata commerce to pay duties at the city.[106] The expedition up the Paraná river, which they were planning for the purpose of making connections with the enemies of Rosas, would also provide an outlet for goods accumulating at Montevideo. The Commissioners had already agreed upon the tentative recognition of Paraguay, when they announced, on September 22, the strict blockade of the port of Buenos Ayres.[107]

The blockade of the Argentine capital enabled Rosas greatly to strengthen his local position. The trading community

[103] F. O. 6, 104, O. to A., Aug. 9, 13, 16, 1845.
[104] F. O. 6, 104, O. to A., Aug. 30. Ouseley spent £1500 for equipping ten vessels. Garibaldi commanded this Montevidean fleet. F. O. 6, 105, O. to A., Sept. 2 and 3; Vedia, op. cit., pp. 130-131; Pereyra, op. cit., pp. 173-174; Durand, op. cit., pp. 153-156.
[105] F. O. 6, 104, O. to A., Aug. 27. National Intelligencer, Oct. 6, 1845. Niles Register, 69, p. 83 records that a petition signed by 15,000 British and French residents in the Plata urged a cessation of interference.
[106] Durand, op. cit., p. 163. The customs receipts rose from 12,000 piastres per month to 30,000 in September, 1845 and to 75,000 in January, 1846.
[107] F. O. 6, 105, O. to A., Sept. 9, 1845; Nov. 26 and enclosure, Ouseley to Lopez, Sept. 23. Ibid., 114, A. to O., June 25, 1846, disapproving of this offer.

heartily supported him. He secured and published various statements from the diplomatic representatives of the United States, Portugal, Bolivia, and even France, testifying to his protection of foreigners.[108] Upon the departure of Chargé Mareuil in October, Rosas persuaded the French agent to transmit a proposal of peace to the Commissioners.[109] The terms of this treaty provided that Oribe should be installed at Montevideo with full powers as President of Uruguay. As such, he should authorize the return of his Argentine troops as soon as the Europeans should withdraw. Martín García and all captured vessels should be returned, and the claims advanced by Argentina for the illegal interruption of her blockade of Montevideo should be arbitrated. Finally, France and England should explicitly renounce, without affecting the treaty of 1828, all right to interfere in the Plata and all pretense that they were guarantors of the sovereignties of the two Republics. The proposed treaty would have to be approved by Oribe.[110]

By the Mareuil treaty, Rosas cleverly shifted his quarrel with the Europeans to ground of his own choosing. He could now pose before the people as defending the principle of the exemption of America from the interference of Europe. The Commissioners were almost beside themselves with anger toward Mareuil. They could do nothing but reject the treaty, since they were already committed by their July ultimatum to demand the withdrawal of the Argentine troops before they would negotiate.[111]

The atmosphere in which Ouseley and Deffaudis found themselves at Montevideo greatly increased their hostility toward Rosas. They had become convinced by the middle of October

[108] *Correspondencia con los Ministros de Inglaterra y de Francia, Archivo Americano.* (Buenos Ayres 1846) pp. 1-41. Brent gratuitously volunteered counter-charges concerning British scalp buying and the massacre of the River Raisin.

[109] F. O. 6, 105, O. to A., Sept. 23, 1845; *National Intelligencer,* Dec. 12, 1845. Rosas tried in vain to bribe Garibaldi to betray Montevideo. Mareuil departed from Buenos Ayres because he said that the blockade brought about a state of war. *Aff. Etr.,* Buenos Ayres, 33, p. 366.

[110] F. O. 6, 106, Mareuil's treaty, Oct. 26, 1845.

[111] *Aff. Etr.,* Buenos Ayres, 34, pp. 320-328, Nov. 10, 1845. Calvo, *Le Droit International,* 1, pp. 233-234.

that there was no hope of a return of peace or prosperity to the Plata until the Dictator had been overthrown. Ouseley began to urge Aberdeen to declare war on Argentina. No step short of that, he insisted, would be sufficient to overcome the paralyzing scepticism of the enemies of the Dictator in regard to European assistance, the latter having already failed them in 1840 and in 1843.[112] The Commissioners received, later in the same month, the unexpected assistance of a portion of the 45th regiment of British infantry, which had been diverted to the Plata from its South African destination on the responsibility of the British Minister at Rio de Janeiro. Its arrival at Montevideo produced an excellent effect, and Ouseley urged that additional forces might be sent.[113]

The home governments were informed, for the first time, concerning the intended Paraná expedition in a letter of October 12. A distant diversion, the Commissioners argued, was the only possible way by which they could hope to secure the recall of the Argentine troops "by Naval means alone." It was their hope that General Paz might supply the military assistance which they lacked from Brazil. The move would at least open up an avenue of communication to Paraguay, and provide access to the products and the markets of the interior.[114] In late October, the interventionists were greatly encouraged by the news that Corrientes and Paraguay were about to conclude a military alliance against Rosas. Ouseley immediately urged the London government to recognize the independence of these two states. He said:

"The recognition of Paraguay, together with that possibly of Corrientes and Entre Rios, and their erection into different independent states would secure the navigation of the Paraná and Paraguay. The difficulty of insisting on a free navigation, which we

[112] F. O. 6, 105, O. to A., Oct. 18, 1845.
[113] F. O. 6, 105, O. to A., Oct. 25, 27, 29; vol. 106, ibid., Nov. 25, 1845. The Commissioners were obliged to guarantee the faithful administration of the Montevidean customs for 1848 in a cash sale of ¼ of them to a private company. See F. O. 6, 106, O. to A., Nov. 26, 1845 and Dec. 27, 1845. Parliamentary Papers, Accounts and Papers, 1849, xxxii (110). These 650 troops were followed by an equal number in December and January.
[114] F. O. 6, 105, O. to A., Oct. 12, 1845; ibid., 106, Nov. 26, enclosures 1 and 3.

ourselves deny in the case of the St. Lawrence, might thus be obviated."[115]

Meanwhile, no letters had reached the Commissioners which would interfere in the least with the contemplated program. Guizot's instructions of October 8 approved the early resistance to Oribe and the defense of Montevideo.[116] Never were the Foreign Ministers more concerned that their joint undertaking should succeed than in the early autumn of 1845. Their directions urged harmony of action and the faithful execution of the original instructions.[117] Not until November did Aberdeen begin to insist that his agent should observe a strict neutrality between the native factions within Uruguay. Oribe's rights as an Oriental citizen should be respected, he said, provided always that he was unsupported by Argentine forces.[118]

The Paraná expedition did not get under way until November 17. The delay had given Rosas ample time to prepare a rather formidable reception for the invading fleet along the bluffs which line the right bank of the river as it turns northward about a hundred miles from the mouth. The combined squadron of some twelve or fifteen vessels [119] arrived on the third day before a fortified promontory by the name of *Obligado*. It was armed with four batteries placed so as to defend a line of twenty-four vessels chained together to block the passage of the river. A sharp fight ensued. It was only after a cannonade of seven hours duration, which was accompanied by several rather daring exploits on the part of the European forces, that the chain was cut and the shore batteries silenced. The battle cost the invading forces not a few lives and considerable

[115] F. O. 6, 105, O. to A., Oct. 27, 30, 31, 1845. The Alliance was concluded at Asunción, Nov. 11, 1845. *British Foreign and State Papers,* 35, 293-295.

[116] *Aff. Etr.,* Buenos Ayres, 34, p. 277. To Deffaudis, Oct. 8, 1844.

[117] The *British Foreign and State Papers* for this year present a staunch defense of coercive measures, and bitterly attack Oribe and Rosas. Vol. 34, p. 1265 ff.

[118] *Aff. Etr.,* Buenos Ayres, 34, p. 308. To Deffaudis Oct. 31, 1845. F. O. 6, 102, to Ouseley, Oct. 8, Nov. 5, 1845.

[119] The number is variously reported from 11 vessels to as high as 7 steamers plus 15 men-of-war. See the *National Intelligencer,* Aug. 31, 1845. W. Hadfield, *Brazil, the River Plate, and the Falkland Islands.* (London 1854) p. 277.

damage to their vessels. After a short delay, the expedition proceeded on its way, serving now as an escort for a vast fleet of more than one hundred merchantmen of every flag, which had been collecting for some time at Montevideo.[120] No further resistance was encountered. The commanders operated under instructions to avoid all engagements unless an attempt were made to cross the river.[121]

The attitude which the invaders encountered in the inter-river Provinces was very disappointing to them. Governor Madariaga of Corrientes seemed friendly enough; but the people everywhere were very suspicious of the foreigners.[122] General Paz's small force was facing the alarming prospect of an attack from Entre Rios by an army under General Urquiza, formerly a lieutenant of Echagüe. The crisis was, in fact, very serious. Much depended upon what Paraguay would do. Captain Hotham, the British leader, who carried an important letter from Ouseley to President Lopez, pushed on with all speed to Asunción by the aid of a small steamer. He reached the city in the middle of January, 1846.[123]

Hotham lost no time in presenting his credentials to Lopez. He invited the Asunción Government to make treaty overtures to the allied agents, on the basis of an assurance that they had recommended to the authorities at Paris and London the establishment of closer relations with Paraguay.[124] The task of treating with Lopez was undoubtedly made more difficult, because of other influences operating at Asunción, notably the pressure exerted by the resident Brazilian agent, and the promises held out to the President by a representative of the United States, who had left the city only a fortnight before Hotham's arrival. These factors will be considered in a later connection. All the exchanges that passed between the British Cap-

[120] Brossard, op. cit., pp. 156-162. 150 men were killed and three vessels seriously damaged at Obligado. Durand, op. cit., pp. 156-162.

[121] Aff. Etr., Buenos Ayres, 36, pp. 65, 202-203. National Intelligencer, Aug. 31, 1846.

[122] L. B. Mackinnon, Steam Warfare in the Paraná. 2 vols. (London 1848) vol. 1. This account is not wholly trustworthy, however.

[123] F. O. 6, 118, O. to A., May 17, 1846.

[124] Ibid., 106, Nov. 26, 1846. Enclosure no. 3, Ouseley to Lopez, Sept. 23, 1845.

tain and Lopez are not revealed. In the end, the Paraguayan
President made the following preliminary demands which, he
said, would have to be met before he would consider the conclusion of the desired treaties:

> "1st. The acknowledgment of the independence of Paraguay.
> 2nd. The free navigation of the rivers Paraná and Paraguay
> for all nations.
> 3d. That Great Britain, in securing the freedom and inde-
> pendence of the Banda Oriental from the dominion of
> Rosas, should include Paraguay."

Hotham, of course, had no authority to grant these conditions. He could do no more than arrange several treaties in
a tentative form, and urge Lopez to send agents to treat with
the Commissioners at Montevideo. The Captain assured Ouseley, in an advance letter, that the moment was remarkably opportune for securing an alliance with Paraguay.[125]

The two agents whom Lopez later sent to Montevideo accomplished nothing. The Europeans had difficulty in treating with
the men, and soon came to distrust them. The Commissioners,
nevertheless, did go as far as to announce their recognition
of Paraguay, *ad referendum*, in early March, 1846.[126] For
reasons that will be more apparent later, Paraguay failed to
come to the aid of General Paz. The Unitarian resistance in
Corrientes disintegrated before the advance of Urquiza. Paz
himself was obliged to find refuge in Paraguay, never again to
be an important factor in Argentine affairs.[127]

The river expedition contributed nothing toward realizing
the purposes of the intervention.[128] The effort was also a dis-
mal failure from a commercial standpoint, many of the vessels
returning with their entire cargoes.[129] The most important

---

[125] F. O. 6, 118, O. to A., May 17, 1846. Enclosed are reports of Capt.
Hotham, dated January 15 and 31. Another letter of Feb. 4, gave an
extended review of the commercial opportunities of Paraguay. The religious freedom clause in one treaty was to be nullified by a secret article.
[126] F. O. 6, 115, O. to A., Mar. 4 and 10, 1846. Lopez to Ouseley, Jan.
22, 1846.
[127] *National Intelligencer*, June 24, 1846. News from Montevideo.
[128] It did win some glory for the participants. Hotham was knighted for
his services in this expedition. See Wilfred Latham, *The States of the
River Plate*. (London 1856 and 1868), p. 266. Ouseley was later rewarded
with the same honor, in 1853. Hadfield, *op. cit.*, pp. 241-2.
[129] *National Intelligencer*, July 17, 1846. From Montevideo, news to
May 20. S. D. Arg. Rep., Desp. 5, Brent to Buchanan, Jan. 16, 1846.

consequence was that it aroused the national patriotism of the Argentine people to an unprecedentedly high pitch. All parties united in opposing the foreigners who were trying to dismember their country. Rosas had even been able to secure the assistance of a number of British volunteers, who had manned his most effective battery at *Obligado*.[130] Concerning the popular feeling, Brent wrote as follows, in January, 1846:

"I am thoroughly persuaded that at no foregoing period of the history of these countries has the spirit of patriotism been so generally aroused, and internal divisions so much allayed and destroyed." [131]

It was not possible to get the caravan started back down the river until April. The progress of so many vessels was necessarily slow. After being held up for several days at the fortified heights, the squadron ran past them in safety, and arrived finally at Montevideo on June 14, 1846.[132] By this time both European governments were ready to withdraw from the affair. They had in fact already embarked upon that series of negotiations which were to continue for four years. Their struggle with Rosas had just begun. Concerning the later phases of this episode, an eye-witness has left the following testimony:

"There is not in the history of the intercourse of nations, nor in the annals of diplomacy, any parallel to the ever-varying phases and extraordinary character of this Anglo-French intervention." [133]

Before proceeding with the discussion of the attempts of Paris and London to extricate themselves from their unfortunate entanglements, we must digress to consider the rôle which the South American agents of the United States and the government at Washington had played in the intervention.

[130] F. O. 6, 107, O. to A., Dec. 27, 1845. These British volunteers repudiated the charge that they were traitors, on the ground that war had not been declared by England.

[131] S. D. Arg. Rep., Desp. 5, Brent to Buchanan, Jan. 16, 1846. *Archivo Americano*, III, Nov. 30, 1845, p. 67. Paraguay alone was apathetic toward the foreign invasion.

[132] *National Intelligencer*, Aug. 31, 1846; Mackinnon, *op. cit.*, 1, p. 281 ff.; 2, pp. 1-25.

[133] S. D. Arg. Rep., Desp. 7, Harris to Clayton, April 10, 1850.

CHAPTER VI

THE POLICY OF THE UNITED STATES TOWARD THE INTERVENTION

The United States took very little interest in Argentine affairs for more than a decade after the unfortunate Falkland Island quarrel in 1832-33. The friendly mission of General Alvear to Washington, in 1838, ran aground on this question, and it continued for several years longer to be a barrier to diplomatic relations.[1] President Tyler was not sufficiently interested in Plata affairs in 1842 to take advantage of the offer of a commercial treaty with Uruguay.[2]

But the policy of aloofness on the part of the United States could not continue indefinitely. Numerous claims were calling for settlement, and the growth of North American commerce to the Plata[3] was attracting increasing attention to the tremendous potentialities of the region. The State Department became particularly concerned in 1843 over a change in the tonnage regulations at Buenos Ayres, which placed North American shipping at a disadvantage to that of the British.[4] The news of the assembling of a Congress of representatives

---

[1] S. D. Arg. Rep., Notes to Legation, 6. To Gen. Alvear, Oct. 10, 1838, Dec. 4, 1841. Sec. Webster asked that the matter be postponed pending the solution of the quarrel with Britain over possession of the Islands. F. O. 6, 64. Mandeville to Palmerston, June 4, 1838.

[2] Ellauri, J., *Correspondencia, etc.,* pp. 385-386. Cass to Ellauri, Dec. 16, 1841, Mar. 5, 1842.

[3] *Merchant's Magazine and Commercial Review,* 14, p. 367. La Plata trade was still only 16% of U. S.-South American trade, *ibid.,* 7, pp. 481-82. The figures show an increase from less than 1.5 millions in 1840 to 2.8 in 1841, and 3.5 in 1842. *Ibid.,* 12, pp. 567-568; 9, p. 90; 13, p. 202; 14, p. 367. Rice and breadstuffs went to Montevideo; hides and wool came from Buenos Ayres. This trade was practically unaffected by the Montevidean blockade. See S. D. Arg. Rep., Desp. 5, Watterson to Calhoun, Sept. 8, 1844.

[4] *Merchant's Magazine,* 13, p. 294. Foreign vessels were obliged to pay $4 per ton as against $3 for national vessels, to which latter group the British ships were assimilated by the treaty of 1825. S. D. Arg. Rep., Instr., 15, p. 3.

from the principal Latin-American states at Lima, Peru, early in 1843, where Mexican-United States relations were to be considered,[5] may also have made Washington more concerned about their prestige in South America.

Meanwhile, the development of European interference at Montevideo in 1842 caused Rosas to forget his quarrel with the United States. He made known, through North American naval officers, that he was not indisposed to the resumption of diplomatic relations.[6] Secretary of State Upshur, accordingly, despatched Mr. H. M. Watterson to Buenos Ayres as special agent, in September, 1843. Watterson was directed to gather information concerning the domestic and foreign affairs of the Confederation, and particularly any which might affect the interests of American citizens. He should work to secure the restoration of United States shipping to an equal status with that of England, and prepare the way for a general settlement of claims. His exertions might also be directed unofficially to the end that peace be restored, and he should take care to ascertain the scope and the objectives of the policies of England and France.[7] Watterson was almost overwhelmed by the cordiality and flattery with which he was received by Rosas. The Governor, he decided, was a real General Jackson of a fellow, a great man of the people, one of nature's noblemen. By April, 1844, he was glad to announce that the Argentine Government desired very much that diplomatic relations should be reëstablished.[8]

The opportunity was immediately taken advantage of by the State Department. Secretary Calhoun appointed Mr. Wm.

[5] *National Intelligencer,* May 8, July 1, Oct. 26, 1843; Feb. 3, 26, 1844. J. M. Callahan, "Statements . . . of the Monroe Doctrine . . . from 1845 to 1870." *Proceedings of the American Society of International Law,* 8, p. 60. (Washington 1914.) S. D. Venezuela, Desp. 2, no. 20. J. Q. Adams, *Memoirs,* 12 vols. (Philadelphia 1876) Vol. 11, p. 340. The Mexican representative was to take to Lima both French and Spanish translations of the U. S.-Mexican correspondence from May to Sept., 1842, and a recent speech of J. Q. Adams.

[6] N. D. Officers, Ships of War 32, Upshur to Com. Chas. Morris, Mar. 24, 1842. F. O. 6, 83, Mandeville to Aberdeen, Feb. 26, Apr. 23, 1842. N. D., Brazilian Squadron, to Com. Turner, Jan. 24, 1844.

[7] S. D. Arg. Rep., Instr. 15, pp. 1-5. To H. M. Watterson, Sept. 26, 1843.

[8] S. D. Arg. Rep., Desp. 5, from Watterson, April 27, 1844.

Brent, mentioned above, as *Chargé d'affaires* at Buenos Ayres. Brent was an elderly man of no previous diplomatic experience, a typical Democrat, with a strong animus toward everything British. His instructions were practically the same as those which Watterson had carried. Claims must be acknowledged; tonnage dues must be equalized; information should be secured concerning the reported change of policy toward foreigners on the part of Paraguay.[9] Mr. Brent departed for his post on August 13, 1844.[10]

While the new Chargé was *en route*, an incident occurred, in connection with the Argentine blockade of Montevideo, which threatened to wreck the promised restoration of diplomatic relations. One Captain Voorhees of the United States frigate "Congress" took offense in October, 1844, when a schooner associated with the blockading squadron carelessly but harmlessly fired a few musket shots into an American merchantman, during the pursuit of a blockade runner. In retaliation, Voorhees surprised and seized the entire Argentine squadron. He secured further satisfaction by liberating a number of captured fishing vessels and releasing several American citizens of the crews. The Captain promptly released the Argentine vessels after satisfactory explanations had been received, but he detained the offending schooner and its crew on a charge of piracy, because of the false use of the Uruguayan flag.[11]

The situation was very embarrassing for Watterson. He did his best to allay the popular excitement, and attempted to alleviate the indignation of the Argentine authorities by expressing his regrets, on October 11, 1844, over the rash action of the naval officer.[12] But the situation soon became

[9] S. D. Arg. Rep., Instr., Calhoun to Brent, July 15, 1844.

[10] *Niles National Register,* 66, p. 397.

[11] S. D. Arg. Rep., Desp. 5, Watterson to Calhoun, Oct. 11, 1844, and enclosures. The temper of Voorhees may be appreciated from the following explanation to the U. S. Minister at Rio: "There was no alternative between disgrace to myself, and the correction of the Argentine squadron. . . . These people are a set of sanguinary barbarians. . . . They fire away, no matter where, hit or miss, not caring if they kill a dozen of their neutral friends, so they kill one of their enemies." N. D. Brazilian Squadron, Com. Daniel Turner, April '44 to April '45, Voorhees to Wise, Nov. 1, 1844.

[12] S. D. Arg. Rep., Desp. 5, Watterson to Calhoun Oct. 11, and enclosures.

worse. Before orders could arrive from Commodore Turner, the commander of the Brazilian squadron, Voorhees announced that he would no longer permit the molestation of any North American vessel by the blockade, as long as the French and British were permitted to examine all vessels flying their flags.[13] The situation was not relieved until Turner arrived from Rio de Janeiro on October 28, bringing Brent with him. An apology was immediately presented to the Argentine Government, and the authority of the blockade was again acknowledged.[14] Turner did not, however, disapprove the capture of the schooner. It was finally returned on November 20, 1844, out of respect for the Argentine Government.[15] The promptness of this redress arranged matters so that Brent encountered no difficulty in getting his credentials accepted by Rosas on November 15.[16]

The authorities at Washington also made prompt amends for the ill-considered action of Voorhees.[17] The Captain was court-martialed and sentenced to a reprimand and suspension from the navy for three years. When the Secretary of State later notified the Argentine Minister at Washington of this action, he expressed the hope that it would demonstrate the disposition of the United States to "respect the rights of Buenos Ayres." [18]

The perennial failure of the Washington authorities to provide adequate instructions for their representatives in the Plata gave rise to a most unseemly quarrel between Brent and the successor of Voorhees in early 1845. The difference arose

[13] N. D. Brazilian Squadron, Com. Daniel Turner, 1844-45. On the 24th Voorhees declared the measure to be "no more than a paper blockade."
[14] *Ibid.* Turner to Adm. Toll, Nov. 3; same to Sec. Mason, Nov. 4, 1844.
[15] *Ibid.*, Turner to Capt. Baltierrs, Nov. 20, 1844.
[16] S. D. Arg. Rep., Desp. 5, Brent to Calhoun, Dec. 11, 1844, Jan. 15, 1845, with an enclosed copy of Rosas' annual message of Dec. 27, 1844.
[17] S. D. Arg. Rep., Instr. 15, pp. 12-14. Calhoun to Brent, Dec. 28, 1844.
[18] For Voorhees' extended defense, see the *National Intelligencer* for July 10, 1845. The same paper for Aug. 15, 1845, contains a statement by Secretary Bancroft. J. B. Moore, *The Works of James Buchanan*, 12 vols. (Phila. 1909) vol. 6, pp. 283-284.

in connection with the strict blockade of Montevideo which
Rosas decreed in January. Acting in accordance with his
firm conviction that France and Britain entertained some dark
purposes behind their opposition to Oribe, Brent employed
almost threatening language in his protest to Admiral Lainé
against the postponement of the application of the blockade.[19]
The United States naval officer, Captain Pendergast, adopted
the attitude of the British leader, and refused himself to recognize the strict blockade. He even went so far as to forbid any
further molestation of American vessels entering Montevideo
while those of France and England were exempt.[20] In the friction which resulted, Brent was temporarily over-ruled, since
Pendergast enjoyed the support of his naval superior and the
United States consul at Montevideo.[21]

When the question was referred to Washington, Brent's position was upheld. The State Department ruled that the naval
officers were obligated to respect the belligerent rights of
Buenos Ayres.[22] Turner was advised as follows by the Secretary of the Navy:

"The department would have been pleased if, on the occasion of
an infraction of the rights of an American nation by a European
squadron, the armed vessels of the United States had set the example of respect for the rights of the weaker power." [23]

After a protracted and acrimonious correspondence with Pendergast, the naval authorities dismissed the matter with the
following statement:

"The doctrine that the besieging power must be strong enough
not only to resist its enemy, but to overpower neutrals, cannot be
admitted, inasmuch as it would confine the right of blockade to
those nations only, which have decided preponderance on the
ocean." [24]

[19] S. D. Arg. Rep., Desp. 5, Brent to Calhoun, Jan. 28, 1845. S. D.
Brazil, Desp. 14, Wise to Buchanan, May 2, 1845.
[20] 29, 1st Sess., H. Ex. Doc. 212; *Niles Register,* 67, pp. 208-209.
[21] 29, 1, H. Ex. Doc. 212. Pendergast wrote to Brent on Mar. 1, 1845,
that Buenos Ayres lacked one of the prime requisites of any blockade,
i.e., "the force and power to resist effectively all opposition." N. D.
Brazilian Squadron, Com. Dan. Turner, 1844-1845. To Sec. Mason, April
9, 1845. S. D. Arg. Rep., Desp. 5, Brent to Buchanan, Feb. 15, 1846.
[22] S. D. Arg. Rep., Instr. 15, pp. 17-18. To Brent, May 26, 1845.
[23] 29, 1, H. Ex. Doc. 212, p. 39. May 27, 1845.
[24] 29, 1, H. Ex. Doc. 212, pp. 31-50

The approval of Brent's contention in regard to the blockade had the one unfortunate result of encouraging the already violent partisanship of the Chargé for the Argentine cause. During the attempted mediation of Ouseley and Deffaudis, he undoubtedly allowed himself to be used as a shield for the Governor,[25] as has already been seen.

When the open break between the European Commissioners and Rosas developed at the end of July, Brent became thoroughly convinced that the time had arrived for his Government to take a hand in the matter. In a letter of August 2, to Secretary Buchanan, he reproduced for the edification of the State Department the famous letter from Jefferson to President Monroe in October, 1823, together with pertinent passages from the still more famous message of the President himself which followed in December. Tyler's statement in 1842 was also included. Brent asserted, with all the emphasis at his command, that the United States was traditionally opposed to the meddling of European powers in cis-Atlantic affairs.[26] Not content to stop with this unsolicited lecture to Buchanan, the Chargé sent on the same day [27] a letter to the editor of the *Daily Union* of Washington, the official organ of the Democratic party. The letter appeared in the paper anonymously in October, 1845, and ran in part as follows:

"There has long been, and now exists, a settled determination more particularly in the British Government to get a foothold in these countries. . . . The government of the United States and the people of the United States should be aroused to the critical situation of these republics. . . .

"Is not now the time to see *what is meant* by the United States in the letter of Mr. Jefferson of 24th October, 1823, to Mr. Monroe, by the message of Mr. Monroe of December, 1823, and of Mr. Tyler's message, August 11, 1842? . . . Shall the countries of La Plata be suffered to arrange their own affairs, without the intermeddling of European powers? Or shall they be ruled by them, under a commercial vassalage certainly, or perhaps by such a rule as India, Barbary, and Greece (and China too perhaps) are now

[25] S. D. Arg. Rep., Desp. 5, Brent to Buchanan, July 1, Aug. 2, 1845. This offer, at first confidential, was made public at Rosas' request.
[26] S. D. Arg. Rep., Desp. 5, Brent to Buchanan, Aug. 2, 1845.
[27] The letter came from Buenos Ayres, and the coincidence in date and identity of contents show that it could only have emanated from the U. S. legation.

governed? . . . The United States can at least extend some moral influence against this European intermeddling in American affairs. What they can, or will, or ought to do, is for those who are at the fountain head to determine." [28]

Brent opposed the operations of the Europeans at every turn. In regard to the blockade of Oribe's ports, he tried to get Pendergast to engage the allied commanders in a discussion concerning the alleged illegality and inconsistency of the policy which they were pursuing. He ordered Pendergast to inform the British and French leaders that the declaration of a blockade by the agencies of a non-belligerent government was contrary to the law of nations, and that those guilty of such an offense were liable to indemnity claims for any injury sustained by an honest neutral in consequence of it. But, waiving this question of legality, he should ask if the allied commanders would admit the same reservations and postponements which they themselves had recently exacted from Rosas in regard to the Montevidean blockade.[29]

The arguments of Brent, which were buttressed with numerous references to authorities, would perhaps have been in order in an academic debate in proof of the proposition that the European powers had forfeited their neutral standing. But under the circumstances, they were entirely gratuitous. These recommendations would have been wise only on the condition that the North American government had been ready to force the issue by arms. Such a program was far from the minds of the authorities in Washington. The Chargé was acting as the agent of Rosas, not as that of Buchanan and Polk.

The United States was saved considerable embarrassment when Pendergast refused to obey the orders of Brent. The Captain was not interested in international law, and was under orders from his superior to observe a strict neutrality.[30] The actual policy which Pendergast adopted, however, was even less dignified than that which Brent would have conducted.

[28] *Daily Union,* Oct. 7, 1845.

[29] S. D. Arg. Rep., Desp. 5, Brent to Buchanan, Sept. 23, 1845, and enclosures; 29, 1st Sess., H. Ex. Doc. 212.

[30] N. D. Brazil Squadron, Com. Turner, 1845-46. To Pendergast, Aug. 22, 1845.

After he had formally recognized the blockades of Oribe's ports, he tried to claim additional privileges for American shipping on the basis of the earlier demands which the Europeans had made upon Rosas. His arguments, though presented with great heat, were so ill-considered that the two Admirals paid no attention to them. The Captain could only swallow his wrath.[31] The commander who later suceeded Pendergast was ordered to respect the blockades and in no event to come into collision with any foreign power, except in self-defense.[32]

This second quarrel with Pendergast only increased the violent hostility of Brent toward the intervention. He chose the occasion of the establishment of the blockade of Buenos Ayres on September 22, to issue the following public statement to the Admirals:

"For the United States of America, Sir, I do not acknowledge this decision of the Plenipotentiaries of France and England, . . . as having any validity whatever to declare the blockade of the coasts and ports of the Province of Buenos Ayres.
"Nor do I acknowledge the right of the combined Squadron, or of the Commanders of such Squadron of France and England to establish such blockade.
"Nor do I acknowledge any validity whatever in any such misnamed blockade, by virtue of such decision thus taken."

Brent concluded his declaration of defiance by promising reclamations for losses to United States citizens occasioned by the blockade.[33]

The acute attack of anglophobia from which the Chargé was suffering eventually threw him into a complete panic on the question. The entire Argentine country, he reported, was about to be subjected to British misrule. Martín García in the hands of England would become more important than Gibraltar, the Cape of Good Hope, or Hongkong. It would provide a place where Chartists and Irish repeal men could be sent. It would command the river markets and, worst of all,

[31] *Ibid.*, to Bancroft, Nov. 12, 1845 and enclosures; 29, 1st Sess. H. Ex. Doc. 212, p. 17 ff.
[32] N. D. *ibid.*, Turner to Bancroft, Nov. 12, 1845.
[33] N. D. *ibid.*; 29, 1, H. Ex. Doc. 212, p. 35; S. D. Arg. Rep., Desp. 5, Brent to Buchanan, Sept. 23. The British Minister returned the letter. F. O. 6, 105, Ouseley to Aberdeen, Oct. 3, 1845.

would secure for Great Britain a cotton country, "equal, if not superior to that of the United States."[34] He pointed out that if the intervening powers should secure commercial concessions from Paraguay and Corrientes in return for guarantees of the independence of these states—which seemed to be their purpose—they would always have an excuse to interfere. The extension of Republican principles in America would be defeated, and England would have secured a source for cotton in spite of her failure in Texas and India. Brent wrote that he viewed "with horror indescribable the interference in any possible way of any European Monarchy in the affairs of the American Republics."[35]

Final evidence of the sincerity and naïveté of the Chargé is to be found in a long dissertation which he sent to Governor Rosas in February, 1846, through the medium of Manuelita.[36] Brent was convinced that a divine purpose had brought him to the Plata to be the instrument of repelling the diabolical machinations of Europe. Taking his cue from a random passage to which he happened to turn in the Old Testament, where it was recorded that Israel had been delivered from an invader by prayer and fasting, he proceeded to expand upon this inspiration. He recommended with great earnestness that a similar policy be adopted by Rosas. He undertook to prove both from experience and the scriptures the efficacy of such exercises. The concluding statement which follows will illustrate the spirit of the document:

"They [the Argentine people] will pray for that day when God in his Providence shall permit no foreign government to intrude itself in any way whatever, into the affairs of others; when no foreign nation shall insolently, and arrogantly, and infamously, and hellishly, by bribes and by mercenary and hired bands assume

[34] S. D. Arg. Rep., Desp. 5, Brent to Buchanan, Nov. 14, 1845.
[35] *Ibid.*, same to same, Feb. 2 and 15, 1846. Brent's ineffective objection to the participation of American merchantmen in the Paraná expedition was later approved by Buchanan. See J. B. Moore, *Works of Buchanan* vol. 7, p. 67.
[36] *La Gaceta Mercantil*, Feb. 14, 1846. An enclosure in S. D. Special Missions, E. A. Hopkins. Brent accompanied this document with a most affectionate and not exactly fatherly letter to the daughter of Rosas, explaining how this work had been his occupation for many Sabbaths, and asking her to make a copy of it for him in her own handwriting.

it to be *'their duty'* to interfere in the domestic institutions and political concerns of any nation or people." [37]

Brent had indeed gone the limit in his effort to secure aid for the Argentine cause.

In the meantime, the United States Minister at Rio de Janeiro, Mr. Henry A. Wise, had been following an independent policy on his own initiative, which has considerably more significance for our story than do the fulminations of the American Chargé at Buenos Ayres.

The attention of Wise was first directed toward the question of a possible European intervention in the Plata, by an interesting conversation which he had with the Brazilian Foreign Minister in November, 1844—just at the time, it will be recalled, that Abrantes reached London. França told Wise confidentially that:

"Montevideo was so reduced as to be knocking at the doors of England and France for assistance; and [França] asked whether the United States would not unite with Brazil in putting an end to that war by force, if necessary, rather than permit England and France to interpose and acquire a dominant influence in the Platte country."

Wise reported his reply as follows, not appreciating the double game which the Brazilian Minister was playing:

"I said that the United States had long assumed and acted on the policy to prevent European intervention in the wars of North America, and that they had ever interposed to protect South American states, and I had no doubt that they would approve the same course on the part of Brazil in this instance, and would interpose their good offices to arrest the war of Montevideo and Buenos Ayres." [38]

Although careful to maintain a reserved attitude toward the Brazilian Government on the Argentine question, Wise was enthusiastic over the suggested project. He forwarded glowing reports to Washington in regard to the opportunity af-

[37] S. D. Special Agents, Hopkins, enclosure. F. O. 6, 116, Ouseley to Aberdeen, Feb. 27, 1846, enclosures no. 1, 2, 3, and 4.
[38] S. D. Brazil, Desp. 13, Wise to Calhoun, Nov. 1, 1844.

forded the United States to play a leading rôle in South American affairs. His local program he explained in the following
manner:

"An *American* policy is a favorite topic with those whom I meet.
That means with them what I would have it mean. The U. States
and Brazil are the two elder sisters of North and South America,
and are in a moral sense responsible for the whole family of states
in the new World. They urge upon me the interposition of the
U. States in the affairs of Montevideo and Buenos Ayres,—my
invariable reply is that Brazil has precedence of friendly offices or
of interposition in South America. The U. States had enough to
do to protect American policy in the North American Continent." [39]

During the Spring of 1845, Wise developed a scheme by
which he hoped that the European settlement of the Plata dispute might be avoided. His idea was that Brazil should sum-
mon Rosas to redeem the promise given by Argentina in the
Convention of 1828 to conclude a definitive treaty with the
Imperial Government covering both the independence of Montevideo and the freedom of river navigation. Wise became
rather intimate with Ouseley during the latter's visit at Rio de
Janeiro in April, 1845. He accordingly suggested that Britain,
as the mediator in 1828, should reënforce Brazil's demand
upon Rosas, this to the great bewilderment of Ouseley. The
United States, not having had any part in the question, would
merely stand by,[40] according to Wise.

If the two Governments to whom this suggestion of Wise was
made, had been in a position to co-operate in the Plata, the
policy proposed might have been productive of good results.
After it later became apparent to Wise that he had been deceived by Ouseley in regard to the purposes of the British,
he urged the Brazilian Government all the more strongly to
make a direct approach to Rosas, rather than leave the matter
entirely to the arbitrament of European force.[41] The danger-
ously tense relations between the Imperial Government and

[39] S. D. Brazil, Desp. 13, Wise to Calhoun, Jan. 12, 1845.
[40] S. D. Brazil, Desp. 13, Wise to Calhoun, Feb. 25, 1845; to Secretary
of State, Mar. 28, 1845; vol. 14, to Buchanan, May 2, 1845. The first
alarm which Wise had felt over the European defiance of Rosas' blockade
of Montevideo was allayed by Ouseley's visit to Rio de Janeiro in April,
1844. See Chapter I, note 29.
[41] S. D. Brazil, Desp. 14, Wise to Buchanan, July 31, 1845.

Rosas were such as to make impossible the execution of the idea, but there can be no doubt of the fact that the pacific counsels of Wise aided materially in preventing a break between them.[42]

Wise was much irritated throughout the first half of 1845 because his instructions obliged him to limit his activities to this advisory capacity,[43] although he appreciated, as Brent did not, the unwisdom of entangling his government in the quarrel. The danger, which the Minister at Rio de Janeiro foresaw, was that the inevitable South American struggle over the river navigation question should be precipitated by the European intervention. In such a situation, France and England could easily wield the balance of power, dictate their own terms, and establish more firmly their objectionable pretensions as guarantors and arbiters in Plata affairs.[44] Wise appreciated, in other words, the supreme importance of persuading Brazil and the up-river communities not to play into the hands of the interventionists. The arrival at Rio de Janeiro in late July, 1845, of one Edward A. Hopkins, who was under appointment as special agent of President Polk to visit Paraguay, provided Wise with both the authorization for his policy and the means of executing it.[45]

The mission of Hopkins had, in its inception, no connection whatever with the European intervention. It had been author-

[42] *Ibid.* Also same to same, Sept. 6, 1845, and enclosures. "The United States cannot interpose," Wise warned. "I can only advise that the Imperial Government must not allow Guido to depart." War between them, he insisted, was just what the Europeans wanted.

[43] *Ibid.*, same to same, July 31. "I have been autocrat in all these matters," he complained. "Please to guide me, Sir, in the best and most politic course to serve our country. . . . The stakes in South America are worthy of our regard."

[44] *Ibid.*, May 19, and July 2, 1845. If driven from Uruguay, Rosas would certainly attack Corrientes and Paraguay, and it would be impossible for Brazil to stay out of such a struggle, according to Wise.

[45] N. D. Brazil Squadron, Com. Dan Turner, 1844-45. Turner to Mason, June 22, 1844 and enclosures. The selection of the agent was most unfortunate. Hopkins had been expelled from the navy only the year before because of flagrant misconduct and insubordination. After having been put ashore at Rio de Janeiro, he got into serious trouble with the police, and Com. Turner was obliged to advance $100 to him so that he could return home. *Hunt's Merchant's Magazine*, 21, pp. 80-87. Hopkins was the son of the Methodist Bishop of Vermont. C. A. Washburn, *The History of Paraguay*, 2 vols. (Boston 1871) Vol. 1, pp. 353-356.

ized by Polk only at the instigation of a commercial group, for which Hopkins himself was promoter, who were urging the government to recognize Paraguay and to secure the free navigation of the Paraná river.[46] The instructions carried by the agent, nevertheless, fitted the situation remarkably well. They included one statement of particular importance to the effect that Hopkins should seek the advice of Mr. Wise in regard to the course which he was to pursue. The agent was also charged with the duty of assuring the President of Paraguay that the United States was deeply interested in the independence and prosperity of his country, and of warning him against granting special privileges or engaging his country in any entangling alliances. In case Hopkins should find that the Argentine Government intended to reduce the state to a status of dependence, cutting off its commerce with the outside world, he should assure the authorities at Asunción that:

"the Government of the United States, should this become necessary, will freely interpose its good offices with that of Buenos Ayres to induce it to open that great river to the trade of other nations. . . .

"Should the Government [at Asunción] have proceeded in regular order, maintaining the rights and performing the duties of an Independent Power, more especially, should it have been treated as such by the surrounding nations, the President will not fail to recommend to Congress at its next session the recognition of its independence. Should it have acquired, in your opinion, the firmness and consistency of an independent nation, you might suggest that the President would be pleased to see a diplomatic agent from Paraguay in the United States on the meeting of Congress in December, next, and that he entertains not the least doubt but that its independence would be recognized by that enlightened Body. The President would then be prepared to enter into commercial relations with Paraguay on the most liberal terms." [47]

Wise proceeded immediately to appropriate the mission of Hopkins to his own purposes. He flattered himself that it would be possible for his government, by an entirely peaceful and impartial policy, to establish itself as the great protector of the American states. The United States, he prophesied, could:

[46] S. D. Special Missions, Instr. 1, p. 222. To Hopkins, June 10, 1845.
[47] Ibid., pp. 218-221. To Hopkins, June 10, 1845.

"secure a vast extension of their commerce without departing in the least from their established and wise policy of non-intervention and avoiding all entangling alliances, and without committing themselves to any guarantees which may hereafter involve or embarrass our foreign relations."

He was directing Hopkins, he wrote, to assure Paraguay that she would enjoy the support of every commercial nation in behalf of her independence if she would only abstain from going to war at this time. Wise would volunteer his good offices in transmitting any communication which Paraguay might wish to make to the Imperial Government or to Rosas through Mr. Brent.[48]

The news of the initiation of hostilities by the European forces in August placed a severe strain on the conviction held by Wise that the Washington government should not go beyond the peaceful policy which he had previously recommended. He was especially angered at having been deceived by Ouseley, and did not like the idea of the United States looking tamely on at such a spectacle. Hopkins was sent off with all speed to urge upon the Asunción authorities a neutral policy. At the same time, Wise redoubled his activity at Rio de Janeiro.[49] He secured an assurance from the Brazilian Government that it would be true to the American policy,[50] and he even elicited a favorable reaction from General Guido, the Argentine Minister at Rio, to his suggestion that Buenos Ayres should be willing to make sacrifices rather than risk the European domination of the rivers.[51] Guido even said that the acknowledgment of the independence of Paraguay by the United States would not be considered by Rosas as an unfriendly act; the Dictator, he thought, would probably be willing to take similar action.[52]

[48] S. D. Brazil, Desp. 14, Wise to Buchanan, July 31, 1845.
[49] S. D. Brazil, Desp. 14, Wise to Buchanan, Aug. 24, 1845. Again Wise asked for definite instructions.
[50] Ibid. Wise was at this time aided in arousing the suspicions of Brazil against Britain and France by the Russian Minister at Rio, one Lomonsoff. Ibid., Wise to Buchanan, Dec. 16, 1845.
[51] Ibid. Same to same Sept. 6, enclosure; Wise to Guido, Aug. 27.
[52] Ibid. It is difficult to believe that Guido was not better informed than this would indicate as to the attitude of Rosas toward Paraguay. At any rate he encouraged Wise on a false lead.

The North American Minister was greatly discouraged at the news that Paraguay and Corrientes were about to conclude an alliance against Rosas. He regretted very much that Hopkins had not departed sooner. He confidently predicted that the European forces could now name their own price for relinquishing their control of the rivers. In regard to the prosecution of hostilities without an acknowledgment of belligerency, he wrote:

"I should not like to be either Mr. Brent or the Commander of the U. States naval forces at the river Plate, because responsibilities might be thrown on me which I would reluctantly but surely take at all hazards, if there were no instructions to the contrary." [53]

The appeals of Wise for additional instructions became much more urgent:

"I call again the most earnest attention of the President to the affairs of the river Plate. . . . The armed intervention has brought nothing but war and devastation instead of peace, and is our commerce not in danger of losing its equal privileges? . . . If not before, next to the Oregon question, the issues of the River Plate are the most important to the U. States." [54]

Nothing could have better suited the egotistical temperament of Hopkins than did the mission with which he was charged. The prospect of the United States defeating the machinations of the hated king-craft of Europe, while supposedly afraid to interfere, fired his imagination.[55] Before he departed from the Brazilian capital, he strongly recommended to Washington the immediate recognition of Paraguay. He wrote reassuringly from Rio Grande do Sul that he would have no difficulty in persuading President Lopez to correct the serious blunder of the Corrientes alliance. The dramatic details of his strenuous ride across the country in a race with a phantom French steamer coming up the Paraná lost nothing of color in his

[53] S. D. Brazil, Desp. 14, Wise to Buchanan, Nov. 24, 1845. Note that this was an objection to illegal hostilities, not against European interference as such. *Ibid.*, Dec. 23.

[54] *Ibid.* Same to same, Dec. 16, 1845. U. S. vessels at Montevideo, Wise said, should refuse to give the required bond upon departure.

[55] S. D. Special Missions, Hopkins. To Buchanan, Aug. 5, 26, 1845. Hopkins distrusted Brazil, also.

account to the State Department.[56]   Once within Paraguay, Hopkins was most extravagant in his praise of the wealth and industry of the country.   He arrived at Asunción on November 8, three days before the Paraguay-Corrientes alliance was formally concluded.

Hopkins immediately applied himself to the task of dissuading Lopez from any thought of co-operating with the European forces.   He discovered to his great satisfaction that the Brazilian agent at the city had recently received orders to advocate the same policy, on the basis of American principles.[57]   Hopkins was lavish in his promises.   He committed his own government fully to the recognition of Paraguay.   Forgetting the limitations to his power as a mere special agent, he tendered the good offices of the United States, in his own name, in the quarrel between Asunción and Buenos Ayres.[58]   He then proceeded to dazzle Lopez with his picture of what North American capital and enterprise could do for the country, if steamships and factories were introduced.

The President was so delighted with Hopkins personally, and so attracted by the prospects held out to him, that he finally granted the Yankee promoter a monopoly of the steam navigation of Paraguay waters, together with exclusive commercial and industrial privileges.[59]   In return for Hopkins' promises of mediation at Buenos Ayres and pressure upon Rosas for the freedom of the rivers, Lopez agreed to limit the force which he was sending to Corrientes to 4,000 men, and to order that they remain entirely inactive, unless attacked, for at least four months or until he heard from Buenos Ayres.[60] Lopez would not agree to repudiate the Corrientes alliance, but

[56] *Ibid.*   To Buchanan, Aug. 26, Sept. 16, 19.

[57] *Ibid.*, Nov. 15.   Hopkins was completely taken at Asunción by the lies of the Brazilian agent concerning the Abrantes mission.   He was told that England wanted control of the rivers and France a colony in Uruguay.

[58] *Ibid.*   To Buchanan, Nov. 31, 1845.   Wise considered Hopkins to have been authorized by his instructions in these acts.—S. D. Brazil, Desp. 15, Wise to Buchanan, Jan. 11, 1846.

[59] C. A. Washburn, *The History of Paraguay*, vol. 1, pp. 353-364; S. D. Arg. Rep., Desp. 5, Brent to Buchanan, Mar. 31, 1846.   The "United States and Paraguay Navigation Co." was organized upon Hopkins' return, with a charter under the legislature of Rhode Island.

[60] S. D. Special Missions, Hopkins to Buchanan, Nov. 31, 1846; S. D. Arg. Rep., Desp. 5; Brent to Buchanan, Mar. 31, 1846, and enclosures.

he would consent to treat with Rosas on the basis of the independence of Paraguay and a United States guarantee of a subsequent treaty of limits and one of navigation with Argentina.[61] Until the influence of the Brazilian representative is known, it is not possible to say how far the American agent alone was responsible for the failure of Paraguay to support General Paz in Corrientes. Hopkins was very confident upon his departure on December 31 that Lopez would not assist the Europeans; [62] the real problem, however, was how to avoid a clash between the Paraguay troops and the advancing Argentine forces of Urquiza.

The arrangement which Hopkins made at Asunción was to no small extent responsible for overcoming this latter danger. Brent was informed of the matter by a letter from Wise, dated January 12, that Lopez had promised to suspend hostilities awaiting the outcome of the mediation by the United States.[63] He immediately brought the matter to the attention of the Dictator. The representations of the Chargé finally bore fruit, for Rosas made known his acceptance of the North American mediation on February 26, directly after the news of the collapse of Paz's resistance had reached Buenos Ayres. The Governor sent orders to Urquiza on the following day "not to invade Paraguay under any consideration." [64]

This happy avoidance of a clash which would certainly have set all the up-river country ablaze with war would not have been foreseen by Hopkins in December. So alarmed was he over the situation, that he left Asunción about two weeks be-

[61] S. D. Arg. Rep., Desp. 6, enclosure of Harris to Buchanan, Oct. 17, 1847. *El Paraguay Independiente* for Aug. 2, 1846. Special Missions, *ibid.,* Lopez to Hopkins, Dec. 5, 1845.

[62] S. D. Special Missions, Hopkins, No. 7. From the "Saratoga" at sea, Feb. 1846: "There is no fear of an envoy of the Ministers of the intervention being able to procure anything from Paraguay."

[63] S. D. Arg. Rep., Desp. 5, Brent to Buchanan, Mar. 31, 1846, and enclosure.

[64] S. D. Brazil, Desp. 15, Wise to Buchanan, Apr. 14, 1846. Enclosure, R. M. Walsh to Wise, Feb. 23, 1846. Urquiza defeated only the advance guard of Paz's army on Feb. 4. Gov. Madariaga immediately made terms with Urquiza, and the 4000 Paraguay troops returned home. Gen. Paz fled to Asunción. See Pelliza, *Historia argentina* vol. 2, pp. 328-330. José Maria Paz, *Compañas contra Rosas.* (Buenos Ayres 1917), pp. 285-288.

fore Hotham arrived, and hurried back to Rio de Janeiro. He took Wise completely by surprise when he appeared at the city on February 10.[65] When the Minister learned of the alarming news of the advance of the Argentine army, he decided not to wait for the expected instructions from Washington, but to send Hopkins immediately to Buenos Ayres.[66] By a presumptuous extension of his advisory capacity, Wise directed that Hopkins should obtain access to Rosas through Mr. Brent, and should urge upon the Governor the extreme necessity of avoiding a war with Paraguay. Wise concluded his instructions with the following admonition:

"Let Genl. Rosas fall, if he will not do justice to a sister Republic whom it is his true interests to recognize in the bonds of peace. . . . Do nothing, I suggest, without consultation and advice with him [Brent]; but act decisively and promptly. Wait a reasonable time, but dally not a second with any apparent procrastination. . . . I would not remain in Buenos Ayres over ten days." [67]

Hopkins reached the Argentine capital on February 27, the very day on which the order was sent to Urquiza not to invade Paraguay. The young man was thoroughly convinced, by this time, that he was about the most important personage in South America.

The egotism of Hopkins was to suffer a hard jolt at the hands of Rosas. The agent was received informally by Arana on February 28, 1846, but was not permitted thereafter to participate in any of the conferences concerning the mediation because of his lack of diplomatic credentials. Arana refused to communicate with the special agent except through Brent, while the abjectly subservient attitude of the Chargé toward Rosas was disgusting to Hopkins. The latter regarded his treatment as a deliberate personal insult, and declared that he would rather have had his horse die under him than to have been obliged to endure such humiliation. He had no illusions what-

[65] S. D. Special Missions, Hopkins to Buchanan from Rio, Feb. 12, 1846.
[66] S. D. Brazil, Desp. 15, Wise to Buchanan, Feb. 18, 1846.
[67] *Ibid.,* enclosure, Wise to Hopkins, Feb. 11; Arg. Rep., Desp. 5, Brent to Buchanan, Sept. 6, 1847. Gen. Guido was asked to prepare the way for Hopkins. Wise was confident that Washington would approve the mediation.

ever about the fact that it was he and not Brent who was best able to see the mediation through.[68]

The announcement which Rosas made on March 16 of the terms on which he would make peace with Paraguay was more than Hopkins could endure. Rosas said that Paraguay would be allowed to enjoy territorial integrity, independence in internal affairs, and freedom of river transport on a basis of equality with every other member of the Argentine Confederation. The precise territorial limits could be fixed later.[69] On March 18, Hopkins announced abruptly that he would depart on the following day, his presence, apparently, being no longer required. Upon his departure, he left a letter for Governor Rosas, which was delivered after the agent was safely aboard a war vessel in the river.

For sheer audacity and impudence, this letter of Hopkins probably has no equal in the annals of American diplomacy. The agent announced at the beginning that, since the countrymen of the Dictator dared not speak, he himself would render some much-needed advice. The country of Rosas, he said, richly deserved the contempt which it then enjoyed. Its credit was gone, freedom was paralyzed, the Executive power was a despotism, the Judiciary the "rotten tool of oppression," and the legislature the "cringing puppet" of the Dictator. Why did not the Governor rise to the occasion, forget the past, clean up the scurrilous press, make a treaty with Brazil, recognize the independence of Paraguay as the United States will do, and confide the question of river navigation to a general Congress? Continuing:

"Now is the time when like the Greeks of old . . . [South American states should cease] their domestic wars to combat the common enemy. . . . Why not declare boldly war [sic] against G. Britain and France, and confiscate all property belonging to either nation? . . .

"I have yet to hear that sincerity in anything but revenge and hatred can characterize any Government of Buenos Ayres. . . .

"Would it be more agreeable to your soul as it wings its flight to

[68] S. D. Arg. Rep., Desp. 5, Brent to Buchanan, Mar. 31, 1846 and enclosures. Brazil, Desp. 15, Hopkins to Wise, Mar. 27, 1846.
[69] S. D. Brazil, Desp. 15, Wise to Buchanan, Apr. 14, 1846. Enclosure, Arana to Brent, Mar. 16.

other regions, to hear the frantic joy occasioned by your death, or the sorrowing moan of a weeping people that they had lost their father? . . .

"You know the motives of this letter, you know that they spring from a Love born in me, a love pure and holy beyond all other loves, the love of one who would, were it possible, sacrifice ten thousand lives for America by deaths of keenest torture, and still be inestimably indebted to her that she had given him birth but once.

"This country and this man are now your warmest friends, and would, if they be allowed, do the most for you of all others upon earth. Pause before you add them to the list of your enemies. Life is easily purchased among anarchy and Confusion; it is a small gift with *dishonor*. Then it is a *curse*, still the *deeper*, still the more awful, by each hour that it is prolonged." [70]

Brent contributed the final blow in the complete destruction of the prestige of the United States in South America. The Chargé foolishly disclosed his entire correspondence with Wise on the Paraguay question, in an effort to appease the angered Dictator. The latter immediately published the material, much to the embarrassment of the Minister at Rio de Janeiro.[71] Wise was greatly exercised in defending his policy to the Washington authorities, especially his later ill-advised instructions to Hopkins.[72] When the special agent returned to Rio de Janeiro, after having announced that *his* mediation had been withdrawn, Wise was obliged to lecture him in regard to the limitations of his powers. Hopkins thereupon withdrew his announcement,[73] and returned to the United States to berate the Government and to preach the cause of Paraguay far and wide.

The Washington authorities cannot escape a large share of the blame for the unfortunate aspects of the Hopkins mis-

[70] S. D. Arg. Rep., Desp. 5, Brent to Buchanan, Mar. 31, enclosure Y,— Hopkins to Rosas, Mar. 19. This letter was reproduced in a Montevidean newspaper, *El Nacional*, on June 26, 1846,—*ibid.*, 6, Harris to Buchanan, July 14, 1846.

[71] S. D. Brazil, Desp. 15, Wise to Buchanan, Apr. 29, June 19, 1846. See *Gaceta Mercantil* for Mar. 31, Apr. 28, May 7, 1846. In Zinny, *op. cit.*, 3, pp. 132, 137, 142.

[72] For the newspaper account, see the *National Intelligencer* for Sept. 8, 1846.

[73] S. D. Arg. Rep., Desp. 5, Brent to Buchanan, Sept. 6, 1847; enclosures, Hopkins to Brent April 1, 1846 from Montevideo, April 14, from Rio de Janeiro. Special Missions, Hopkins to Lopez, April 20, 1846, contained a scathing attack upon Rosas, but cautioned the President of Paraguay to avoid co-operating with Europe.

sion. It was their mistake, in the first place, that a man of the temper of Hopkins was selected for his task. For a second thing, they provided no instructions whatever to guide the actions of the agents who were struggling so desperately to sustain what they conceived to be the traditional policy of their country. Secretary Buchanan was for months in possession of information concerning the plans of the Minister at Rio de Janeiro before the question of the recognition of Paraguay was ever considered by the Cabinet. This was not done until February, 1846, and then only at the instance of the Brazilian representative.[74] The question was referred to General Alvear the Argentine Minister, and in consequence of the protest of this gentleman, the entire idea embodied in the original instructions to Hopkins was repudiated and the agent recalled.[75] In an effort to recover the good-will of Rosas, Buchanan directed the successor of Brent to explain that the recognition of Paraguay had been suspended:

"purely from regard to the Argentine Republic and in consideration of the heroic struggle which it is now maintaining against the armed intervention of Great Britain and France in the concerns of the Republics on the La Plata and its tributaries." [76]

When the Hopkins letter to Rosas became known at Washington, the President hastened to present his humble apologies to General Alvear with the assurance that the offending agent had already been recalled.[77] That Polk had no sympathy whatever for the mediatory program which his representatives had sponsored in South America is revealed by the following entry in his diary:

"The conduct of Mr. Wise at Brazil and Mr. Brent at the Argentine Republic in interfering in the internal contests of the South

[74] James K. Polk, *Diary . . . during his Presidency, 1845-1849.* 4 vols. (Chicago 1910) Vol. 1, pp. 238-9. Feb. 19, 1846.
[75] S. D. Arg. Rep., Desp. 6, Harris to Buchanan, July 14, 1846. In enclosure of *Gaceta Mercantil* for July 1, 1846, the entire report from Alvear on the matter is given. The United States was promised, in return, equal trading privileges with Europe on the rivers. S. D. Special Missions, Instr. 1, pp. 235-238. To Hopkins, Mar. 30, 1846. Buchanan erroneously seemed to think Hopkins responsible for the league between Paraguay and Corrientes against Rosas, and therefore accused him, upon no grounds, of co-operating with the European forces.
[76] S. D. Arg. Rep., Instr. pp. 19-23. Vol. 15.
[77] Moore, *Works of Buchanan,* 7, pp. 57-59.

American Governments, and especially in the tender of the mediation of their Government, was not only unauthorized, but was calculated to do much mischief. Mr. Brent has been superseded by Mr. Harris, and Mr. Wise will return during the next winter. Their successors will be instructed to avoid embarrassing and involving their Government in a similar manner. It is indeed provoking that any foreign representatives should have acted with so little discretion and judgment as Mr. Wise and Mr. Brent have done." [78]

The responsibility which had been left with Brent to conclude the effort to mediate between Asunción and Buenos Ayres was discharged rather ingloriously. Since it was certain that Paraguay would not consent to enter the Argentine Confederation,[79] the Chargé decided to send a delegation to Lopez with the proposal that hostilities be generally suspended while a Commission should be named to treat with a similar group from Argentina.[80] The two emissaries, Brent's own son and consul Graham, found Lopez bitterly angry against the United States Government for having repudiated the promises of Hopkins and for adopting so friendly an attitude toward the arch enemy of Paraguay.[81] The President broke out in coarse epithets at the very mention of the name of Rosas and disdained the protestations of the two men concerning the goodwill of the United States. When the agents finally departed from Asunción in October, 1846, Lopez was still giving evidence of his inveterate hatred of Rosas, but he had no intention of joining himself to the now discredited European intervention.[82]

The authorities at Washington were greatly relieved to be

[78] *Polk's Diary* 2, p. 155, Sept. 25, 1846.

[79] S. D. Arg. Rep., Desp. 6, Harris to Buchanan, July 14, 1846. Rosas insisted that Paraguay was still in the Confederation by the 1811 treaty. To allow it to leave at the instigation of Europe would, he said, destroy the Confederation. Harris foresaw that a general war would develop as soon as the intervention ceased, and he advised a policy of friendly sympathy toward all the parties.

[80] *Ibid.*, 5, Brent to Buchanan, from Fairfax County, Va., Sept. 6, 1847.

[81] S. D. Brazil, Desp. 16, Wise to Buchanan, Dec. 9, 1846, enclosing Graham to Wise, Sept. 16, 1846.

[82] S. D. Arg. Rep., Desp. 6, Harris to Buchanan, Oct. 17, 1847, and enclosures. G. L. Brent and Graham to Harris, Dec. 7, 1846. They reported an insidious attempt of Brazil to fan this hatred of Lopez for Rosas.

rid of the embarrassment of the mediation.[83]   The evidence
brought back by Brent and Graham indicated that most of the
stories concerning the great wealth and productivity of Paraguay were myths, and that the United States had nothing to
gain either politically or commercially from recognizing the
state.   The people, for the most part, were in a very backward
state of civilization, and the prospects of trade were of the
meagerest.   The cotton of the country was very inferior in
quality, and there was little or none for export purposes.[84]
The subsequent vehement agitation of Hopkins in behalf of the
recognition of Paraguay, with himself as the first Chargé,
found the State Department not interested.   Secretary Clayton, in 1849, felt called upon to disavow to the Argentine Government the activities and pretentions of the former special
agent.   He commented drily:

"In pursuing this course, he [Hopkins] must have supposed that
the Department kept no records." [85]

That the Washington government showed no appreciation
of what their agents had accomplished in opposing the European intervention is very apparent.   What, then, was the official policy of President Polk toward this violation of American soil?

The press of the United States, during the latter half of
1845, was unanimous in its condemnation of the operations
of the British and French forces in the Plata.   To the Demo-
crats, the incident was but another demonstration of the diabolical machinations of those powers who had recently attempted
to rob the Union of Texas.[86]   The Whig papers, on the whole,
were less violent in attacking the European program, but they

[83] S. D. Arg. Rep., Instr. 15, pp. 31-33.   To Harris, Nov. 12, 1846, pp.
31-33.   Moore, *Works of Buchanan* 7, pp. 113-114.
[84] *Ibid.,* Desp. 6, Harris to Buchanan, Oct. 17, 1847.
[85] S. D. Arg. Rep., Instr. 15, pp. 39-40.   Clayton to Harris, Dec. 26, 1849.
See *De Bow's Commercial Review* 14, pp. 238-251.
[86] *The Daily Union,* Oct. 3, Aug. 5, Sept. 13, 1845.   Almost all the news
in the U. S. press came from Buenos Ayres, and hence was pro-Rosas
in attitude.

seized eagerly upon the incident as an opportunity to criticise the administration for its lack of a foreign policy. Public opinion, lamented *Niles Register*, had become so engrossed in political struggles at home that Monroe's words had become a dead letter. More vigilant nations were now assuming the place of leadership in South American affairs which rightfully belonged to the United ,States. When would such measures, asked the editor, encounter the solemn protest of the government? [87]

The attitude of the press became a matter of international significance when Brent's letter of August 2, 1845, from Buenos Ayres appeared in the *Daily Union* of Washington in October.[88] An editorial accompanying the letter demanded that the Government challenge this effort of Great Britain to reduce the Argentine country to commercial vassalage, if not to territorial domination. Two paragraphs ran as follows:

"This is the commencement of their European system of making and unmaking Governments at pleasure—of establishing on the American continent the same system that they have in Europe. They disclaim any intention of acquiring territory; but that territory must be governed as they dictate.

"Our commercial stake in the river is too great to permit us to see it sacrificed. It is of yet more vital concern to our avowed national policy to keep this continent safe and sacred from aggressive foreign dictation." [89]

The British Ambassador could not allow such representations in the official administrative organ to go unchallenged. He called upon Secretary Buchanan on October 13, 1845, and protested against the *Daily Union* articles. The report of this interview which Pakenham sent to London is very interesting. The Secretary, he said, did not appear to be aware of the publications in question, and disclaimed all responsibility for them. Continuing:

[87] *Niles Register* 68, June 7, 1845. The editor said that British mediation meant "the oyster to the mediator,—a shell each to the mediated." *Ibid.*, 69, p. 113, Oct. 25, 1845. *The National Intelligencer*, Sept. 25, praised the attitude of Brent. See E. B. White, *op. cit.*, pp. 114-115. Reports from Boston, New York, and Mobile all demanded a vigorous remonstrance from the Government.

[88] See above, note 28, for the substance of Brent's letter.

[89] *Daily Union* for Oct. 7 and 9, 1845. E. B. White, *op. cit.*, pp. 115-116. Later editorials declared Britain to be exclusively responsible for this high-handed interference. *Ibid.*, Oct. 17, 28, 1845.

"He [Buchanan] added that the Government of the United States had no intention of interfering with or opposing in any way the efforts of Her Majesty's Govt. and the Government of France for the pacification of the two South American Republics."

Pakenham had been assured that Brent's instructions told him only to recognize the blockade of Montevideo by Rosas, if it were legally applied.[90]

In the meantime, Ouseley's complaint concerning the obtrusive opposition of the American Chargé had produced a reaction from London. Instructions were received by Pakenham soon after his first protest, directing him without delay to:

"draw the attention of the United States Government to the conduct of Mr. Brent, and invite them to furnish him with such instructions as shall insure his future abstinence from interference unless invited to do so by all the Parties to the pending negotiation." [91]

Pakenham should explain to Buchanan that their intention was not to secure territory, but simply to put an end to the barbarous war, so damaging to the commerce of everyone. This would be done "by mutual agreement of the Parties, if possible; if not by compulsion. . . . We are determined . . . that it shall cease." [92]

The report of the conference which was held in pursuance of these instructions throws more light on the attitude of the Washington government. Pakenham wrote as follows:

"Mr. Buchanan repeated to me in a more positive manner what he had told me in a former conversation respecting the President's determination to recall Mr. Brent immediately on the opening of the approaching session of Congress. . . . But I must observe to your Lordship that on this last occasion Mr. Buchanan's language in disclaimer of Mr. Brent's unauthorized proceedings was less

[90] F. O. 5, America, 429. Pakenham to Aberdeen, Oct. 13, 1845. Note that this promise is conditioned on the pacific purpose of their efforts.

[91] F. O. 5, 423, Aberdeen to Pakenham, Oct. 3, 1845. The original draft of Aberdeen, almost unfriendly, was corrected to include the statement that the co-operation of the United States in the mediation would have been requested, had that Government been a party to their earlier efforts.

[92] *Ibid.* It was at this time that Aberdeen told the French ambassador that a success in the Plata was indispensable for their general policy after failure in Texas. *Aff. Etr.,* Buenos Ayres, 34, pp. 278-280. Jarnac from London, Oct. 9, 1845. See above, chapter 5, note 32. On Oct. 3, Aberdeen criticized Pakenham for allowing the offered 49° settlement of Oregon to be recalled. On Nov. 28, he said that Britain was ready to "incur the risk of great sacrifice for the preservation of peace and friendly relations with the U. S." F. O. 5, 428, Aberdeen to Pakenham.

open and satisfactory than during our early communications on the same subject. He talked of the jealousy with which the American people viewed any European interference in the affairs of this Continent, and he added that the idea began to prevail that the British and French Governments intended to retain possession of the Island of Martín García for the purpose of securing for themselves the exclusive Commercial advantages in that part of the World. . . . No such suspicion as that . . . was entertained by the United States Government, . . . he had referred to it merely as a proof of the susceptibility of the American people on all [such] questions."

The British Ambassador said that he was exerting every effort to secure the preparation of satisfactory instructions for Brent's successor. The President, he thought, would have something to say on the question in the coming annual message.[93]

President Polk's annual message of December 2, 1845, is of great significance in defining his policy toward the European intervention. It contained three distinct ideas in reference to the American Doctrine. In the first place, he denounced in the most thorough-going manner the proposed application of the principle of the balance-of-power to check the expansion of the United States. Any such interference from Europe in North America, he declared, would be resisted "at any and all hazards." He next asserted that all of the American states by virtue of their sovereignty and independence had a right to be free from foreign interposition in the matter of making war, concluding peace, and regulating internal affairs. This obvious reference to the South American intervention carried with it only the feeble sanction that the people of the United States could not be indifferent to such violation of the sovereign rights of these states. Polk thus avoided committing his government to any policy, and merely repeated what Buchanan had said to Pakenham a few weeks before.

Polk's final word on the American policy was an affirmation of his concurrence in the wisdom and soundness of Monroe's earlier prohibition of future colonization in America. But in the same sentence, the President limited the application of this

[93] F. O. 5, 429, Pakenham to Aberdeen, Nov. 13, 1845.

principle to the northern half of the hemisphere. Within these
limits, he would forbid the extention of European *dominion* as
well as colonization. This statement was intended primarily
for the situation on the Pacific coast.[94] Even the previous
assurances given by Pakenham that England and France desired to annex no territory in the Plata country did not influence the President to refrain from restricting to North America
the application of the original anti-colonization principle of
Monroe. This deliberate restriction is far more meaningful
than the lip-service given to Monroe's message.

Secretary Buchanan made it perfectly clear in later conferences which he held with the British Ambassador that the
United States had no intention whatever of interfering in the
Plata affair. Shortly after the annual message, Pakenham
questioned the Secretary of State in regard to Brent's defiance
of the European blockade of Buenos Ayres, which the *Daily
Union* was praising as in harmony with the ideas expressed by
the President.[95] Buchanan's reply was reported as follows:

"Mr. Buchanan spoke in terms of entire disapproval, and he said
that it had increased the President's desire to remove Mr. Brent
from his appointment. . . . He added clearly and explicitly that
the Gentleman intended to succeed Mr. Brent would be instructed
to abstain from all interference with the operations of the British
and French Governments in that part of the World." [96]

The Washington government was apparently making a virtue
of the necessity incumbent upon it to allow matters in the
Plata to run their course, especially since it appeared that the
intervention was encountering unexpected difficulties. In
March, 1846, Pakenham quoted Buchanan as saying in reference to the successor of Brent:

[94] Jesse Reeves, *American Diplomacy under Tyler and Polk.* (Baltimore
1907) p. 258. Polk "reaffirmed the Monroe Doctrine, with an eye, as he
said, as much on California with the fine bay of San Francisco as to Oregon." See Richardson, J. D., *Messages and Papers of the Presidents.* (1899)
vol. 4, p. 398 ff.

[95] *Daily Union*, Dec. 3 and 8, 1845. See note 33, above.

[96] F. O. 5, 430, Pakenham to Aberdeen, Dec. 13, 1845, enclosing copies
of hostile articles in the *Daily Union* and *New York Sun.* In the same
despatch was included a copy of Sec. Walker's famous argument for a
reduction of the tariff, which, Pakenham said, "will be read with most
satisfaction by Her Majesty's Government."

"Mr. Harris' instructions . . . will be to observe the strictest neutrality, to interfere in no way whatever with the operations of England and France in the River Plate. 'We want to have nothing to say to it.' " [97]

These unqualified assurances on the part of the State Department, which contrast so markedly with Polk's war-like utterances condemning interference of any description in North America, are particularly significant because they came at a time when the Paraná expedition and the efforts to revolutionize the interior of Argentina made mockery of any pretense that France and Britain were acting merely as mediators. It would have been one thing, moreover, for Polk to have adopted a policy of non-interference under such circumstances; it was quite another for him to inform the British Government explicitly concerning that decision. Polk's rather unsuccessful effort to make an accommodation with the traditional policy of his country was clearly secondary to his purpose of buttressing the program which he himself was contemplating in Texas, New Mexico, and California. The engagement of a large British naval force far up the Paraná river was a veritable God-send to the United States in 1845-46, when a war with England over Oregon and perhaps California seemed almost inevitable.[98] What was even more important, the Argentine intervention provided an opportunity for the United States gracefully to yield to a coercive program of England and France in one quarter of America of such a character as to make absurd any later pretention by these latter nations that the rights of small states would justify them in protecting Mexican territory from an attack by the North American republic.[99]

As final evidence of the fact that Polk's Government was deliberately conniving at a violation of the American doctrine,

[97] F. O. 5, 447, Pakenham to Aberdeen, Mar. 29, 1846.
[98] J. H. Smith, *The War with Mexico*, 1, pp. 325-334. Polk's *Diary*, 1, pp. 62-65. Moore, *op. cit.*, 6, p. 404, to Slidell, Mar. 12, 1846. *Daily Union*, Sept. 13, 1845; *Niles Register*, Feb. 29, 1846; v. 69, p. 403.
[99] That Buchanan feared European opposition on just such grounds is indicated in Polk's *Diary*, 1, pp. 397-399, May 13, 1846. Mexico fully expected European aid. Smith, *War with Mexico*, vol. 1, pp. 111-115; 121-122. E. D. Adams, *op. cit.*, pp. 219-225. Whitelaw Reid, *The Monroe Doctrine, the Polk Doctrine, and the Doctrine of Anarchism*. (N. Y. 1903).

we have the following excerpt from the March 30th instructions to Mr. Harris, the new Chargé at Buenos Ayres. Buchanan wrote:

"The late annual message of the President to Congress has so clearly presented the great American Doctrine in opposition to the interference of European Gov'ts. in the internal concerns of the nations of this continent that it is deemed unnecessary to add another word on this subject. That Great Britain and France have flagrantly violated this principle by their armed intervention on the La Plata is manifest to the whole world. While existing circumstances render it impossible for the United States to take a part in the present war, yet the President desires that the whole moral influence of this Republic should be cast into the scale of injured party. We cordially wish the Argentine Republic success in its struggle against foreign interference. It is for these reasons that, although the Government of the United States never did authorize your predecessor, Mr. Brent, to offer his mediation in the affairs of Great Britain, France, and the Argentine Republic, this act has not been publickly disavowed. His example, however, is not to be followed by you without express instructions. . . .

"It will be your duty closely to watch the movements of these two powers in that region, and should either of them, in violation of this [afore-mentioned] declaration, attempt to make territorial acquisitions, you will immediately communicate the fact to this Gov't. . . . A spirit should be cherished among all the nations on the continent to resist European interference and maintain the freedom and independence of each of their Gov'ts. The gov't. and people of the Argentine Republic have manifested to all the world by their conduct that they feel the importance of asserting these principles and that they have the courage to maintain them against two of the greatest powers of Europe. It should, therefore, be your constant effort, both in your public and private intercourse to impress upon that Gov't. and the people how deep an interest we feel in their success, and how anxious we are to cultivate with them the most friendly relations." [100]

The defiant reaction which Polk's message of December, 1845, aroused in Europe [101] prompted several Democratic Senators to advocate that Congress adopt a resolution in support of the President's American policy. Because of the known unwillingness of the Senate Committee on Foreign Relations to recommend such a move, Senator Allen of Ohio, the Chair-

[100] S. D. Arg. Rep., Instr. 15, pp. 23-25. A distinct reflection of the American Doctrine of Mr. Wise is apparent in these instructions.
[101] Niles Register, 68, pp. 366-367; 70, pp. 25-28, 48. F. O. 27, France, 748, Cowley to Aberdeen, Jan. 22, 1846. Smith, op. cit., 2, pp. 294-301.

man, forced the question before that body by introducing a resolution on his own initiative. He proposed, on January 14, 1846, that Congress should declare that the recent warning against European interference in America was demanded in the interests of the preservation of peace between the Old World and the New. They should therefore:

"solemnly declare to the civilized world the unalterable resolution of the United States to adhere to and enforce the principle that any effort of the powers of Europe to intermeddle in the social organization or political arrangements of the independent nations of America or further to extend the European system of Government upon this continent by the establishment of new Colonies, would be incompatible with the independent existence of the nations, and dangerous to the liberties of the peoples of America, and therefore it would incur, as by right of self-preservation it would justify, the prompt resistance of the United States." [102]

Such a declaration would have definitely committed the government to responsibilities in South America which Polk had determined to avoid.

Allen's resolution immediately drew an attack from Calhoun. The latter questioned the right of the Senator from Ohio to introduce the proposal apart from his Committee, and also challenged the wisdom of making the declaration. His remarks were reported in part as follows:

"As far as his [Calhoun's] information went, the interference of France and England with the concerns of the Government of Buenos Ayres was an outrage, high-handed in its character, and without precedent in the history of nations. But the great question presented by this resolution was, whether we should take under our guardianship the whole family of American States, and pledge ourselves to extend to them our protection against all foreign aggression. . . . Had we arrived at that state of maturity to do so? . . .

"With great deference to the Senator from Ohio, if he was really in earnest in his desire to carry into effect the principle involved in his resolution, instead of introducing it in a general form, he ought to introduce one calling on the Government at once to interfere in behalf of Buenos Ayres, to be prepared to take that Republic under our protection and repel the interference of France in her concerns. . . . True dignity consists in making no declaration which we are not prepared to maintain." [103]

[102] *Congr. Globe,* 15, p. 197. Note the appeal to Calhoun followers in the term "social organization."
[103] *Ibid.,* pp. 197-8.

A motion for leave to introduce the resolution was laid upon the table, from which it was not withdrawn until January 26.[104]

The final debate on the Allen resolution resolved itself into a duel between Senators Cass and Calhoun. The Michigan Senator, speaking in support of the resolution, declared that nothing could be more appropriate at a time when the avowed European balance-of-power system was actually being put into operation in South America. The proposal, he said, did not necessarily involve war; it left the government free to regulate its conduct by future circumstances, if protest proved to be inefficient. He continued:

"We are young, but we are every day becoming stronger as we become older. . . . What we now want is to prevent any future pretense that by our acquiescence we have recognized this new-fangled doctrine of interference. . . . To give proper weight and solemnity to any measure upon this great question under consideration requires the action of Congress. The declaration of the President will be as barren as that of Monroe unless adopted by the National legislature." [105]

Calhoun's reply was devastating. Speaking as the only surviving member of the Cabinet of Monroe in 1823, he declared that the famous declaration was intended to refer only to a specific situation; that "Monroe was a wise man, and had no design of burdening the country with a task which it could not perform." A more general declaration, sponsored by Adams, he said, was never considered by the Cabinet.[106] More effective was the direct frontal attack of the South Carolina leader upon the wisdom of the proposed action. He said:

"By the adoption of the principle of the resolution we would be called on to interfere whenever a European nation, right or wrong, should bring on a conflict of arms between one or another nation on this continent. . . . Would it not be better to wait for the emergency in which we would have sufficient interest to interfere, and sufficient power to make that interference influential? Why make any such declaration now? What good purpose can it

[104] The question of the right to propose the resolution was long debated, but it is not pertinent here. *Congr. Globe* 15, pp. 239-248.
[105] *Congr. Globe* 15, pp. 240-242.
[106] *Ibid.*, p. 245. Calhoun's interpretation is at variance with Adams' own idea of the declaration. See J. Q. Adams, *Memoirs,* vol. 6, pp. 451-452.

serve? Only to show to the men who are to come after us that we were wiser and more patriotic than we feared they might be! . . . Will mere vaporing bravado have any practical effect? . . . Will it not create jealousy on the part of England? Will it not militate against the formation of alliances on the part of nations favorably disposed toward us? . . . We must meet each particular case by itself, and according to its own merits, always taking care not to assert our rights until we feel ourselves able to sustain our assertions." [107]

The attempts to answer the arguments of Calhoun were almost puerile. For formal reasons, leave was granted Allen to introduce the resolution, but it was immediately interred by the Committee of Foreign Affairs.[108]

For several months subsequent to the message of Polk, the Democratic press continued to fulminate in most intemperate fashion concerning the activities of France and England in the Plata.[109] Repeated attempts were made to stretch the words of the President to cover the question. The *Daily Union* said: "His message, it is true, stops with North America, but its enlarged principle equally rebukes the flagitous interference and murderous attack upon the shores of the Paraná." A week later, the same paper declared that Congress should at least go so far as to assert, with the President, that "north of the Isthmus of Darien, such atrocities . . . shall not in any event or at any hazard be tolerated.[110] The press of the United States progressively moderated its tone, until it finally ceased to discuss the intervention as a violation of the American Doctrine. The episode continued to serve, however, as a stock example of the ambition and cupidity of Great Britain.[111]

[107] *Ibid.,* pp. 245-246.

[108] *Ibid.,* pp. 245-248. It was pointed out by Clayton that in April, 1826, Polk had opposed in Congress any declaration involving an obligation to defend South America. Allen resigned as Chairman of the Committee soon after. White, *op. cit.,* pp. 116-117. Later reference to the matter in Congress called up no debate.—29, 1, Sen. Journal, p. 254; 29, 1. H. Journal, pp. 411,746.

[109] White, *op. cit.,* p. 117 ff. *United States Magazine and Democratic Review,* 18, pp. 369-382, May, 1846.

[110] *The Daily Unión,* Feb. 10, 17, 18, 1846. The language here used is extreme.

[111] See an article by Caleb Cushing in *The United States Magazine and Democratic Review* 18, pp. 163-184, March, 1846. "English and French Intervention in the Rio de la Plata." See also the *National Intelligencer,* Jan. 24, 1846; *Niles Register,* Mar. 21, May 2, June 27, 1846.

Polk's policy of complete non-interference in the Argentine quarrel was maintained throughout the intervention.[112] A formal protest which Mr. Harris made in July, 1847, which will be considered in a later connection, was made without instructions. By a dignified neutrality, the United States representative at Buenos Ayres was able to gain the respect of the European leaders, but he could never recover for his country the prestige among the native parties which had been sacrificed by the blunders and follies of his predecessors. The failure of Washington to redeem the extravagant promises of Brent, and the simultaneous attack upon Mexico left the United States enjoying neither the confidence nor the respect of Argentina, and put Washington in the same class with Paris and London in their eyes.[113] The withdrawal of the naval forces of the United States from the Plata for service against Mexico cut short several well-founded protests of Harris against the irregularities of the blockade.[114] The North American republic became a mere spectator of the proceedings.

[112] Moore, *op. cit.*, vol. 7, pp. 131-152; 466-474. The annual messages of 1846 and 1847 did not mention it. The best contemporary account of the situation is one by S. F. Streeter, "Rosas and the Argentine Republic" *North American Review* 69, pp. 43-93. (July, 1849). The theme is a laudation of the capacity and determination of Rosas.

[113] F. O. 6, 119, Ouseley to Aberdeen, June 29, 1846. S. D. Arg. Rep., Desp. 6, Harris to Buchanan, July 14, Sept. 15, 1846.

[114] F. O. 6, 120, Ouseley to Aberdeen, July 12, 1846; *ibid.*, 114, Palmerston to Ouseley, Dec. 4, 1846.

CHAPTER VII

THE FIRST ATTEMPT TO MAKE PEACE

Lord Aberdeen's friendly policy toward France became steadily more unpopular in England during 1845. Within his own party, the considerable number who had come to share the apprehensions of Wellington concerning the evil designs of the French Government, especially in case trouble should arise in America, was strengthened by a larger group who believed with Peel that it was unwise to stake the safety of England on the continuance of the health of a seventy-year-old French King and the precarious tenure of Guizot. Others were of the opinion that the recent concession made by the Foreign Office in regard to the slave-trade treaty smacked too much of subservience to the demands of the French Chambers.[1] So hopelessly out of sympathy with his party did Aberdeen find himself by September, 1845, that he offered to resign from the Cabinet. He withdrew his resignation only when Peel insisted that the unavoidable disclosure of the real cause of such a break would produce a most unfortunate increase of public alarm.[2] This same uneasiness in regard to French relations made the Whigs unwilling to entrust the Foreign Office to Lord Palmerston in December, 1845, when Russell attempted to form a Ministry. A revamped Peel Government was given six months more of sailing before the inevitable shipwreck on the issue of the Corn Laws.[3]

Aberdeen enjoyed even less support in the new Conservative

[1] C. S. Parker, *Sir Robert Peel.* (London 1899) Vol. 3, pp. 207-216. Spencer Walpole, *The Life of Lord John Russell,* 2 vols. (London 1899) Vol. 2, pp. 13-25.
[2] Parker, *op. cit.,* 3, pp. 400-411.
[3] G. P. Gooch, *The Later Correspondence of Lord Russell, 1840-1878.* (New York 1925) Vol. I, pp. 81-82. Hall, *op. cit.,* pp. 381-382. Trevelyan, *John Bright,* pp. 139-141, says that the objection to Palmerston was a welcome excuse for Lord Russell.

Cabinet than before.[4] He was therefore obliged to resign himself to the dreary task of retrenchment,—attempting to resolve all outstanding disputes, and salvaging what he could from the wreck of his foreign policy.[5] It is only in the light of the abandonment of his earlier attitude toward French relations that Aberdeen's later actions in regard to the Plata intervention become intelligible.

The news of the initiation of hostilities in the Plata in August, 1845, had made the British Foreign Office decidedly uneasy. While Aberdeen still entertained high hopes that a brilliant success might vindicate his foreign policy, his instructions to Ouseley lost all of their earlier belligerent character. He cautioned his agent to remain strictly neutral between the Oriental factions, and to restrict his coercive measures to naval activities alone. The troops destined for South Africa should be sent on, he said, as soon as possible. The British Minister also secured Guizot's co-operation in forbidding their agents to guarantee a loan to Montevideo. Ouseley was even told that the money he had spent in fitting out a fleet of small boats at Montevideo should be regarded as a loan to the city.[6]

The London authorities were greatly annoyed when they learned of the Paraná expedition. Why, asked Aberdeen, had such an aggressive measure been undertaken before the full effects of the severing of the communications of Oribe were ascertained? Aberdeen realized that it was too late to order the abandonment of the enterprise; but Ouseley was warned that he was not to employ British vessels thereafter in violation of Argentine territory except when "directly and absolutely necessary to prevent aggression by Buenos Ayres upon the independent Rights of Montevideo."[7] These misgivings did not, however, prevent the British Government from des-

[4] Parker, op. cit., 3, pp. 411-412. Guizot pretended that these warlike preparations were being directed exclusively against America. Journal de Débats, Dec. 1, 1845. Quoted by Cass in Cong. Globe, 15, p. 242.

[5] Hunt's Merchant's Magazine 17, pp. 19-33. Guyot, op. cit., pp. 267-280. Hall, op. cit., pp. 369-380.

[6] F. O. 6, 102, Aberdeen to Ouseley, Nov. 5, 17, Dec. 3, 1845. Vol. 114, Jan. 13, 21, 1846. Aff. Etr., Buenos Ayres, 35, pp. 131-132. Repeatedly, Guizot expressed the fear that Rosas might separate the allies. F. O. 27, 748, Cowley to Aberdeen, Jan. 12, 1846.

[7] F. O. 6, 102, Aberdeen to Ouseley, Dec. 27, 1845.

patching an additional steam vessel to assist Hotham in forcing the passage of the river.[8]

The policy adopted by the Paris Government toward these later developments of the intervention was affected to a surprising extent by that of England. Guizot enjoyed a moment of popularity in France when the first news arrived concerning the bold advance of their forces up the Paraná; and the Foreign Minister was at first inclined to share the prevailing enthusiasm.[9] He prepared approving instructions for Deffaudis, and drew up an extended justification of the river expedition in reply to the protest of the Argentine agent at Paris. All this was changed after he was informed concerning the attitude of Aberdeen. The instructions to Deffaudis were considerably altered to agree with the British point of view, and the letter intended for the Argentine agent was never delivered.[10]

Aberdeen had by this time lost all his zest for the French *entente*, and was retreating from the Plata war much more rapidly than was Guizot. The difference in the reactions of the two men to the news of the battle of *Obligado*, which arrived in February, 1846, was very noticeable. The French Minister was highly elated. He spoke of the victory as "most creditable to both services," and was eager to learn what effect it would have on the obstinacy of the Dictator. He assured the British Ambassador that such an example of loyal co-operation between their forces "could not fail to improve the good feeling" between France and England.[11] In striking contrast to the enthusiasm of Guizot was the grave concern expressed by Aberdeen lest this gratuitous aggression by the

[8] Mackinnon, *op. cit.*, 1, pp. 19-27.

[9] *Revue des Deux Mondes*, 1845, vol. 3, pp. 164-167. Sept. 30, 1845. The editor thought that the break had been too hasty.

[10] F. O. 27, 745, Aberdeen to Cowley, Jan. 23, 1846; 748, C. to A., Jan. 26. *Aff. Etr.*, Buenos Ayres, 36, p. 10 ff.

[11] F. O. 27, 749, Cowley to Aberdeen, Feb. 2, 13, 15, 1846. The official account of the battle appeared in the *Moniteur* for Feb. 14, 1846. The *National Intelligencer* for June 22, 1846, contained the following news from Paris: "The colors taken at the battle of *Obligado* in the La Plata war have been pompously carried to the *Hôtel des Invalides* . . . National pride relishes the French share in that aggression; the *sycee* silver from Canton was welcomed in London as a better trophy than the laurels gained by the British at *Obligado*. O ye peace-makers, opium heroes, and joint mediators."

allied forces should make a settlement all the more difficult. The two Ministers were still sufficiently in agreement, however, to declare that the terms of the Mareuil treaty were entirely unsatisfactory.[12]

Other political considerations were driving the two governments apart. Guizot was finding an almost indispensable support for his tottering foreign policy in this much-praised effort to succor French nationals in Uruguay.[13] The only objection that appeared in the Chambers was that the intervention was not sufficiently independent and effective.[14] On the other hand, forces had been gathering in England in opposition to the intervention which were soon to turn the cautious retreat of Aberdeen into a complete rout. The financial and commercial interests who had expected so much from the intervention found themselves more embarrassed than ever. Private debts to British creditors at Buenos Ayres were unpaid, and the interest on the public debt of Argentina had been definitely suspended.[15] Said a report to Parliament on the subject:

> "The great prospects indulged in England, before the expedition to the Plata, of immense profits by trade to that river, have generally ended in ruin; very few indeed of the speculators have escaped without considerable loss." [16]

The British Foreign Office had found itself flooded since early December with petitions asking that the intervention be discontinued.[17] A pamphlet was widely circulated declaring that the operations had only prolonged the war, and that the

[12] F. O. 6, 114, Aberdeen to Ouseley, Feb. 4, 1846. As to Mareuil's treaty, Aberdeen objected that Oribe could not be addressed as President; the safety of foreign and native belligerents was not guaranteed; and the blockade could not be disallowed as a precedent, as had been demanded. Guizot approved these objections. F. O. 27, 749, Cowley to Aberdeen, Feb. 13, 1846.

[13] *Le Moniteur Universel*, Dec. 28, 1846. Jan. 9, 15, 16, 1846. The most cutting criticism came from one Saint-Priest ridiculing Guizot for sending Page, whose letter from Mackau had been published by Rosas. The opposition in the Chamber of Peers was divided, one man even defending Rosas. Guizot was thrown violently on the defensive on the Texas question during the January debates.

[14] *Ibid.*, Jan. 13, Feb. 5, 1846.

[15] F. Durand, *op. cit.*, pp. 163-167. *National Intelligencer*, Jan. 8, 1846.

[16] MacGregor, *op. cit.*, p. 298.

[17] F. O. 6, 113, Domestic Corresp., Canning to various, Dec. 3-17. Between these dates no less than 15 protests against the intervention were answered.

interests of merchants in Argentina had been flagrantly sacrificed for the benefit of a few speculators who had purchased the customs receipts at Montevideo. The only alternative to complete withdrawal before Oribe, the paper argued, was open war; and one "more causeless,—more hopeless,—more unjust, impolitic, and inglorious, will never have been waged." [18] This British agitation was supplemented by an effective piece of Argentine propaganda in the form of a public letter to Lord Aberdeen from a fictitious Alfred Mallalieu. It was a clever apology for the régime of Rosas, and included a thoroughgoing defense of his policy toward Uruguay. This letter, also, enjoyed a wide hearing, for it carried the endorsement of Mandeville and other English friends of the Dictator. [19]

The opposition began to come to a focus in late February. The arguments of Mallalieu were forced upon Aberdeen's attention in the House of Lords. Oribe's authority in Uruguay, said one speaker, was more legal than that of Montevideo, and Rosas had a perfect right to defend himself from his enemies. It was also remarked that the opening of the Paraná river was a dangerous precedent for England in view of the current quarrel with the United States over the use of the St. Lawrence. The attack culminated in a motion directing that the correspondence with France concerning the intervention should be laid before the House. The Foreign Minister was not over-careful with the facts in his reply. He insisted, in the first place, that Oribe was nothing more than the agent of Rosas. France and England were fully justified, after two years of patient forbearance, in taking measures to enforce their demand of 1842 that the "senseless war" should cease. The requested disclosure of the French correspondence, he concluded, "might prove exceedingly mischievous," especially since the

[18] F. O. 6, 128, L. Lucas to Canning, Jan. 27, 1846. "An Appeal on behalf of the British subjects residing and connected with the River Plata against any further violent Intervention by the British and French Governments in the Affairs of that Country." Printed by Norris and Son (London 1846).

[19] *Archivo Americano*, Nov. 30, 1845, p. 4 ff. *Papeles de Rozas*, in 2 vols., vol. 2, pp. 75–77, Mandeville to Manuela, Sept. 27, 1850. Brossard, *op. cit.*, pp. 340–348.

Dictator had recently made encouraging proposals of peace. The motion was finally withdrawn.[20]

Aberdeen developed a complete panic on the question of the river expedition a few days later. Without a word of consultation with Guizot, he sent the following peremptory order to Ouseley on March 4:

"Take what steps you may deem the most advisable to assure the prompt and unconditional recall of the squadron under the command of Capt. Hotham."

He could not approve the river expedition, Aberdeen explained to his agent, because it was an act of aggression against a state with whom Great Britain was not at war.[21] The Paris authorities were not informed of this move until Aberdeen's letter was two days on the way. Guizot was then invited to make a similar decision, on the ground that he had already expressed his disapproval of the Paraná expedition.[22]

A quarrel ensued between Paris and London over the question. Guizot was both surprised and offended at the discourtesy shown him. He declared that he knew of no recent alarming development which called for an action so precipitate that France could not have been consulted. Were the British forces still to act in concert with the French? Perhaps other orders had been sent without the knowledge of France. The French Ambassador at London was directed to remind Aber-

[20] *Parliamentary Debates,* 3d Series, 83, p. 1152 ff. Feb. 19, 1846. This reference to the Mareuil treaty sounds strange.

[21] F. O. 6, 114, to Ouseley, Mar. 4, 1846. It is more than possible that this sudden decision was caused by the likelihood of an American war developing over Oregon. Buchanan's conciliatory suggestion that Britain might again propose the 49° settlement, made on Feb. 26, could not have been known in London by Mar. 4; and even as late as Apr. 1, Aberdeen doubted a favorable outcome. The 3000 sailors and 16 major British war vessels in the Plata could have been of considerable assistance to Admiral Seymour in the Pacific, who was at Valparaiso at the time insisting that he be sent reënforcements. Seymour's request did not reach London until June, 1846, at which time Aberdeen refused to send the vessels asked for, on the grounds that it would make the home fleet inferior to the French, and also because danger of war with U. S. was passed. See Moore, *Works of Buchanan,* 6, pp. 377-383. *Peña y Reyes, op. cit.,* pp. 65-68. *National Intelligencer,* Dec. 12, 1845. *Le Moniteur,* Jan. 15, 1846. E. D. Adams, *op. cit.,* pp. 254-260. *Accounts and Papers,* 1849, XXXII, (110) Parl. Papers.

[22] *Aff. Etr.,* Buenos Ayres, 35, p. 376. Aberdeen to Cowley, Mar. 6, 1846, and enclosure.

deen emphatically that their agents had been fully authorized to employ coercion against the party which refused to make peace. A too hasty retreat now would render a solution practically impossible.[23] Aberdeen's attempted justification for his admitted discourtesy was far from convincing. The receipt of the news that a merchant vessel had been pursued up a tributary of the Paraná, he said, had convinced him that he must immediately put an end to acts which altered the character of the expedition, and left the Government without means of replying satisfactorily to the announced interpolation of Lord Russell. The immediate departure of the mail packet had been responsible, he alleged, for his inability to communicate with Paris on the subject. Aberdeen agreed, however, that their concert should not be broken.[24]

The supplementary instructions to Ouseley, which Aberdeen immediately sent, directed the agent to "lose no opportunity of renewing those unreserved and confidential relations which should characterize the joint intervention." [25] But the previous order was not rescinded, nor was it made conditional on the acquiescence of the French. When Guizot finally sent orders on March 20 for the French forces also to withdraw from the Paraná, it was on the condition that the holding of the upper river should not be indispensable to the purposes of the intervention.[26]

The dreaded interpolations of the Whig leaders in the British Parliament took place on March 11 and 23. Palmerston was at his best in ridiculing the pretensions of Peel that they were still at peace with Argentina. He asked the Government to explain the nature of the recent occurrences on the Paraná. The Prime Minister argued first that a blockade did

[23] *Aff. Etr.*, Buenos Ayres, 35, p. 376. Aberdeen to Cowley, Mar. 6, 1846, London, Mar. 11, 1846.

[24] *Aff. Etr.*, Buenos Ayres, 35, pp. 401-402. St. Aulaire to Guizot, Mar. 16, 1846. The necessity of sending the 1300 soldiers at Montevideo on to Cape of Good Hope was an added reason for the return of the marines to replace them. Aberdeen yielded to the Admiralty on this point on April 8. F. O. 6, 114, A. to O., Jan. 7, 14, Apr. 8; vol. 128, to Canning, Jan. 31, 1846.

[25] F. O. 6, 114, to Ouseley, Mar. 17, 1846. *Aff. Etr.*, Buenos Ayres, 35, p. 404.

[26] *Aff. Etr.*, Buenos Ayres, 35, p. 407. To Deffaudis, Mar. 20, 1846.

not necessarily mean war. He then repudiated all responsibility for the river expedition by the very questionable affirmation that the Government had never contemplated such an action.[27] It is evident that the British authorities had ceased making any attempt to defend their policy in Argentina.

Aberdeen discovered a ray of hope that he might free himself from the embarrassing complications of the Plata in a proposal brought forward by T. S. Hood, formerly British consul at Montevideo.[28] On the basis of his intimate acquaintance with both Rosas and Oribe, Hood took the liberty to express his conviction to Aberdeen that the Argentine Government would be ready to withdraw their forces from Uruguay and meet every other reasonable demand, if only their belligerent rights were acknowledged, Martín García and the fleet restored, and the foreigners at Montevideo disarmed.[29] Hood convinced the Foreign Minister that he himself was the one best qualified to negotiate the question.[30] He was ably assisted in his cause by pressure from the employed agent of commercial and banking firms having interests in Argentina. This agent insisted in a letter of April 22 to Aberdeen that the intervention should be discontinued at once. Shipments from Liverpool, he said, had fallen to one-seventh of their normal volume, and debts due British merchants at Buenos Ayres, amounting to £700,000 had already been cut in half because they were payable in the depreciating paper money. Losses from this cause would become increasingly greater if the interference were continued, and in the end, all British property at Buenos Ayres might be appropriated outright. The letter concluded with the following observation:

[27] *Parliamentary Debates,* 3d Series, 78, pp. 639-44; 83, pp. 1432-1439. That Aberdeen had prepared himself for an even more elaborate defense is proven by two Memorandums in F. O. 6, 128. In January, 1840, Aberdeen had maintained that: "the right of blockade was strictly a belligerent right. . . . France was at war with Buenos Ayres." *Ibid.,* 51, p. 572.

[28] F. O. 51, Montevideo, 24, Canning to Hood, May 31, 1843. *Ibid.* Vasquez to Aberdeen, July 2, 1843. Hood's recall had been demanded because of his partiality for Oribe and Rosas.

[29] F. O. 6, 129, Hood to Aberdéen, Apr. 6, 1846.

[30] Durand, *op. cit.,* pp. 167-168. French writers all assert that Hood was the agent of the Baring Banking house. He had personally negotiated the Baring loan of 1825.

"We feel that it is much to be lamented that the opportunity which was afforded by the Argentine Government in October last [through Mareuil] for the resumption of negotiations was slighted by Mr. Ouseley. . . . Some Gentleman acquainted with Buenos Ayres and its people [Mr. Hood should] go and settle this matter." [31]

The French Government was informed of the new idea of Aberdeen in a letter from St. Aulaire, dated April 24. The Ambassador reported that the British Government was so annoyed by the incessant complaints against the Argentine intervention and by the fact that it presented such a vulnerable target for the Whigs that they would not hesitate to recall the British forces immediately if it were not for their agreement with France. Since he felt that it was probable that Rosas would not treat with the agents who had made themselves his personal enemies, Aberdeen had suggested that a Mr. Hood, a sagacious man with favorable local connections, should be entrusted with the negotiation of a settlement. The regular Commissioners could be directed to conclude officially the peace which he would arrange. If Oribe could be released from his dependence on Argentine troops and have his authority confirmed by a regular election, the war would at least be brought to an end. The British Government, concluded St. Aulaire, was anxious that the matter be arranged by the first of May.[32]

In spite of the fact that Hood was known from his previous career to be rabidly anti-French and an intimate friend of Oribe, the Paris Government accepted the proposal of Aberdeen. Guizot apparently did not relish the idea of having to settle the affair with the terrible Palmerston.[33] A joint memorandum was accordingly drawn up, and the signatures of

[31] F. O. 6, 129, L. Lucas to Aberdeen, Apr. 22, 1846, writing from 13 New Broad St., London.

[32] *Aff. Etr.*, Buenos Ayres, 36, pp. 83-92. St. Aulaire to Guizot, Apr. 24, 1846.

[33] St. Aulaire, from London, submitted his mild protest against this too easy acquiescence by Guizot. He doubted the wisdom of allowing a British agent, the friend of Oribe, to speak for France. Nor was it right that they desert a Government recognized by both Powers, without guaranteeing a true expression of the will of the people. *Aff. Etr.*, Buenos Ayres, 36, p. 136. To Guizot, May 16, 1846.

the two Ministers attached on May 5. The terms were approximately those of the Mareuil treaty. Foreigners within Montevideo should be disarmed and the Argentine troops withdrawn from Uruguay simultaneously. Immediately thereafter, the European forces should raise the blockade of Buenos Ayres, evacuate Martín García, and restore captured vessels. The independent rights of Argentina, including her exclusive control over the Paraná, should be fully recognized, as well as the application under similar circumstances to Great Britain and France of the principles underlying their interruption of the belligerent rights of Buenos Ayres. Oribe must agree to abide by the outcome of a free Presidential election;—but nothing was said concerning the question of the person who should conduct the election. Argentine émigrés at Montevideo would be obliged to remove to a foreign port or to withdraw into the interior. In case Montevideo should refuse to disarm the foreigners after Rosas and Oribe had accepted the terms proposed, all European intervention should cease.[34]

The preparation of the more detailed instructions for Hood was left to Aberdeen. What passed between these two men in their many oral conversations referred to in the instructions can only be conjectured. The brief written directions given contained at least two important departures from the terms of the May 5 memorandum. In the first place, the mere *substantial* acceptance of their proposal by Rosas and Oribe was said to be sufficient. Second, instead of the order to maintain the blockade until after the execution of the disarmament at Montevideo and the withdrawal of the Argentine troops, Aberdeen wrote:

"It would appear that as soon as the proposition shall have been accepted by General Rosas and General Oribe, and the armistice declared, it would be just and expedient at once to raise the blockade of Buenos Ayres."

Although Guizot was furnished with a copy of these instruc-

[34] F. O. 6, 125. Identical documents, dated May 5, in English and French, signed by Aberdeen and Guizot respectively. *Aff. Etr.*, Buenos Ayres, 37, pp. 371-373.

tions,[35] the changes made were never incorporated into the original memorandum.

The two Commissioners were told nothing concerning the nature of the Hood mission, except that they were to conclude the settlement which the new agent was authorized to negotiate, withdrawing all of their support from Montevideo if that government refused to accept it.[36] In Aberdeen's final instructions to Ouseley, he maligned the luckless agent most unmercifully. He charged that Ouseley had deliberately violated his instructions in embarking upon open hostilities and in urging his government to declare war against Rosas. The Commissioner had allowed himself, said Aberdeen, to be unworthily influenced by feelings of personal enmity toward Rosas. The tentative recognition accorded Paraguay and the financial assistance given Montevideo extended entirely beyond his authority and were contrary to the wishes of his superiors.[37]

Later, in the same month that the Hood mission was agreed upon, the French Government found itself attacked in the Chambers for having failed to act with sufficient vigor in its operations against Rosas. Thiers led out in the demand that the Government cast aside the foolish pretense of being at peace with Buenos Ayres, and adopt adequate measures for the quick relief of French commerce and the fulfillment of their obligations to Uruguay, that "veritable French colony." Further delay, he argued, would only play into the hands of Rosas, while a few thousand men could easily raise the siege of Montevideo.

The Government was not without a reply. Guizot called attention to the broader interests of France, represented by

[35] F. O. 6, 125, Aberdeen to Hood, May 19, 1846. *Aff. Etr.*, Buenos Ayres, 36, pp. 139-140. F. O. 6, 129, Smythe to Capt. W. A. B. Hamilton of the Admiralty, May 18, 1846, directing a steamer to convey Mr. Hood to the Plata with the utmost speed.

[36] F. O. 6, 114, Aberdeen to Ouseley, May 5, 1846. *Aff. Etr.*, Buenos Ayres, 36, pp. 110-111. To Deffaudis, May 5.

[37] F. O. 6, 114, Aberdeen to Ouseley, Apr. 28, June 25, 1846. The French agent was informed that his Government had abandoned all thought of rendering further assistance to Montevideo. *Aff. Etr.*, B. A., 36, pp. 170, 218-221. To Deffaudis, May 30; to Lainé, June 30.

the many petitions recently sent to him opposing the blockade. He flatly denied that they had any obligation toward Montevideo, and again referred to the instructions which Thiers himself had prepared in 1840. He finally asserted his unalterable determination not to allow the situation to revert to the unhappy state of affairs from which they had been freed by those instructions. Mackau came to the support of his chief. He declared that he would have resigned from the Cabinet had there ever been any intention of undertaking a hazardous military expedition into the interior. Such a move, he insisted, would immediately unite all Americans against the French, and would expose their own nationals to further danger. Thiers became angry when he attempted to reply. Interruptions and personal jibes were frequent. Disorder prevailed. When the question was finally made a matter on confidence, the Government emerged with a fairly comfortable majority of eighty-five votes.[38] Subsequent attacks of a similar character were not participated in by Thiers,[39] but the Argentine issue had ceased to be a great source of strength for the Government.

When the fact of the Hood mission became generally known in Paris, late in June, Guizot was again thrown on the defensive. He was asked to explain why a foreigner, inimical to French interests, had been entrusted with such an important negotiation in preference to their own agent already on the ground. In order to escape from this predicament, Guizot resorted to a questionable subterfuge. Hood had been chosen, as had Page previously, he said, because he was personally qualified to use his influence to contribute to the ends which the governments had in view. In neither case was there any contradiction with the mission which was confided to the official agents. Since England had not objected to the use of Page, he concluded, France therefore had no reason to complain of the present employment of Hood. The opposition was power-

---

[38] *Le Moniteur Universel,* May 14, 1846. Brossard, *op. cit.,* p. 241. Thiers continued his attempted explanation through the press.
[39] *Le Moniteur Universel,* May 30, 1846.

less, of course, to disprove this not overscrupulous representation of the facts, and the Government again saved itself.[40]

While the Cabinets of Europe had been repudiating, the earlier policy, their agents at Montevideo were struggling with problems which accumulated faster than they could be solved. The friction within the city between the native Orientals and the Europeans developed into an open insurrection in April, 1846. The outbreak was precipitated when Rivera suddenly appeared in the harbor and sought in vain for permission to land.[41] The excitement was fanned by the rumor that the British troops within the city were about to withdraw. The black regiments on the outer defenses fired on their officers and abandoned their positions. The disorder quickly spread throughout the city. For several days, the leading men of the government were obliged to conceal themselves in Ous>ley's garret. Had it not been for the presence of the British regulars and the French marines, who put a stop to pillaging and manned the inner defenses so as to forbid the entrance of any troops from without, the city would have fallen into a state of complete anarchy. When the French Basques themselves began to declare for Rivera, and the European leaders were faced with the disagreeable alternative of firing into the refractory regiments, they finally permitted the ex-President to come ashore. Rivera immediately assumed the post of Minister of War, while a friend and supporter, one Magariños, arrived from Rio de Janeiro shortly thereafter to take the position of Foreign Minister.[42]

[40] *Ibid.*, June 26, 1846. Hood carried official credentials and instructions signed by both Ministers, while the Page mission was private and confidential.

[41] A. Palomeque, *op. cit.*, pp. 114–119. Brazil had permitted Rivera's departure from Rio out of sympathy for his hostility to the Europeans. His party was seeking to organize a local coalition against Rosas, and the presence of the Europeans greatly delayed this movement. S. D. Brazil, Desp. 15, from Wise, Mar. 6, 1845. *Aff. Etr.*, Buenos Ayres, 34, p. 345. The British Admiral had vetoed the proposed return of Rivera in August, 1845.

[42] F. O. 6, 117, Ouseley to Aberdeen, Apr. 3, 7, 16, 19, 1846. *Ibid.*, 118, May 28, 1846. S. D. Brazil, Desp. 15, Wise to Buchanan, Apr. 29, 1846

The interventionists were never able to recover their standing in Montevideo. In an effort to regain the confidence of the Foreign Legion, they published the statement appearing in Ouseley's first instructions that:

"when once obliged to resort to coercive measures, the Intervening Powers will not desist until their objects are affected." [43]

Finding themselves subjected to daily attacks from Rivera's press, the Commissioners were obliged to present a formal protest to Magariños. They solemnly declared that, however much they should dislike to withdraw, their co-operation could not continue under the existing circumstances.[44] Relations improved somewhat, but the new party in control did not surrender its conviction that the salvation of Montevideo and Uruguay was not to be expected from European assistance. With Rivera again taking to the open country up the Uruguay river at the head of a group of Oriental deserters from Oribe's forces and supported by a naval force under Garibaldi, the Montevidean Government began to bend all of its efforts toward interesting the surrounding states and the inter-river provinces in a coalition against their common enemy at Buenos Ayres.[45]

No sooner had order been restored at Montevideo than it became necessary to take measures to revive the prostrate credit of the city. Direct financial assistance must be provided if the Europeans wished to avoid the seizure and confiscation of a vast amount of foreign property which had accumulated at the port. It was perfectly evident, as Ouseley pointed out in his despatch, that troops with arms in their hands would not be content to starve when food could be had

---

and enclosure. Durand, *op. cit.*, pp. 168-169. Contemporaneous quarrels within Oribe's forces probably prevented an attack on the town during this insurrection.

[43] F. O. 6, 117, Ouseley to Aberdeen, Apr. 23, 1846.

[44] *Aff. Etr.*, Buenos Ayres, 36, pp. 66-67. Ouseley and Deffaudis to Magariños, Apr. 28, 1846. The Montevidean Government was almost entirely personal. The Assembly of Notables met only 4 or 5 times a month and never did very much business. See *Actas de to honorable Asamblea de notables Años, 1846, 47, 48, 49, 50, 51.* (Montevideo, 1897.)

[45] Durand, *op. cit.*, pp. 170-173. Palomeque, *op. cit.*, pp. 119-130; 163; 176-200.

from pillage.[46] The Commissioners therefore agreed to underwrite a fourth part of a loan of $60,000 a month to the government, the remaining 75% being covered by private contributions and by the sale of a portion of the customs receipts for 1849. A clandestine trade to Buenos Ayres, which had gained considerable proportions during the absence of the fleet up the Paraná, was largely connived at, and came to provide a partial outlet for the goods which paid duties at Montevideo.[47]

After all the strenuous exertions on the part of the Commissioners in combating these difficulties, it is not strange that they were thoroughly disgusted at the precipitate retreat staged by their governments. Charged with the double responsibility of protecting Montevideo and of obliging Rosas to withdraw his troops from Uruguay, they found themselves under the necessity of sending away the only regular troops under their direct control, and of confining their operations to a perfectly useless blockade.[48] It was impossible to disembark the troops destined for South Africa until the Paraná expedition had returned. Even then, Admiral Inglefield refused to spare the marines required to replace them because of the "great apparent probability of a war with the United States," which, he said, might require his immediate departure. Only the increasing number of desertions from Oribe's camp, where serious friction between Argentines and Orientals had developed, made it possible in July, 1846, to embark the two British regiments.[49]

When Aberdeen's unfair criticisms reached Ouseley, the latter could not refrain from making a spirited rejoinder. He indignantly denied that his course had been determined by personal hostility toward Rosas. He contended that the Dic-

[46] F. O. 6, 118, Ouseley to Aberdeen, May 6, 1846.

[47] *Ibid.*, 119, June 5, 1846. British goods alone in Montevideo amounted to more than a million sterling. S. D. Arg. Rep., Desp. 5, Brent to Buchanan, Sept. 7, 1847, from Fairfax County, Va.

[48] F. O. 6, 117, Ouseley to Aberdeen, Apr. 7 and 9. *Ibid.*, 118, May 6, 1846. Deffaudis complained that the withdrawal from the river surrendered their most effective means of coercion, and repudiated the only action which carried any glory with it. *Aff. Etr.*, Buenos Ayres, 37, p. 211.

[49] F. O. 6, 119, *ibid.*, June 5, 20, 25, 29; 120, July 7, 26. The two regiments left on July 3 and 26 respectively.

tator's position as Governor of Buenos Ayres gave him no
authority whatever to claim exclusive control of river navigation. In such matters all the provinces of the Confederation
shared equally. Recently, he said, a distinct coolness had
developed between Urquiza and Rosas on that very question.
The Entre Rian leader flouted the orders issued by the Dictator, and allowed vessels to clear openly from Montevideo for
his province. The occupation of the Paraná river, continued
Ouseley, had been contemplated from the very beginning as
a part of the blockade of the Province of Buenos Ayres. Furthermore, he had seen no evidence of the reasonableness on the
part of the Governor to which Aberdeen's letter referred.[50]
Recent desertions from Oribe, he pointed out, had left that
leader entirely dependent upon his Argentine forces, while
Rivera's activities, along with those of Garibaldi, in the north
were decidedly encouraging.[51]

The arrival of Hood at Buenos Ayres on July 2, an event
which was loudly acclaimed by Rosas,[52] threw the Uruguayan
capital into a state of indescribable turmoil. The defenders
of the city, embittered by long privations and now exasperated
at the apparent repudiation of the solemn promises of the
Commissioners, were in no humor to submit tamely to the triumph of their hated enemy. The entire future of the Basque
soldiers was dependent upon the survival of the government
which had promised to repay them by grants of land.[53] The
following excerpt from a report of Hood, on July 25, gives an
idea of the state of affairs:

"Montevideo appears to be in a perfect Pandemonium. . . .
Everything is topsy-turvy. . . . In Truth, Insanity has usurped

[50] F. O. 6, 119, Ouseley to Aberdeen, June 29, 1846; 117, *ibid.,* Apr. 19;
118, May 6; 119, June 6, July 9 and 20, 1846. Urquiza abandoned his
operations in both Corrientes and Uruguay, and refrained from any attempt to resist the Paraná expedition from the Entre Rian side. A new
coalition including Paraguay was definitely projected.

[51] F. O. 6, 120, O. to A., July 11, 26, 1846. Wages of $8 to $10 a day
could be had in Rio Grande, and they attracted many deserters. *Ibid.,*
122, Sept. 22; 123, Oct. 31, 1846.

[52] F. O. 6, 125, Hood to Aberdeen, July 18, 1846. Exchange at Buenos
Ayres rose within two weeks from 454 to the gold dollar to 275.

[53] F. O. 51, Montevideo, 41, F. Hamilton to Aberdeen, July 13, 1846;
S. D. Brazil, Desp. 15, Wise to Buchanan, June 19, 1846.

the place of Reason and Chaos the place of Order, and what is to
be done to get things back to their old place, God only knows. . . .

"Baron Deffaudis declares that he will on *no conditions* make
peace with General Rosas, and Mr. Ouseley declares that, without
positive and *specific* orders, he will adhere to his Instructions to
act in unison with his French Colleague. . . . I much fear that
under some pretext or other, . . . the basis agreed upon by England and France, and accepted with very slight alterations, will
be referred back to the Allied Governments." [54]

The substantial agreement of Rosas and Oribe to the proposals of Hood was obtained without difficulty. Following the
suggestion of Aberdeen, it was agreed that the blockade should
be lifted and the Argentine vessels restored as soon as the
armistice should be declared. Another departure from the
May 5 memorandum was an arrangement by which Oribe's
consent to the treaty was indicated by the signature of one
Villademoras, who assumed the title of "Foreign Minister of
the Oriental Republic." [55] Hood presented both his instructions and the negotiated treaties to the Commissioners at
Montevideo about the middle of August.

As the negotiator had anticipated, the treaties encountered
anything but a favorable reception. Ouseley kept himself
conveniently in the background while the not unwilling Deffaudis took the initiative. The French agent denied that he was
bound by anything but the strict letter of the May 5 memorandum; he paid no attention to the personal assurances of
Hood, and would not admit the separate instructions signed
by Aberdeen. He would therefore accept neither the time
specified for raising the blockade nor the approval of the
treaty by the pretended Foreign Minister of the Government
of Oribe.[56] An embarrassing complication arose when Magariños, probably only too ready to indicate his separation from
the European faction, accepted the Hood proposal, with the
single reservation that the Oriental troops should not be
obliged to evacuate Martín García along with the European

[54] F. O. 6, 125, Hood to Aberdeen, July 25, 1846.
[55] F. O. 6, 125. From an undated Memorandum of Hood. See *Documentos relativos a la Misión del Honorable Sr. D. Tomás Samuel Hood*,
(Buenos Ayres 1846), pp. 4-15. Pereyra, *Rosas y Thiers*, pp. 184-186.
[56] *Aff. Etr.*, Buenos Ayres, 36, pp. 336-354. F. O. 6, 125, Hood to Aberdeen, Aug. 1, 13, 20, 26, 27, 1846.

forces.[57] Ouseley refused to break with Deffaudis, as Hood demanded that he should. The only thing to be done was to send the negotiator back to Buenos Ayres to see if the Dictator would agree to the necessary alterations.

The effort to persuade Rosas to alter his terms was fruitless. He announced that he would never consent to an unfair armistice which left the European squadron in control of the situation until after the pacification was completed. He suggested that the European Cabinets first come to some agreement on their instructions.[58]

The negotiations were brought to an abrupt end on September 9, by action of Deffaudis. The French agent took violent exception to a statement which Hood had made to Arana to the effect that the French had ulterior motives, and were solely responsible for the rejection of the terms agreed upon.[59] Ouseley was, in fact, equally hostile with Deffaudis to the treaty, and freely admitted that the French had ample room to complain of the partisanship of the negotiator.[60] The Hood bases would have been almost impossible to execute if for no other reason than because of the fact that Oribe clearly understood that he should assume immediate control of the government and have charge of the new election.[61]

As soon as Ouseley learned that Aberdeen had retired from the Foreign Office, his despatches assumed the form of a series of bitter tirades against the recent policy. He complained to Palmerston that Hood's secret negotiations had entirely undermined the morale of Montevideo at the very time that Oribe's power was crumbling away.[62] The negotiator, he said, had

[57] F. O. 6, 122. Ouseley to Aberdeen, Sept. 1. Palomeque, *La Jurisdicción del Plata*, pp. 176-178. Durand, *op. cit.*, pp. 173-175.

[58] F. O. 6, 125. Hood to Aberdeen, Sept. 13. Enclosure, Arana to Hood, Sept. 6, 1846. Durand, *op. cit.*, p. 175. *Documentos relativos a la Misión del Honorable Sr. T. S. Hood*, pp. 15-51.

[59] *Aff. Etr.*, Buenos Ayres, 36, pp. 405-406, 433. Ouseley to Hood, Sept. 10; Deffaudis to Ouseley, Sept. 9. S. D., Arg. Rep., Desp. 6, Harris to Buchanan, Sept. 10.

[60] F. O. 6, 122, Ouseley to Palmerston, Sept. 6, 1846. *Aff. Etr.*, Buenos Ayres, 36, p. 352. Deffaudis to Guizot, Aug. 28, 1846. Adm. Inglefield made Hood furious by charging him to his face with being interested in a private speculation.

[61] Brossard, *op. cit.*, p. 348. F. O. 6, 122, Ouseley to Palmerston, Sept. 4, 1846.

[62] F. O. 6, 122, Ouseley to Palmerston, Sept. 4.

openly boasted that he himself was responsible for Aberdeen's change of policy. He had also kept Rosas informed of his actions in London for months before his arrival. The charge which he had circulated that France entertained designs upon Uruguay, Ouseley continued, was entirely without foundation; Deffaudis had in fact little or no control over the Basque population. It had finally been proved that Hood himself was interested in speculative shipments from Liverpool.[63]

The entire episode certainly does little credit to Lord Aberdeen.

Two significant facts came to light during the Hood negotiations. It became perfectly apparent, in the first place, from the prodigious preparations for war made by Brazil that a conflict between the Imperial Government and Rosas would surely follow the European withdrawal.[64] A development of still greater significance was an agreement entered into between Governors Urquiza and Madariaga that they would endeavor to establish a Constitutional government for the Confederation and would remain strictly neutral in all "wars or military enterprises which may be entered into by Genl. Rosas without the consent of their people." This latter decision had been communicated to the other Argentine provinces, and was a source of great anxiety to the Dictator.[65] But the ultimate outcome, which was definitely foreshadowed in these developments, was not to be achieved for several years. For the time being, local operations came to a complete standstill, while everyone waited to see what policy Lord Palmerston and the new Whig Government at London would pursue.

[63] *Ibid.*, Sept. 11, 1846. M. T. Hood, son of the agent, and vice-consul at Montevideo, was continually reporting news unfavorable to Ouseley. F. O. 51, 48, Palmerston to Ouseley, Feb. 4, 1847.

[64] S. D. Arg. Rep., Desp. 6, Harris to Buchanan, Aug. 1, Sept. 10, 1846; *National Intelligencer,* Sept. 8, Nov. 25, 1846.

[65] S. D. Arg. Rep., Desp. 6, Harris to Buchanan, Oct. 10, 1846. *National Intelligencer,* Dec. 5, 1846. Harris feared that Urquiza and Madariaga had come to terms with Hotham.

CHAPTER VIII

GUIZOT AND PALMERSTON, 1846-1848

The accession of the Whig Government to power in July, 1846, with Lord Palmerston in the Foreign Office, was the death blow to the faltering Franco-British *entente*. Rather than await the outcome of the suspicious activities of Palmerston's agent at the court of Madrid,[1] Guizot himself precipitated a break by consummating his own arrangement for the Spanish marriages. The action thus taken was in open violation of a previous promise made to Aberdeen, and its disclosure in late August aroused a storm of anger in England. So alarming did the international situation appear that Aberdeen volunteered to support Palmerston if the latter would only strive to keep the peace.[2] Those who distrusted France were now fully vindicated. Suspicion and hatred revived on both sides of the Channel.

Guizot gained no substantial advantage from this bold move. The immediate triumph, of course, was his; but the masterful Palmerston, with his country solidly behind him, was not to be denied his way from this time forward. The support which the French Cabinet gained from the Anglophobe element in the legislative Chambers[3] was more than balanced in the long run by the damaging accusation which they incurred from the Left Center and the Republicans to the effect that Guizot had sacrificed the only friend of France on the altar of dynastic ambition.[4]

The estrangement which developed between the former allies served only to sharpen their common desire to extricate them-

[1] Hall, *op. cit.*, pp. 382-393. Cecil, (*British Foreign Secretaries*, pp. 159-161) attempts to justify Guizot. Guyot, *op. cit.*, pp. 283-298.

[2] G. P. Gooch, *The Later Correspondence of Lord John Russell*, 2 vols. (New York 1925) Vol. 1, pp. 129-130.

[3] *Le Moniteur Universel*, Jan. 19, 1847. The Marquis de Boissy.

[4] Hall, *op. cit.*, pp. 393-396.

selves from the embarrassment of their joint enterprise in the river Plata. With the *entente* destroyed, one of the principal arguments in behalf of their intervention no longer existed. Guizot desired to withdraw as soon as possible.[5] On the British side, Palmerston heartily approved the Hood mission and was committed to the relief of British commerce in Argentina.[6] The new Foreign Minister was also convinced that the intervention was illegal. To his Ambassador in Paris he wrote as follows:

"The real truth is, though we had better keep the fact to ourselves, that the French and British blockade of the Plata has been from the first illegal. Peel and Aberdeen have always declared that we have not been at war with Rosas; but blockade is a belligerent right, and unless you are at war with a state, you have no right to prevent ships from other states from communicating with the ports of that state—nay, you cannot prevent your own merchant ships from doing so. I think it is important, in order to legalize retrospectively the operations of the blockade, to close the matter by a formal convention of peace between the two powers and Rosas."[7]

The desirability of sending a new mission to the Plata was suggested by Palmerston as soon as the outcome of the Hood mission was known in late November.[8] No difficulty was encountered in securing Guizot's consent to his proposal that the Governments should concede the demand of Rosas in regard to the time of raising the blockade. Their first idea, which was merely to notify their respective agents at Montevideo concerning their decision,[9] was abandoned when Palmerston discovered that several alterations in the Hood terms would be

[5] *Aff. Etr.,* Buenos Ayres, 36, p. 222 ff. and 360. To Deffaudis July 4 and Aug. 29, 1846. Guizot disapproved the loan to Montevideo and now declared the war in Uruguay to be a *bona fide* civil war.

[6] F. O. 6, 114, Palmerston to Ouseley, Aug. 12, Sept. 30, Oct. 10, Nov. 4, 1846; *ibid.,* 138, London Merchants to Palmerston, Oct. 18, and reply, Oct. 21,—published on Nov. 9; *ibid.,* 125, Palmerston to Hood, Nov. 25, 1846. F. O. 51, 48, P. to O., Mar. 4, 1847.

[7] H. Lytton Bulwer, *Life of Henry John Temple, Viscount Palmerston,* 3 vols. (London 1871) vol. 3, p. 327, Dec. 7, 1846.

[8] F. O. 27, 747, Palmerston to Normanby, Nov. 20, 1846.

[9] *Aff. Etr.,* Buenos Ayres, 37, pp. 56, 107-110. St. Aulaire to Guizot, Dec. 9, 1846. Bulwer, *op. cit.,* vol. 3, pp. 326-327. Palmerston to Normanby, Dec. 7.

desirable. It would be better, he thought, if Oribe were referred to in the treaty not as President of Uruguay, but merely as the claimant of the Presidency. It also occurred to the British Minister that, in view of the fact that a new alignment of the Argentine Provinces in the future might deprive the present Confederation Government of the left bank of the Paraná, it would be preferable to avoid admitting the absolute control of Buenos Ayres over that river. He would have the treaty acknowledge, instead, only the rights of control over interior waters as derived from the general principles of international law. The sharing of the Oriental state in the control of the Uruguay river should also be specified. In return for these alterations, the Europeans could agree that the allied forces should assume the responsibility of disarming the foreigners within Montevideo and permit the raising of the blockade at the beginning of the armistice. They might also agree to restore Martín García to Buenos Ayres, instead of merely evacuating it as Montevideo desired.[10] Palmerston was confident that such terms would be acceptable.[11]

Guizot's part in determining the character of the new mission was very small indeed. Even if his desires had differed markedly from those of the British Minister, which was probably not the case, he well knew that Palmerston was in no mood to be crossed.[12] The French Minister's one suggestion, to the effect that their agents should be left some discretionary power in view of the unwisdom of concluding the formal Convention until they were assured of the actual pacification and a free election in Uruguay, was immediately vetoed by his suspicious British colleague.[13] After having successfully weathered the debates on the address to the King, in January, 1847,

[10] F. O. 27, 747, Palmerston to Normanby, Dec. 31, 1846; *ibid.*, 773. Same to same, Jan. 19, 25, 1847. *Aff. Etr.*, Buenos Ayres, 38, pp. 18-19, 22-23, 25-29. Normanby to Guizot, Jan. 3, 1847. *Ibid.*, pp. 84-90. Palmerston disliked several of the other articles, also.

[11] *Parliamentary Debates,* 3d Series 89, pp. 508-510.

[12] *Aff. Etr.*, Buenos Ayres, 37, pp. 164-166. Mackau to Guizot, Dec. 27, 1846; vol. 38, pp. 40-41. A protest from the Chamber of Commerce of Bordeaux, to Guizot, dated Dec. 29, 1846.

[13] F. O. 27, 748, Palmerston to Normanby, Feb. 9, 1847.

Guizot approved the terms *in toto* as Palmerston had outlined them.[14]

The plan of entrusting the mission to their new naval commanders[15] was given up when it became apparent that difficulties might arise in negotiating the treaty. Palmerston thereupon suggested that the matter be confided solely to Lord Howden, the new British Minister to Brazil.[16] But Guizot preferred to have his own agent. Count Walewski was finally chosen to accompany Howden. Both Deffaudis and Ouseley were recalled.[17]

The instructions prepared for Walewski reflect clearly the conciliatory attitude of the French Government. Guizot suggested that if any difficulty should arise in designating Oribe as "claiming to be President" and Suarez at Montevideo as "Provisional President" of Uruguay, the Convention might assume a purely military character, or might be made into a three-cornered affair in which Rosas should speak for Oribe and the allies for Montevideo. Whatever form the treaty should take, all parties must be committed to the independence of Uruguay. If Montevideo should decline the terms which had been accepted by Rosas and Oribe, the city was to be allowed three days to consider the matter before the blockade was to be raised and the intervention discontinued. In this latter case, full amnesty and security of the persons and property of foreigners was to be required from Oribe, and Walewski's chief concern should be to prevail upon the French population to abstain from the fighting. If, on the other hand, the Convention was accepted by all parties, the agents of France were to assume responsibility for disarming the foreign-

[14] *Le Moniteur Universel,* Jan. 21, and Feb. 4, 1847. La Plata affairs ceased to be a major subject for discussion during the remainder of 1847. See *ibid.,* May 6, June 24, Aug. 3, 1847.

[15] Durand, *op. cit.,* pp. 175-177. Capt. LePrédour replaced Lainé, and Com. Herbert, an intimate friend of Rosas, replaced Adm. Inglefield. *Aff. Etr.,* Buenos Ayres, 37, pp. 170-171. Guizot to Deffaudis, Jan., 1847; 38, pp. 80-81. Same to Capt. LePrédour, Feb. 8, 1847.

[16] F. O. 27, 773, Palmerston to Normanby, Jan. 25, 1847.

[17] *Aff. Etr.,* Buenos Ayres, 38, pp. 71-72. Guizot to the King, Feb. 20, 1847. *Ibid.,* 37, pp. 271-272. To Deffaudis, Mar. 10, 1847. F. O. 51, Montevideo, 48, to Ouseley, Mar. 4 and 22. Ouseley was severely criticized.

ers, restoring Martín García, and securing the evacuation of Uruguay by the Argentine troops.[18]

Lord Howden's instructions were practically identical with those of the French agent with whom he was charged to act in the fullest confidence. If the negotiations with Rosas should finally break off, Howden was assigned the additional task of trying to arrange an armistice at Montevideo preparatory to the election of an acknowledgeable government.[19] The exact form which the various possible treaties should take was set forth in great detail. The preamble pledged the signers to the independence of Uruguay, and Article V guaranteed to Argentina the territorial rights over the rivers "which, according to the general law of nations, are applicable to interior waters." An accompanying statement from the Advocate General explained the British interpretation of the complete jurisdiction of riparian states.[20]

Howden also received additional oral instructions the nature of which is not revealed. The agent requested, on one occasion, that he be given particular information concerning the course he should pursue in case Walewski attempted to employ the up-river discontent to coerce Rosas or should insist, against the objection of Oribe, that the French population of Montevideo should be permitted to vote in the election.[21] From other sources, it is known that the British Admiralty was

[18] *Aff. Etr.*, Buenos Ayres, 38, pp. 81-96. To Walewski and to Capt. Le-Prédour, Mar. 8, 1847. These instructions were approved by Palmerston. F. O. 6, 132, Palmerston to Howden, Feb. 26.

[19] F. O. 6, 132, Palmerston to Howden, Mar. 22.

[20] *Ibid.*, and three enclosures. Article I provided that the armistice should begin with the signing of the terms. Art. II and III concerned disarmament of Foreign Legion by the Allies, and the withdrawal of the Argentine forces. Article IV stipulated the restoration of the Argentine navy, Martín García, flags, cannon, vessels and cargoes to Buenos Ayres. Art. VI affirmed the rights of both Republics in peace and war equal to those of France and Britain. Art. VII concerned a free election in Uruguay and Art. VIII provided for general amnesty, rights of foreigners, acknowledgment of legitimate claims, and the possible removal from Uruguay of Argentine émigrés endangering the peace of the Plata. It was later agreed that Art. VIII might be omitted if Rosas placed little value on it, or objected to it.

[21] F. O. 6, 133, Howden to Palmerston, Mar. 25, 1847.

bringing pressure to bear for the immediate return of the fleet from the Plata.[22]

The situation which the agents encountered when they arrived at Buenos Ayres in May, 1847, was far from promising. The Hood mission had left Rosas and Oribe in a very powerful position. The cause of Montevideo was hopelessly discredited, and the city was now entirely dependent on the foreign population for its defense. The ferment in the inter-river provinces had died down. It was apparent, moreover, that the continuance of the intervention would be advantageous to Rosas because it assured him of the support of his own people and gave him respite from the impending attack on the part of Brazil and Paraguay. The North American Chargé prophesied that it would be impossible to make peace with Rosas unless the new Commissioners were prepared to offer concessions considerably in advance of those made by Hood. Rosas was also fully aware that the Franco-British *entente* had been broken and was prepared, said Harris, to act as independently as if he had an armed force behind him equal to that of France and England combined. The agent added:

"This contest of the weak with the strong for the mastery is certainly an interesting, and would be an amusing spectacle, if it were not for the fact that whilst the contest lasts, the business and interests of all commercial nations were suffering." [*sic.*] [23]

Howden recognized, upon his arrival, the same discouraging features in the situation. He wrote that Rosas was confident of the strength of his position, and seemed much indisposed to negotiate with them at all on the Uruguay question. Commenting on the extreme hostility which the Argentine people manifested toward all foreigners, he said:

"There is no Country in the Universe where European Diplomacy will always find itself so helpless, and indeed hopeless, as here. . . . There are many points of possible collision, without one of sympathetic contact, unless we abandon every idea of intervention in their affairs." [24]

[22] Gooch, *op. cit.*, 1, pp. 247-8. A memorandum of Lord Auckland, Apr. 2, 1847.
[23] S. D. Arg. Rep., Desp. 6, Harris to Buchanan, May 11, June 4, 1847.
[24] F. O. 6, 133, Howden to Palmerston, May 9, 26.

The relations between the two European agents were from the beginning so inharmonious that the possibility of an open break between them was never remote. The French leaders could not help but resent the persistent efforts of the British to throw upon their country the entire responsibility for the intervention. Because of the French interests at stake in Montevideo, Walewski would be obliged to insist upon the strict execution of his instructions. Howden, on the other hand, was apparently ready to withdraw from the affair at almost any cost. He was by no means sure that the dark rumors of French intrigue circulated by Rosas were without foundation. He told Harris that he thought France was supporting the efforts of Montevideo to secure aid from Brazil, and said that Britain was prepared to sustain the cause of Oribe if such an arrangement developed.[25] In case the Foreign Legion should seize control at Montevideo, the British squadron was under express orders to render "every assistance short of hostilities" to enable Oribe to enter the city.[26] Howden would not consent to the suggestion of his associate that they shift all responsibility for failure directly upon Rosas by first securing the agreement of the two parties at Montevideo to their terms.[27] The Commissioners were able to co-operate at all only because they both much desired that a general settlement should take place.

The first developments were nevertheless encouraging. The agents were received at Buenos Ayres with enthusiasm, and their Admirals were able promptly to arrange temporary armistices between the forces in Uruguay.[28] The first objections which Rosas raised had been anticipated in their instructions. The Commissioners met them by agreeing to eliminate the amnesty clause and to salute the Argentine flag, and by suggesting that they make the negotiation a three-cornered affair,

---

[25] S. D. Arg. Rep., Desp., 6, Harris to Buchanan, May 11, 25, 1847. This same rumor was current at Rio de Janeiro,—Brazil, Desp. 16, Wise to Buchanan, June 27.

[26] F. O. 6, 133, Howden to Com. Herbert, May 13.

[27] *Ibid.*, Howden to Palmerston, May 14, and May 30.

[28] *Ibid.*, May 11, 14, 21, and enclosures.

and thus avoid the Dictator's objection to treating with Montevideo.[29]

But Rosas was not satisfied, and he had meanwhile become angry because he had not been consulted in arranging for the cessation of hostilities in Uruguay.[30] He immediately suggested more serious alterations in a counter-proposal, presented on May 30. The Dictator omitted from the preamble the clause guaranteeing the independence of the Oriental Republic. He explained that such a provision in a treaty with a European state would, in his opinion, violate the American doctrine, which was the pivot of his entire foreign policy. He based his refusal, he said, on the "determination never to admit the right of any Transatlantic Power to intervene in the affairs of the Continent under any shape, be it Hostility or Protection."[31] All efforts to persuade Rosas to reinsert the clause were futile.[32] The Governor also objected to the wording of the article on the navigation of the rivers. He required that the Paraná river should be explicitly recognized as subject only to the laws and regulations of the Argentine Confederation and that the Uruguay river be similarly controlled in common with the Oriental state.[33]

It is fairly clear that Rosas was deliberately preventing a settlement. He had been previously informed by his agents in Europe that France and England would refuse to tie their hands in the matter of river control.[34] He probably did entertain some suspicion that they had secret designs, but he certainly knew that his demand for absolute control of the rivers would defeat the negotiation. Still another difficulty came to light during the month of futile conversations. The Commissioners discovered that Rosas had never contemplated abandoning Oribe until the latter was installed as President at

[29] *Ibid.*, May 23.
[30] *Ibid.*, June 16. Rosas considered himself betrayed by Oribe and outwitted by the Europeans in this move.
[31] *Ibid.* The United States agent considered Rosas' action to be a definite confirmation of his opinion, long entertained, that the Dictator purposed to bring all the Provinces of the Plata under a single Government. S. D. Arg. Rep., Desp. 6, to Buchanan, June 16.
[32] F. O., 6, 133, H. to P., June 1.
[33] *Ibid.*, June 16.
[34] See F. O. 6, 134, H. to P., July 25, 1847.

Montevideo. Hood had given him to understand that Oribe himself should superintend the new election.

The obstinacy of the Dictator was proof against the combined efforts of the Commissioners and co-operating neutral agents.[35] On June 30, the negotiation ran firmly aground on the question of river control. The agents finally waived all objections and proposed that they return to the exact terms of the Hood Convention. But Rosas would agree to no terms which did not explicitly grant to the Argentine Convention unqualified control over the rivers.[36]

The representatives of the British Government cannot escape a large measure of the responsibility for the failure of the negotiation. While they tried very hard indeed to achieve a general settlement, they made no effort, at the same time, to conceal from Rosas their distrust of the French. Commodore Herbert had long been a friend of the Dictator, and Howden became infatuated with the attractive Manuelita.[37] As a result of the intimacies exchanged during the frequent visits of these two men to the estate of Rosas at Palermo, the Governor was made confident that a break between the two intervening powers was inevitable. Howden repeatedly assured him that the French connection alone prevented a settlement.[38] So cordial did their relations become that Rosas volunteered

[35] F. O. 6, 133, H. to P., June 5, Brossard, *op. cit.*, pp. 351-357. See the *National Intelligencer* for Sept. 10, 1847. S. D. Arg. Rep., Desp. 6, Harris to Buchanan, June 16, 1847. The United States Chargé attributed the failure directly to Rosas.

[36] F. O. 6, 133, H. to P., June 25 and 30. "I beg your Lordship not to suppose," he wrote, "that any erroneous ideas are to be corrected by any asseverations or arguments. An idea once adopted here is imperishable." Brossard, *op. cit.*, pp. 357-360; Durand, *op. cit.*, pp. 177-178.

[37] Saldías, *op. cit.*, vol. 4, p. 377 ff. Ouseley and Herbert developed a bitter quarrel in July over the latter's partiality to the Argentine cause. See F. O. 6, 138, Ouseley to Howden, Oct. 11, 1847. See A. Saldías, *Papeles de Rozas*, 2 vols. (La Plata 1904), vol. 1, pp. 252-253, vol. 2, pp. 85-87. The first is an affectionate letter from Howden to Manuelita, May 27, 1847, and the second a friendly letter from Herbert, dated Nov. 4, 1850, to his "dear, dear friend Manuelita." Carlos Ibarguren, in *Manuelita Rosas* (Buenos Ayres 1926), pp. 67-72, relates that Lord Howden made a proposal of marriage to the daughter of the Governor on May 31, 1847, and that their affecionate correspondence continued after his departure.

[38] F. O. 6, 134, H. to P., July 3, 1847. Rosas showed Howden his correspondence from Rio de Janeiro. It proved the intimacy existing between Brazil and Montevideo but exonerated the French of any share in their intrigue.

to provide Herbert's vessels with fresh provisions.[39] Formal regrets were exchanged between them on June 23 and 24, over the battle of *Obligado*,[40] and the Governor, a few weeks later, returned a British flag and cannon taken in that engagement.[41]

Another phase of the game by which Howden was conspiring to reëstablish the dominant position of his Government at Buenos Ayres concerned the United States Chargé. Mr. Harris had joined with other neutrals in notifying the Commissioners that, in case they should fail to reach a settlement, formal protests would be lodged against the outrageous blockade of the Argentine capital. The problem of formulating a reply worried Howden. He saw no way to defend the illegal system then in operation, and wanted particularly to avoid a damaging quarrel with the influential American Chargé.[42] The plan which he finally hit upon is foreshadowed in the following report which Mr. Harris sent to Washington:

"After a great deal of conversation with Lord H[owden] . . . . I found that his Lordship was willing to withdraw the blockade, if he had any creditable pretext to do so. I had told him before that if negotiations were broken off without a settlement, I should feel it my duty to address to the Count and himself, a note remonstrating and protesting against a further continuance of the present blockade. His Lordship desired me at once to send him such a note, and said that he was sure that it would be followed by the best consequences." [43]

Harris was only too glad to find this opportunity to restore the prestige of the United States, which had practically been destroyed as a result of the Mexican war.[44] With Howden's

[39] F. O. 6, 133, H. to P., June 3, 1847.
[40] *National Intelligencer*, Sept. 4, 1847.
[41] F. O. 6, 134, H. to P., July 11.
[42] F. O. 6, 133, H. to P., June 16, 25. "The sooner it is got rid of, the better," said Howden, speaking of the blockade. He refused to back a new Montevidean loan and denied to Walewski that the government at that place had any greater claim to legality than had Oribe's.
[43] S. D. Arg. Rep., Desp. 6, Harris to Buchanan, July 3. Howden showed Harris despatches to Palmerston just prepared and promised to raise the blockade as soon as he reached Montevideo.
[44] *Ibid.*, June 16. Harris wrote: "The strongest feelings and prejudices exist here, with all classes of Spaniards, against our people and government in regard to the Mexican War. The best informed of them have not hesitated to tell me, that we are doing toward Mexico precisely what England and France are doing toward this country. They look upon the war as one of mere conquest, and as an act of the grossest and most cruel oppression."

explicit encouragement to spur him on, he proceeded, on July 1, to deliver to the Commissioners identical protests of an extremely vigorous nature. The blockade, he affirmed, had proven itself valueless as a means of securing peace. Its only effect was to substitute for legitimate commerce a spurious trade to Buenos Ayres paying tribute to the anomalous government at Montevideo. The United States, he said, with its strict policy of non-interference, could never approve such a program as the intervention in the Plata. Especially was this the case when the action was prosecuted in America by governments not recognizing "the great conservative principle that the people are the only true and legitimate source of all political power." His government, he said, could not be expected to conform indefinitely to an alleged blockade, which had permitted, within the course of fifteen months, no less than 4012 entries and departures at Buenos Ayres. Harris concluded as follows:

"A longer continuance of the blockade in its present form would probably give some color to the opinion, long since entertained, that one or both of the Governments of England and France have . . . some purpose to establish a permanent political influence in the Banda Oriental which might control or change the form of that government. . . . I must be permitted to declare it as my opinion, that the government of the United States could not sanction for a moment, the establishing of any governments or colonies as political communities in any of the provinces of the Plate, by any European Government. . . .

"I do therefore . . . most respectfully but solemnly protest against any further continuance of the present blockade." [45]

Harris defended his bold departure from the careful neutrality enjoined by his instructions on the ground that the failure of the Europeans to end the disgraceful situation had afforded him an opportunity which he felt obliged to take advantage of. The military prowess which the United States forces were displaying in Mexico would assure them a respectful hearing, and with a single stroke they could regain the

[45] S. D. Arg. Rep., Desp. 6, Harris to Buchanan, July 14, 1847 and enclosed *Gaceta Mercantil* of July 13. The editor of the *Gaceta* declared that Mr. Harris' statement merited a prominent place among the most distinguished documents of North American diplomacy. See also *Niles Register*, 73, pp. 94-95.

goodwill of the Argentine people. It was particularly necessary, he insisted, that he interpose some counter-weight to the influence of Lord Howden, who, by playing a double rôle with Rosas, was shifting the entire responsibility for the failure of the negotiations to the French agents and endeavoring in this way to regain Britain's former ascendency at Buenos Ayres. If the State Department would only follow up his protest, he continued, by authorizing formal inquiries at Paris and London in regard to the matter, and also send a small naval vessel to the river, the prestige of the United States in Argentina could be entirely reëstablished.[46]

It is evident from the explanation made by Harris, that his protest was intended primarily for the benefit of the Argentine people rather than for the European agents. The authorities at Washington apparently made no move whatever to follow out his recommendations. Certainly no inquiries were instituted at the European capitals, and no war vessels were sent to the Plata.

The protest of the American Chargé was turned to clever account by Lord Howden. The Britisher immediately addressed a short reply in which he denied the implication of ulterior motives and at the same time praised the candor and moderation of the letter of Harris. He concluded his statement as follows:

"I am sure that you will hold me excused from discussing the legality of any acts of my Government at the moment when my mission here is terminated. . . .

"With regard to your remarks on the inutility of the blockade and its pernicious effects on the commerce of neutrals, you may rest assured that I have given them my deepest attention. But as it is expressly enjoined to me in my instructions to act in entire concert with the Plenipotentiary of his Majesty the King of the French, you will see the propriety of my not giving any insulated opinion on a subject embracing so many interests." [47]

Walewski fell directly into the trap which Howden's refusal to defend the intervention had set for him. The Count's reply

---

[46] S. D. Arg. Rep., Desp. 6, Harris to Buchanan, July 15.
[47] Ibid., enclosure, Howden to Harris, July 2. Niles Register, 73, p. 95, Oct. 9.

to Harris on July 3 was an extended effort to justify the allied
attempt to pacify the river states. He said that he would
gladly relieve commerce if Rosas would only give him the
opportunity to do so. He also made a formal statement to the
effect that France had never entertained any intention of
compromising the independence of the two Plata states.[48] It
can easily be seen how damning this letter of Walewski would
be to the standing of France in Argentina when it appeared
in the *Gaceta Mercantil* a few days later side by side with
Harris' protest and Howden's reply.

The next step in the program of the British agent was taken
at Montevideo, to which place the Commissioners had gone
following the failure of their negotiations with Rosas. Howden
proposed to Walewski on July 5 that, since it was apparent
that Rosas would not permit Oribe to accept an election commission jointly chosen, they should propose an arrangement
which he would accept. If the foreign element who dominated
Montevideo should decline to capitulate on Oribe's terms, they
might be threatened with the alternative of the withdrawal of
European assistance. The allies could still retain Martín
García and the Argentine war vessels until further orders were
received.[49] Walewski flatly refused to consider the raising of
the blockade unless an equitable armistice, providing for the
free communication of Montevideo with the interior, was arranged. He would consent to the capitulation proposal, he
said, only if requested to do so by the authorities at Montevideo.[50]

When the two agents repaired to Oribe's camp at Cerrito
on July 9, they found, as they had expected, that an armistice
on any basis of equality was out of the question. Oribe refused to raise the siege and insisted upon the recognition of his
position as legal President. He would consent to a five month's

[48] S. D., *op. cit.,* enclosure, Walewski to Harris, July 3. Harris was invited to exert more pressure on Rosas, although his previous assistance
was acknowledged.
[49] *Aff. Etr.,* Buenos Ayres, 38, pp. 251-254. Howden to Walewski, July 5.
[50] *Ibid.,* p. 255 ff. Walewski to Howden, July 7. Brossard, *op. cit.,* pp.
362-363.

armistice and agree to provide the city with 1500 beeves per month only on condition that the blockade be raised on both sides of the Plata.[51] To the astonishment of the French agent, Howden announced on July 10 that he intended to order the British squadron to retire if Oribe's armistice was not accepted by Montevideo. In vain did Walewski protest that their orders were to arrange an armistice, not to impose one, and that the operation of the penalty clause against Montevideo applied only in case of the city's rejection of a *treaty* already accepted by Rosas and Oribe. The proposition, he said, would be manifestly unfair to the unoffending party, and acquiescence would make him liable to official reprimand for violating his instructions.[52] The British agent, however, would not be moved from his decision. After Montevideo definitely rejected the armistice on July 14,[53] Howden announced, on the following day, that since the blockade could no longer serve any useful purpose and the offer of Oribe had been refused by the city, the British squadron would refrain from all further participation in the intervention.[54]

The British Minister explained, in a private letter to Palmerston, some of the considerations which prompted him to make this decision. He admitted that his instructions did not apply to the existing state of affairs, but he thought them at least applicable in spirit to the situation. He realized, he said, that British commercial houses were seriously embarrassed because of large shipments made to the river under the conviction that peace was about to be restored. Since he had become, moreover, thoroughly disgusted with the state of affairs at

[51] F. O. 6, 134, H. to P., July 8, 15, 1845. Durand, *op. cit.,* pp. 178-180. Brossard, *op. cit.,* pp. 364-365. The armistice term was later changed to six months.

[52] *Aff. Etr.,* Buenos Ayres, 37, pp. 358-359.

[53] Brossard, *op. cit.,* pp. 364-371. Brossard himself, as assistant to Walewski, conducted the negotiations at Cerrito. He gave it as his opinion that Oribe would have made an acceptable peace, if it had not been for orders from Rosas. F. O. 6, 134, H. to P., July 10 and 15. Howden did not make clear the real issue of the French protest in his reports.

[54] *Aff. Etr.,* Buenos Ayres, 38, p. 300 ff. Howden to Herbert, July 15, 1847. *National Intelligencer,* Sept. 11, 1847.

Montevideo, he had therefore "determined to take advantage of the refusal" of that government in order to withdraw.[55]

Howden was not mistaken in assuming that his action would be approved. Two months later Palmerston replied that the decision arrived at was "in perfect Conformity with the spirit of your Instructions and with the Intentions of your Government." On this same occasion, the Foreign Minister also approved the order given to Commodore Herbert to seize Colonia in case the French should take control at Montevideo.[56] The Spanish marriage injury was partially atoned. for.

Not content with having shifted the entire responsibility for the defense of Montevideo to the French forces, Howden sought to crown his efforts by securing the entrance of Oribe into the Uruguayan capital. Such a conclusion of the affair, he exultantly explained, would "crush forever French ambition and intrigue, and give England that legitimate influence which she ought to have as the great Commercial Power in these waters." [57] A few days later Oribe was secretly persuaded to agree to the following terms for the capitulation of the city: (1) amnesty for all who would lay down their arms; (2) restoration or indemnification for confiscated property; (3) the return of the Argentine troops simultaneously with Oribe's entrance into the city; (4) the immediate arrangement for a constitutional election, free from intimidation.[58] These terms were transmitted to the Montevidean Cabinet by consul M. T. Hood, Howden himself not daring to go ashore.[59] Arrangements were made for a visit of Señor Pereira, the head of the Cabinet, to a British vessel in the harbor.

A conference between Pereira and Howden took place on

[55] F. O. 6, 134, H. to P., July 15. Previous American treatments of this point are in error. See J. M. Callahan, in *Proceedings of the American Society of International Law*, April, 1914, p. 60 ff. and E. B. White, *op. cit.*, p. 118.

[56] F. O. 6, 132, P. to H., Sept. 21, 22, 1847. *Archivo Americano*, 2nd series, no. 5.

[57] F. O. 6, 134, H. to P., July 20.

[58] F. O. 6, 134, H. to P., July 20, and an enclosure, Howden to Hood, July 17. Oribe refused to dismiss the Argentine troops immediately for fear of offending Rosas.

[59] F. O. 6, 134, H. to P., July 16. The foreigners threatened to kill Lord Howden if he came ashore.

July 19. The Oriental leader reported that with the single exception of the Provisional President, Suarez, the Government was in favor of accepting Oribe's offer. But they must be assured of British support in case difficulties arose. Howden reported his reply in part as follows:

"As far as my moral support went in guaranteeing merciful and just measures on the part of General Oribe, and as far as material support went in putting both the Vessels of Her Majesty and their Crews at the disposal of the proper authorities to prevent outbreaks, or to repress murder and pillage, I promised these unreservedly." [60]

But Walewski and the French population were not to be left out of consideration entirely. They were decidedly in no mood to acquiesce in any more underhand work by the British. The two European forces were, in fact, perilously near to hostilities.[61] When the Count's secretary inquired of the Montevidean Government whether secret negotiations with the British were in progress, the Foreign Minister assured him that such was not the case and that the Cabinet had no desire to come to terms with Oribe. Walewski himself finally obliged two members of the Government to admit the fact of the negotiations with Howden. But his informers were most emphatic in asserting their loyalty, and attributed the move to treachery on the part of Pereira.[62] In the face of the French opposition, the matter quickly ran aground. The Government did not dare announce a bold capitulation, a move which Commodore Herbert later suggested to them, because of the fact that the commander of the French Legion would have to be consulted on the question. Lord Howden was disgusted at the lack of courage on the part of the Montevidean authorities, but he was glad to send the following optimistic message to his chief, upon his departure for Rio de Janeiro:

[60] *Ibid.*, July 20.
[61] S. D. Arg. Rep., Desp. 6, Harris to Buchanan, July 21, 1847. Any move of Oribe to take the city would have resulted in open warfare between the European forces.
[62] F. O. 6, 134, Howden to Palmerston, July 25. "You will see," commented Howden, "the difficulty, if not the impossibility of working out any result with such pusillanimous beings as the men composing the self-called Government of Montevideo,"

"The good will of *all* the Native Inhabitants toward England on both sides of the River Plate was never so strong, or so surely fixed as it is at this moment." [63]

The exposure of the secret intrigue with Howden and the banishment of its promoters so greatly strengthened the French influence at Montevideo that observers generally believed that an attempt would be made to convert the Banda Oriental into a French colony. Walewski's party was certainly in favor of such a move.[64] The Count departed for Paris in August with the announced purpose of demanding an expedition of 6,000 men to raise the siege of Montevideo.[65] Another possibility, which seemed no less remote, was that France and Brazil would join hands in an effort to reëstablish Brazilian suzerainty over Uruguay and perhaps extend the dowry lands of the Prince de Joinville southward from Santa Catharina.[66] But the extreme unpopularity of the French Government in South America, and the certain hostility of England to such programs made them practically out of the question. Guizot was simply left in the unenviable dilemma of being unable to withdraw without dishonorably betraying the cause of his nationals, and yet of having no feasible objective which would justify the risks of going to war.[67] Political and military affairs in the Plata came to a complete standstill following the withdrawal of the British forces. All pretense of maintaining an effective blockade of Buenos Ayres was abandoned. Overseas commerce destined for Argentina was merely required by the French squadron to pay import and export duties at Montevideo both in entering and in leaving the river.[68]

[63] F. O. 6, *op. cit.* Howden was too optimistic, for Rosas was angry when he heard of the secret negotiations. Palmerston later ordered the Admiralty to restore to Rosas the guns taken at Obligado. F. O. 6, 138, Palmerston to Admiralty, Sept. 24, 1847.
[64] Brossard, *op. cit.,* pp. 1-5.
[65] S. D. Arg. Rep., Desp. 6, Harris to Buchanan, Sept. 16, 1847. F. O. 13, Brazil, 244, Howden to Palmerston from Rio, Aug. 24, 1847. F. O. 6, 134, H. to P., July 25.
[66] F. O. 13, Brazil 244, H. to P., Aug. 24, 1847.
[67] S. D. Arg. Rep., Desp. 6, Harris to Buchanan, July 15.
[68] S. D. Arg. Rep., Desp. 6, Harris to Buchanan, Sept. 16, 1847. Rosas would have spoiled this game by closing Buenos Ayres to all trade passing through Montevideo, if Urquiza could have been persuaded to do the same for Entre Rios. Rosas did it anyway in early 1848.

Against such an indefensible system, which possessed, as Harris repeatedly declared, every characteristic of piracy, the government at Washington did not raise a single protest. North American trade was left entirely without protection.[69] With the manifold problems arising from the Mexican war to be attended to, as well as the alarming expansion of the territory of Palmerston's protegé, the King of the Mosquitos, into Nicaragua,[70] the State Department found no time for South American affairs. Even the prospect of a major French expedition to Uruguay attracted no more than casual notice from the apathetic North American press.[71] In spite of the bold utterance made by the United States Chargé at Buenos Ayres on July 1, 1847, the Plata affair remained entirely a matter for the settlement of France and England.[72]

Letters sent from the French Foreign Office during the summer of 1847 indicate how anxious Guizot was to avoid a difference with England on the Plata question.[73] When discouraging news began to arrive from Buenos Ayres in late August, the French Minister immediately suggested to London that they concert in the sending of new instructions. A letter sent to Walewski on August 31 commended that agent for his success in defeating the persistent attempts of Rosas to separate the two negotiators.[74]

It can only be surmised with what serious misgivings Paris learned that the French forces had been entirely abandoned

[69] *Ibid.*, Oct. 17, 1847. The apathy of the United States toward this abuse is in striking contrast with the firm attitude of Secretary Clay in 1827, when the Brazilian blockade of Buenos Ayres developed irregular features. See W. R. Manning, "An early Diplomatic Controversy with Brazil," *Hispanic American Historical Review*, I, pp. 123-145.

[70] R. Rivas, *Relaciones Internacionales entre Colombia y los Estados Unidos, 1810-1850.* (Bogotá 1915), pp. 105-128.

[71] *National Intelligencer*, Feb. 22, 1848. A book written by J. A. King, *Twenty-four Years in the Argentine Republic* (N. Y., Phila., Cincinnati, 1846) probably did much to disabuse the public mind of the prevalent adulation of the régime of Rosas.

[72] Hopkins still demanded a more active policy. See *DeBow's Commercial Review*, 14, pp. 238-251.

[73] Guizot could not co-operate with reactionary Europe because of the vigilance of the banqueteers. See Allison, *op. cit.*, p. 324 ff.

[74] *Aff. Etr.*, Buenos Ayres, 38, pp. 348-50. Guizot to Broglie, Aug. 19, 1847; B. to G., Aug. 29; *ibid.*, p. 354, to Walewski, Aug. 31.

by the British in their operations against Buenos Ayres. The full details of the affair were known by the middle of September. The offense was so flagrant in character that Ambassador Broglie in London was immediately directed to question the British Government concerning it. The matter was brought to the attention of Lord Russell on September 16, the Foreign Minister being absent from London at the time. Broglie presented to him a convincing exposition of the French point of view. He insisted that Howden's unjustifiable misapplication of their joint instructions had left France completely abandoned in an enterprise which she had undertaken only at the request of Great Britain. Reference should at least have been made to the home governments before such a move. If the existing situation were not relieved, the Paris authorities would have no alternative but to ask for new credits and disclose to popular indignation the full details of the shameful treatment which they had received. Russell had no excuse to offer and frankly admitted that the action of the British agent had been highly irregular. He promised to confer with Palmerston immediately on the subject.[75]

But Palmerston had made other plans. On the same day as the Broglie interview, he directed Normanby at Paris to deliver the following statement to the French Government:

"H. M.'s Gov't. having taken all the circumstances into their serious consideration, and adverting to the Fact that the Blockade had long ceased to be a measure of coercion upon Buenos Ayres, and had become nothing but an illegitimate method of raising Money for Montevideo . . . ; and H. M.'s Gov't. further reflecting that the continuation of such a Blockade would be futile, while any attempt now to convert it into a real Blockade would probably raise inconvenient and embarrassing Questions between the two Allies and Neutral Powers; they have determined to approve and confirm the decision of Lord Howden, and therefore not to order any Renewal of the Blockade by the British Force in the River Plate."

[75] Aff. Etr., Buenos Ayres, 38, pp. 363-374. See the same in M. O. d'Haussonville, Histoire de la politique Extérieure du Gouvernement Français, 1830-1848. 2 vols. (Paris 1850) Vol. 2, pp. 285-292.

Normanby was ordered to ask the French Government to adopt a similar course, and to co-operate with the British in restoring the captured war vessels and Martín García to Buenos Ayres.[76] The simultaneous arrival at Paris of these contradictory reactions from the two British Ministers left Guizot to choose between two alternative courses. Instead of making the most of the significant admission made by Lord Russell, the French Minister apparently became frightened at the boldness of his own agent. He did tell Broglie to ask that the discrepancy be explained, but the Ambassador should also not fail to assure Palmerston that France was willing to reëstablish the accord with England.[77] The British Foreign Minister quickly took advantage of the opening thus offered to him. Without conceding anything in regard to the unwarranted character of the action of Howden, Palmerston secured Broglie's consent, on September 24, to a proposal that they should deliberate on a new policy "exactly as if there had been manifested no dissent between the two Commissioners." [78] The following letter to Normanby reveals Palmerston's gratification over the outcome:

"I have had a long conversation with Broglie about River Plate affairs, and have granted him as a favor that which I must have claimed as a right, namely, that England and France should finish in concert the bad business which they began together. It would never do to leave France to settle the matter single-handed; if she did so she would occupy Montevideo. . . . The blockade . . . is piracy; it is equivalent to stopping neutral vessels on the high seas and making them pay blackmail. I am very glad that we are out of such a system, and if the French do not make haste to get out of it too, they will get into trouble with other countries.

"As to the protection of the independence of Montevideo, we are still bound with France to provide for that. . . . My belief is that the only danger to Montevideo springs from her foreign garrison,

[76] F. O. 27, France, 776, Palmerston to Normanby, Sept. 16, 1847. *Aff. Etr.*, Buenos Ayres, 38, pp. 376-8. Howden's actions were approved in every detail. F. O. 6, 132, Sept. 17, 18, 19.

[77] *Aff. Etr.*, Buenos Ayres, 38, pp. 387-390. Guizot to Broglie, Sept. 20, 1847. The original draft ordered Broglie to *insist* upon a satisfactory explanation, but it was greatly moderated when corrected.

[78] *Ibid.*, Broglie to Guizot, Sept. 24. Palmerston explained later that Russell had had imperfect information. F. O. 27, 776, to Normanby, Oct. 8, 1847.

and that her best safety would be to let Oribe take quiet possession of the town."[79]

The new agreement which was finally arrived at in early December, indicates the extent of the surrender made by the Paris Government. Instead of attempting another negotiation with Rosas, it was decided that the new mission should merely arrange with the two Oriental parties for the capitulation of Montevideo. Rosas would be regarded merely as the auxiliary of Oribe.[80] The city was to be surrendered to the Oriental troops of Oribe upon a promise of personal security to all and general indemnification for confiscated property. The withdrawal of the Argentine troops and the disarmament of foreigners within the city were to be accomplished simultaneously and with the assistance of the allied commanders. The French blockade of Buenos Ayres would be lifted as soon as both operations had been completed.[81] If Montevideo should refuse to treat, or should decline to accept the terms proposed, the intervention should be discontinued on both sides of the river. If, on the other hand, Oribe should prove to be the obstinate party, Palmerston agreed that:

"the British squadron in the River Plate will again unite with the French Squadron in taking measures to intercept any communication or intercourse whatever between those ports of the Oriental territory which were occupied by his [Oribe's] army, and the two Banks of the River Plate."[82]

Under no condition, however, would the British establish again their blockade of Buenos Ayres. The French agent carried separate instructions that he also should discontinue at the most convenient time the blockade of his own squadron at the same port.[83]

The Commissioners chosen were Mr. Gore, the new British

[79] H. L. Bulwer, *op. cit.*, vol. 3, pp. 324-326.

[80] *Aff. Etr.*, Buenos Ayres, 38, pp. 403-423; 39, pp. 4-33. Guizot refused to agree with Palmerston's assertion that blockade was strictly a belligerent right. This, he said, would have destroyed the principle of armed mediation.

[81] *Aff. Etr.*, Buenos Ayres, 39, pp. 48-49. Guizot to Gros, Dec. 15. F. O. 51, 51, Palmerston to Gore, Dec. 18, 1847. Large discretionary power was permitted the agents.

[82] F. O. 51, 51 Palmerston to Gore, Dec. 18, 1847.

[83] *Aff. Etr.*, Buenos Ayres, 39, pp. 48-55. Guizot to Gros, Dec. 15.

Chargé at Montevideo, and one Baron Gros for France.   In order to avoid the danger of unfavorable pressure from Rosas, the agents were charged to observe the strictest secrecy in their negotiation. They should announce to the Dictator, at the close of their mission, that France and England were depending upon Oribe to fulfill the obligations of the Government of Uruguay. They were also to remind Rosas that he was bound by several formal instruments, notably the Brazilian treaty of 1828 and the Mackau Convention of 1840, to respect the independence of the Oriental Republic.[84]   Gore departed from England on December 31, and Gros immediately followed him.[85]

A private memorandum of Guizot, prepared during his early conversations with Palmerston in regard to the Gore-Gros mission, contains an interesting statement of the considerations which led the French Minister to accept the new arrangement. It was apparent, he wrote, that a new negotiation with Rosas could not possibly succeed. On the other hand, if France undertook an armed expedition to drive Oribe out, they could not avoid making a French colony out of Uruguay. Guizot meditated:

"Are we prepared for that development and for all the consequences which will be the inevitable result of it?   I hold, as far as I am concerned, that the expedition is a folly which M. Thiers can well sustain on the tribune, but which he would not undertake himself if he were in power."

It would be better, he concluded, to allow Palmerston to reenter the common action, if only by a mere promise that he would reëstablish the British blockade. Guizot surmised as follows: "There is a hundred thousand to wager against one that he will not execute it." But if Palmerston should refuse such a conciliatory offer, or should later fail to keep his promise and oblige France to act alone, the Paris government would

[84] F. O. 51, 51, Palmerson to Gore, Oct. 14, Dec. 18, 1847. It was finally enjoined to Gore to do nothing to impair the good understanding with France. The Montevidean agent in Paris had more confidence in Gros than in Gore. M. Herrera y Obes, *Correspondencia Diplomática*, 1, pp. 91-92. From J. LeLong, Jan. 7, 1848.

[85] F. O. 51, 51, Gore to Palmerston, Dec. 31, 1847.

then have strong ground on which to defend its policy. He said:

"When we will be attacked before the public, we will expose in simple and severe language, the conduct of Lord Howden first, then that of Lord Palmerston, to popular reproof. We will throw back upon him all the consequences of the abandonment in which he has left us. We will have for ourselves all the diplomacy of Europe, all the Conservative and Peelite party, Lord Aberdeen at their head, probably five-sixths of the Whig party and the Cabinet itself.

"In my opinion, it is the best chance for us; if it were permissible to desire evil in order that good might come out of it, one could wish that Lord Palmerston persisted in the line of conduct which he is following in that affair." [86]

The very caution of Guizot was destined to defeat his plan. When the opportunity came to execute his threat, he was no longer in control of the government.[87]

In that devastating attack of the opposition in the French Chambers upon the foreign policy of Guizot which was staged in the early months of 1848, the fiasco of his program in the Plata came in for its full share of attention. The issue was raised in the Chamber of Peers on January 18. Violent objection was made to the optimistic paragraph in the address to the King predicting the early restoration of commercial relations with Buenos Ayres.[88] The entire enterprise, it was said, had been ill-advised. France had no quarrel with Rosas, and yet had allowed herself to be entangled in the affair by England, and then abandoned by the same power. The opposition insisted that they had a right to know what had been the points of difference between the agents at Buenos Ayres in the previous July, and which government had made the surrender in the new mission. Guizot refused to make any explanation. The information asked for, he said, would greatly embarrass

[86] *Aff. Etr.*, Buenos Ayres, 38, pp. 4-9. A Memorandum, wrongly dated Jan. 1847. From internal evidence, probably Oct. 1847.

[87] *Parliamentary Debates*, 3d Series, vol. 95, pp. 967-968, 1437-1438; 96, pp. 82-83. Palmerston had no difficulty in replying to questions from Parliament in December, 1847, and in February, 1848. He boasted of the new French agreement and refused to submit Howden's instructions, when Disraeli demanded them. British trade journals severely attacked Palmerston's vacillating policy. *The Economist*, 1, pp. 1273-4, 1448, Nov. 6 and Dec. 18, 1847, respectively.

[88] *Le Moniteur Universel*, Dec. 29, 1847, Jan. 11 and 18, 1848.

the negotiations then in progress. The paragraph could not, of course, be defeated on mere speculations, and the debate finally shifted to other matters.[89]

When the same question came up before the Chamber of Deputies a few days later, the opposition was better prepared. They had discovered from some secret source the exact nature of the instructions which had been confided to Gore and Gros. The group who favored war were materially assisted by a Frenchman who had returned with Walewski from Uruguay, and was now pleading the cause of 250 of his fellow nationals who had been held at the town of Durazno as hostages since Oribe's first invasion of the Oriental Republic in 1843.[90] The announcement which Guizot made at the outset, that he would not participate in the discussion, made his opponents more determined to force him to do so.

The attack was launched with great vigor. The Government, they charged, had already allowed Great Britain an inestimable advantage by acquiescing in her earlier withdrawal. If this new mission now accomplished its purpose, the French nationals in Uruguay would be abandoned and the interests of their country in that region damaged beyond repair. Should they wait, it was asked, until their prestige had entirely disappeared before they demonstrated, as ultimately they must, the energy which France could display after long patience? Could the Chambers ever be justified, in the face of their overwhelming social problems at home, in sacrificing that magnificent outlet for surplus population and goods in Argentina? Should they weakly surrender to the savagery of a man who would "embellish with the name of the 'American system' the expulsion of Europeans and of French in particular from the Plata country?"[91] What evidence did the Government offer to support their optimistic attitude? On what terms had their cooperation with England been restored? Nothing had been said

[89] *Ibid.*, Jan. 18 and 25, 1848.

[90] Benjamin Poucel, *Les otages de Durazno; souvenirs du Rio de la Plata pendant l'intervention anglo-française, de 1845 à 1851.* (Paris 1864.) Poucel succeeded in getting identical resolutions introduced into both Chambers on the subject.

[91] *Le Moniteur Universel,* Feb. 5, 1848. M. Lavavasseur.

concerning any disavowal of Howden's action in the previous July, the orator continued, and recent copies of the *Gaceta Mercantil* proved that Rosas had not retracted one whit of his arrogant demands. It was declared, in conclusion, that the Chamber had a right to refuse, in an affair employing one-tenth of their naval force and costing three millions a year, meekly to repeat the chimerical hopes held out to them by the Government, while no adequate effort was being made to resolve the situation. An amendment to the paragraph was finally moved which omitted the reference to the British co-operation in the new mission.[92]

Guizot was finally obliged to take the tribune in his own defense. It was not from any lack of respect for the rights of the Chamber, he said, that he had refused to discuss the question. He could not afford to embarrass the negotiations then in progress. He finally secured the withdrawal of the amendment by pledging his word that every precaution had been taken for the security of their nationals.[93] The pressure on the Government in behalf of the hostages at Durazno was not discontinued until February 18, and then it was done only because of the serious nature of the gathering storm which was soon to engulf the Orleans Monarchy.[94] The Plata intervention contributed a considerable share to the lamentable failure of the foreign policy of Guizot, which was one of the principal reasons for his downfall.[95]

When the new Commissioners arrived at Montevideo, in March,[96] they found the city in a state of complete despair. The customs revenue at the port had been almost destroyed due to the fact that Rosas had recently declared an embargo for Argentina against all trade coming from the Uruguayan capital. The inhabitants were weary of the struggle. One of the ablest leaders among the enemies of Rosas had recently been

[92] *Le Moniteur, op. cit.* Drouyn de Lhuys and Lacrosse.
[93] *Ibid.* Curtis, E. N., *French Assembly of 1848 and American Constitutional Doctrines* (1918), pp. 21-22.
[94] Poucel, *op. cit.*, pp. 315-317.
[95] *Hunt's Merchant's Magazine* 18, pp. 497-499.
[96] F. O. 51, 54, from Gore at Montevideo, Mar. 17.

assassinated.[97] A large proportion of the Basque population had already sought refuge in Argentina, and Garibaldi, with some three score of his followers, was preparing to leave for Italy.[98] There was no immediate prospect of securing aid from Brazil. The city was in desperate straits, and the time seemed ripe for the settlement of the vexing problem.[99]

The mediators proceeded immediately to their task. They readily secured the acceptance of their good offices by both parties at Montevideo. The precautions which they had taken in anticipation of an outbreak within the city proved happily to be superfluous. By the second week of April, the terms of the suggested capitulation were in the hands of the rival governments. They specified that Oribe should immediately be recognized as the Provisional President and have charge of calling a new election. Foreigners should be guaranteed safely, but individuals obnoxious to Buenos Ayres might be removed from the country. The French would accompany the lifting of their blockade by a salute to the Argentine flag of 21 guns.[100] Oribe indicated his acceptance of the allied terms on April 21, with but a single alteration. The clause providing for allied participation in the disarming of the foreigners and the withdrawal of the Argentine troops was stricken out. Oribe also explained that he would have to confer with Rosas in regard to the retirement of these forces.[101] It was apparent that Montevideo could not long continue its resistance, and hopes were high that a settlement was near at hand.

But the wishes of Rosas in the matter were still to be taken into consideration. The Dictator had no intention of seeing

[97] S. D. Arg. Rep., Desp. 6, Harris to Buchanan, Jan. 14, and Mar. 26, 1848. The victim, Florencio Varela, was referred to by Harris as "by far the most talented and accomplished gentleman, native or foreigner, that I have met in this part of the world." For Herrera's attitude see Palomeque, *De la Diplomacia de la Defensa de Montevideo*, pp. 164-168. Herrera y Obes, *op. cit.*, 1, pp. 18-19. To LeLong in Paris, Dec. 24, 1847.

[98] G. Garibaldi, *Autobiography*, vol. 3, pp. 254-262. Garibaldi left on April 15. The revolutionary outbreak in Italy was not known to him at the time. F. O. 51, 54. From Gore, Apr. 22.

[99] Herrera y Obes, *op. cit.*, 1, pp. 19-23; F. J. Pereira, *Colección de varios documentos oficiales extraídos de la memorias de ministero de relaciones exteriores del Brazil.* (Caracas 1857), pp. 3-24. The Unitarian refugees raised serious objections to the surrender.

[100] F. O. 51, 54, Gore to Palmerston, April 14, 1848, and enclosures.

[101] F. O. 51, 54, Gore to Palmerston, Apr. 22, 1848.

himself eliminated by a trick of diplomacy as the arbiter of affairs in the Plata. Any gesture of independence on the part of Oribe at this time would be exceedingly damaging to his waning authority. The recently inaugurated embargo policy was causing serious unrest in Buenos Ayres, and only a few months before, Urquiza had refused to take orders from the Dictator during a military excursion into Corrientes. If the interventionists should now be allowed to withdraw without coming to terms with Buenos Ayres, Rosas knew that his prestige would evaporate and his power collapse like a house of cards. He would prefer open hostilities with the European forces rather than permit himself to be ignored.[102]

When news reached the Plata in the first week of May that all Europe was ablaze with revolution, Rosas delayed his action no longer.[103] On May 8, he sent a peremptory order to Oribe to break off all negotiations with Montevideo, and to hold no further communication with the Europeans unless they were prepared to make a definitive settlement with the Argentine Government on the Hood bases. Oribe was roundly berated for his attempted betrayal of the interests of his friend and ally.[104] The Dictator attempted to justify this action on the basis of his favorite American policy. To permit the recognition of the European governments as mediators when they had, up to this time, negotiated as belligerents, he said, would amount to a sanction of the intervention and would therefore be fatal to the future well-being of all the South American states.[105]

The explanation given by Rosas can hardly be taken seriously. The settlement which the allies were offering to Oribe

[102] S. D. Arg. Rep., Desp. 6, Harris to Buchanan, Mar. 26, 1848. Urquiza had crushed a new uprising in Corrientes in November, 1847, but had refrained from attacking an army under President Lopez on the Paraguay border. He thus passed up an excellent opportunity to subdue Paraguay. Rosas was greatly annoyed. Ibid., Oct. 17, 1847, Jan. 14, 1848. Herrera y Obes, op. cit., 1, pp. 11-14. National Intelligencer, Mar. 8, 1848.
[103] S. D. Arg. Rep., Desp. 6, Harris to Buchanan, May 11.
[104] Brossard, op. cit., pp. 375-383. The news of the upheaval in Europe was hardly the cause of his refusal, as Durand states, op. cit., pp. 181-184.
[105] F. O. 51, 55, Gore to Palmerston, Aug. 4. Herrera y Obes, op. cit., 1, pp. 88-89, 94-96, 101-107. From John LeLong in Paris, Mar. 1, 1848; to LeLong, May 15, 1848.

was in fact their own surrender. The purposes of the Dictator would in reality be better served if he would keep his enemies begging from him indefinitely.[106] Whether it was more prejudicial to the independence of Uruguay for Rosas to refuse to permit the rival factions there to make peace, or for the European agents to arrange the terms of the withdrawal of their intervention, anyone can judge.

The news of the overthrow of the Government of Guizot had meanwhile revived hope within Montevideo that deliverance might still be had. The French Legion, which had previously voted to surrender, now reconsidered their action. The government of the city began to procrastinate in regard to Oribe's proposal of April 21 and, on May 15, embarked secretly upon a final endeavor to organize a coalition against Rosas.[107] The city was saved from its embarrassing position by Oribe's announcement on May 18 that his former acceptance of the capitulation terms was recalled and that any further negotiation must be made on the Hood bases. The armistice came to an end four days later, and hostilities were resumed.[108]

Difficulties immediately arose between the two Commissioners. When Mr. Gore was called upon to reëstablish the British blockade of Oribe's ports, as provided in his instructions, he suddenly developed serious scruples over the fear that the February revolution had deprived his French associate of all authority. Gros raised strong objections against such a conclusion, and the British agent finally agreed, on May 28, to enforce the penalty which had been provided in case Oribe should refuse their terms. But Gros must allow him to wait until the arrival of the next mail packet. The mail of June 2 brought no communication from Paris or London, whereupon Gore flatly refused to execute his instructions. Neither would he consent to an alternative suggestion that they subsidize the

[106] S. D. Arg. Rep., Desp. 6, Harris to Buchanan, June 17, 1848 and Jan. 15, 1849.
[107] F. O. 51, 54, Gore to Palmerston, May 15. Herrera y Obes, *op. cit.*, 1, pp. 88-89, 94-96, 101-107. From John LeLong in Paris, Mar. 1, 1848; to LeLong, May 15, 1848.
[108] F. O. 51, 54, Gore to Palmerston, June 12, 1848.

garrison at Montevideo.[109] The following is Gore's explanation to Palmerston:

"We had nothing more to do but to carry out our Instructions, and prevent all intercourse between Oribe and Rosas. . . . It was quite evident to me that a great effort was making [being made] to get the English once more in the Intervention, which I was just as anxious to prevent if I had the opportunity to escape it, and the chance of my colleague being left without any confirmation of his instructions by the New Government of France was the only legitimate objection I could make; and one that it was my duty to take advantage of, although . . . it would place me in a most disagreeable position. [sic]" [110]

The flimsy character of Gore's pretense that a change of government in France made his own instructions inoperative is demonstrated, in the first place, by the fact that he had given no evidence of such scruples as long as it appeared that Montevideo would be the party to refuse. Furthermore, a statement made by Palmerston in Parliament, on May 8, shows how groundless was his contention. The British Minister, in reply to a query on that very point, asserted that the revolution in France had not made necessary any new communication with reference to the Plata mission, and that he had no reason to suppose that the instructions to Gros had been withdrawn.[111]

The French agents were left again with the proverbial bag to hold. They had no choice but to take whatever steps were necessary to make possible the continued resistance of Montevideo. Since Gros was himself under instructions to raise the now useless blockade of Buenos Ayres, their most convenient course was to pledge the French Government to a monetary subsidy. A Convention was accordingly arranged on June 12, providing for a monthly subsidy to Montevideo from the French treasury of 40,000 piastres (approximately dollars). The French Commissioner reserved the right to reclaim the amount

[109] F. O., op. cit. Gore went so far over to Rosas' side as to declare that the Dictator had been justified in his objection of May 8. F. O. 51, 55, Gore to Palmerston, Aug. 22, 1848.

[110] F. O. 51, 54, Gore to Palmerston, June 16.

[111] Parliamentary Debates, 3d series, vol. 98, p. 764. Current criticisms of France in British periodicals were most unfair. See Edinburgh Review, 87, pp. 534-565.

advanced in case his action should not be approved.[112] The blockade of Buenos Ayres was lifted a few days later, and the French squadron under Admiral LePrédour was ordered to confine its activities thereafter to the interception of all communication between Oribe and the Argentine Confederation. Gros immediately returned to Paris where he urged upon the Provisional Government the importance of saving what little prestige remained to their country in the Plata by ratifying the subsidy treaty.[113]

The lifting of the French blockade brought Rosas face to face with serious difficulties at home. The remarkable increase in prosperity at Buenos Ayres, which accompanied the resumption of trade, multiplied the local discontent with his despotism. Vigorous measures would be required if the Dictator intended to maintain his control. So infuriated was Rosas because of the refusal of the Europeans to treat with him that he embarked deliberately upon a policy of defiance, using the menace of foreign attack as a pretext for placing the city under martial law.[114] On July 15, he forbade all contact of British and French war vessels with the Argentine coast. On the following day, he exasperated the new British consul to the city, M. T. Hood, by refusing to grant his Exequatur, on the grounds that the recent negotiations had aggravated the injuries of Buenos Ayres beyond endurance.[115] The Governor began extensive preparations for war. Harris was convinced that Rosas was trying to provoke an overt act of hostility on the part of the British forces which would provide him with an excuse to abrogate the perpetual British commercial treaty.[116] All foreigners within Buenos Ayres were placed under the strictest surveillance. The Sardinian agent, who had been in charge of the

[112] Aff. Etr., Buenos Ayres, 39, pp. 250-253. A report of LePrédour, June 12, 1848, signed also by Gros. Durand, op. cit., pp. 184-185. Colección de tratados . . . de la República Oriental de Uruguay, Vol. 1, 171-2.
[113] Brossard, op. cit., pp. 385-386. Aug. 23, 1848, from Gros.
[114] F. O. 6, 139, Southern to Palmerston, Nov. 21, 1848.
[115] F. O. 51, 55, Gore to Palmerston, July 16, 22, and 27 and enclosures. F. O. 6, 140, Hood to Palmerston, Aug. 8, 9, 1848 and enclosures. An exception was made for Herbert's own vessel. Montevideo was at this time trying to come to terms with Rosas.
[116] S. D. Arg. Rep., Desp. 6, Harris to Buchanan, July 28, 1848.

British and French consulates, was forcibly expelled from the city in September, because he refused to curb the patriotic demonstrations of his Italian countrymen over news of happenings in Europe. Harris wrote that the interventionists had no choice but to "fight,—and fight hard,—or surrender their pretentions absolutely and unconditionally."[117]

The government at Montevideo, at the same time, was having more than its share of trouble. Colonia fell into the possession of Oribe, and Admiral LePrédour, who had no enthusiasm for his blockading task, withdrew his support from the Montevidean garrison at Martín García. Within the Oriental capital itself, the French consul was engaged in a bitter quarrel with the government over the expenditure of the subsidy.[118] So disorganized did the defenses of the city become, that it was necessary to send 400 French marines ashore to man the almost deserted batteries. The only encouraging factor in the situation was the news which arrived in November that Paris had decided to approve the subsidy treaty.[119]

Señor Herrera y Obes, the Foreign Minister of the Montevidean Government, tried in vain during 1848 to secure military assistance from the former European allies. He suggested that the powers should assume a joint protectorate over Uruguay for an indefinite period and argued that the freedom of river navigation could be secured if all interested parties would unite for that purpose.[120] France, of course, was overwhelmed with domestic problems. Palmerston would not listen to Herrera's pleas and replied by cautioning Montevideo concerning the dangers connected with their continued acceptance of the

[117] Op. cit., Sept. 23, 1848. Harris pled for the sending of an American war vessel. F. O. 6, 140, Hood to Palmerston, Sept. 10 and 20, 1848.
[118] F. O. 51, 55, Gore to Palmerston, Aug. 22, 1848. Palomeque, Martín García, pp. 159-60, 173-174.
[119] Herrera y Obes, op. cit., 1, pp. 197-198, 213-214. Correspondencia Confidencial de Sr. D. Gabriel Pereira, 2 vols. (Montevideo 1896) vol. 1, p. 547. Approval of the subsidy came on Dec. 26, 1848. Brossard, op. cit., p. 384.
[120] Herrera y Obes. op. cit., vol. 1, p. 132 ff.—To Adolpho Pfeil in London, June 14, 1848. Vedia, Martín García, pp. 133-135. F. O. 51, 56, Gore to Palmerston, Nov. 29; Palmerston to Gore, Nov. 13. Herrera asked that they send out an expedition to act in concert with Brazil or else leave at once.

French subsidy. He asserted emphatically that neither Britain nor France would despatch any troops.[121]

The only remaining hope for the relief of Montevideo lay in the gradual drawing together of the inter-river Provinces, Paraguay, and Brazil in opposition to the domination of the Plata by Buenos Ayres. An overturn which occurred in the government at Rio de Janeiro in September, 1848, was a distinct step in that direction.[122] But in the absence of an urgent necessity, the progress made in forming the coalition was painfully slow. Nothing could be expected from it until France and England had made their peace with the now defiant Rosas.

[121] F. O. 51, 56, Palmerston to Gore, Oct. 20, Nov. 15; vol. 61. Jan. 31, 1849. Gore's action was approved Oct. 11, 1848.

[122] Herrera y Obes, op. cit., 1, pp. 41-44, 215-219. Durand, op. cit., pp. 187-189. In 1846-7, the Imperial Government had refused to interfere unless the independence of Uruguay should be seriously threatened. See Palomeque, De la diplomacia, pp. 189-230.

CHAPTER IX

THE END OF THE EUROPEAN INTERVENTION

So determined was Palmerston to avail himself of the full advantage gained by the earlier withdrawal of the British forces from in front of Buenos Ayres that he despatched a diplomatic agent to that city in June, 1848, before the outcome of the Gore-Gros mediation was known to him. The man chosen for the delicate task of the restoration of diplomatic relations with Rosas was an experienced diplomat by the name of Henry Southern. He had been thoroughly informed regarding the Plata situation as a result of frequent conversations with Mr. Mandeville. The former British Minister had also prepared the way for him by several letters to Manuelita, and had provided the agent with a flattering personal introduction to Rosas.[1] Southern was left almost entirely upon his own resources by his instructions. He should seek to have himself received by Rosas, and to impress upon the Governor the great importance of maintaining friendly relations with Great Britain. He should explain that London was no longer worried over the independence of Montevideo, but that questions of illegal interference with British commerce, of the destruction of property, and of the unpaid claims to British creditors were still points which called for settlement.[2]

In spite of the discouraging news which Southern received at Rio de Janeiro concerning the belligerent attitude of Rosas, the British agent proceeded directly to Buenos Ayres, arriving in early October, 1848. When he requested permission to come ashore as British Chargé, he was met by an almost vicious refusal. The Governor declared that he would receive no official

[1] Saldías, op. cit., 5, pp. 147-148, 390-392. Letter from Mandeville to Manuelita, Mar. 3 and July 29, 1848.
[2] F. O. 6, 139, Palmerston to Southern, June 29 and July 20, 1848.

British agent until amends were made for the injuries which he had suffered. Nevertheless, in deference to the personal credentials presented by the agent, Southern was permitted to land as a private citizen, and was courteously received by the Governor and his daughter.[3] At the same time, Rosas became more violent than ever in his public declarations, going so far as to announce before the *Sala* that all treaties with France and England were abrogated.[4] Although it was a rather painful experience for the dignity of British residents, Southern took no offense at his rebuff, and calmly announced that he would avail himself of the permission of Rosas to remain in the city as a private individual until instructions arrived.[5]

The Dictator had finally met his master in the art of negotiation, for the clever and unscrupulous Britisher did not hesitate to take advantage of every weakness of his opponent. Instead of proceeding as heretofore by threats and demands, Southern disarmed the belligerency of the Governor by presenting as a target nothing but his own inoffensive patience and flattery. His despatches to London reveal almost nothing concerning the methods which he employed, except that he successfully enlisted the powerful moderating influence of Manuelita and deliberately played upon the strong prejudice of the Dictator against the French. Within less than a week the British agent was conversing unofficially with Arana concerning their differences.[6] At the end of six weeks, the Argentine Foreign Minister was busy at the task of defining what he meant by the Hood terms. By the first of the new year Rosas had agreed to submit a definite proposal of peace, and had made a public acknowledgment of the return of the Argentine war vessels and cannon held by the British.[7]

The terms which finally came to Southern's hand on Janu-

[3] *Ibid.*, Southern to Palmerston, from Rio de Janeiro, Sept. 6; from Buenos Ayres, Oct. 14, 1848. The most recent grievance of Rosas had been a definite move of the British to occupy lower Patagonia. Pereyra, *op. cit.*, pp. 201-202.

[4] S. D. Arg. Rep., Desp. 6, Harris to Buchanan, Oct. 26, 1848.

[5] *Ibid.*, Jan. 15, 1849. Harris did not think that Southern could possibly make any headway against the stubbornness of Rosas.

[6] F. O. 6, 139, Southern to Palmerston, Oct. 14 and 18, 1848.

[7] *Ibid.*, Nov. 21, 24, Dec. 17; vol. 143, Jan. 4, 1849 and enclosures.

ary 12, 1849, being for the most part those which Howden and Walewski had refused, became the subject of a long negotiation.[8] The agent immediately made objection to the specified requirement of a separate peace between the British and Oribe. He said that since their opposition had already ceased, there was nothing to settle between them. For two months the steady pressure of argument, cajolery, and flattery continued. To the astonishment of all who knew him, Rosas yielded point after point, until the treaty which was finally agreed upon in early March possessed little resemblance indeed to the Hood bases.

The most significant characteristic of the instrument was that Britain escaped entirely from the responsibility of terminating the trouble at Montevideo. The provisions made for the evacuation of Martín García, the salute to the flag, and the reciprocal return of captured vessels and cargoes were the same as before, as was the explicit acknowledgment of local control over the rivers. But Rosas agreed that his troops would return from Uruguay only after the French had disarmed the foreigners, evacuated all territory, and concluded a treaty of peace. In securing the French treaty, the Governor was to enjoy the assistance of Great Britain. To the Argentine Government was reserved the privilege of free discussion in the future concerning the application to England and France of the principles on which they had violated the independent rights of Argentina. The settlement would constitute the reestablishment of friendly relations when it was approved by Oribe and ratified by the London government.[9]

British relations at Buenos Ayres immediately improved. Consul Hood received his Exequatur in May, and the decree interdicting the communication of war vessels with the coast was repealed.[10] The middle of July found the situation approaching normalcy again, when Southern began to express his confidence in the integrity of Rosas to meet the public

---

[8] F. O. 6, 143, S. to P., Jan. 14, 1849. The Spanish version read *President* Oribe and the English, *General* Oribe.
[9] *Ibid.*, Mar. 6, 1849; *British Foreign and State Papers*, 37, pp. 7-11.
[10] F. O. 6, 143, S. to P., May 16.

obligations of his government toward the Messrs. Baring of London.[11] The unenviable burden of negotiating with Rosas for the pacification of Uruguay was shifted completely to the shoulders of France.

In Paris, there had been little opportunity amid the turbulence and uncertainties of the first months of the revolutionary régime to give any attention to a problem as remote as that of the Plata.[12] The first hurried note of May 27, 1848, to Citizen Admiral LePrédour merely expressed the hope that a settlement had already been reached, and explained that, since decisive measures were out of the question, the conduct of the affair was entrusted entirely to the commander's sagacity.[13] A report of a Committee of the National Assembly, in July, 1848, recommended the adoption of a more vigorous policy in the Argentine, although it admitted with regret that they were bound for the time being by the acts of the previous Government.[14] It was not until October, 1848, that formal instructions were finally sent to LePrédour. These instructions gave evidence of a complete lack of understanding of the previous negotiations, for there were many omissions as well as several inadmissible demands. For one thing, the terms suggested did not specify the time for the raising of the blockade, or for the restoration of Martín García and the Argentine fleet. Oribe was not to be admitted as President of Uruguay until installed as a result of a free election. Another provision went so far as to require the indemnification of all French nationals suffering loss from the war. If these terms were refused, LePrédour was directed to notify the Dictator that France would know how to make her engagements respected. The Admiral was assured that he could expect full support in any action which he might take in behalf of the honor of the flag. An important oversight in the instructions was the failure to provide the Admiral with any credentials.[15]

[11] *Ibid.*, July 16.
[12] Durand, *op. cit.*, pp. 185-187.
[13] *Aff. Etr.*, Buenos Ayres, 39, pp. 188-190. To LePrédour, May 27, 1848.
[14] Poucel, *op. cit.*, pp. 308-321. *Le Moniteur Universel*, July 12, 1848; *Journal des Débats*, July 13.
[15] *Aff. Etr.*, Buenos Ayres, 39, p. 282 ff. To LePrédour, Oct. 3. Durand, *op. cit.*, p. 187.

Admiral LePrédour had no enthusiasm whatever for the mission which he was thus called upon to execute at Buenos Ayres in January, 1849. His own earlier recommendations to the Paris authorities had been to abandon Montevideo, which was now largely deserted by the French, and to make peace with Rosas even at the price of indemnifying Argentina for injuries sustained as a result of the blockade.[16] The purposes of Rosas were much too well served by the continuance of European interference at Montevideo for anyone to expect him to agree easily to a settlement. This was especially true since he was confident of British support as a check to any French attack. It was therefore no surprise when the Dictator declared that the terms were entirely unsatisfactory, and made objection to LePrédour's lack of credentials.[17] Appreciating the unwisdom of the threatening tone of his instructions, and influenced no doubt by his intimate contacts with Manuelita [18] and with Southern, the French leader determined to postpone a break with the Dictator by imitating the tactics of the British negotiator. He consequently asked Rosas to prepare for him the terms on which peace could be secured by France, while he himself would remain in the city to await the arrival of his full powers.[19]

The treaty which was finally signed by LePrédour on April 4, 1849, marks the greatest triumph which the diplomacy of Rosas had yet attained. The French Admiral would be allowed to arrange an immediate armistice at Montevideo if he would at the same time raise his blockade of the ports of Oribe. Following the ultimate disarmament of the defenders of Montevideo, Rosas would give his consent to the return of the Argentine forces, providing they were no longer needed by

[16] *Op. cit.*, pp. 256-259, LePrédour to Minister of Marine, Aug. 16, 1848.
[17] F. O. 6, 143, S. to P., Mar. 1, 1849. *Aff. Etr.*, Buenos Ayres, 40, p. 16 ff. From LePrédour, December, 1848 to February, 1849. Brossard, *op. cit.*, p. 274. Harris thought that Rosas wished to keep his troops in Uruguay as a menace to the Brazilian frontier. S. D. Arg. Rep., Desp. 6, from Harris, April 9, 1849.
[18] See Saldías, *Papeles de Rozas*, 1, p. 308. LePrédour to Mademoiselle, Feb. 15, 1849. Manuelita had acquired the desire to learn the French language, and he the Spanish, and they were rendering mutual assistance.
[19] *Aff. Etr.*, Buenos Ayres, 40, p. 64. From Le Prédour, April 2. S. D. Arg. Rep., Desp. 6, Harris to Secretary of State, Mar. 14, 1849.

President Oribe. If Montevideo should refuse to disarm, it was provided that the French forces would withdraw their support from the city. The other articles corresponded to the previous Argentine proposals. The treaty would have to be accepted by Oribe, and all questions between that leader and the French Government should be regulated in a separate Convention.[20] LePrédour himself admitted to the United States Chargé that it would be difficult, if not impossible, to execute the treaty;[21] it was obvious that the submission of such a document to Paris could serve no useful purpose except that of killing time.

The required negotiation of the French Admiral with Oribe was immediately undertaken, a treaty being concluded between them by the middle of May, 1849. This second treaty was for the most part a reaffirmation of the terms just made with Rosas. The only significant feature was a secret article which provided that Oribe himself should have full control of the arrangements for the election of a new Uruguayan Assembly, which would choose the new President.[22] A six months' armistice at Montevideo was agreed to on May 24, on which date the French blockade was entirely withdrawn. Nothing remained of the European intervention except the French subsidy to Montevideo, the occupation of Martín García, and the retention of a few dilapidated Argentine war vessels.[23]

The relative position in which the two European governments found themselves in 1849 in regard to the ratification of their respective Argentine treaties demonstrates clearly the advantage which Great Britain enjoyed in the Plata affair. The approval of the Southern treaty, in the first place, was

[20] *Aff. Etr., ibid.*, pp. 42-46, 69-79, 102-106. F. O. 6, 143, S. to P., April 4, 1849. In the Spanish version, Oribe was entitled *President,* and Montevideo was referred to as a *de facto authority.*

[21] S. D., *ibid.*, April 9, 1849.

[22] *Correspondencia Confidencial de Sr. D. Gabriel A. Pereira,* 1, pp. 529-535. F. O. 6, 143, S. to P., May 18, 1849. It is significant that the *British* agent was advised of this *secret* article by the Argentine authorities.

[23] S. D., Arg. Rep., Desp. 6, Harris to Clayton, June 4, 1849.

entirely within the competence of the British Cabinet, who were under no necessity whatever of disclosing its terms. An attempt of the opponents of the Government, in August, to make the issue of the British abandonment of Montevideo and the desertion of their French associates a question of confidence in Parliament was easily turned aside by Lord Palmerston. No one could deny the assertion which he made that the independence of Uruguay was not sacrificed by the new treaty. He had, moreover, an unanswerable argument in the fact that British commerce was rapidly recovering under the new arrangement.[24]   The unstable French Government, on the other hand, was obliged by the Constitution of the second Republic to present every treaty to the Assembly for ratification. For them to have attempted to defend the humiliating surrender of LePrédour in an open debate might easily have proven fatal to the entire Bonapartist régime. The expensive subsidy policy was, of course, utterly futile; and yet to embark upon the difficult task of forcibly exacting the kind of Argentine treaty which would permit the discontinuance of the subsidy would arouse certain opposition for France both in England and America.

During the first half of 1849, Napoleon's Government, which was far more conservative than its revolutionary predecessor had been, did little but mark time on the Plata question. It was too late to protest at London against the action of Gore in the previous year.[25] Such confusion obtained at the office on the Quai d'Orsay that the October, 1848, instructions to LePrédour were not even discovered until the following April.[26] When the Argentine issue was raised by several members of the French Assembly, later in this same month, in connection with a supplementary appropriation bill, it was crowded out by the

[24] *Parliamentary Debates*, 3d. Series, 102, pp. 767-8; 104, pp. 602-617; 105, pp. 780-1; 106, pp. 732-3; 107, pp. 90-100. February to July, 1849. Lord Howden was viciously attacked in July, and his own defense lacked much of frankness, if not something of honesty, in his treatment of facts.

[25] *Aff. Etr.*, Buenos Ayres, 40, pp. 61-62. To Adm. Cecil in London, Mar. 29, 1849. See Article 53 of the French Constitution.

[26] F. O. 27, 843, Normanby to Palmerston, April 22, 1849.

press of other business.[27] The speech of President Bonaparte before a newly elected Assembly, on June 1, revealed indirectly his concern over the inevitable Montevidean problem. On this occasion, he carefully emphasized the fact that many French nationals had recently migrated from Uruguay to the Argentine side of the Plata.[28] In the meantime, Palmerston had become so uneasy over the encouragement which the name of Napoleon had given to French imperialists, both at home and in South America,[29] that he had definitely warned Paris that England would not be indifferent toward any attempt to annex Uruguay.[30] Southern had been ordered in April, 1849, to render every assistance to the negotiation of LePrédour, because, as Palmerston remarked in the same letter:

"It is indeed evident that if England were to make a separate arrangement and to leave France with her differences with Rosas unsettled, the British Government would lose all right of objecting to the french [sic] occupation of Montevideo, and yet a prolongation of that occupation, ending possibly in the conversion of the Country into a french Colony, would be very adverse to British Interests, both Commercial and Political." [31]

When the Southern treaty reached London in early June, its ratification was indefinitely delayed in the hope that France might be persuaded to withdraw at the same time.[32]

A project came to light in early July which greatly alarmed the British Government. It was learned that a private company in Paris was contemplating the collection of an "emigrant body," consisting of some 5,000 men, from among the restless spirits thrown up by the revolution—men of whom the police

[27] *Le Moniteur Universel*, Apr. 24, 25, May 2, 1849. The sum voted was 480,000 francs.
[28] *Annual Register* for 1849, pp. 226-246, 256. The Socialists had gained 116 seats in the new election, and Barrot, formerly the leader of the Third Party, became head of a new Cabinet.
[29] F. O. 13, 265, Hudson to Palmerston, Jan. 13 and Feb. 24, 1849.
[30] *Aff. Etr.*, Buenos Ayres, 40, pp. 110-116. From Adm. Cecil at London, Apr. 7, 1849. F. O. 6, 27, 843, Palmerston to Normanby, Apr. 20, 1849; Normanby to Palmerston, Apr. 22. Guillemot, the over enthusiastic French Chargé at Rio de Janeiro was recalled in disgrace, and his pretended intimacy with Napoleon's imperialistic purposes was declared to be without foundation.
[31] F. O. 6, 142, to Southern, April 21, 1849. Mr. Gore at Montevideo was also warned of French ambitions. F. O. 51, 61, May 3 ff.
[32] F. O. 6, 142, Palmerston to Southern, June 4, July 4, Aug. 4, 1849.

would gladly be rid—for the purpose of colonizing Uruguay. The men were supposed to go unarmed, and the expedition was to be entirely unofficial.[33] Palmerston immediately directed Normanby at Paris to inform the French Foreign Minister that, under the circumstances, such an expedition:

"could only be considered as a Part of a scheme long suspected, but never avowed, to convert Montevideo into a French colony . . . [and] would form a grave Consideration for the Gov't of Great Britain." [34]

The British Ambassador, who was more confident than Palmerston of the pacific intentions of Napoleon's new Government, softened the statement considerably;[35] but the assurance which he received in reply that no aggression had been contemplated by the emigration proposal was not entirely convincing.[36] The matter was, however, definitely dropped for the time being.

The impossibility of accepting the LePrédour treaties was apparent as soon as they reached Paris, in late July. An immediate difficulty arose in connection with the postponement of their consideration because of the fact that the Commission on appropriations refused to replenish the exhausted credits covering the subsidy until the Government should announce its new policy.[37] The predicament of the French Cabinet was made immeasurably worse by the appearance of a news item in the *London Times* of August 1, 1849, which described accurately the terms of the French treaty with Rosas and emphasized especially that by it the independence of Uruguay had been sacrificed.[38] A perfect furor developed in the French press over the question. Normanby, who had consistently advocated the acceptance of the treaties, made the following confession to Palmerston on August 16:

[33] F. O. 27, 846, Normanby to Palmerston, July 2, 1849. This emigration scheme emanated from the Montevidean agent at Paris.
[34] F. O. 27, 837, P. to N., July 3, 1849.
[35] F. O. 27, 846, N. to P., July 3.
[36] *Ibid.*, July 9.
[37] *Ibid.*, July 2 and 23. *Aff. Etr.*, Buenos Ayres, 40, pp. 239-243. The full text of the treaties is given, pp. 276-282. A Memorandum raises many objections to the treaties.
[38] *London Times*, Aug. 1, 1849. The announcement also created a stir in the British Parliament. *Parliamentary Debates*, 3d, 107, p. 1157.

"I cannot say . . . that the step which I thought abstractly the best might not have led to consequences directly the reverse of what one should have wished, and by a combination of Parties, would have ended in the rejection of the treaty and the overthrow of the Government." [39]

The subsidy was temporarily continued by a decree of the President on August 19, and the Assembly adjourned with the question still unsettled.[40] When Palmerston became convinced that early action on the French treaties was not to be expected, he determined to delay no longer his acceptance of the one which Southern had negotiated. Without taking the trouble to notify even his own Ambassador at Paris, the Foreign Minister sent full powers to his agent at Buenos Ayres on August 31, with orders to conclude the ratifications with Rosas.[41] Unaware of this action, Normanby continued for three months his persuasion that the French Government should resist the pressure of the war party in the Assembly and should try to negotiate the necessary alterations in the treaties, all the while acting on the assumption that London was holding up their settlement with Rosas.

A serious crisis developed in the relations between France and England when it was discovered, in early December, by the Paris authorities that the Southern treaty had already been ratified.[42] Foreign Minister la Hitte was highly offended at the unwitting deception which Normanby had practiced upon him, and the British Ambassador himself did not hesitate to raise a strong protest at having been kept in the dark by Palmerston.[43] There was now no possibility of hiding the fact

[39] F. O. 27, 847, N. to P., Aug. 16, 19, and 20, 1849. Pres. Bonaparte was trying to quiet the opposition to the treaties by suggesting qualifications. The Montevidean agent in Paris was informed on Aug. 24 that the treaties would not be ratified. See Palomeque, "Melchor Pacheco y Obes" *Revista histórica* 4, pp. 296-298. (1911.)
[40] *Le Moniteur Universel*, Jan. 8, 1850.
[41] F. O. 6, 142, P. to S., Aug. 30, Sept. 3, 1849. The British agent's ability was highly commended. The signing of the treaty took place on Nov. 24 and the ratifications were exchanged May 15, 1850. *Accounts and Papers*, 1850, lvi, p. 1, (1253).
[42] F. O. 27, 848, Normanby to P., Nov. 26, 29, Dec. 2, 1849.
[43] *Ibid.*, Dec. 2 and 6; P. to Normanby, Dec. 3, 6. Normanby would have none of Palmerston's excuses that the incident was due to a clerical oversight. He cited numerous instances in his recent correspondence which would have indicated to the Foreign Minister that he was unaware of the order to Southern.

that France had been completely abandoned by Britain in Uruguay. To the prevailing popular unrest,[44] which made the Plata issue under any circumstances dangerous, there was now added a wave of intense hostility toward Great Britain to complicate the question. The debate upon the subject developed into one of the most serious crises that Napoleon's various Governments had yet been obliged to face.

The subject of the LePrédour treaties was brought before the Assembly on December 21, 1849, in connection with the recommendation of appropriation bills to cover amounts already drawn for the Montevidean subsidy. The Chairman of the Commission, M. Daru, reported that his group had come to the conclusion that France must either send an armed expedition at once or else abandon Montevideo entirely. The increasingly unreasonable nature of Rosas' demands, of which the LePrédour treaties were conclusive evidence, proved the futility of entering upon further negotiations. On the other hand, he continued, complete withdrawal would be preferable to the present hopeless and expensive program. In spite of the undeniable facts that the sending of an army to South America would endanger the interests of many French nationals in Argentina, and might precipitate either a domestic crisis in France or an international one with England and the United States, the Commission, said Daru, had leaned toward the alternative of action for the reason that they could not recommend abandonment. Pertinent documents from previous missions were deposited with the report, and the particularly objectionable features of the treaties were indicated.[45] The question came up for general debate a week later.

The belligerent party took the initiative at the outset, and presented a strong case for an immediate expedition to Montevideo. Britain, they declared, had deliberately sought to ruin the interests of France in the river, and Rosas was obviously trifling with them. Admiral Lainé himself lent his support to

[44] F. O. 27, 847, N. to P., Oct. 6, 22, 1849. Moderate leaders predicted that an insurrection would occur in France within a few months.
[45] *Le Moniteur Universel*, Dec. 22, 1849. The emigration proposal was also mentioned, but it did not receive much support.

the statement that a small but energetic force could, with some local support, rescue the prestige of France and secure an acceptable treaty.[46] To acknowledge Oribe as President, after France had been committed from the very first to a rejection of his claims, they declared, would leave Britain supreme in the Plata. The inevitable struggle between Brazil and Rosas, which would result from French withdrawal, would be more damaging to trade than their own effort to settle with the Dictator.

The Foreign Minister made his first statement near the end of the second day. He said that he advocated neither the acceptance of the treaties nor the sending of 10,000 troops, the number which would now be required because of the practical decimation of the French population at Montevideo. Such an expedition would be sure to excite the powerful American spirit against France, and would inevitably arouse the opposition of every commercial nation in Europe. The opportunity for negotiation was not yet closed, he insisted, and France had "no right to establish a colony at Montevideo."[47] M. Daru immediately came to the defense of his report. He admitted that the French Republic might sacrifice her only two friends by the suggested expedition; but England would surely be fair, and after the Mexican war, the United States would certainly have no right to object. Action, he said, was the only feasible policy, but the Government should perhaps not be denied their right to weigh the political considerations and determine the nature of the measures.[48] Taking advantage of the latter qualification introduced by Daru, the Minister of Justice, Rouher, took the tribune on the following day and denounced the Commission's attempt to evade the responsibility of considering the political consequences of their decision,—in calling for *action* instead of *war*. By stressing this point, a wedge was cleverly driven between the more radical and the

[46] *Ibid.*, Dec. 29.
[47] *Ibid.*, Dec. 30. Of the former 15,000 French inhabitants of Montevideo, only 2,200, he said, were left.
[48] *Ibid.* Daru deplored the descent from the high point of French prestige in America which had obtained after the storming of San Juan d'Ulloa.

moderate elements of the opposition. Daru was finally forced by the war party to admit that he would prefer an armed nego- tiation to immediate hostilities. Rouher was thereby given the opportunity to drive home the basic contention of the Gov- ernment that something might still be expected from nego- tiation.

The first test of the strength of the moderates came during the general uproar which followed the rebuttal speech of the Minister of Justice. The radicals made every effort to secure an immediate decision on the various amendments which had been proposed; but in this they were thwarted by the arbitrary ruling of the President of the Assembly that the amendment selected would have to be referred back to the Commission for consideration. The choice was bitterly contested, for some of the proposals demanded immediate hostilities. It was only by the narrow margin of 315 to 312 that the moderates secured the selection of the none too pacific amendment of one M. Rancé, which ran as follows:

"A credit of ten millions is open to the Ministers of war and marine to support, in case of need, the negotiation pending be- tween the French Republic and the Argentine Republic." [49]

The report on the Rancé amendment which the Commission brought back on January 4, 1850, was in the nature of a defi- nite recommendation that the Government should be invited to employ whatever forces were necessary to secure the success of the negotiation and to protect French nationals. Fifteen hundred to eighteen hundred troops, it was thought, could hold Montevideo temporarily in case of failure, and thus prepare the way for a larger expedition. But the Foreign Minister was still not satisfied. He objected to being drawn into entangle- ments which would almost inevitably mean war.[50]

As the radical leaders saw the increasing success of the tac- tics of the Government, they became more violent in their attacks. They denounced the Cabinet for the betrayal of the honor of France and for the abandonment of their commercial interests in the Plata. They attempted in vain to persuade

[49] *Le Moniteur Universel*, Jan. 1, 1850.
[50] *Ibid.*, Jan. 5, 1850.

the Government to outline the definite modifications of the treaty which they expected to secure from Rosas; la Hitte steadfastly refused to do that which would force him to negotiate by ultimatum. Finally Adolph Thiers advanced to the tribune, to speak for his first time in opposition to the Government of Napoleon. He based his forceful argument on the old theme of the sacred obligations of France toward Montevideo and upon a graphic representation of the wonderful future possibilities for French commerce in the Plata and in all South America. All of these, he insisted, were at stake in the present decision. His eloquence seemed to electrify the Assembly, for the speech was frequently punctuated by long applause. When he concluded with a stirring patriotic appeal demanding that a military expedition be sent without delay against the tyrant whose provocations had given France such an undeniable right to make war, the Assembly was in an uproar. From many quarters came the demand for a vote on the question.[51]

But the Government still had their last card to play against the inflammatory eloquence of Thiers. When order was eventually restored, the Minister of Justice took the tribune and began to read from the instructions prepared for Mackau on July 21, 1840. The previous orator became so excited in his frequent interruptions and attempted explanations that the presiding officer was obliged to quiet him. But the fact that Thiers himself had refused war in 1840 and had explicitly repudiated their obligations toward Montevideo could not be denied. Rouher then proceeded to demonstrate from recent despatches that a large majority of their countrymen then living on the banks of the Plata wanted peace. The Foreign Legion, he said, might deserve their protection, but such a minority group should not be allowed to dictate a policy which would injure many others and the international results of which would be incalculable. The question of war should therefore be adjourned for three to six months, at least until every opportunity of accommodation had been exhausted.[52] The

[51] *Ibid.*, Jan. 5 and 6. Some speakers of the Left demanded an expedition, but declared that colonies were undesirable.
[52] *Ibid.*

puncturing of the argument of Thiers by the Minister left the warmongers completely discredited. Only the armed negotiation proposal of the Commission remained as an alternative to leaving the hands of the Government perfectly free in a new negotiation.

The Cabinet finally achieved its full triumph on January 7, 1850. Over the strenuous objections of the Left wing, the President of the Assembly gave precedence to a new motion of M. Rancé [53] to the effect that the body pass to the order of the day, in view of the facts that the treaties were not being presented for ratification, and that the Government proposed to continue the negotiation for the purpose of safeguarding the interests and honor of France and of protecting their fellow nationals in the Plata. The motion carried by a vote of 338 to 300, and the appropriations for the subsidy were approved immediately thereafter.[54] The settlement of their score with Rosas had been postponed for a time, and the Government had gained a breathing space.[55]

Every precaution was taken that the new instructions might be sent off under the most favorable auspices. A private letter from Mackau to Arana told of the difficulties which the Government was encountering. He entreated Argentina to come to terms.[56] The British Ambassador at Paris was assured that the fifteen hundred regular troops, which were to accompany the new instructions, were intended for replacement only and did not constitute a military expedition. Paris also said that their objections to the treaties were not of a serious nature, and, most encouraging of all, that the pacifically-minded Le-Prédour was again to conduct the negotiation.[57] Normanby

[53] F. O. 27, 868, N. to P., Jan. 31, and an enclosed copy of the *National* of Paris, containing a letter from Rancé to the Montevidean agent in Paris. It told of confidential assurances from la Hitte that the Uruguay city would be protected. Rancé was apparently acting as stalking horse for the Government during the debate.

[54] *Le Moniteur Universel,* Jan. 8. Saldías, *Historia Argentina,* 5, pp. 183-196.

[55] Brossard's book was published in 1850, and it was a direct attempt to arouse France to fulfill her duty to civilization by making a colony of Uruguay. See pp. 1-5, 371-2, 396-407.

[56] Saldías, *op. cit.,* 5, p. 97.

[57] F. O. 27, 868, Normanby to P., Jan. 21, 1850.

appreciated the situation, and wrote to Palmerston deprecating the hostile attitude of the British press, which was causing a very unfortunate reaction in France. He warned that a failure of the new mission would make it impossible for the French Government to avoid going to war even at the risk of disrupting their valued understanding with Great Britain. The British Foreign Minister unhesitatingly pledged the hearty co-operation of Southern.[58] Another disquieting incident for London was the declaration made by Aberdeen and Lansdowne in Parliament that the British Government's disgraceful abandonment of France had left the latter perfectly free, and that permanent French control of Uruguay would be preferable to its surrender to Rosas.[59]

The instructions sent to LePrédour on January 26 show that the possibility of a war with Rosas was being seriously contemplated by the French Government. La Hitte wrote that he did not want to resort to such extreme measures until it had been proved to England and America that France had reached the "limit of moderation, patience, and long suffering"; but that if Rosas and Oribe should refuse the necessary modifications, hostilities would become imminent.[60] The Minister required, in the first place, that the French treaties with Uruguay in 1836 and with Argentina in 1840 should be referred to explicitly in the preambles and elsewhere. Second, the Argentine forces outside Montevideo must withdraw to the Uruguay river when the disarming of the foreigners began, and should cross the river when notified of the completion of that operation. The war vessels and Martín García were not to be restored until after these first arrangements were executed. Third, it would be necessary for Rosas to guarantee an amnesty at Montevideo. Fourth, France would admit no liability for indemnity arising from the intervention. Finally, in regard to the Argentine treaty, LePrédour should sign no

[58] Ibid., Jan. 28; Palmerston to N., Jan. 29. F. O. 6, 148, to Southern, Feb. 4, 1850.
[59] Parliamentary Debates, 3d., 108, pp. 1278-1286. By Lansdowne and Aberdeen in the House of Lords, Feb. 22, 1850. National Intelligencer, Mar. 13, 1850.
[60] Aff. Etr., Buenos Ayres, 41, pp. 4-9. To LePrédour Jan. 26, 1850.

statement describing Oribe as the President of the Oriental Republic, or referring to Montevideo as a mere *de facto* authority, as had been the case in the previous document. The secret article of Oribe's treaty was declared entirely inadmissible; the new election must be managed either jointly or by a provisional authority. The foundation arrangement for the settlement of French claims on both sides of the Plata should also be laid. In case the negotiations should break off, the Admiral was directed to land all his troops at Martín García and at Montevideo and await further instructions.[61]

The arrival of the reënforcing French squadron before Montevideo in April, 1850, found Rosas in a most diabolical frame of mind. A break with Paraguay and Brazil had just been narrowly averted,[62] and it seemed only a question of a short time until that inevitable conflict should begin. The despotism of Rosas had never been more absolute.[63] In connection with his recent election to another term of dictatorship, his puppets in the *Sala* had placed all the resources of Argentina at his disposal for accomplishing the reincorporation of Paraguay into the Confederation.[64] The extreme irritability of Rosas, resulting from the physical strain of working day and night, was aggravated by a chronic affliction of the gout.[65] With the Dictator exasperated almost beyond expression at the appearance of the 1500 additional troops, and with LePrédour deter-

[61] *Aff. Etr., op. cit.,* pp. 11-36, 40-41, dated Jan. 29.

[62] S. D. Arg. Rep., Desp. 7, Harris to Clayton, Aug. 23, Sept. 20, Oct. 10, Nov. 4. S. D. Brazil, Desp. 17, Tod to Clayton Oct. 17, Dec. 17. F. O. 6, 143, S. to P., Aug. 16, 1849. A Hungarian officer named Weisner commanded the Paraguayan forces. Mr. Hopkins was back in Paraguay by this time.

[63] S. D. Arg. Rep., Desp. 7, Harris to Clayton, Jan. 20, 1850.

[64] F. O. 6, 149, S. to P., Mar. 10; vol. 150, Mar. 19, April 19, May 4, 18. The *Archivo Americano* during this period is largely taken up with the defense of the Buenos Ayres position in regard to the control of the river. Open fighting frequently occurred along the borders of Uruguay and Brazil.

[65] F. O. 6, 145, S. to P., Oct. 11, 1849. Southern had recently encountered great difficulty with Rosas in concluding the ratification of the British treaty. *Ibid.,* Nov. 25, Dec. 13, 17, 1849; vol. 149, same to same, Jan. 26, 1850. S. D. Arg. Rep., Desp. 7, Harris to Clayton, Jan. 26.

mined not to risk a repetition of his previous humiliation, the outlook for an agreement was far from promising.[66] The first advances of the Admiral elicited only violent and inarticulate explosions of temper from the Governor. When the British agent very unostentatiously allowed his opinion to be known that it would be madness for Buenos Ayres to prefer war to the acceptance of the reasonable French terms, Rosas flew into another rage. During the Governor's first conference with the French leader, only a remarkable exhibition of self-control on the latter's part prevented an open rupture. Nevertheless with the aid of the astute Mr. Southern, LePrédour finally placated Rosas by a written explanation to the effect that the new troops had been sent only for the purpose of preventing outbreaks and disarming the foreigners at Montevideo.[67] But the direct negotiations had hardly started before they ran firmly aground on the question of the manner of the withdrawal of the Argentine troops from Uruguay. The Governor became impervious to all arguments on that point.[68]

Just when it began to appear inevitable that the exasperating obstinacy of Rosas would force the French to make war upon him, two significant incidents occurred. In the first place the United States Chargé, Mr. Harris, took it upon himself to notify both the Governor and a prominent member of the Assembly of Buenos Ayres that there was not the slightest ground for any hope that the United States would assist Argentina in case of a conflict with France. When Rosas insisted that the northern republic was obligated to aid him in maintaining the American Doctrine, Harris replied that "the only support which they [the United States] could properly lend him was a moral one, and . . . that had been done, as far as it was deemed useful or necessary."[69] A still more significant

---

[66] F. O. 6, 150, S. to P., April 14, 18, 1850.

[67] Ibid. Also Saldías, op. cit., 5, p. 201-205.

[68] Ibid., May 1, 3, 4, 16. Southern wrote that Rosas was "a man capable of involving the whole world in ruin and misery for the sake of a comma."

[69] S. D. Arg. Rep., Desp. 7, Harris to Clayton, May 14, 1850. Harris distrusted Southern, declaring that his diplomacy was "corruption in all its forms, unscrupulousness, mystery, and intrigue." As to Rosas, he said, "The effort of his whole life [has been] to try how far he can constrain all . . . men to abate from the fair demands of justice."

occurrence was to be found in the fact that Rosas received a communication from the Montevidean authorities saying that they would much prefer the entrance of Oribe into the city rather than have it fall into the hands of the French. The Dictator was asked to give his consent to that arrangement.

Rosas decided that he would use this latter proposal as an excuse for discontinuing his negotiations with the French. But in making a declaration to that effect he clearly over-reached himself. On the advice of Southern, Le Prédour very skillfully surprised and defeated his opponent's insincere pretentions by indicating his own hearty agreement and urging Rosas immediately to grant the request made by Montevideo. Both the British and French agents were rightly confident that Rosas did not wish to settle the trouble in Uruguay immediately, and that if the affair had to come to an end, he would much prefer that it be accomplished by a regular treaty with France.[70] The outcome of the incident was that Rosas became more amenable to reason, and the patient LePrédour was finally able, on June 25, to arrive at an agreement with him. Considerable delay was occasioned thereafter by a serious illness of the Governor, and it was not until early August that Oribe's consent to the new treaty was secured.[71] The final signatures were affixed at Buenos Ayres on August 31, and at Cerrito on September 13, 1850.[72]

The new treaty represented a distinct retreat from Rosas' previous position, but it nevertheless fell considerably short of the demands indicated as essential by the French Government. In regard to the withdrawal of the Argentine troops from Uruguay, it was specified that a body of them equal in number to the sum of the regular French troops and one-fourth of the marines should remain at Montevideo for two months after the armistice, at the end of which time the French forces would also depart. Oribe was given the title of President in the Spanish version and that of Brigadier-General in the French, while a separate article explained that the titles used implied no obliga-

[70] F. O. 6, 150, S. to P., May 16.
[71] Ibid., June 9, 25, July 24; vol. 151, Aug. 9, 1850.
[72] C. Calvo, Le Droit International 6 vols. (1896). Vol. 1, pp. 335-6.

tion upon either government. A satisfactory understanding was also reached in regard to the claims. But at least four other demands were not complied with, namely, the reference in the preamble to the previous French treaties, the retirement of the Argentine troops before the return of Martín García and the Argentine war vessels, the guarantee of amnesty at Montevideo, and the joint control of the election in Uruguay.[73] With the apparently successful termination of the second negotiation of LePrédour, the French Government ceased to be a determining factor in the affairs of the Plata, although the subsidy and the retention of Martín García later gave material aid to the enemies of Rosas.[74] The grand coalition against the Dictator, so long delayed in its organization, now took command of the situation.[75] Brazil broke off relations with Rosas in October, 1850;[76] she formed an alliance with Paraguay in December, and came to an understanding with Gov. Urquiza of Entre Rios during the early part of 1851. In every case, the defense of the independence of the Banda Oriental was recognized as a primary objective of the allies. Entre Rios declared war on Rosas in April, 1851, and Corrientes followed suit a few weeks later. A formal league between Brazil, Entre Rios, and Montevideo, established on May 29, 1851, was later expanded to include Corrientes and Paraguay, the general purpose being to overthrow their common enemy at Buenos Ayres.[77] Operations in Uruguay were begun in June, and the long siege of Montevideo had been terminated by the end of July.[78] The rapid march of these events had meanwhile been a God-send to the authorities in Paris.

[73] *Aff. Etr.*, Buenos Ayres, 41, pp. 219-222. Pereyra, *op. cit.*, pp. 216-7.
[74] S. D. Arg. Rep., Desp. 7, Harris to Webster, May 4, 1851. The Island was later surrendered to Urquiza.
[75] Vedia, *op. cit.*, pp. 139-152. Sarmiento, *Life in the Argentine Republic*, pp. xvi-xviii. The coalition was largely the product of the Unitarian propaganda.
[76] S. D. Arg. Rep., Desp. 7, Harris to Clayton, Oct. 5, 24, 1850.
[77] F. P. Pereira, *Colección de documentos*, pp. 24-36. Brazil's promise to support Montevideo was made on Mar. 16, 1851. Carlos Oneta y Viana, *La diplomacia del Brasil en el Río de la Plata*, p. 24 ff. Durand, *op. cit.*, pp. 192-196. Vedia, *op. cit.*, pp. 152-153. *British Foreign and State Papers* 110, pp. 1135-1140.
[78] Durand, *op. cit.*, pp. 197-201. S. D. Arg. Rep., Desp. 7, Harris to Webster, May 4, 1851.

During the ten months' time which had been consumed by the second LePrédour negotiation, the danger that France would undertake more serious operations in the Plata had become very imminent. The war party was strong,[79] and the French Foreign Minister would only reply to the constant pressure from London for an early settlement by saying that he would do everything that he could, consistent with his responsibility to the will of the Assembly.[80] The news that Brazil was seeking to enroll French officers in her army, which reached London in the autumn of 1850, was very disquieting. Palmerston became thoroughly alarmed in December when Paris began to plead the impending conflict between Brazil and Rosas as a reason for postponing their action on the new treaty.[81] The British Ambassador was ordered to announce that such a demur would give color to the suspicion that France was seeking an excuse to continue indefinitely her occupation of the important port of Montevideo, and that such a development could not under any circumstances be regarded with indifference by England.[82]

But Palmerston was mistaken in his judgment of the motives of the French Government in this delay. They would only too gladly have been rid of the embarrassing problem.[83] After many conversations with various members of Napoleon's Cabinet on the question, Normanby reported to his chief, on December 26, 1850, as follows:

"I cannot flatter myself that there is any quarter in which the future use of these arguments will materially influence the result.

[79] Poucel, *op. cit.*, pp. 320-321. Interested parties, imperialists, and Chambers of Commerce were all bringing pressure to bear. Montevideo also was still seeking French assistance. See Andrés Lamas, *Notices sur la République Orientale de l'Uruguay.* (Paris 1851.) This appeal is dedicated to Thiers in the French translation.

[80] Palmerston himself, at this very time, was contemplating the seizure of the Straits of Magellan and Patagonia. See F. O. 6, 148, P. to Southern, July 19, 1850. F. O. 27, 873, N. to P., Aug. 5, 1850.

[81] F. O. 27, 876, N. to P., Dec. 13, 1850. The Paris press was almost unanimous in opposing the treaty. Poucel, *op. cit.*, p. 321.

[82] F. O. 27, 867, P. to N., Dec. 20, 1850. Britain exerted all her influence to prevent this war between Brazil and Rosas. F. O. 6, 156, January, July, November, 1851,—numerous instructions.

[83] That the French Cabinet was ready to accept the treaty because of dangers in Europe is proved by a long memorandum in the Argentine correspondence. *Aff. Etr.,* Buenos Ayres, 41, pp. 239-274.

With the President and the Cabinet I believe them to be unnecessary. They seem to be sincerely anxious to bring this affair to a satisfactory conclusion; . . . but the whole rests absolutely with the National Assembly, and as [in view of] the temper shewn upon all recent occasions by that body upon questions connected with the Rio Plata, I am afraid that any overt indication of the interest which England takes in the adoption of a particular course by France would be likely to have an injurious effect." [84]

The nebulous state of affairs in the river enabled the Government to postpone the treaty decision; it was not until May, 1851, that the necessity of making some provision to cover the drafts for the subsidy at Montevideo brought the question up before the Assembly.[85] The Foreign Minister introduced at this time three measures for the consideration of that body, two of them appropriation bills to continue the subsidy through July, 1851, and the third a motion for the approval of the LePrédour treaty. The Minister agreed to submit pertinent documents in connection with the latter instrument, although he refused when asked to disclose the text of the instructions given to the Admiral.[86] The appropriation measures were promptly reported by the Commission, with the amendment that the limit of the subsidy should be set at the last of March. They were approved.[87] The treaty question was kept under consideration for several weeks longer. When the recommendation for the acceptance of the Convention was finally presented on June 28, the news of the beginning of actual hostilities in the Argentine country made it inadvisable to take any action upon the matter. The session of the Assembly closed without the treaty being ratified, and it was never formally approved.[88]

The triumph of the coalition forces commanded by Urquiza was so rapid that little was left of the régime of Rosas by the

[84] F. O. 27, 876, N. to P., Dec. 26, 1850. Even the Count of Chambord and his legitimist followers had been lined up to oppose the treaty. See Poucel, *op. cit.*, pp. 321-324. An ably written article by Thomas Page, advocating peace, appeared in the *Revue des Deux Mondes*, April, 1851, pp. 126-169.

[85] F. O. 27, 900, N. to P., April 21, 28, 1851. This was the fifth Cabinet with whom Napoleon had discussed the Argentine question.

[86] *Le Moniteur Universel*, May 2.

[87] *Ibid.*, May 13, 15.

[88] *Ibid.*, June 29. F. O. 6, 156, P. to S., Aug. 8, 1851. *Parliamentary Debates*, 3d, 118, pp. 1857-1858.

end of 1851. Oribe surrendered on October 7,[89] and the Dictator, now practically deserted, was powerless to check the conqueror's advance. The final victory at Monte Caseros just outside Buenos Ayres, on February 3, 1852, found arrangements already made by Rosas for the reception of himself and his daughter on board a British war vessel in the river. They departed for England a week later, never to return to the shores of the silver river.[90]

That the terrible Dictator deserves much of the odium which has since gathered around his name, no one can deny. But when it has been admitted that he was ruthlessly cruel and that he governed by terror, that his outlook was more barbarian than civilized, and that his despotism and ambition were for two decades a scourge to both banks of the Plata, the proposition might still be defended that the results might have been much worse if his strong hand had not been available to bring a semblance of order out of the chaos which threatened the Argentine Confederation in his day. No one has ever questioned the personal honesty of Rosas, his prodigious industry, or his fervent patriotism. His shrewdness and foresight have been greatly underestimated. None contributed more than he to the establishment of the American policy in Argentina.[91] That Rosas was not exclusively responsible for the many evils which plagued the Plata during his era is finally proved by the fact that they did not cease with his departure.[92]

Immediately following the triumph of Urquiza, the old quarrel between Buenos Ayres and the interior provinces was revived.[93] An accord was reached at a meeting of the various Provincial Governors at San Nicolas shortly after the fall of

[89] Durand, op. cit., pp. 201-210. A great proportion of Oribe's army deserted to Urquiza.

[90] Vedia, op. cit., pp. 153-155. Durand, op. cit., pp. 212-233. An interesting quarrel occurred in each House of Parliament in regard to the nature of the reception accorded Rosas and his daughter by the port officials at Plymouth. Parl. Deb., 3d, 121, pp. 1-7.

[91] Pereyra, op. cit., pp. 230-233. Appendix, No. 5.

[92] Manuel Oliveira Lima, Evolution of Brazil as compared with that of Spanish and Anglo-Saxon America. (Palo Alto 1914) Vol. 17, Leland Stanford Jr. Publications, pp. 92-93.

[93] D. F. Sarmiento, Compaña en el ejercito grande de Sud América. (Rio de Janeiro 1852). An attack on the Federalism of Urquiza.

Rosas, which chose Urquiza as provisional President of the Confederation, decreed freedom of interior transit and river navigation, and recognized the independence of Uruguay and Paraguay.[94] But this arrangement was promptly repudiated at Buenos Ayres. No sooner had Urquiza departed from the city in September, 1852, after having restored his authority there, than the former capital again asserted its independence of all Federal control. The President invited foreign powers to have nothing to do with the insurrectionary authorities within the city, and proceeded with his task of organizing a general Confederation government at Santa Fé.[95]

The opportunity offered by the overthrow of Rosas to negotiate for the freedom of river navigation had been immediately appreciated in Paris and London. Special agents were sent to the Plata for that purpose in April, 1852.[96] At the invitation of the two European governments, a United States agent was also sent to the river during the same month, with instructions to participate in any negotiations concerning the navigation of the streams, and to arrange commercial treaties with the three Plata Republics.[97] The turmoil around Buenos Ayres delayed for more than a year the desired arrangement with Urquiza for freedom of river navigation. It was not until July, 1853, after the Argentine leader had definitely abandoned his endeavor to force the city into submission,[98] that the matter was consummated. Identical treaties with France, Great Britain, and the United States, providing for the free navigation of the Paraná and Uruguay rivers in perpetuity, were signed

[94] José Bianco, *Organización Nacional.* (Buenos Ayres 1903.)

[95] S. D. Arg. Rep., Instructions, pp. 68-69, Marcy to Peden, Jan. 29, 1854. Durand, *op. cit.,* pp. 237-242. José L. Bustamante, *Memoirs sobre la revolución de 11 de septiembre de 1852.* (Buenos Ayres 1853.)

[96] *Parliamentary Debates,* 3d., 120, pp. 17, 782.

[97] S. D. Arg. Rep., Instructions, Webster to Pendleton, April 28, 1852. See Fillmore's message of Dec. 6, 1852, in Richardson. The treaties were secured with Uruguay and Paraguay without difficulty. Both of them provided for free river navigation. S. D. Arg. Rep., Instructions, Dec. 2, 1852, July 30, 1853.

[98] S. D. Arg. Rep., Desp. 8, Pendleton to Secretary of State, Jan. 1, July 14, 24, 1853. A. H. Guernsey, "La Plata," *Harpers Magazine,* 18, pp. 327-9.

by Urquiza on board a vessel in the Plata on July 10, they being officially concluded in Entre Rios several weeks later.[99]

With the acquisition of the privilege of direct access to the ports of Argentina and to the markets of the interior, one primary consideration responsible for the intervention of France and England was eliminated for all time. Many difficult problems still remained to vex this quarter of South America in subsequent decades, for example, the control of Martín García,[100] the determination of the territorial limits of the states,[101] and the unification of Argentina.[102] But the governments at London and Paris were quite content to leave these questions for the settlement of the local parties.

The tangled story of the preceding pages needs no retelling here, but a few observations may serve to throw the salient facts into bolder relief. It is apparent, in the first place, that the geography of the Plata valley was far more important as a determining factor in the episode than was the whim of any ruler or diplomat. Behind Rosas and his policy were the *gauchos* who were responsible for his régime; back of the *gauchos* were the boundless Pampas which bred them and made them all but unconquerable by foreigners. Similarly, the importance of the river system itself, together with the resources and potential markets of the vast empire which it drained, made the manner of its regulation a question of inevitable concern to commercial nations as well as to the provinces and states of the interior of the Continent. With the interests of the two latter groups identical in favoring the free use of the rivers, a combination between them for the purpose of wresting control from the man who would stand astride the mouth of the Plata and throttle its trade should easily have been pos-

[99] S. D., *op. cit.,* July 14, Aug. 1, 1853. The date for the signature is given as July 13, with concluding negotiations made in Entre Rios three weeks later. Centeno, *Tratados,* . . . 8, pp. 143-160, 234-242, 327-334.

[100] Vedia, *op. cit.,* pp. 169-176.

[101] *British Foreign and State Papers,* 110, pp. 1140-1145. Vedia, *op. cit.,* pp. 158-163. Durand, *op. cit.,* pp. 169-176.

[102] A. Deberle, *Histoire de l'Amerique du Sud.* (1878, 1897), pp. 199-202. Buenos Ayres remained outside the Confederation until 1859.

sible. That such was not the case was due to the fact that the suspicion entertained by the long isolated native population toward foreigners and the contempt of a rural people for the advantages of trade were not sufficiently taken into account at Paris and London. The indifference of the United States toward the episode only demonstrates the comparative weakness of avowed political principles when divorced from real economic interests.

But political considerations nevertheless played no inconsiderable part in determining the policies at both Paris and London. From the original decision of Molé in 1838 to give an exhibition in America of the power of France, until the last frantic postponement of the action on the LePrédour treaties by the Government of Napoleon, it was necessary for the Paris authorities to take strict account of the political consequences of every decision made in reference to their policy in the Argentine. Only the accidental fact that the troublesome Thiers was the author of the instructions given to Mackau in 1840 saved Guizot and his successors from much more serious embarrassment on the question than they actually encountered in the Chambers. The desire of Aberdeen and Guizot to strengthen their political *entente* in 1845 was undoubtedly an important factor in bringing about the blunder of the second intervention. Moreover, the danger to British interests from complications arising on the Pacific coast of North America may well have influenced Aberdeen in his precipitous retreat in 1846. But with the British policy, especially, it is almost impossible to separate the political from the economic factors. The powerful influence which the organized commercial and financial groups exercised directly upon Aberdeen throughout his tenure is perfectly evident; and the fact that Palmerston's unscrupulous policy served the interests of these parties left very little to be said in Parliament in opposition to his shameful treatment of France.

Two bitter experiences had taught England her lesson that commercial advantages in Argentina were not to be promoted

by political interference.[103]   France, on the other hand, felt
that she had a humiliation to be wiped off the slate, a damaged
prestige to be restored; and a powerful group within the country was still enamored by the hope of reëstablishing their political, if not their territorial, stake in the new world.[104]   In this
respect, the failure to take advantage of their opportunities in
the Plata from 1848 to 1851 undoubtedly had a definite bearing on Napoleon's policy a decade later in Mexico, the place
where the victory had been so easy in 1838 and where the stubborn *gaucho* was not to be encountered.[105]

Several facts also emerge which throw new light on the subject of the traditional attitude of the United States toward
the international affairs of South America.   The stubborn hostility toward European interference, which Rosas so completely
embodied, was latent in the Argentine people themselves, and
had been entirely indigenous in its development.   The South
American agents of the United States, when acting upon their
own initiative and without restraint from Washington, did
much to encourage this American spirit and contributed not a
little in the way of obstacles to the European program.   But
the policy of the North American government was clearly
one of non-interference.   Polk and Buchanan repudiated the
early unauthorized actions of their agents, and went so far as to
promise the British Ambassador that they would not oppose
the intervention in the Plata.   They carefully avoided any
public commitment on a question which was admitted to be a
flagrant violation of the principles of Monroe, as then understood.   To conclude that the United States would have interfered if territorial acquisition had been attempted is a speculation which finds considerably more support in the sacrosanct
political creed which posterity has built up than in the actual
facts themselves.   Neither the press nor the government of the
United States showed any noticeable alarm in 1849-50, when
such a move on the part of the French Republic appeared im-

[103] *Frasers Magazine*, 45: 596-602, "Rosas the Dictator of Buenos Ayres."
[104] N. Peuchgaric, *La Plata de 1851 à 1854.* (Paris 1856).   This is an
attempt to stimulate French colonization to the Plata.
[105] Poucel, *op. cit.,* pp. 327-348.   A direct comparison is here made between their prospects in Mexico and in Uruguay.

minent. The actual forestalling of a possible French colony at Montevideo was the work of the British Foreign Office, not that of the American State Department.

It is, at the same time, difficult to imagine just how the course of events could have been materially influenced for good if the United States had entangled themselves in the miserable quarrel. It would merely have complicated the affair more than ever, and would have gained for the northern republic the enmity of one or the other of the opposing local parties. Alberdi, the Unitarian statesman, has criticized the Washington government for denying to Argentina at this time the legitimate aid which France and England might have afforded in her political regeneration; [106] but this Polk certainly did not do. Señor Pereyra has more recently damned the North American authorities for not assisting Rosas in the defense of American soil,[107] when it was apparently not necessary that they do so. It appears that the real quarrel of both of these gentlemen is not so much with the policy as with the pretentions of their neighbor to the north.

[106] *Hispanic American Historical Review*, 3, pp. 362-374. W. W. Pierson, "Alberdi's views on the Monroe Doctrine."
[107] Pereyra, *op. cit.*, pp. 234-246.

BIBLIOGRAPHY

I. SPECIAL BIBLIOGRAPHICAL GUIDES

Biblioteca nacional. Catálogo methódico. Buenos Aires, 1911.
Calvo Carlos, *Le Droit international.* 2 vols. Paris, 1870. An excellent general account, close to the sources.
Cambridge History of British Foreign Policy, 1783-1919. Cambridge, 1922-23. Extensive bibliographies, uncritical and largely unused.
Coester, Alfred, *Literary History of Spanish America.* New York, 1916.
Fernández y Medina, B., *La imprenta y la prensa en el Uruguay, 1807-1900.* Montevideo, 1900.
Hispanic American Historical Review. Baltimore and Durham, N. C., 1918 ff. Vol. 6 contains a formal bibliography.
Lafinur, Luis Melian, *Las Charreteras de Oribe.* Montevideo, 1895. Contains a critical discussion of the historical writing of the period.
Lamas Andrés, *Biblioteca del Río de la Plata. Colección de Obras, documentos y noticias . . . para servir á la historia, física, política, y literaria del Río de la Plata.* Buenos Aires, 1873.
Rodkey, F. S., *The Turkish-Egyptian Question in the Relations of England, France, and Russia, 1832-1841.* Urbana, 1924. Good formal bibliography.
Williams, J. K., *The International Trade of the Argentine under incontrovertible paper money, 1880-1900.* Harvard Studies, 22, 1920.
Zinny, Antonio, *Efemeridografía argirometropolitana hasta la caída del gobierno de Rosas.* Buenos Aires, 1869. A survey of the periodical literature of Buenos Ayres from 1801 to 1852.

II. SOURCE MATERIAL

A. Primary Sources

Adams, J. Q., *Memoirs of John Quincy Adams, comprising portions of his Diary from 1795 to 1848.* 12 vols. Philadelphia, 1876. Edited by C. F. Adams. An interesting reference to the Lima Congress of 1843 is found in vol. 11.
Argentina:
Archivo Americano y Espíritu de la Prensa del Mundo. Series

1, 32 numbers, Buenos Ayres, 1843-46; series 2, 29 numbers, 1847-1851. A propaganda medium edited by Pedro de Angelis, printed in Spanish, French, and English. It reproduces much correspondence pertaining to the various missions. The most important numbers are included in the French, British, and American diplomatic correspondence. The Church Collection in the Library of Brown University contains a remarkable collection of twenty-five numbers, many of them autographed by Rosas himself. No. 26 of the second series contains an index.

Buenos Ayres, Sala de representantes, *Manifiesto . . . á los gobiernos y ciudadanos de las provincias hermanas de la Confederación Argentina.* Buenos Ayres, Sept. 19, 1852.

Contestaciones de los Exmos. Gobiernos de las Provincias de la Confederación Argentina á las notas relativas á la correspondencia oficial particular. . . . Buenos Ayres, 1838.

Correspondence between . . . the Governor of Buenos Ayres . . . and Mr. John B. Nicolson. . . . Buenos Ayres, 1839. The Nicolson mediation. Printed also in Spanish and French.

Documentos relativos á la organización constitucional de la República Argentina. 4 vols. Buenos Aires, 1911-1914. They cover from 1851 to 1883.

Mensaje del Gobierno de Buenos Aires. Buenos Aires, 1840-1841.

Oficio del consulado encargado interinamente del Consulado general de Francia en Buenos Aires al Sr. ministro de relaciones exteriores de la Confederación Argentina. Buenos Ayres, 1838. Roger's correspondence.

Oribe, Manuel, *Manifiesto sobre la infamia, alevosía, y perfidia con que el contra-almirante Francés Mr. Leblanc, y demás agentes de la Francia residentes en Montevideo han hostilizado y sostenido a la tiranía del rebelde F. Rivera al Estado Oriental del Uruguay.* Buenos Ayres, 1838. A French edition, 1839.

Ramos, J. P., *El poder ejecutivo en los estatuos, reglamentos, y constitucionales.* Buenos Aires, 1912.

Ultimatum adressé par Mr. Aimé Roger, consul de France, au gouvernement de Buenos Aires. . . . Buenos Ayres, 1838. Printed also in Spanish and English.

Calhoun, J. C., *The Works of John C. Calhoun.* 6 vols. New York, 1851-1870. Edited by R. K. Crallé.

Correspondence of Nicholas Biddle dealing with National affairs, 1807-1844. Edited by R. C. McGrane. New York, 1919. Contains a letter from Clay in regard to the French blockade of Mexico, 1838.

France:
Affaires Étrangères, Ministère des, manuscript archives. Paris.

(Abbr. *Aff. Etr.*): Brésil, 18, 23; Bolivie, 1-2; États Unis, 102; République Argentine and Buenos Ayres, 23-41. The correspondence between Paris and London in regard to the Plata interventions is bound with the Argentine material.

Archives parlementaires de 1789 à 1860. 127 vols. Paris 1862-1913. The series is incomplete, stopping in July, 1839.

Le Moniteur Universel, 1839-1851. Daily newspaper containing full reports of all debates in the Chambers.

Guizot, F. P. G., *Histoire parlementaire de France, 1819-1848. Recueil complet des Discours prononcés dans les Chambres de 1819 à 1848.* 5 vols. Paris 1863-1864. Valuable as a sort of an index to the debates, especially after July, 1839.

Thiers, Adolphe, *Discours Parlementaires de M. Thiers.* 16 vols. Paris, 1879-1883. Edited by M. Calmon.

Gooch, G. P., *The Later Correspondence of Lord John Russell, 1840-1878.* 2 vols. New York, 1925. Disappointing on South America.

Great Britain:

Adams, E. D., "British Diplomatic Correspondence concerning the Republic of Texas, 1838-1846." *Quarterly of the Texas Historical Association,* and *Southwestern Historical Quarterly,* vols. XV-XXI. Austin, 1912-1917.

British Foreign and State Papers. London, 1812 ff. Vols. 15, 20, 22, 26-42. A most valuable source, as far as it goes.

Foreign Office Archives, manuscript correspondence:

F. O. 5, America, vols. 403-511, scattering.

F. O. 6, Argentina, vols. 56-156.

F. O. 13, Brazil, vols. 151-214, scattering.

F. O. 27, France, vols. 555-872, scattering.

F. O. 51, Montevideo, vols. 14-66, omitting occasional volumes.

F. O. 84, Slave Trade, vols. 467-9; 523-5.

Hansard's *Parliamentary Debates,* 3d. series, vols. 47-121.

Parliament, *Accounts and Papers:* 1846, XXIX, no. 36; 1849, XXXII, no. 110; 1850, LVI, no. 1253; 1847, LXIV, no. 769. The last document cited is in the King Collection, vol. 40. All are accessible in the New York Public Library. The 1847 document is an extensive study by John Macgregor, *Commercial Tariffs and Treaties.* Part 18 and 19 concern *Statistics of the Spanish American Republics of South America.*

Martens Ch. de, *Nouveau Recueil Général de Traités.* Gottingue, 1855. Vol. 13 contains some pertinent documents on the Plata intervention.

Paraguay, Ministerio de Relaciones Exteriores, *Archivo Diplomático y consular.* Vol. 1. Asunción, 1908.

Peel, Sir Robert, *Biographical Memoir of Sir Robert Peel. Opinions expressed in Parliament and in public.* London, 1850.

Peel, Sir R., *Sir Robert Peel from his private papers.* 3 vols. London, 1899. Edited by C. S. Parker. Interesting in regard to French relations.

Peña y Reyes, Antonio de la, *Lord Aberdeen, Texas, y California.* Vol. 15 of the *Archivo Histórico Diplomático Mexicano.* Mexico, 1925.

Vol. 23, *ibid., La Primera Guerra entre México y Francia.* Mexico, 1927.

Pereira, F. J., *Colección de varios documentos oficiales extraídos de las memorias del Ministerio de relaciones exteriores del Brazil y que, formando una intersante página de la historia de la diplomacia de la América del Sur.* Caracas, 1857. Correspondence from leaders at Montevideo asking for Brazilian aid, collected for the purpose of refuting charges of Brazilian ambition.

Peireira, G. A., *Correspondencia confidencial y política del Sr. Gabriel A. Pereira desde el año 1821 hasta 1860, acompañada de algunos documentos históricos.* 2 vols. Montevideo, 1896. Vol. 2 is especially valuable for information concerning Montevidean affairs in the late years of the intervention.

Polk, James K., *Diary . . . during his Presidency.* Chicago, 1910. Edited by M. M. Quaife.

Rodríguez, José Ignacio, *American Constitutions.* 2 vols. Washington, 1907.

Rosas, Juan Manuel, *Papeles de Rozas, publicados con una introducción y notas por Adolfo Saldías.* 2 vols. La Plata, 1904-1907. Large folio volumes of plates from photostatic copies. Valuable for intimate information concerning the family of Rosas.

Taschereau, *Revue Rétrospective ou Archives secrètes du dernier gouvernement, 1830-1848.* Paris, 1848. Correspondence between Louis Philippe and Victoria in 1844.

The Daily Union of Washington, October, 1845 to February, 1846. The official Democratic organ. Its editorial policy was the subject of several diplomatic exchanges.

Treaty collections of South American states:

Calvo, Carlos, *Colección completa de los tratados, convenciones, capitulaciones, armisticios, y otros actos diplomáticos de todos los estados de la América latina . . . desde el año de 1493 hasta nuestra días.* 11 vols. Paris, 1862-69. A French edition as well.

Centeno, Francisco, *Tratados, convenciones, protocoles, y acuerdos internacionales.* 11 vols. Buenos Aires, 1911-12. Arranged by countries.

Colección de tratados por la República Argentina con las naciones extrangeras. Buenos Aires, 1863-1877. 3 vols., 1884.

Colección de tratados, convenciones, y otros pactos internacio-

nales de la República Oriental del Uruguay. 3 vols. Montevideo, 1923-25.

O Tratado de 24 de Março de 1843 entre o Brazil e a Confederação Argentina. Rio de Janeiro, 1845.

Pereira Pinto, Antonio, *Apontamentos para o dereito internacional, ou, Collecção completa dos tratados celebrados pelo Brazil com noticia, e documentada sobre as convenções mais importantes.* Rio de Janeiro, 1864-65.

Tratados, convenciones, protocolos, y otros demás actos internacionales vigentes celebrados por la República Argentina. 2 vols. Buenos Aires, 1901. 3 vols., 1901-1905.

Varela, Florencio, *Tratados de los estados del Río de la Plata.* Montevideo, 1847-48.

United States:

Congressional documents:

25, 3, House ex. doc. 211. The 1838 blockade.

25, 3, House jol., p. 159. Cushing's resolution on the 1838 blockade.

25, 3, House jol., p. 520. Cushing asks for information.

29, 1, House ex. doc. 212. Brent vs. Pendergast at Montevideo.

29, 1, House jol., p. 411, 746.

29, 1, Senate jol., p. 254.

29, 2, Senate jol., p. 124, 145. Senator Hannegan calls for information.

48, 2, Senate ex. doc. 47. Argentine treaties of July 10 and 27, 1853.

Congressional Globe:

29, 1, p. 197 ff.; 240 ff. The Allen resolution debate.

32, 2 p. 91. Reference of Senator Cass to the Plata trouble.

Manning, W. R., *Diplomatic Correspondence of the United States concerning the independence of Latin-American Nations.* 3 vols. New York, 1925.

Moore, J. B., *The Works of James Buchanan.* 12 vols. Philadelphia and London, 1909. Includes all of the instructions sent out by Secretary Buchanan, 1845-49.

Naval Department, manuscript archives (Abbr. N. D.):

Captain's Letters, May to August, 1838; December, 1838; April, 1839.

Instructions, Officers of Ships of War. To Nicolson, July 8, 1839; to Morris, Mar. 4, 1842.

Brazilian Squadron, Commodore Turner, 1844-1846.

Richardson, J. D., *Compilation of the Messages and Papers of the Presidents, 1789-1881.* 9 vols. Washington, 1896-99.

State Department, manuscript archives (Abbr. S. D.):

Argentine Republic: Instructions, 1843-1853; Despatches, vols. 5-8; Notes to Legation vol. 6.

Brazil: Instructions, 1838-1852; Despatches, vols. 8-17.

Buenos Ayres, Consular Letters, vols. 4-6.
Bureau of Rolls and Library, no. 43, Buenos Aires: *Correspondence of Capt. Voorhees, Commodore Turner, and others in 1844.*
Special Missions, Edward A. Hopkins.
France: Instructions, 14.
Uruguayan Republic:
Actas de la Honorable Asamblea de notables, Años 1846-51. Montevideo, 1897.
Archivo y Museo histórico nacional. Montevideo, 1907 ff. Vols. 3, 4, and 6 contain valuable articles and documentary material.
Ellauri, José L., *Correspondencia del doctor José Ellauri, 1839-1844.* Montevideo, 1919. Ellauri was an agent for the Montevidean Government at Paris.
Herrera y Obes, Manuel, *Correspondencia diplomática del doctor don Mañuel Herrera y Obes con los Principales hombres públicos americanos y europeos de 1847 á 1852.* Montevideo, 1901. Very important for the story of the defense of Montevideo. 3 vols. Edited by A. Palomeque.
Mascaro, Pedro, *Revista del Archivo general administrativo, ó colección de documentos para servir al estudio de la historia de la República Oriental del Uruguay.* 11 vols. Montevideo, 1885-1922. A very pretentious undertaking, still unfinished, beginning with the founding of Montevideo. Vol. 11 goes only to 1814.

B. Contemporaneous Source Material—Memoirs, Propaganda, Etc.

Alberdi, J. B., *Acción de la Europa en América.* Date unknown.
Escritos póstumos. 16 vols. Buenos Aires, 1895, 1901. Vol. 3 is entitled *Política exterior de la República Argentina.* 1896.
Obras selectas, nueva edición. 18 vols. Buenos Aires, 1920. Vol. 6 and 7.
Organización de la Confederación. Buenos Aires, 1913. Alberdi was a brilliant journalist, enemy of Rosas, and later President of the Argentine Confederation.
An Authentic Narrative of the Proceedings of the Expedition under the command of Brigadier Gen. Crauford. By an officer of the expedition. London, 1808. This is the ill-fated expedition from South Africa to conquer Argentina.
Angelis, Pedro de, *De la conducta de los agentes de la Francia durante el bloqueo del Río de la Plata.* Buenos Ayres, 1839. Propaganda of Rosas.
Bentley's Miscellany 30: 33-43, "Reminiscences of la Plata." London, 1851. An excellent non-political discussion by a member of one of the missions.
British Resident of Montevideo, *Rosas and some of the atrocities*

of his dictatorship; in a letter to the Right Hon. Earl of
Aberdeen. London, 1844. Pressure for British intervention.

Brossard, Alfred de, Considérations historiques et politiques sur
les républiques de La Plata dans leurs rapports avec la
France et l'Angleterre. Paris, 1850. The best contemporary account from the French point of view, by one of the
actors.

Bustamente, José Luis, Memorias sobre la revolución de 11 de septiembre de 1852. Buenos Ayres, 1853. The revolt against
Urquiza.

Los cincos errores capitales de la intervención anglo-francesca en
la Plata. Montevideo, 1849. A criticism of the intervention
by an enemy of Rosas.

Cushing, Caleb, "English and French Intervention in the Rio de
la Plata." United States Magazine and Democratic Review, 18: 163 ff. 1846. Representative of the best informed N. American opinion.

De María, Isidoro, Anales de la defensa de Montevideo, 1842-
1851. 4 vols. Montevideo, 1883-87. An intimate detailed
account, much prejudiced against Oribe.

Díaz, César, Memorias inéditas. Buenos Aires, 1878. A sort of
autobiography of one of Rivera's right-hand men. It shows
the continual friction between parties within the city.

Domínguez, Luis L., Escritos políticos, económicos, y literarios de
Florencio Varela. Buenos Ayres, 1859. Of little value for
the intervention.

Durand, Commandant Ferdinand, Précis de l'histoire politique et
militaire des États de la République de la Plata. Paris,
1853. An excellent narrative, more detailed on local happenings than Brossard, written by one having first-hand
knowledge, as well as access to official correspondence.

Edinburgh Review 87: 534 ff. April, 1848. A review of King's
Argentine Republic made into an argument against the intervention.

El Comercio del Plata, edited by F. Varela and V. Alsina. Montevideo, August, 1846. "The Two Dictators, Francia and
Rosas." Also March, 1851.

Garibaldi, Giuseppe, Autobiography, 1807-1849. 3 vols. London,
1889. A translation by A. Werner from an Italian edition
of 1850. An interesting narrative of his South American
adventures, colored considerably.

Life . . . with sketches of his companions in arms. New York,
1859. Translated by T. Dwight.

Guillemot, Eugène, Affaires de la Plata. Paris, 1849. An agent
of France urging vigorous action in Uruguay on behalf of
civilization.

Guizot, F. P. G., Embassy at the Court of St. James in 1840.

London, 1862. Concerns principally the Eastern crisis of
1840.
Memoirs of Sir Robert Peel. London, 1857. Shows their co-
operation for the sake of the *entente.*
Memoirs pour servir à l'histoire de Mon Temps. 8 vols. Paris,
1858-67.
Hadfield, William, *Brazil, the River Plata, and the Falkland
Islands.* London, 1854. An apology for Ouseley and Hot-
ham, with contributions from these men.
Hogg, W. A., "Rosas." *Democratic Review* 18: 369 ff. U. S.
opinion in 1846.
Hopkins, Edward A., "Navigation of the Confluents of the Rio de
la Plata." *Hunt's Merchants Magazine* 21: 80 ff. 1849.
Bulletin of the American Geographical and Statistical Society,
1, p. 14 ff. 1852.
DeBow's Commercial Review 14: 238 ff. 1853. These are ex-
amples of the activity of Hopkins for the recognition of
Paraguay.
Hunt's Merchants Magazine and Commercial Review. New York
1839 ff. Vols. 1-20 contain valuable commercial statistics.
King, John A., *Twenty-four Years in the Argentine Republic.*
New York, Philadelphia and Cincinnati, 1846. An account
of the horrors of Rosas' tyranny, written to counteract the
adulation of the Dictator.
La Gaceta Mercantil of Buenos Ayres, 1823-1852. Edited by N.
Mariño and Pedro de Angelis. The local propaganda
agency of Rosas.
Lamas, Andrés, *Escritos, políticos y literarios . . . durante la
guerra contra la tiranía de D. Juan Manuel Rosas.* Buenos
Aires, 1877. Printed originally in *El Nacional,* Montevideo,
1845, 1849. One of the ablest émigré enemies of Rosas.
Notice sur la République Orientale de l'Uruguay. Paris, 1851.
An effort to interest Napoleon's Government in an active
intervention. Dedicated to Thiers.
London Times, The. A barometer for the attitude of the Conservative party.
Mackinnon, L. B., *Steam Warfare in the Paraná.* 2 vols. London, 1848. The writer commanded a steamer in the Paraná
expedition. Cannot be taken too seriously.
Magariños Cervantes, A., *Estudios históricos, políticos y sociales
sobre el Río de la Plata.* Paris, 1854. Published originally in 1851. In opposition to the French at Montevideo.
*Memoria del Brigadier General Pedro Ferré, Octubre, 1821 á Di-
ciembre de 1842.* Buenos Aires, 1921. Written in Brazil,
1845. Contains valuable documents. Ferré was bitter for
his abandonment by Lavalle and the French in 1840.
Mignet, F. A. M., "Des Rapports de la France et de l'Europe avec

l'Amérique du Sud." *Revue des Deux Mondes,* 1838, vol. 3. Praises the intervention.

National Intelligencer of Washington, 1838-1850. A leading Whig daily.

Niles National Register, vols. 63-75. Baltimore, 1842-1849. A Whig weekly featuring foreign news. Contains a convenient index.

O'Brien, General, *Correspondence with the British Government.* London, 1845.

Pacheco y Obes, Melchor, *Le Paraguay; son passé, son présent, et son avenir.* Rio de Janeiro, 1848. Paris, 1851. An argument for free navigation of the rivers.

Réponse aux détracteurs de Montevideo. Paris, 1849. Propaganda to secure French assistance.

Page, Thomas, "Affaires de Buenos Ayres, Expédition de la France contre la République Argentine." *Revue des Deux Mondes,* 25, February, 1841, p. 301 ff. An excellent defense of the Mackau Convention.

Parish, Sir Woodbine, *Buenos Ayres and the provinces of the Rio de la Plata.* London, 1825 and 1839. A Spanish edition, 2 vols., Buenos Aires, 1852. A sympathetic treatment, pro-Rosas.

Paz, José María, *Memorias póstumas.* 3 vols. La Plata, 1892. *Compañas contra Rosas. Memorias póstumas, tercera y última parte.* Buenos Aires, 1917. A very satisfactory narrative of the struggles of this Unitarian leader.

Pereira, Antonio N., *Recuerdos de mi tiempo.* Montevideo, 1897. A piecing together of disconnected memoirs. Of little value.

Pétition et document du commerce français de la république orientale de l'Uruguay à S. E. M. le Ministère Secrétaire d'État. . . . le 2 décembre, 1843. Paris, 1844. Asking for Government aid.

Pfeil, A. R., *Résumé des Affaires de la Plata.* Paris, 1849. Propaganda from the Montevidean consulate in London.

Poucel, Benjamin, *Les otages de Durazno.* Paris, 1864. Tells of the Uruguay war and of activities in 1850-51 on behalf of French hostages held by Oribe.

Rivera Indarte, José, *Rosas y sus opositores.* Montevideo, 1843. Buenos Ayres, 1853. A tirade against Rosas and a demand that France and England fulfill their promises to Montevideo.

Rosas, Juan Manuel (above his signature), *Quelques Réflexions en réponse à la Brochure publiée à Montevideo par D. Florencio Varela.* Buenos Ayres, 1841. An attempt to reply to Varela's trenchant attack on the Mackau Convention.

Russell, John Earl, *Recollections and Suggestions, 1813-1873.* London and Boston, 1875. Disappointing on South American affairs.

Saint Robert, Chevalier M. de, *Le général Rosas et la question de la Plata*. Paris, 1848. A valuable little book by a member of Deffaudis' mission.

Sarmiento, D. F., *Arjiropolis; ó La capital de los Estados Confederados del Río de La Plata*. Santiago de Chile, 1850. A proposal to locate the Argentine capital on Martín García. *Compaña en el ejército grande aliado de Sud América*. Rio de Janeiro, 1852. An attack on Urquiza's Federalism. *Política Arjentina, 1841-1851*. Vol. 6 of *Obras de Sarmiento*. 48 vols. Santiago de Chile, 1887. 53 vols. Paris, 1889-1909. A series of articles defending European intervention.

Strain, Isaac G., *Cordillera and Pampa*. New York, 1853. Of little value.

The Economist,—Weekly Commercial Times, etc. London, 1847 ff. Vol. 1: 1273, 1448. Criticizes Palmerston for failure to relieve Commerce in the Plata.

Varela, Florencio, *Sobre la convención de 29 de Octubre de 1840*. Montevideo, 1840. Denounces the betrayal of Montevideo and Lavalle. *Observations on occurrences on the river Plate, as connected with the foreign agents and the Anglo-French intervention*. Montevideo, 1843. Published in French and Spanish also. A powerful argument based on the promises of Mandeville and Lurde in December, 1842. *Auto-biografía de D. Florencio Varela*. Montevideo, 1848. A partial diary of his trip to Europe, 1843-44, is valuable.

Wrigth, A., *Montevideo, apuntes históricos de la defensa de la República*. Montevideo, 1845.

III. SECONDARY AUTHORITIES

Adams, E. D., *British Interests and Activities in Texas, 1838-1845*. Baltimore, 1910.

Adams, Jane E., "Abolition of the Brazilian Slave Trade." *Journal of Negro History* 10, October, 1925. A good discussion, but unfair to Brazil because of failure to treat commercial aspects.

Allison, John M., *Thiers and the French Monarchy*. Boston, 1926. Valuable, but distorted in emphasis.

Alvarez, Alejandro, *The Monroe Doctrine, its importance in the International Life of the New World*. New York, 1924. A symposium of opinions; scarcely dependable for reference. See p. 258.

Annual Register, The. London, 1838-51. The summaries of political events in England and France are very useful.

Anonymous, *Les Dissensions des républiques de La Plata et les machinations du Brésil*. Paris, 1865. A general survey attacking Brazil.

Antokoletz, D., *La Doctrine de Monroë et l'Amerique latine.* Paris, 1905.

Araújo, Orestes, *Gobernantes del Uruguay.* 2 vols. Montevideo, 1903. A good account, attacking Rosas and Oribe.

Arcas, Santiago, *La Plata, étude historique.* Paris, 1865. An account based on Brossard, partly.

Armas, José de, "Rosas and Doctor Francia." *International America* III, October, 1919. An interesting, but superficial comparison.

Báez, Cecelio, *La tiranía en el Paraguay.* Asunción, 1903. Contains a brief critical account of the régimes of Francia and the Lopezs.

Balfour, Lady Frances, *Life of George, Fourth Earl of Aberdeen.* 2 vols. London, 1922.

Bemis, S. F. and others, *The American Secretaries of State and their Diplomacy.* 10 vols. New York, 1927-29. Vols. 4 and 5.

Bentley's Miscellany 31:487 ff. "Don Manuel Rosas." 1852. An apology.

Bianco, José, *Organización nacional; preliminares del Acuerdo de San Nicolás.* Buenos Ayres, 1903. A good treatment.

Bingham, Hiram, *The Monroe Doctrine; an Obsolete Shibboleth.* New Haven, 1913, 1915. A highly critical treatment.

Blanc, J. J. C. L., *The History of Ten Years, 1830-1840.* 2 vols. London, 1844-1845. A discussion of domestic politics in France.

Bourgeois, Émile, *Manuel Historique et Politique Étrangère.* 4 vols. Paris, 1919-20, 1927. Vol. 2 and 3 are very useful for reference, and have good bibliographies.

Bourne, E. G., "The History and Determination of the Line of Demarkation established by Pope Alexander VI." *Annual Report of the American Historical Association for 1891.* Washington, 1892.

Bulwer-Lytton, Henry, Lord Dalling, *The Life of Henry John Temple, viscount Palmerston.* 3 vols. London, 1870-4. Contains some valuable quotations from private papers to 1847.

Callahan, James Morton, "Statements, Interpretations, and Applications of the Monroe Doctrine and of more or less allied Doctrines from 1845 to 1870." *Proceedings of the American Society of International Law,* 8, p. 59 ff. Washington, 1914. Based upon a partial examination of the material in the State Department.

Calvo, Carlos, *Le Droit international.* 2 vols. Paris, 1868, 1870, 1880-1, 1887-8, 1896. Contains one of the best brief accounts of the episode.

Campbell, John G., *Viscount Palmerston.* London, 1892. Does not mention the Plata affair.

Carranza, Ángel J., *La revolución del 39 en el sur de Buenos Aires.*
Buenos Aires, 1880. A good account, with a valuable documentary appendix.

Cass, Lewis, *France, its King, court and government.* New York
and London, 1840. Impressionistic, and of little value.

Cecil, Algernon, *British Foreign Secretaries, 1807-1916.* London,
1927. The adulation of Lord Aberdeen is carried entirely
too far.

Cervantes, A. M., *Estudios históricos políticos y sociales sobre el
Río de la Plata.* Paris, 1854.

Chase, L. B., *History of the Polk Administration.* New York,
1850. Of little value, for lack of perspective.

Cobos Daract, J., *Historia argentina.* 2 vols. Buenos Aires, 1920.
A patriotic narrative of an elementary character. Very
clear.

Cooper, C. S., "The South American Gaucho." *The South American,* New York, 1918. A fair discussion.

Costa, J. A., *Rosas y Lavalle.* Buenos Aires, 1926. Treated from
a domestic viewpoint.

Curtis, E. N., *The French Assembly of 1848 and American Constitutional Doctrines.* New York, 1891. *Columbia University Studies,* vol. 29, no. 2.

Deberle, Alfred, *Histoire de l'Amérique du Sud.* Paris, 1876,
1897.

Debidour, A., *Histoire diplomatique de l'Europe.* 4 vols. Vol. 1,
Paris, 1891. A standard work by a leading French scholar.

Díaz, Antonio, *Historia política y militar de las Repúblicas del
Plata.* 10 vols. Montevideo, 1877-1878. Vols. 3-8 are
very valuable for this study. Contain many documents.

Dickinson, G. L., *Revolution and reaction in Modern France.*
London, 1892.

Dublin University Magazine, 39 p. 663 ff. "Rosas and la Plata."
1852. Typically British in viewpoint; unfair to France.

Éstrada, J. M., *La Política Liberal bajo La Tiranía de Rosas.*
Buenos Aires, 1897, 1927. A sort of philosophical treatment.

Fraser's Magazine, 45: 596. "Rosas the Dictator of Buenos
Ayres." 1852.

Fournière, Eugène, *Le règne de Louis Philippe, 1830-1848.* Paris,
1906. Vol. 6 of Jean Jaurès, *Histoire socialiste, 1789-1900.*
12 vols. Stresses foreign policy and clericalism.

García Merou, Martin, *Juan Bautista Alberdi.* Buenos Aires, 1890.
A critical essay on his life and works.

Goebel, Julius, *The Struggle for the Falkland Islands.* New
Haven, 1927. A thorough piece of research which all but
demolishes the British claim.

Gordon, G. H., *Thirty Years of Foreign Policy.* London, 1855.
A blind eulogy of British policy.

Guedalla, Philip, *Palmerston*. London, 1927. The definitive biography of Palmerston, although references to minor diplomatic questions are omitted.

Guitiérrez, E., *Juan Manuel Rosas; La Mazorca; Una Tragedia de 12Años; El Puñal del Tirano*. Buenos Aires, 1892. A popular account from the Argentine point of view.

Guyot, Raymond, *La Première Entente Cordiale*. Paris, 1926. Very useful.

Hall, Major John, *England and the Orleans Monarchy*. New York and London, 1912. The authority on the subject, slightly pro-British.

Hart, A. B., *The Monroe Doctrine; an interpretation*. Boston, 1916, 1917. A standard treatment.

Haussonville, M. O.d', *Histoire de la politique Extérieure de la Monarchie de Juillet*. 2 vols. Paris, 1850. A critical account.

Henningson, C. F., *Analogies and Contrasts*. 2 vols. London, 1848. Discusses the difficulties in the way of a British-French *entente*.

Hirst, W. A., *Argentina*. New York and London, 1910, 1912. A general treatment, leaving considerable to be desired.

Hoskins, H. L., "French Views of the Monroe Doctrine." *Hispanic American Historical Review*, 4: 677 ff. 1921. By no means exhaustive.

Hutchinson, T. J., *The Paraná*. London, 1868. Contains a preliminary historical sketch.

Hyde, C. C., *International Law*. 2 vols. Boston, 1922. Contains a good discussion of the pacific blockade.

Ibarguren, Carlos, *Manuelita Rosas*. Buenos Aires, 1926. Documented, and apparently authoritative.

International American Conference, *Reports of Committees and discussions thereon*, 4. *Historical Appendix*. Washington, 1890. Contains a short treatment of the 1846 Congress at Lima, Peru.

James, H. G. and Martin, P. A., *The Republics of Latin-America*. New York, 1923. A standard text. Good bibliographies.

Koebel, W. H., *Argentina, Past and Present*. London, 1910, 1914.
Paraguay. London, 1917.
Uruguay. London, 1911. All are popular accounts, and superficial.

Kraus, Herbert, *Die Monroedoktrin in ihrem beziehungen zur amerikanischen diplomatie und zum voelkerrecht*. Berlin, 1913. Brief, but carefully done.

Lacasa, Pedro, *Vida Militar y Política de General Argentino Don Juan Lavalle*. Buenos Aires, 1858. The author was Lavalle's aid-de-camp. He tries to defend his chief.

La Política Brazilera en el Río de la Plata. Buenos Aires, 1864,

BIBLIOGRAPHY 285

1869. Paris, 1869. Various Argentine writers attack
Brazil.
Latané, J. H., *A History of American Foreign Policy.* New York,
1927. An excellent treatment.
The United States and Latin America. New York, 1920. Not
very satisfactory. Merely discusses several episodes, repro-
ducing an earlier work by the same author.
Latham, Wilfred, *The States of the River Plate; their industries
and commerce.* London, 1856, 1868. A Spanish edition,
Buenos Aires, 1867. By a resident of Montevideo, hostile
to Rosas.
Lavisse, E. et Rambaud, A., *Histoire Générale.* 12 vols. Paris,
1893-1901. Vol. 10 contains a fairly good discussion of
Argentina.
Lawson, L. A., *Relation of British Policy to the Declaration of the
Monroe Doctrine.* New York, 1922. *Columbia University
Studies,* 103. Dependable.
Le Goff, François, *The Life of Louis Adolphe Thiers.* Translated
by T. Stanton, 1879. Not very satisfactory.
Leguizamón, M. P., *Urquiza y la casa Acuerdo.* La Plata, 1909.
Lima, Manuel de Oliveira, *Evolution of Brazil compared with that
of Spanish and Anglo-Saxon America.* Palo Alto, 1914.
Leland Stanford Jr. Publications, 17. The footnotes and
incidental references are particularly valuable.
Lockey, J. B., *Pan-Americanism; its beginnings.* New York, 1920.
Careful in its differentiation between the various sections
of South America.
López, V. F., *Historia de la República Argentina.* 10 vols. Buenos
Aires, 1883-93, 1911, 1913, 1926. The treatment extends
only to 1828. The final volume contains a good discussion
of social conditions.
Manual de la historia argentina. Buenos Aires, 1907, 1920. A
valuable work, close to the sources.
MacKnight, Thomas, *Thirty Years of Foreign Policy.* London,
1855. Scarcely touches South America.
McCormac, E. I., *James K. Polk.* Berkeley, 1922. A standard
biography.
Manning, W. R., "An Early Diplomatic Controversy with Brazil."
Hispanic American Historical Review, 1: 123 ff. 1918.
"Statements, Interpretations, and Applications of the Monroe
Doctrine. . . ." *Proceedings of the American Society of
International Law,* 8: 34 ff. Washington, 1914. Scholarly.
Martin, C. E., *The Policy of the United States as Regards Inter-
vention.* New York, 1921. *Columbia University Studies,*
93, no. 2.
Masefield, John, *Rosas.* New York, 1918. A sort of epic poem
about Rosas.
Mazade, Charles de, *Monsieur Thiers, cinquante années d'histoire*

contemporaine. Paris, 1884. Judicious and fair, though brief.

Melian, Lafinur, L., *Las Charreteras de Oribe.* Montevideo, 1895. A critical discussion of the career of Oribe.

Miranda, J. D., *Compendio de historia nacional, 1830-1894.* Montevideo, 1905.

Moore, J. B., *Digest of International Law.* 8 vols. Washington, 1906.

Moses, Bernard, "Social Revolution of the 18th Century in South America." *Annual Report of the American Historical Association,* 1915.

South America on the Eve of Emancipation. The Southern Spanish Colonies in the last Half-Century of their Independence. New York and London, 1908.

Spain's Declining Power in South America, 1730-1806. Berkeley, 1919.

The Intellectual Background of the Revolution in South America. 1810-1824. New York, 1926. Excellent treatises.

Muir, R., *The Expansion of Europe.* New York, 1923. The author falls into some inaccurate generalizations regarding South America.

Murray, Thomas, *The Story of the Irish in Argentina.* New York, 1919. Interesting sketches of Admiral Brown and others.

Oneta y Viana, Carlos, *La diplomacia del Brazil en el Río de la Plata.* Montevideo, 1903. A good account, but lacking in references.

Oranjo, Orestes, *Gobernantes del Uruguay.* 2 vols. Montevideo, 1903.

Page, William, *Commerce and Industry.* London, 1919. Contains excellent summaries of the discussions of Parliament on trade.

Palomeque, Alberto, *De la diplomacia de la defensa de Montevideo.* Montevideo, 1898. Very dependable, though admittedly incomplete.

La Jurisdicción del Plata. Martín García. La Laguna Merin. Montevideo, 1909. A survey of the antecedents of a live current problem.

Oríjenes de la Diplomacia Arjentina. Buenos Aires, 1905.

Parker, Charles S., *Sir Robert Peel.* 3 vols. London, 1899. Contains some valuable letters.

Pascual, A. D., *Apuntes para la historia de la República Oriental del Uruguay.* 2 vols. Paris, 1864. One of the best treatments of the tangled history of Uruguay up to 1838.

Pelliza, M. A., *Historia argentina desde su origen hasta la organización nacional.* 5 vols. Buenos Aires, 1888. 2 vols., 1910. A smooth running narrative, not over-detailed.

La Dictatura de Rosas. Buenos Aires, 1917. Excellent.

Peña, David, *Juan Facunda Quiroga.* Buenos Aires, 1917. Quiroga was one of the unfortunate rivals of Rosas.

Peña y Reyes, A. de la, *La Diplomacia Mexicana.* Mexico, 1923.

Pereda, S. E., *Garibaldi en el Uruguay.* 2 vols. Montevideo, 1914. Good, but entirely from the local point of view.

Pereira, A. N., *La invasión inglesa en el Río de la Plata.* Montevideo, 1877.

Pereyra, Carlos, *Rosas y Thiers; la diplomacia europea en el Río de la Plata, 1838-1850.* Madrid, 1919. A disappointing effort. Prejudiced against the United States and France.

"Rosas enseñándole à Monroe los rudimentos del Monroisme." *Nuestro Tiempo* 16: 151-164. 1916.

La Doctrina de Monroe; el destino manifiesto y el imperialismo. Mejico, 1908. Yankeephobia seems to be Pereyra's obsession.

Perkins, D., "Europe, Spanish America, and the Monroe Doctrine." *American Historical Review* 27. 1922.

Peuchgaric, N., *La Plata de 1851 à 1854.* Paris, 1856. A pro-Urquiza account; encourages French immigration to the region.

Ports de la Capitale et de la Plata. La Plata, 1905. A map of the river.

Poucel, Benjamin, *Le Paraguay Moderne.* Marseille, 1867. From limited sources.

Pierson, W. W., "Alberdi's Views on the Monroe Doctrine." *Hispanic Amer. Historical Review,* 3: 362 ff. 1920. Alberdi erroneously asserted that the United States deprived Argentina of legitimate assistance from Europe in her regeneration.

Quesada, Ernesto, *Historia diplomática nacional. La política argentino-paraguaya.* Buenos Aires, 1902. Contains valuable letters.

La época de Rosas, su verdadero carácter histórico. Buenos Aires, 1898. An early appreciation of the work of Rosas.

La guerra civil de 1841 y la tragedia de Acha. Córdoba, 1916. A carefully documented work.

"Social Evolution of the Argentine Republic." *Annals of the American Academy* 37: 707 ff. 1911. Excellent.

Urquiza y la integridad nacional. Córdoba, 1920. A eulogy.

Quesada, Vicente G., *Historia diplomática latino-americana.* 3 vols. Buenos Aires, 1919. Vol. 2 covers the Plata policy of Brazil.

R. C., *History of South America.* Translated by Adnah Jones in 1899 from a Spanish edition, Barcelona, 1878. Many minor inaccuracies.

Ramos Mejía, José M., *Rosas y su tiempo.* 3 vols. Buenos Aires, 1907. An intimate portrait of Rosas, with a critical discussion of the writings concerning him.

Reeves, Jesse S., *American Diplomacy under Tyler and Polk.* Baltimore, 1907. South American questions are ignored.

Reid Whitelaw, *The Monroe doctrine, the Polk doctrine, and the doctrine of anarchism.* New York, 1903. A thoughtful analysis of Polk's policy.

République Argentina, son présent—son avenir. Port du Rosario. 1903.

Rivas, Raimundo, *Relaciones internacionales entre Colombia y los Estados Unidos, 1810-1850.* Bogotá, 1915. A valuable study based on the Bogotá archives.

Robertson, H. B., "Emperor Don Pedro II, the Magnanimous." *Pan American Magazine,* 32: 241 ff. 1921. A good article.

Robertson, W. S., *Hispanic American Relations with the United States.* New York, 1923. A praiseworthy effort to get away from the political approach.

History of the Latin American Nations. New York, 1922, 1925. This standard account shares with that of Shepherd the mistaken assumption that the European intervention weakened Rosas, and assisted in his downfall.

"South America and the Monroe Doctrine, 1824-1828." *Political Science Quarterly,* 30: 82 ff. 1915. Excellent.

Rodkey, F. S., *The Turkish-Egyptian Question in the Relations of England, France, and Russia.* Urbana, 1924. *University of Illinois Social Science Studies.* 11, no. 3 and 4.

Rousset, Camille F. M., *Les Commencements d'une conquête— L'Algérie de 1830 à 1840.* 2 vols. Paris, 1887. Shows the vacillation of the Paris Governments.

La conquête de l'Algérie, 1841-1857. 2 vols, Paris, 1904.

Rowe, L. S., *The Federal System of the Argentine Republic.* Washington, 1921. Good.

Saldías, Adolfo, *Historia de la Confederación Argentina,—Rosas y su Época.* 5 vols. Buenos Aires, 1881-1887, 1892. A work of primary importance. Valuable appendices.

Sarmiento, D. F., *Life in the Argentine Republic in the days of the Tyrants.* New York, 1868. Translated by Mrs. Horace Mann. A French edition, 1853. A valuable book, but it has little appreciation of Rosas.

Schafer, Joseph, "British Attitude toward the Oregon Question." *American Historical Review,* 16: 273 ff. 1911.

Schmieder, Oscar, *Alteration of the Argentine Pampa in the Colonial Period.* Berkeley, 1927. *University of California publications in Geography,* vol. 2, no. 10. A suggestive contribution.

Schuyler, R. L., "British Imperial Preference and Sir Robert Peel." *Political Science Quarterly,* 32: 429 ff. 1917.

"Abolition of British Imperial Preference, 1846-1860." *Ibid.,* 33: 77. 1918. Two excellent articles.

Shepherd, W. R., *The Hispanic Nations of the New World.* New

Haven, 1919. The most readable book on the subject, but it misinterprets the effect of the intervention upon the tenure of Rosas.

Smith, Justin H., *Annexation of Texas*. New York, 1911. *The War with Mexico*. 2 vols. New York, 1919. These definitive works might have been improved by a more general knowledge of Franco-British relations.

Stanmore, A. H. G., *The Earl of Aberdeen*. New York, 1893. Disappointing.

Stewart, G. H., *Latin-America and the United States*. New York, 1922. An excellent discussion, but from limited sources.

Streeter, S. F., in the *North American Review*, 69: 43 ff. 1849.

Temperley, Harold, *The Foreign Policy of Canning, 1822-1827*. London, 1925.

Trevelyan, G. M., *The Life of John Bright*. Boston and New York, 1925. Excellent.

Urrutia, F. J., *Páginas de historia diplomática. Los Estados Unides de América y las Repúblicas hispanoamericanas de 1810 à 1830*. Bogotá, 1917. An authoritative work.

Vedia, Augustín de, *Martín García y la Jurisdicción del Plata*. Buenos Aires, 1908. A work of considerable merit.

Vera y Ganzález, Enrique, *Historia de la República Argentina*. 3 vols. Buenos Aires, 1926. A patriotic treatment which lauds Rosas and attacks the Unitarian emigrés.

Villanueva, Carlos A., *Historia de le República Argentina. Rosas*. Paris, 1914.

Walpole, Spencer, *The Life of Lord John Russell*, 2 vols. London, 1899. In all these standard biographies, reference to South American affairs is conspicuously absent.

Washburn, A. H., "The Legality of the Pacific Blockade." *Columbia Law Review*, 21: 55 ff., 227 ff., 442 ff., 1921. A thoughtful treatment of the Plata blockades, though from a too meager basis of fact.

Washburn, Charles A., *The History of Paraguay*. 2 vols. Boston, 1871. Valuable but not definitive. Written by a Minister Resident of the United States at Asunción.

White, Elizabeth B., *American Opinion of France from LaFayette to Poincaré*. New York, 1927. A very valuable reference work.

Willson, Beckles, *The Paris Embassy, a narrative of Franco-British Relations, 1814-1920*. London, 1927. An interesting study in personalities.

Zeballos, E. S., *Argument for the Argentine Republic upon the question with Brazil in regard to the territory of Misiones*. Washington, 1894. Contains excellent maps.

Zinny, Antonio, *La Gaceta Mercantil de Buenos Aires, 1823-1852*. 3 vols. Buenos Aires, 1912. An invaluable summary of the contents of this important newspaper of Buenos Ayres.

INDEX